MW01014500

Peoples of the Past

PHOENICIANS

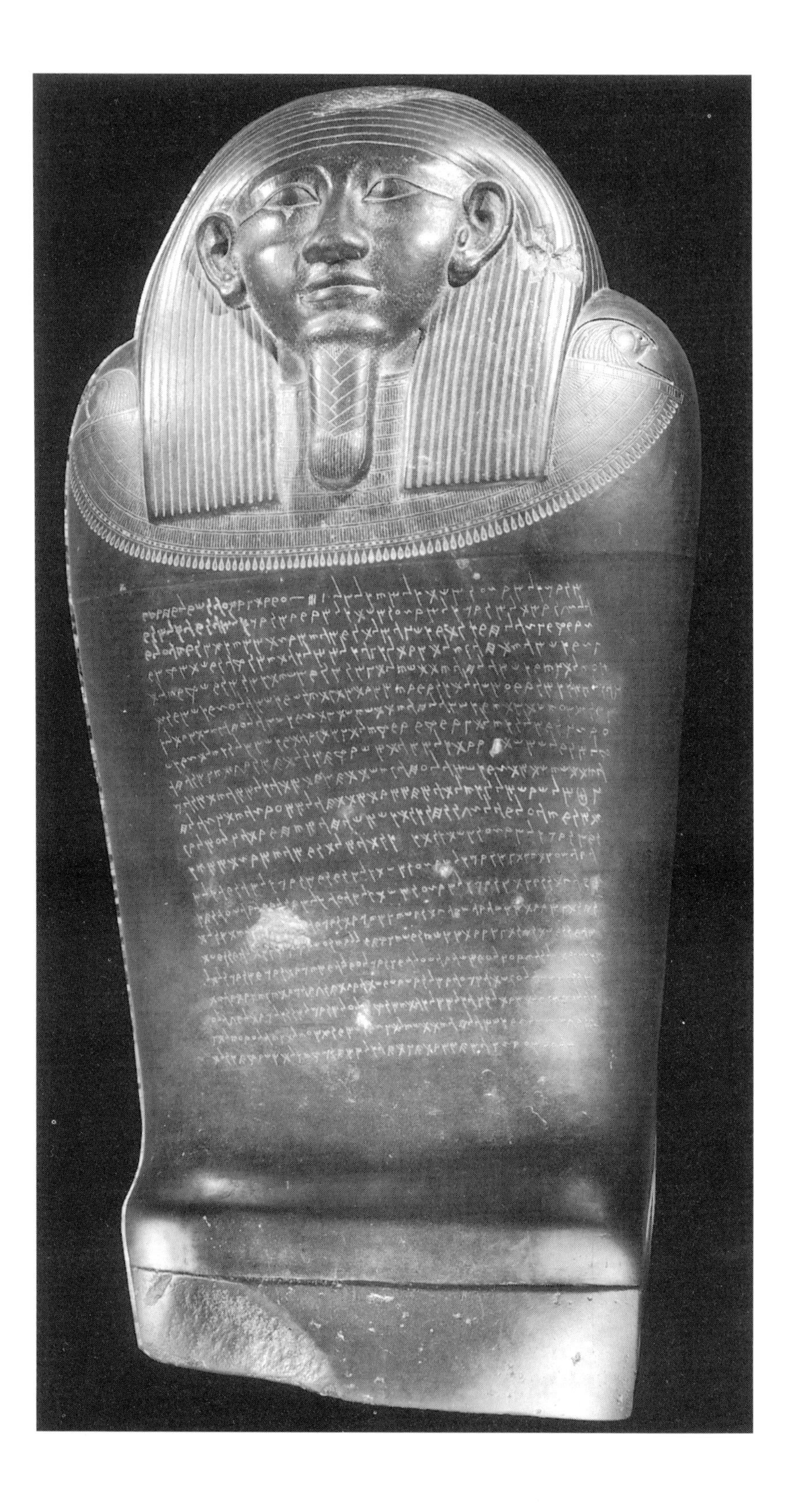

PEOPLES OF THE PAST

PHOENICIANS

GLENN E. MARKOE

University of California Press
Berkeley · Los Angeles

Frontispiece
Inscribed mummiform sarcophagus of Eshmunazar II, king of Sidon, Lebanon. From Magharet Ablun, Sidon, first half of the fifth century BC.

To my sister, Merrill, and my sons, Carey and Noah.

University of California Press
Berkeley and Los Angeles, California

Published by arrangement with British Museum Press

ISBN 0-520-22613-5 (cloth)
ISBN 0-520-22614-3 (paperback)

Designed and typeset in Bembo by Grahame Dudley

Printed in Great Britain by The Bath Press, Avon

9 8 7 6 5 4 3 2 1

Contents

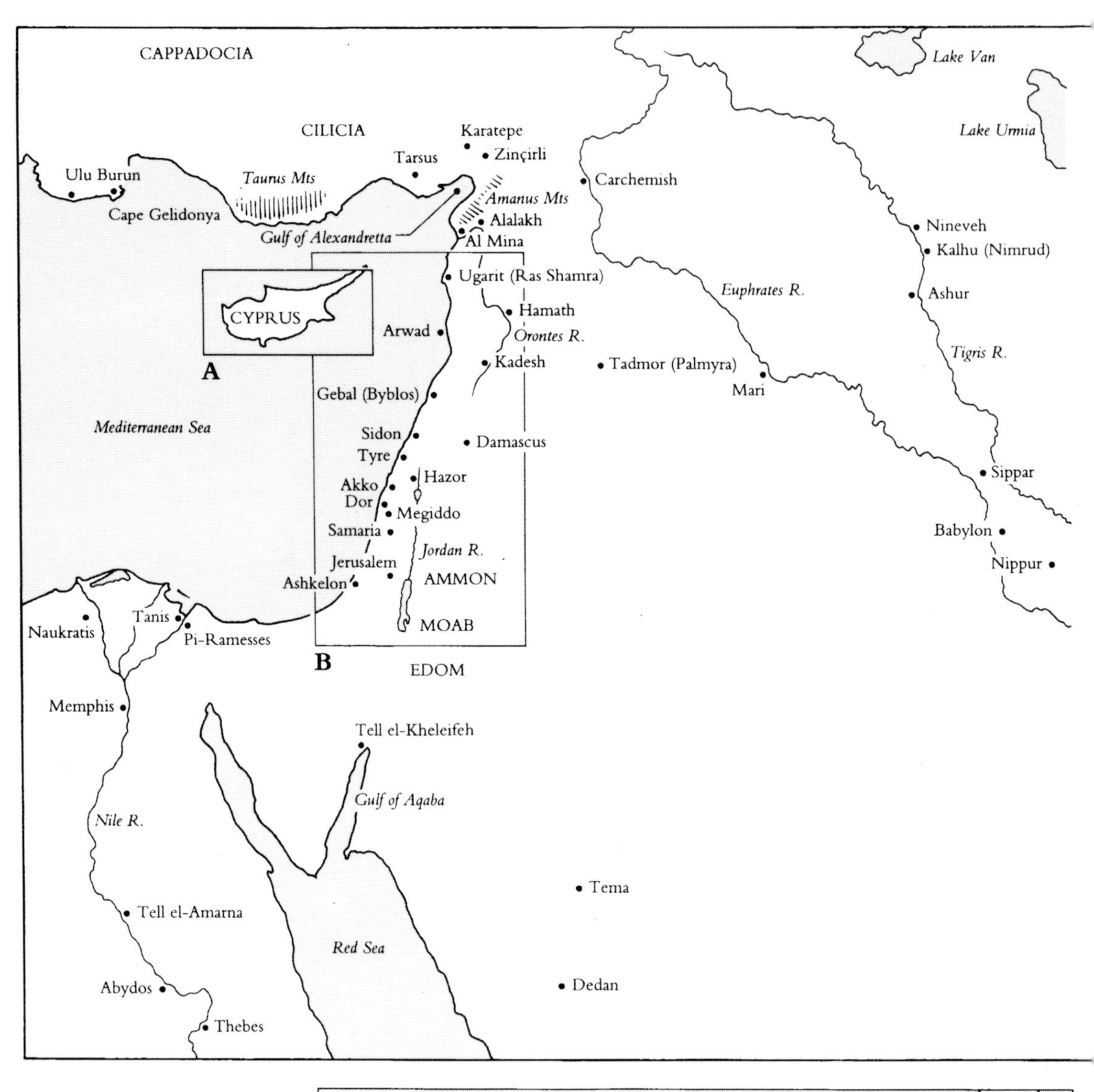
CAPPADOCIA
CILICIA
Karatepe
Zinçirli
Tarsus
Ulu Burun
Taurus Mts
Cape Gelidonya
Amanus Mts
Alalakh
Gulf of Alexandretta
Al Mina
Carchemish
Lake Van
Lake Urmia
Nineveh
Kalhu (Nimrud)
Ashur
Euphrates R.
Tigris R.
Ugarit (Ras Shamra)
Hamath
Orontes R.
CYPRUS
Arwad
A
Kadesh
Tadmor (Palmyra)
Mari
Gebal (Byblos)
Mediterranean Sea
Sidon
Damascus
Tyre
Akko
Hazor
Dor
Megiddo
Samaria
Jordan R.
Jerusalem
Ashkelon
AMMON
MOAB
Naukratis
Tanis
Pi-Ramesses
B
EDOM
Sippar
Babylon
Nippur
Memphis
Tell el-Kheleifeh
Gulf of Aqaba
Nile R.
Tema
Tell el-Amarna
Red Sea
Abydos
Dedan
Thebes

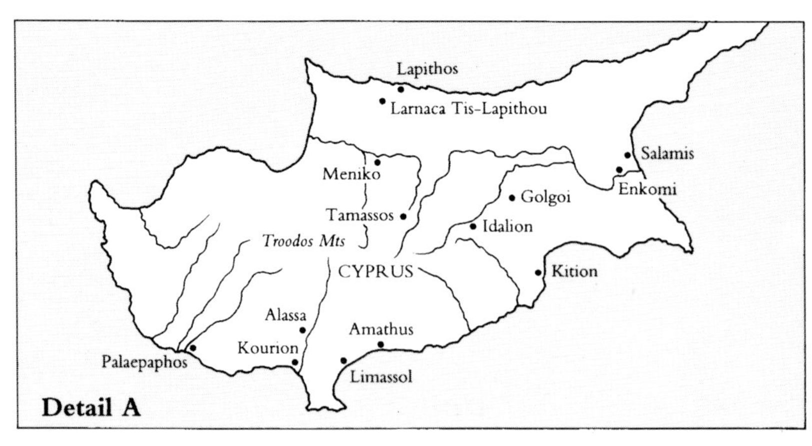
Lapithos
Larnaca Tis-Lapithou
Meniko
Salamis
Enkomi
Golgoi
Tamassos
Idalion
Troodos Mts
CYPRUS
Kition
Alassa
Amathus
Kourion
Palaepaphos
Limassol
Detail A

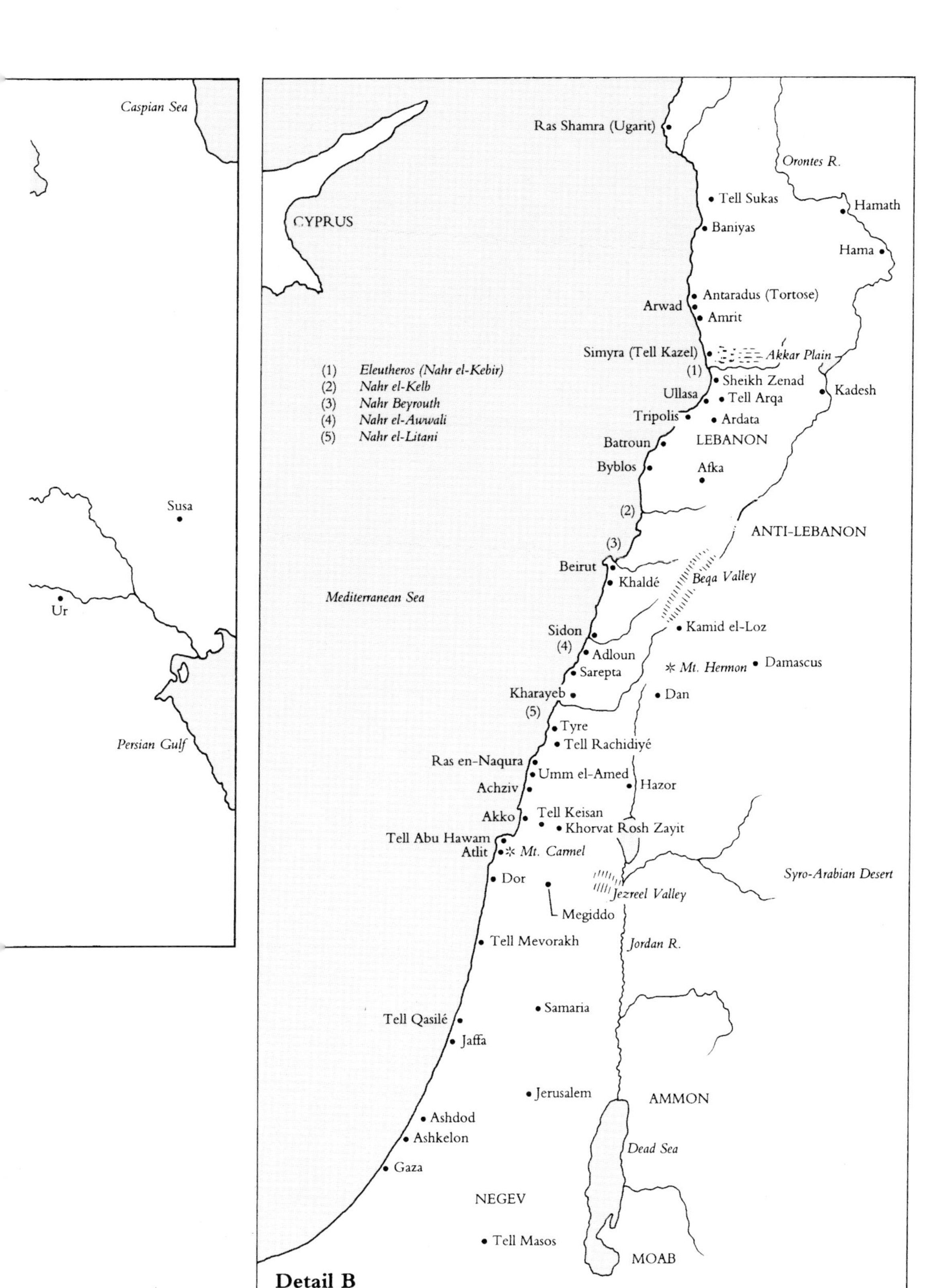
Caspian Sea
Susa
Ur
Persian Gulf
Ras Shamra (Ugarit)
Orontes R.
Tell Sukas
Hamath
CYPRUS
Baniyas
Hama
Antaradus (Tortose)
Arwad
Amrit
Simyra (Tell Kazel)
Akkar Plain
(1) Eleutheros (Nahr el-Kebir)
(2) Nahr el-Kelb
(3) Nahr Beyrouth
(4) Nahr el-Awwali
(5) Nahr el-Litani
(1)
Sheikh Zenad
Ullasa
Tell Arqa
Kadesh
Tripolis
Ardata
Batroun
LEBANON
Byblos
Afka
(2)
ANTI-LEBANON
(3)
Beirut
Khaldé
Beqa Valley
Mediterranean Sea
Kamid el-Loz
Sidon
(4)
Adloun
Mt. Hermon
Damascus
Sarepta
Kharayeb
Dan
(5)
Tyre
Tell Rachidiyé
Ras en-Naqura
Umm el-Amed
Achziv
Hazor
Akko
Tell Keisan
Khorvat Rosh Zayit
Tell Abu Hawam
Atlit
Mt. Carmel
Dor
Syro-Arabian Desert
Jezreel Valley
Megiddo
Tell Mevorakh
Jordan R.
Samaria
Tell Qasilé
Jaffa
Jerusalem
AMMON
Ashdod
Ashkelon
Dead Sea
Gaza
NEGEV
Tell Masos
MOAB
Detail B

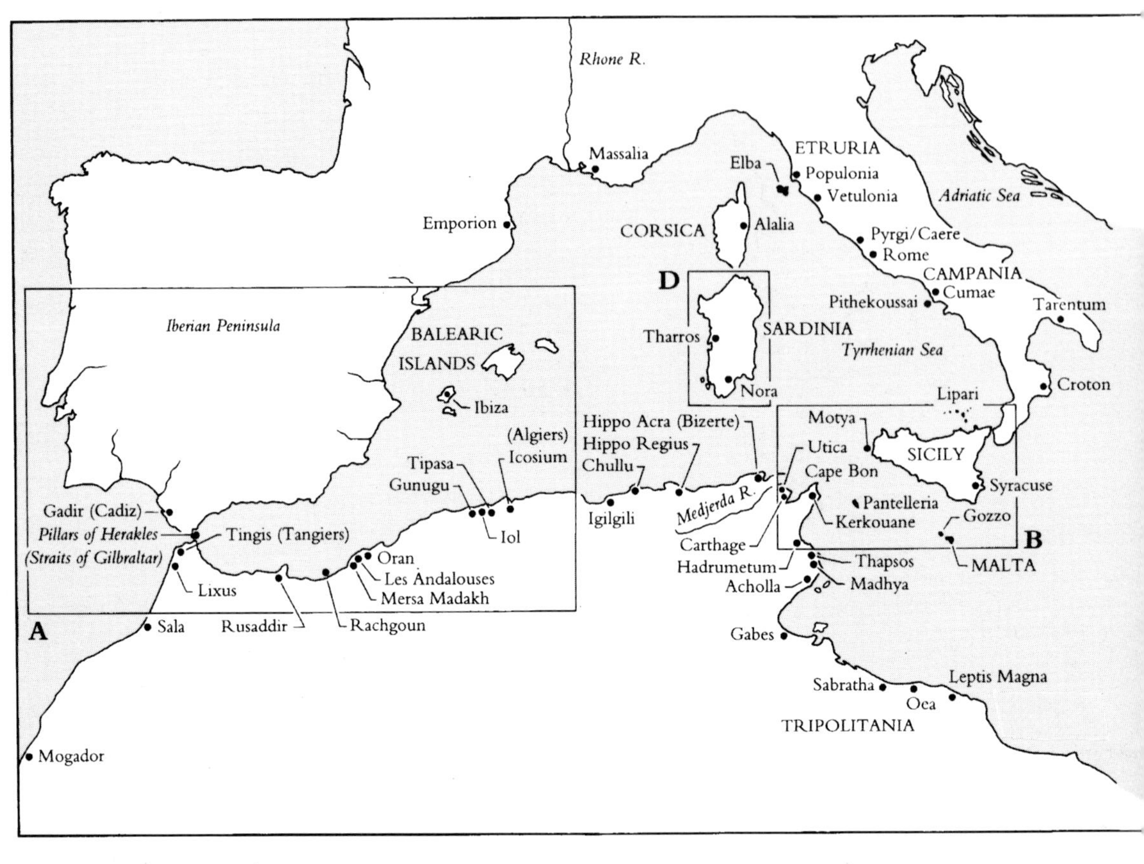
Rhone R.
Massalia
ETRURIA
Elba
Populonia
Vetulonia
Adriatic Sea
Emporion
CORSICA
Alalia
Pyrgi/Caere
Rome
CAMPANIA
Cumae
Pithekoussai
Tarentum
D
Iberian Peninsula
BALEARIC ISLANDS
Tharros
SARDINIA
Tyrrhenian Sea
Nora
Croton
Ibiza
Lipari
Hippo Acra (Bizerte)
Hippo Regius
Chullu
Motya
Utica
SICILY
(Algiers) Icosium
Tipasa
Gunugu
Cape Bon
Syracuse
Pantelleria
Gozzo
Kerkouane
Medjerda R.
Igilgili
Iol
Gadir (Cadiz)
Pillars of Herakles
(Straits of Gilbraltar)
Tingis (Tangiers)
Oran
Les Andalouses
Mersa Madakh
Lixus
Carthage
Hadrumetum
Thapsos
Acholla
Madhya
B
MALTA
A
Sala
Rusaddir
Rachgoun
Gabes
Sabratha
Oea
Leptis Magna
TRIPOLITANIA
Mogador

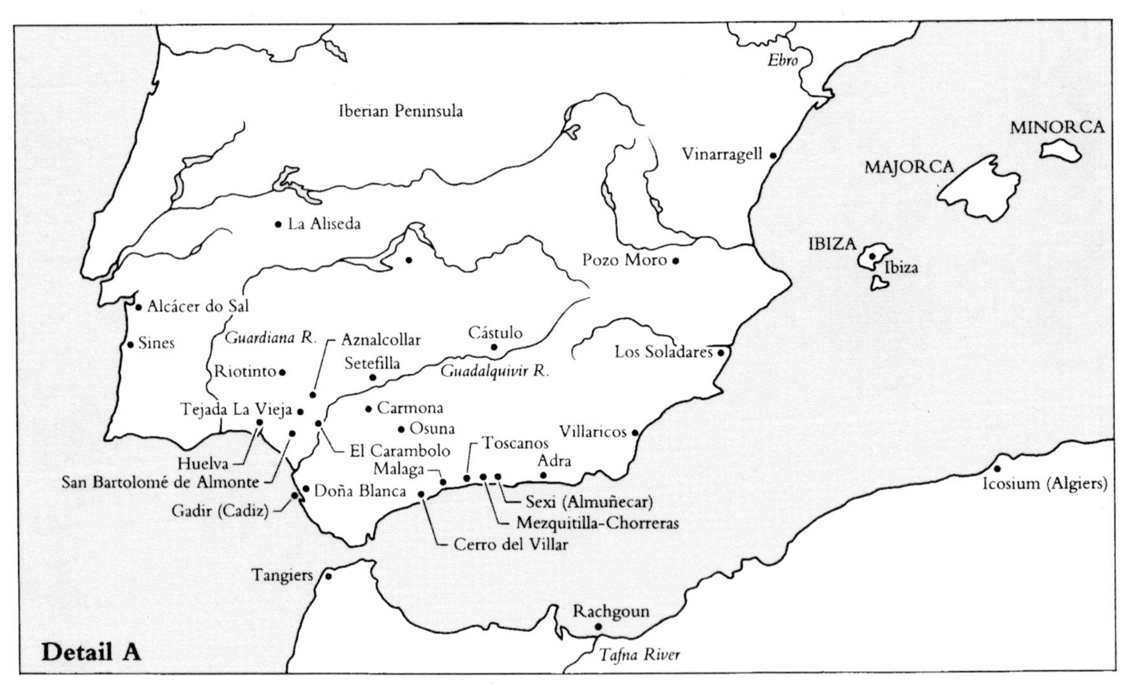
Ebro
Iberian Peninsula
MINORCA
Vinarragell
MAJORCA
La Aliseda
IBIZA
Ibiza
Pozo Moro
Alcácer do Sal
Sines
Guardiana R.
Aznalcollar
Cástulo
Los Soladares
Setefilla
Guadalquivir R.
Riotinto
Carmona
Tejada La Vieja
Osuna
Villaricos
El Carambolo
Toscanos
Huelva
Malaga
Adra
San Bartolomé de Almonte
Icosium (Algiers)
Doña Blanca
Sexi (Almuñecar)
Gadir (Cadiz)
Mezquitilla-Chorreras
Cerro del Villar
Tangiers
Rachgoun
Detail A
Tafna River

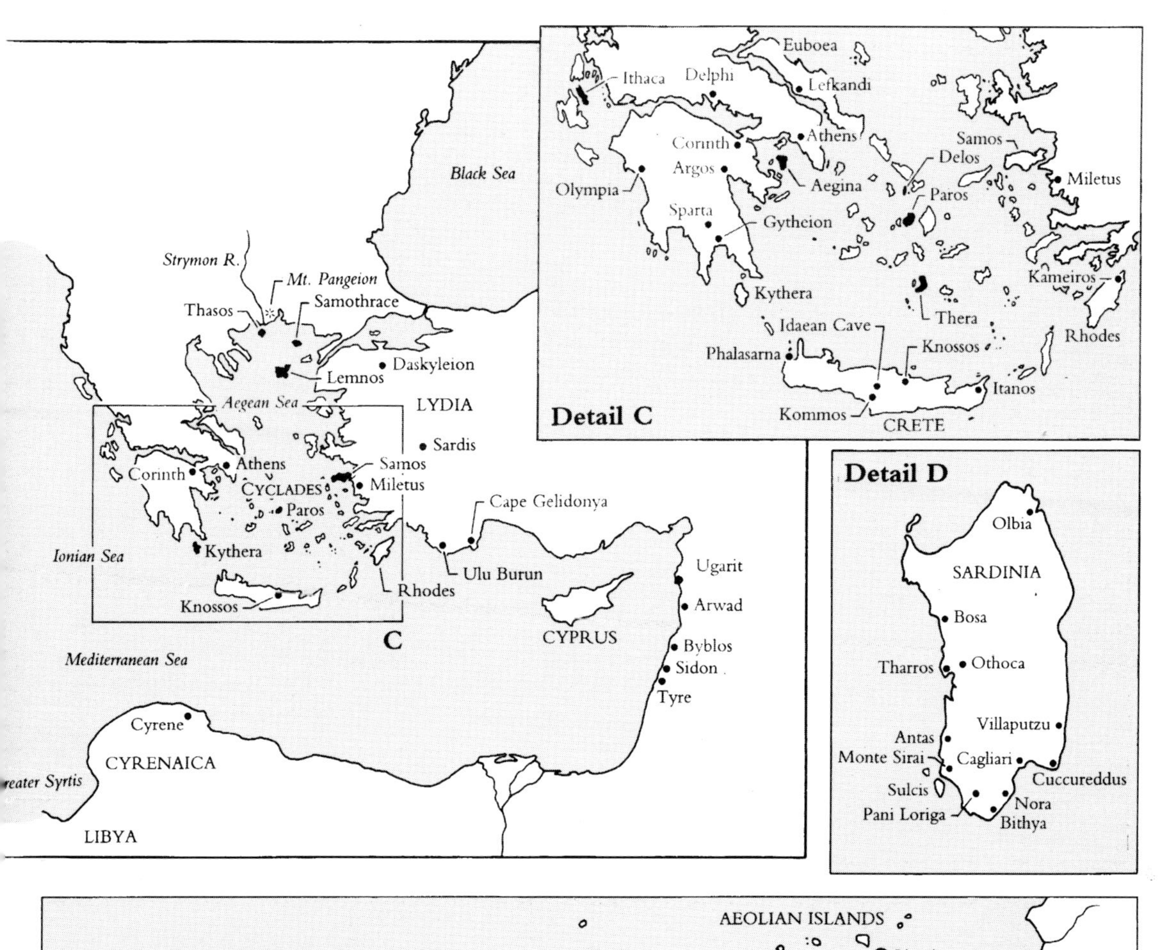
Black Sea
Strymon R.
Mt. Pangeion
Thasos
Samothrace
Lemnos
Daskyleion
Aegean Sea
LYDIA
Sardis
Corinth
Athens
Samos
Miletus
CYCLADES
Paros
Kythera
Ionian Sea
Knossos
Rhodes
Cape Gelidonya
Ulu Burun
C
Ugarit
Arwad
CYPRUS
Byblos
Sidon
Tyre
Mediterranean Sea
Cyrene
CYRENAICA
reater Syrtis
LIBYA
Euboea
Ithaca
Delphi
Lefkandi
Athens
Corinth
Argos
Olympia
Aegina
Sparta
Gytheion
Samos
Delos
Miletus
Paros
Kythera
Kameiros
Thera
Idaean Cave
Phalasarna
Knossos
Rhodes
Itanos
Kommos
CRETE
Detail C
Detail D
Olbia
SARDINIA
Bosa
Tharros
Othoca
Villaputzu
Antas
Monte Sirai
Cagliari
Cuccureddus
Sulcis
Nora
Pani Loriga
Bithya

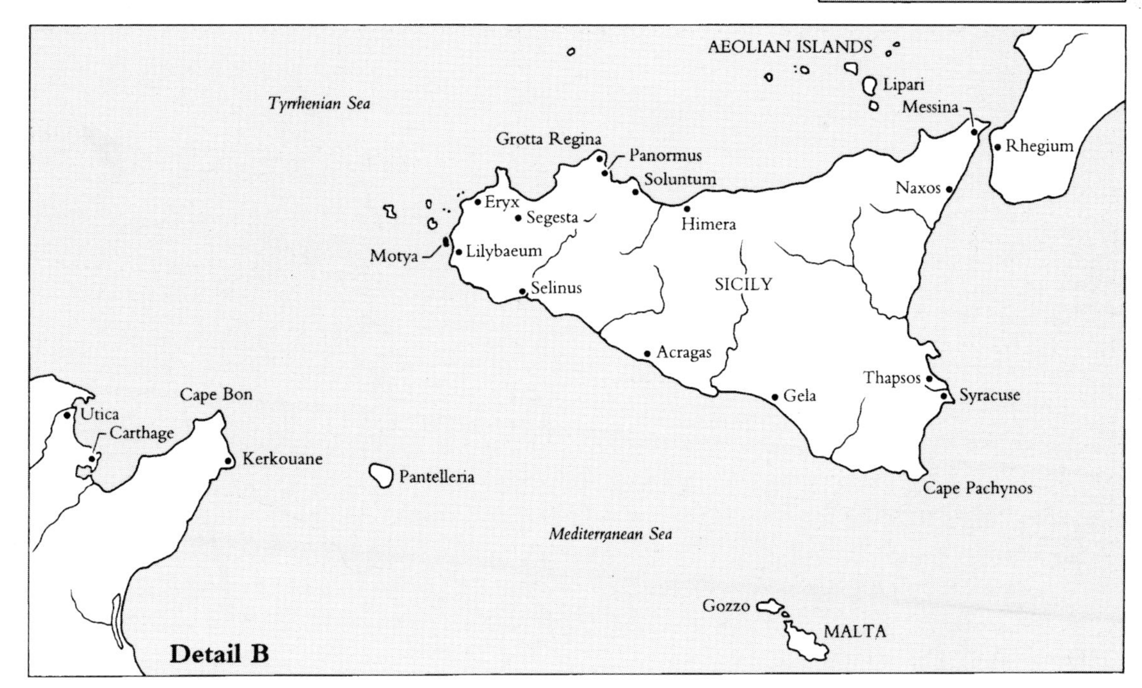
AEOLIAN ISLANDS
Lipari
Tyrrhenian Sea
Messina
Rhegium
Grotta Regina
Panormus
Soluntum
Naxos
Eryx
Segesta
Himera
Motya
Lilybaeum
SICILY
Selinus
Acragas
Thapsos
Syracuse
Gela
Cape Bon
Utica
Carthage
Kerkouane
Pantelleria
Cape Pachynos
Mediterranean Sea
Gozzo
MALTA
Detail B

Introduction

THE 'PHOENICIANS': the name today conjures up a variety of contradictory images – mirrors of an ambiguous past. One of the great enigmas of the ancient world, the Phoenicians were both lauded and despised in antiquity. They were celebrated – as learned scribes, who passed on the modern alphabet; as vaunted seafarers and intrepid explorers, who redefined the boundaries of the ancient world; as skilled engineers, who built monumental harbours and cities; and as gifted artisans, whose skilful creations were the envy of royalty. The Greek poet Homer, writing in the eighth century BC, lauds the superb craftsmanship of the Sidonians, whose silver mixing-bowl, presented by Achilles as prize at the funeral games of Patroklos, was unparalleled in beauty and workmanship.

The very traits for which the Phoenicians were admired, however, brought them contempt and derision. They were despised as cheaters and hucksters, who could not be trusted; as insatiable mongers and unscrupulous profiteers, who kidnapped the helpless and traded in human lives; and as a licentious and morally corrupt race of people, who prostituted their daughters and butchered their infant children in honour of their gods. The Phoenicians' pejorative image as schemers and connivers has survived in the modern vernacular; 'Jezebel', our term for the quintessential shameless woman, was, in fact, a Tyrian princess.

Who were the Phoenicians? Aside from their general Semitic roots, their ethnic identity remains a mystery. Even their ancient name eludes us. The modern term 'Phoenician' is, in fact, a Greek invention, from the word *Phoinix*, whose very meaning is debated among scholars. Among other things, it signified the colour purple-red or crimson – a reference to the reddish colour of their skin, or perhaps to their production of a highly prized purple dye. What the Phoenicians called themselves in antiquity is anyone's guess; the ancient term *Canaanite* represents the most likely possibility. The Phoenicians' origins, too, remain a mystery. Ancient classical tradition associated them with the region of the Red Sea (the ancient name for the modern Persian Gulf); modern scholars tend to reject this account as an attempt to explain their colour association with 'red'.

The issue of ethnic identity raises an even thornier question: did the Phoenicians, in fact, have a national identity? Tyre, Sidon, Byblos, and Arwad were all fiercely independent, rival cities who rarely worked in concert with one another, except under common threat. The Old Testament speaks of Tyrians, Sidonians, Byblians, and Arvadites; there is not a single allusion to a Phoenician confederacy or state. What common bonds, if any, existed between them remains unclear to us today.

Geographically, the Phoenicians are no more easily defined. According to the ancient classical authors, they occupied the entire Levantine coast between the Suez and the Gulf of Alexandretta. In actuality, however, their heartland was considerably smaller, consisting of a narrow coastal strip between the Lebanon mountains and the Mediterranean sea stretching from northern Palestine to southern Syria – a slightly extended version of modern Lebanon. The dichotomy suggests that the term 'Phoenician' in antiquity was broadly applied to any Semitic sea-trader.

Such ambiguity, ironically, may reflect historical reality. Unlike their Syrian or Palestinian neighbours, the Phoenicians were a confederation of traders rather than a country defined by territorial boundaries. Their empire was less a stretch of land than a patchwork of widely scattered merchant communities. Maritime trade, not territory, defined their sphere.

In many respects, the Phoenicians may be considered a lost civilization. Their histories and mythologies, diligently recorded on papyrus scrolls, have all vanished, the victim of human intervention and an uncompromising environment. Indeed, not a single Phoenician manuscript has survived in the original or in translation.

The great libraries of Tyre and Carthage have long since disappeared, the casualty of Macedonian and Roman aggression. So, too, have Phoenician historical and economic records stored in palace and temple archives. An extensive cache of clay papyrus seals recently discovered at Carthage bears ghostly witness to one such collection, lost in the Roman fire that razed the city in 146 BC. It is supremely ironic that the very people responsible for transmitting the alphabet to the West should have left so little in the way of a written legacy.

By default, then, our history of the Phoenicians must rely on the scattered testimony of others, augmented by an ever growing body of archaeological evidence. The primary sources – the Bible, the Assyrian annals, and the Greek and Latin authors – shed light on the military and commercial affairs of the Phoenicians (as they relate to classical or Near Eastern events), but record little of their political, social, or economic development. As for the religious sphere, with few exceptions, the Phoenicians' own memorial inscriptions – formulaic dedications on stone grave markers – offer little more than the names of their dedicants and the gods to whom they were erected. The Old Testament is informative on this subject, but is both limited and biased in its perspective. From scattered Phoenician inscriptions, it is possible to reconstruct, in part, the various ruling dynasties that held sway over Tyre, Sidon, Arwad, and Byblos; but, without associated dates and events, these often represent little more than hollow lists of royal names.

The following presentation will focus on the continuity in tradition that characterized Phoenician history over a period of more than 1200 years, from the beginning of the Late Bronze Age (*c.*1550 BC) – when the Phoenician cities (with the exception of Byblos) first emerge as urban entities – to the start of the Hellenistic period around 300 BC. In this respect, the volume represents a departure from earlier studies, which treat Phoenician culture as an Early Iron Age phenomenon that coalesced at the start of the first millennium BC – the age of Solomon and King Hiram of Tyre. According to these studies, the eleventh century marked the Phoenicians' emergence as a distinct entity characterized by its own language and cultural traditions.

While Tyre clearly entered a new and important political phase under Hiram in the tenth century BC, it is by no means the 'opening' chapter of that city's historical narrative.

As Egyptian and Near Eastern documents record, the preceding Late Bronze Age was a time of economic prosperity for Tyre and its neighbours. Although our knowledge of the period is limited – confined largely to references in ancient correspondence from Syria (Ugarit) and Egypt (Amarna) – the evidence, nonetheless, points to the existence of a group of active, indeed flourishing, commercial emporia along the Phoenician coast. In many respects, they were not unlike their Iron Age successors; both were governed by the same basic institutions and swayed by the same commercial concerns.

Indeed, the archaeological and epigraphical record for the Late Bronze and succeeding Iron Age offers a growing body of evidence for continuity – in the fields of religion, economy, language, and culture. In comparing the Early Iron Age with its precursor, very little is, in fact, entirely new. The early Byblian Phoenician alphabetic script was the product of earlier developments in the Canaanite realm; distinctive Phoenician ceramic and masonry techniques, too, had earlier antecedents; even the celebrated purple-dye industry of the Phoenicians had its roots in the Late Bronze Age.

From all archaeological indications, the transition from the Late Bronze to the Early Iron Age along the Phoenician coast was not accompanied by abrupt or radical change in population make-up or political organization. For reasons not yet fully understood, the massive disruptions caused elsewhere in the Levant by the marauding 'Sea Peoples' in the early twelfth century BC appear to have had a minimal affect upon the Phoenician coastal centres. For all intents and purposes, the Phoenician cities of the Iron Age – from Tyre north to Arwad – were the direct descendants of their Canaanite precursors.

A common thread unites the disparate histories of the Phoenician cities – maritime trade. Confined to a narrow coastal strip with limited agricultural resources, the sea formed their natural outlet. Early on, they realized its potential for economic growth – not only as a vehicle for commercial exchange but as a channel for prospecting abroad. In this respect, the story of the Phoenician cities may aptly be compared with that of the northern Italian principates of Venice, Genoa, and Pisa in the early Renaissance. Like that of the Phoenicians, their histories were marked by intense commercial rivalry. As with Tyre and Sidon, the commercial fortunes of Venice and Genoa were inextricably bound up with the *realpolitik* of their day. Like Tyre, thirteenth-century Genoa formed the seat of a commercial empire that spanned the Mediterranean.

In the final analysis, it is as seafarers that the Phoenicians will be remembered. In an era long before the invention of the mariner's compass, Phoenician sailors mastered the waterways, braving treacherous winds and reefs to explore paths previously uncharted. As archaeology confirms, the Mediterranean was their domain. Just how far beyond it they ventured remains a matter of much speculation. According to the Greek historian Herodotus, Phoenician sailors, at the behest of the Pharaoh Necho (610–595 BC), circumnavigated Africa, a daunting task that took them 3 years to complete. More than 2000 years would pass before the African Horn would again be rounded – by the Portuguese in 1498 under Vasco da Gama. In their ships of 'Tarshish', the Phoenicians sailed beyond the Red Sea to gold-laden Ophir, a distant biblical land whose historical veracity is now vouchsafed by an inscribed potsherd found in Israel. Its location remains the subject of debate; although India has been proposed, southern Arabia or east Africa remain more likely alternatives closer to home.

Phoenician and Carthaginian sea-traders ventured far beyond the Straits of Gibraltar, the ancient 'Pillars of Hercules', along the Atlantic coasts of Spain and Morocco. In pursuit of tin, the Carthaginian navigator Himilco reportedly traversed the English Channel, landing along the southern coast of Britain, perhaps beyond. The vexing question remains: just how far into open waters did the Phoenicians explore within the Atlantic? Did they, in fact, reach the distant Azores, as the alleged (and unverified) discovery of Carthaginian coins, recorded in an eighteenth-century Spanish account, suggests. If so, could they have ventured beyond, driven by the Atlantic trade winds and the Canary Current, to the Americas? The answer will probably never be known. Proof in the form of an inscription, like the celebrated Phoenician text allegedly found at Parahaiba in northern Brazil, remains unlikely. The latter, which recounts the landing of a storm-driven party from Sidon, has long been recognized as a clever forgery.[1] If such a fateful expedition had actually occurred, the proof is more likely to be found in a handful of Phoenician pottery sherds.

The present study encompasses two separate stories – about the Phoenicians in the eastern Mediterranean (the 'Phoenician' horizon) and the Carthaginians in the west (the 'Punic' horizon). By treating the two narratives separately throughout the book, I have attempted to give them both their due. Owing to space constraints, however, primary emphasis has been placed on the history of the Phoenicians in the east, a subject that has, until recent years, been largely overlooked in favour of the Punic west. In the last two decades, extraordinary progress has been achieved on the archaeological and historical front in the mainland, meriting a reassessment of the Phoenicians in their homeland. The present volume will attempt to incorporate these new findings. A word about the interpretation of the biblical sources. The present author acknowledges the ongoing debate over the historical veracity of the biblical texts dealing with kings Hiram and Solomon; in this volume, however, he has chosen to adopt the traditional view that the narrative in its basic elements is historically correct.

As with all studies Phoenician, the present book should be considered a 'work in progress'. No doubt, future discoveries, such as those currently being made at Carthage and Tyre, will add to and perhaps alter some of the conclusions drawn here. It is my sincere hope that this study, by stimulating future debate and discussion, will contribute to a better understanding of the enigma that we call the Phoenicians.

Chapter One

HISTORY

The Late Bronze Age

AS IT WAS throughout the entire Near East, the end of the Middle Bronze Age marked a pivotal point in the history of the Levant. Some time in the first half of the sixteenth century BC, the Hyksos, an amalgam of Canaanite-speaking peoples from Syria–Palestine, fell from power in Egypt. Their removal ushered in a long and prosperous period of native Egyptian dynastic rule known as the New Kingdom. Together with the Egyptians and the Hittites, the Hurrian-speaking peoples in the kingdom of Mitanni in Syria figured prominently in the historical development of the Late Bronze Age Levant.

The numerous levels of burning and destruction uncovered by archaeologists at various Levantine sites document the path of Egypt's military incursion into Syria–Palestine following the expulsion of the Hyksos. Egyptian military intervention intensified under Tuthmosis III (1479–1425 BC), whose war efforts laid the foundation for Egypt's western Asiatic empire.

Tuthmosis' annals are revealing in their focus on the Phoenician littoral. Beginning in his fifth campaign, Egyptian military thrust is directed against the northerly Akkar coastal plain and the cities of the Eleutheros river valley. As the single break-point between Mount Lebanon in the south and the Jabal al-Ansariyeh range in the north, the Akkar served as the main passage between the Mediterranean coast and inland Syria. Early historical records testify to the strategic significance of this river corridor (known today as the Homs Depression), which provided direct and efficient access to the River Orontes and thence to the middle Euphrates. Major Phoenician centres in the region such as Byblos and Arwad proved pivotal to Tuthmosis' attempt to consolidate control of the region of Amurru, then under Mitannian supervision.

Tuthmosis' efforts culminated in the capture of the coastal city of Ullasa (at the mouth of the Eleutheros). From there, the Egyptian monarch directed his attention northward to the harbours and port facilities along the Phoenician coast as far as Amrit. Although it is not specifically mentioned by name, it is likely that the island port of Arwad (modern Roaud) was included in Tuthmosis' tour of inspection. With its twin sheltered harbours, Arwad was the surest and most dependable point of anchorage along the entire Syrian coast north of Byblos. Already a flourishing harbour town in Tuthmosis' own day, it was ideally situated as an entrepot for coastal as well as inland trade.

Like Byblos to the south, Arwad was commercially dependent upon access to the Eleutheros valley, which provided a direct line of communication with the interior.

Through this inland corridor via coastal Tripolis, Byblos (which had no direct access to the interior) became the major outlet for Mesopotamian trade with Egypt in the early second millennium BC.

Byblos, in fact, stood at the median point of two Phoenician commercial spheres. The first, extending northwards from Tripolis, looked primarily towards Syria and Mesopotamia for trade, while the second, extending southwards from Beirut, was oriented towards the southern Palestinian coastal plain and Egypt. As we shall see, the differing orientations of these two spheres figured prominently in the development of the Phoenician coastal cities in the Late Bronze Age.

BYBLOS: AN EXCEPTIONAL CASE

With the possible exception of Arwad (whose archaeological past remains a mystery), Byblos is the only major Phoenician coastal city with a continuous record of occupation from the Early Bronze Age to the first millennium BC. As the historical and archaeological record attests, the city enjoyed the height of its economic prosperity in the early second millennium BC (nineteenth to eighteenth centuries), when it served, alongside Ugarit, as the eastern Mediterranean's primary coastal emporium with direct trade ties to Egypt, the Aegean, and Mesopotamia. (See Plate I.) Byblos apparently continued to prosper in the late Middle Bronze Age, when commercial ties with its Canaanite Hyksos counterparts in the Egyptian Delta appear to have been close.[1]

As the texts clearly document, Egypt's longstanding interest in Byblos was motivated by one dominant factor: the desire for Levantine wood. Relatively devoid of large-circumference trees, Egypt actively sought out foreign sources of supply. As history records, among its primary targets were the forest reserves located behind Byblos in the valley of the Nahr Ibrahim and the adjacent slopes of Mount Lebanon.[2] (See Plate II.)

Not surprisingly, Tuthmosis III, in his Levantine campaigns, saw to it that the Phoenician harbours were adequately stocked with timber and were prepared for annual shipments of cedar wood to Egypt. His account of the on-site construction at Byblos of cedar boats and their overland transport to the Euphrates reveals the scale and intricacy of such state-controlled operations.

THE SOUTHERN PHOENICIAN COASTAL CITIES

By the mid-fourteenth century BC, as the Amarna correspondence between the Egyptian court and the Phoenician coastal cities reveals, the region of Syria–Palestine was incorporated within a loosely defined Egyptian administrative framework involving three areas. The southern Phoenician coast from Akko to Beirut was subsumed within Canaan, a district encompassing the entire Palestinian coast as far as the Egyptian border at Sinai. The second district, Apu, covered the inland regions of present-day northern Israel and Lebanon, from Galilee up through the Lebanese Beqa. The northern Phoenician coastal plain from Byblos to Arwad formed part of a third district, Amurru, centred on the Akkar plain between the coast and the River Orontes. It is this northern coastal strip that the

1 *Cuneiform clay tablet, bearing the text of a letter fro Abimilki, king of Tyre, to the Egyptian court. From Tell el-Amarna, Egypt.*

Egyptians appear to have designated as Djahi in distinction to the southern Phoenician littoral, which was regarded as a northern extension of Canaan itself.

In the Amarna correspondence, the southern Phoenician cities of Tyre, Sidon, and Beirut all appear as developed and relatively prosperous political entities with established dynastic houses, political assemblies, and commercial fleets. While administratively (and, to a large degree, militarily) dependent upon Egypt, they none the less exhibit a considerable amount of autonomy in their inter-regional dealings, which are marked by intense commercial rivalry (especially in the case of Tyre and Sidon). For each of the cities, control of and access to the surrounding hinterland was a critical and often contested factor. Outside of Phoenicia proper, the economic impact of neighbouring emporia, such as Ugarit, Hazor, and Qadesh, is clearly felt, reflecting a complex and vigorous intra-regional network of economic exchange.

Byblos' standing within the Egyptian political hierarchy is clearly attested both in its position of regional territorial oversight and in the volume of its correspondence in the Amarna archives. (See fig. 1.) (Its seventy-plus letters are, in fact, the most extensive in the Amarna corpus.) Tyre and Sidon also figure prominently (although less frequently) in this correspondence. Tyre's economic prosperity is clearly evinced in a letter from Rib-addi, king of Byblos, to the pharaoh Akhenaten, in which the former warns the Egyptian monarch of the enormous wealth of the 'princely house of Tyre', which he compares with that of Ugarit, the most prosperous of eastern Mediterranean trade emporia. (While Rib-addi is clearly using poetic 'hyperbole' to denounce his rival southern neighbour, the comparison is none the less revealing.) In deference to Tyre's political and economic standing, the Byblian monarch initiates a political alliance with the Tyrian king, offering his own sister in marriage to that ruler.[3]

Curiously, none of the Phoenician coastal cities south of Byblos receives any direct mention in the accounts of Tuthmosis III or his immediate successors. Tyre, Sidon, and Beirut, in fact, do not appear until the Amarna correspondence of the mid-fourteenth century BC.

What may be deduced about the status of the southern Phoenician cities in the first half of the Late Bronze Age (sixteenth to fifteenth centuries)? In this regard, the record of earlier occupation in the Middle Bronze Age is of critical importance. An archaeological sounding conducted at Tyre in the 1970s revealed that, following an initial settlement in the third millennium BC, the island was abandoned during the Middle Bronze Age and reoccupied only around the middle of the sixteenth century BC. As for the surrounding cemeteries in the region, all date to the Late Bronze and succeeding Iron Age. To the north, the city of Sarepta has yielded firm evidence for an initial settlement at the same time – in the mid-sixteenth century BC.

Excavations at Sidon and its immediate vicinity have also produced no trace of occupation during the Middle Bronze Age. The same is true of the adjacent coastal site of Dakerman, which served as a primary necropolis for the city throughout most of its history; the Late Bronze Age cemetery overlies a prehistoric, Chalcolithic settlement. The immediate vicinity of Sidon has, in fact, yielded an abundance of Late Bronze Age tombs; earlier burials of the Middle Bronze Age, although attested in the general region, are located further inland. At the neighbouring coastal site of Khaldé to the south of Beirut, excavations have revealed a Late Bronze Age building complex that directly overlay a settlement of the Late Chalcolithic period, once again revealing a hiatus in the record of Middle Bronze Age settlement along the southern Phoenician coast.[4]

The stratigraphic record at Tyre reveals that the city entered a phase of renewed prosperity, marked by extensive architectural development and industrial activity, in the mid-fourteenth century BC. Sarepta, too, enjoyed a period of intensive industrial and architectural growth at this time. What factors contributed to the remarkable expansion of the southern Phoenician cities?

THE PHOENICIAN CITIES AND THE LATE BRONZE AGE COPPER TRADE

Egyptian historical records clearly underscore the economic importance of the tin and copper trade in the eastern Mediterranean during the Late Bronze Age. Beginning in the reign of Tuthmosis III, 'Asiatic copper' is first imported into Egypt in quantity.[5] The primary purveyor, as one would expect, is Cyprus, whose very name, Kypros, means 'copper' in ancient Greek. Next to Cyprus, however, the Phoenician coastal cities appear as primary providers in Tuthmosis' accounts. Phoenician involvement in the copper trade is equally attested in the fourteenth century. In the Amarna correspondence, in fact, copper appears only in the imposts of the Phoenician cities.

As modern geological survey has shown, local sources of copper ore are documented in the region of Byblos,[6] which itself was an active bronze-working centre in the early second millennium BC. Local copper deposits have been identified also in the southern Beqa, where a regional tradition of cast copper statuettes flourished.

During this time, coastal Byblos served as a primary terminus for the lucrative import trade in tin (and lapis lazuli) from Afghanistan to the West. That such trade continued through the Late Bronze Age is clear, and it is very probable that the Phoenician coastal cities benefited economically from it. Egyptian control over the Akkar plain and the Beqa in the fourteenth century provided them with a protected corridor for such trade.

Active Phoenician participation in the Late Bronze Age Mediterranean tin and copper trade is suggested by the quantities of Cypriot and Mycenaean pottery unearthed at Phoenician coastal sites such as Akko, Tyre, and Sarepta. The recently discovered late fourteenth- or early thirteenth-century shipwreck at Ulu Burun off the southern coast of Turkey is illuminating in this regard.[7] Among its varied cargo, which included a large quantity of copper and tin ingots, were many Canaanite amphorae of a type originating in the northern Palestinian and southern Phoenician coastal sphere (from the region of Haifa to Byblos). The Ulu Burun vessel also contained a large pithos with tin fragments that held more than twenty Cypriot vessels and four pottery lamps of mainland variety. The presence of the amphorae and lamps (the latter ubiquitous to the Syro-Palestinian coast but rarely found on Cyprus) along with the cargo – stone and carved ivories, metalwork and wrtiting tablets of boxwood – suggests that the consignment originated along the Phoenician or Syrian coast.

The emergence of the southern Phoenician cities in the fourteenth century may be seen, at least in part, within the context of a major political realignment that now occurred in the Levant – the establishment of entente between Egypt and Mitanni. Peace between the two rival powers was officially sealed by a marriage alliance, about 1415 BC, between Tuthmosis IV and a daughter of the Mitannian king Artatama I. In control both of inland commercial routes along the strategic lower Orontes valley and the entire coast as far as Ugarit, Egypt was now in a position to dominate eastern Mediterranean trade in the Levant. As 'favoured cities' in the eyes of the Egyptians, the Phoenician coastal towns clearly benefited from their role as entrepreneurs in such commerce.

Egyptian historical records and tomb paintings of the period document the diversity of Levantine trade goods that entered Egypt through diplomatic and commercial channels. Not surprisingly, precious commodities and luxury goods predominated, with metals and minerals topping the list. The market for foreign imports was clearly fuelled by Egypt's own burgeoning economy, which witnessed extraordinary growth in the late Eighteenth Dynasty, beginning under Amenhotep III (1391–1353 BC).

Amenhotep's ambitious domestic programme of urban expansion and temple construction reveals the enormous wealth – in both commodities and human resources – that Egypt held at its disposal in the early fourteenth century. Bolstered by peacetime prosperity, agricultural surpluses, and a continuous influx of gold from Nubia and the Eastern Desert, the Egyptian state and temple economy grew at an unprecedented pace, creating enormous reserves which, in turn, lent stability to the economy and provided the wherewithal for substantial foreign trade. Aside from the accumulation of physical wealth, other factors contributed substantially towards an economic climate ripe for Egyptian international trade. One was the re-establishment of an administrative capital in the lower Nile Delta at Memphis, a location well positioned for Mediterranean trade. Another was the marked growth in the number and size of the temple compounds, which, in turn, created an increased demand for outside goods and services. Of the commodities most highly sought after by the Egyptians, one – timber – clearly had an overriding impact on the Phoenician economy.

A case in point: the Late Bronze Age cedar trade

The growth and diversification of the Egyptian economy during the Eighteenth Dynasty created a lucrative market for the Phoenician cities. Nowhere is this fact more evident than in the vigorous Egyptian import trade in timber, which grew rapidly from the time of Tuthmosis III. Once a virtual Byblian monopoly, such commerce appears now to have benefited the majority of Phoenician coastal towns, nearly all of which (with the notable exception of Tyre) had direct access to large reserves of marketable wood. Extensive tracts of cedar, fir, pine, oak, and juniper were located all along the Lebanon range from Sidon north to Tripoli and, beyond, along the slopes of the Jebel Ansariye; additional growth could be found along the western slopes of the Anti-Lebanon and Mount Hermon to the south.[8] (See Plate II.) Of the various Lebanese hardwoods harvested in antiquity, cedar was the most highly prized because of its durability and fragrance. The Egyptian market for cedar was insatiable. In addition to an expanding shipbuilding industry (which included not only seagoing vessels but a variety of river craft), the diversified needs of the Egyptian temple estates (roof beams, columns, doors, portable shrines, and altars) had to be met. The Egyptian funerary industry supplied another lucrative market: cedar was the wood of preference for coffins of the priestly class and the élite, while its resin was used as both an aromatic and an embalming agent. Financial gain for the Phoenicians lay not only in the marketing of the timber itself but in the varied employment it provided Phoenician artisans, traders, and seamen, both on the mainland and in locations abroad.

The Phoenicians: the Post-Amarna and Ramesside periods

The late Eighteenth Dynasty saw a shift in balance of power away from Egypt towards the Hittite realm. The loss of the North Syrian coast – from Ugarit south to Byblos – was a serious economic blow to Egypt. While the precise nature of Egyptian administrative control over the southern Phoenician coast at this period is unclear, there are indications that the region enjoyed a greater degree of independence.

Such political autonomy quickly ended, however, soon after the establishment of the first Ramesside dynasty. In the first year of Seti I (1306–1290 BC), Egyptian control was swiftly reaffirmed over the southern Phoenician coast from Akko to the north of Tyre – a clear demonstration of Egypt's economic interest in this region. Despite repeated attempts by Seti I and his successor, Ramesses II, however, the strategic northern coast and Akkar plain remained in Hittite hands. The division of political control over Phoenicia was affirmed by a treaty negotiated by the Egyptians in 1269 BC. A stone marker, or stele, erected on location by Ramesses II suggests that the boundary was the Nahr el-Kelb, or River Dog, between Beirut and Byblos.

As under Amenhotep III, the long and relatively peaceful reign of Ramesses II (1290–1224 BC) was a period of marked prosperity for both Egypt and the Phoenician realm. To an even greater degree than before, the renewed vigour of Egypt's temple-based economy encouraged the development of state-sponsored Mediterranean trade. That Egypt at least partially undertook the initiative in such exchange seems clear from both the archaeological and the historical record. In his Great Abydos Inscription, Ramesses boasts of having equipped his father's mortuary temple with a seagoing vessel (replete with merchants) for foreign trade. As contemporary texts reveal, private estates were provided also with merchantmen for coastal trade. In the tomb of one such merchant, Pabes, at Memphis, we find a depiction of commercial activity at the city's docks, including the offloading of a copper ingot.[9]

Egyptian interest in Levantine trade is clearly evinced by Ramesses II's building activities at Memphis and at Pi-Ramesses (modern Qantir) in the Eastern Delta. Site of the former Hyksos capital of Avaris, Pi-Ramesses' location along the Pelusiac branch of the Nile gave it direct access to the Levantine coast. Numerous finds of Canaanite commercial amphorae at both cities testify to Egypt's vigorous trade contacts with Ugarit and the Phoenician realm. The archaeological and textual evidence documents the active presence of Levantine merchants in Egypt, above all at Memphis with its extensive dockyards and shipbuilding facilities. The existence there of Ramesside-period shrines to Baal and Astarte clearly suggests that a Phoenician enclave (like that which Herodotus later observed at Memphis in the fifth century BC) existed in Ramesses' day.

THE PHOENICIANS AND CYPRUS IN THE THIRTEENTH CENTURY

At the Phoenician coastal cities, a notable trend may be observed in levels dating to the thirteenth century BC: Cypriot pottery imports show a marked decline compared with that of the preceding fourteenth century. This drop has traditionally been attributed to a decline in Phoenician–Cypriot bilateral trade. The archaeological record on Cyprus, however, reveals a more complicated and, perhaps, contrasting picture. Indeed, as recent excavation has shown, the thirteenth century marked a phase of intense urban and industrial development closely connected with the production and export of copper. At the port facility of Enkomi on Cyprus' east coast, copper smelting reached its peak at this time. The emergence of new sites in the south associated with copper production points to industrial diversification and an expansion of trade.

The copper 'ox-hide' ingots attributable to Cyprus are all of late fourteenth- or thirteenth-century date. Of particular relevance is a large cargo of ingots found aboard a sunken Late Bronze Age vessel off Cape Gelidonya on Turkey's southern coast; laboratory analysis has shown that they, like their counterparts from the Ulu Burun wreck, are of Cypriot manufacture. The vessel's cargo strongly suggests that the ship itself, datable to around 1200 BC, was of mainland Levantine or Cypriot origin.[10] The thirteenth century, in fact, marked Cyprus' emerging role in the central Mediterranean trade with Sicily and Sardinia.

Cypriot involvement in Aegean trade at this time may help to explain a conspicuous pattern in the archaeological record in the Levant: the visible and ubiquitous presence of imported Mycenaean pottery at both coastal and inland sites. The occurrence of such exports has conventionally been attributed to growing Mycenaean trade initiative in the eastern Mediterranean, but the archaeological and historical evidence for Mycenaean presence abroad, aside from the pottery, is negligible. How else may we account for the presence of these Greek imported wares in the Levant? The answer is that they are a by-product of Cypriot trade. At Sarepta, the thirteenth-century occupation levels have revealed large quantities of Mycenaean painted pottery but virtually no imported Cypriot wares. Yet, active Cypriot trade with Egypt and the Levant at this time is clearly indicated by the presence of Cypriot exports in other media (especially bronze and faience). In virtually all thirteenth-century Levantine contexts in which Mycenaean pottery is found, it is accompanied by Cypriot and/or Canaanite wares.

The conspicuous presence of Mycenaean (IIIB) painted wares at Sarepta and other Levantine coastal sites in the thirteenth century may thus be regarded as a direct reflection of bilateral trade between Cyprus and the Phoenician mainland. One may easily imagine how a Cypriot trading vessel like the Gelidonya ship, bound with copper and tin for the Aegean market, might have acquired Mycenaean wares at an intermediate transit station such as Rhodes. Once back in its home port, its cargo could have reached the Levantine mainland either through Cypriot initiative or through the intermediary of a Phoenician merchant. Such entrepreneurs were almost certainly responsible for the Myceanean wares found at inland sites in the Beqa and the Galilee, such as Kamid el-Loz and Tel Dan.

THE PHOENICIANS, UGARIT, AND MESOPOTAMIAN TRADE

Ugarit's vast commercial resources (it controlled a territory of 3500 square kilometres (1350 square miles), comprising some two hundred villages) and its access to the tin- and silver-rich southern Anatolian realm made it both an attractive market and a commercial rival for the Phoenician cities. Ugarit's commercial ties were particularly strong with the northerly Phoenician ports of Arwad and Byblos, with whom it appears to have engaged regularly in commercial trade. In addition to providing finished goods, these cities furnished Ugarit with alternative facilities for industrial production.[11]

As a Hittite dependency, Ugarit's primary economic orientation, however, lay to the north – with the Anatolian realm. Commercial ties were particularly strong with Carchemish and with the Cilician port of Ura, the primary Mediterranean outlet for the Hittites. Economic ties with Cyprus were also close. Throughout the thirteenth century BC, the Eleutheros and Orontes river valleys remained under Hittite control. Hittite authority doubtless ensured safe passage for Mesopotamian trade through the Akkar plain; such commerce clearly benefited the northern Phoenician centres of Simyra, Byblos, and Arwad.

In the middle of the century a shift occurred in the control of overland Mesopotamian trade that clearly benefited the Phoenicians. As a contemporary document reveals, the Hittites, in concert with the merchants of Amurru, instigated a commercial blockade of Assyria. With trade access through the Akkar plain denied, the Assyrians (who were now in control of Babylonia) sought an alternative commercial route to the south, which passed from the Euphrates via Damascus and Tadmor (Palmyra) to the Lebanese coast through the Beqa. This southerly shift placed the southern Phoenician coastal cities in a strategic position commercially. The chance discovery at Tyre of an Assyrian cylinder seal of the late thirteenth century may well document the existence of trade relations between that city and the northern Mesopotamian realm.[12]

THE PHOENICIANS IN THE LATE BRONZE AGE: AN OVERVIEW

As the archaeological and the written records reveal, the Phoenician coastal cities in the Late Bronze Age were relatively prosperous entities. By all indications, their economies were diversified; foreign trade in timber and metals played an especially dominant role. The economic importance of various craft industries is clear. The correspondence from Ugarit reveals that both Tyre and Byblos were commercially active in the textile and garment trade. Late Bronze Age facilities for the production of purple dye from the murex shell have, in fact, been uncovered at Akko and Sarepta, suggesting an active export trade in dyed wool and linen garments. The Tyrians were also involved in the manufacture of faience, a form of vitreous paste made from ground sand; excavations at the site revealed an extensive precinct of faience production. In the Amarna correspondence, Tyre is also recorded to have sent a large shipment of raw glass to Egypt.

As it was later on in the Iron Age, the Phoenician market in luxury goods must already have been an active and a lucrative one. The inventory of finds from the palace complex at Kamid el-Loz in the Beqa offers an indication of the wealth of precious items (including carved ivories and granulated gold jewellery) available to them. Kamid el-Loz itself was located astride two major commercial routes to the Euphrates, extending north from Egypt and east from Phoenicia.

Politically and economically, the Late Bronze Age Phoenician realm comprised two distinct regions: the northern Akkar coastal plain and the southern Phoenician littoral. The island ports of Arwad in the north and Tyre in the south illustrate the differing commercial orientations of these two areas. Arwad looked towards Syria as its primary market, while Tyre looked south towards Egypt and Palestine. Both cities were united by their commercial ties to Cyprus. In the thirteenth century, Arwad and Tyre fell, respectively, under Hittite and Egyptian administrative control.

Byblos occupied the middle ground, geographically, commercially, and politically, trading actively with both the north and south. Despite growing competition from its Levantine neighbours, the city appears to have retained its earlier dominance as the primary Phoenician commercial depot in the Late Bronze Age. Aside from its longstanding reciprocal trade relationship with Egypt, Byblos was unique among Phoenician cities in another important respect: it controlled a considerable stretch of coastal territory extending from Batrun in the north to the Nahr el-Kelb in the south.

Of the Late Bronze Age Phoenician coastal cities, ironically, it is Sidon about which we know least. In contrast to Tyre and Byblos, the historical record reveals little about its commercial activities with either Egypt or Ugarit. Like Beirut, however, it enjoyed direct access through the Beqa to inland trade with Mesopotamia, a factor which may have contributed to its economic rise in the Late Bronze Age.[13]

The Iron Age

THE LATE THIRTEENTH TO EARLY TWELFTH CENTURIES BC: A PERIOD OF TRANSITION

The final quarter of the thirteenth and ensuing years of the early twelfth century marked an extraordinary period of change for the entire eastern Mediterranean. Triggered, in part, by the incursions of foreigners known collectively as the 'Sea Peoples,' this era witnessed the collapse of the Mycenaean and Hittite empires and the decline of Assyria and Egypt as regional powers. The period also witnessed the growing ascendance of semi-nomadic groups, such as the early Israelites in Palestine and the Aramaeans in Syria.

As modern research has shown, the dramatic changes which transformed the political and economic landscape of the Near East in the early twelfth century were the result of a complex variety of factors, both internal and external. Geological evidence points to marked environmental and climatic change, which brought about a gradual rise in temperature and sea level. On a socio-economic plane, the collapse of the Late Bronze Age urban 'palace' system led to a significant change in patterns of livelihood, trade, and communication throughout the region. In both Palestine and Syria, the emergence and growing social dominance of a pastoral element is evidenced by a gradual shift in settlement pattern away from the coastal plain towards the outlying steppes and hill country. The predominantly urban structure of the Late Bronze Age city-state is now replaced by an emerging pattern of village settlement.

How did such change affect the regions immediately surrounding Phoenicia proper? To the north, the cities of Alalakh and Ugarit met catastrophic ends in the early years of the twelfth century BC. The massive destruction level uncovered at Ugarit and the city's subsequent abandonment bear dramatic testimony to this fact. Correspondence in the early twelfth century between Ugarit's last king, Hammurapi, and the king of Alashiya (Cyprus) mentions the presence of enemy boats along the north Syrian coast; this reference has been plausibly associated with the arrival of the Sea Peoples. Archaeological investigation on Cyprus itself has likewise revealed the presence of Aegean newcomers. In all likelihood, the island served as a staging point for sea-based incursions against the Levantine mainland.

On Phoenicia's northern boundary, the Late Bronze Age port of Tell Sukas suffered a destruction that does not appear to have had a devastating impact on the city. Clear evidence for reuse of Late Bronze Age construction at the site points to continuity in occupation; the archaeological record at Ras Ibn Hani to the north points to a similar conclusion. To the south, the various coastal cities along Israel's northern littoral, from Tell Dor northwards, also show continuity in occupation, although with a notable change in material culture that has been traditionally associated with settlements of Sea Peoples. At most of these sites (Abu Hawam, Akko, and Achziv), the earliest Iron Age occupation is, however, architecturally scant, and characterized by installations of local industrial character (furnaces, kilns, stone-lined silos, etc.).

As for the Phoenician mainland, the archaeological record, although admittedly incomplete, does not support the occurrence of massive disruption or destruction at any of the major coastal sites. Soundings conducted at Tyre revealed continuity in construction from the Late Bronze II period to the ninth century BC.[14] Moreover, these same excavations yielded no clear stratigraphic evidence for the city's destruction or abandonment. Indeed, continuity in occupation at the site is evidenced by the city's faience precinct, which saw continued usage into the Iron Age.

To the north, at Sarepta, the stratigraphic evidence likewise attests to uninterrupted occupation and cultural continuity from the Late Bronze through the early Iron Age. This transition is evident both in the ceramic sequence and in the continuity in architectural and industrial usage.[15] At both sites, the twelfth-century occupation levels, like those of their immediate neighbours, yielded very modest architectural remains in association with installations (such as storage silos and kilns) clearly intended for local industrial use. Both sites also revealed a level of cultural impoverishment underscored by a marked decline or absence of pottery imports. To the north, excavations at Tell Kazel (ancient Simyra) in the Eleutheros river valley have revealed evidence for continued, although limited, Early Iron Age occupation; once again, the archaeological evidence does not indicate that a major rupture or hiatus occurred.[16]

Relevant archaeological evidence is, unfortunately, lacking for the coastal sites of Sidon, Byblos, and Arwad. The antiquity of their place names would, however, argue strongly for continuity in their settlement; all of the Phoenician cities – from Akko to Arwad – preserve their Late Bronze Age toponyms.

Cultural continuity with the Late Bronze Age is most clearly evinced by the material culture of the Phoenician coast in the second half of the twelfth and early eleventh centuries BC. The element of continuity is, in fact, so strong that it is often difficult to differentiate the Early Iron Age Phoenician horizon from its Late Bronze Age precursor. Many varieties of pottery characteristic of the thirteenth century, such as the pithos with wavy relief band decoration, continue unabated into the succeeding twelfth century.

Moreover, in contrast to the southern and central Palestinian coast (from Philistia to

Tell Dor), none of the Phoenician cities has preserved any record or literary tradition concerning the influx or settlement of Sea Peoples. The only direct reference to possible hostilities may be found in the accounts of certain late classical authors. The Roman historian Justin, writing in the second century AD, records that the island of Tyre was 'founded' a year before the fall of Troy (1183 BC, according to the dating of Eratosthenes) by Sidonian refugees after their defeat at the hands of an unnamed king of Ashkelon. While this reference has been interpreted by some as evidence for a naval encounter between the Sidonian fleet and the Philistines,[17] the statement itself is vague and open to interpretation. Nothing is recorded about hostilities against Tyre, although the implication is that the island city must have been temporarily abandoned (or significantly depopulated) at the time of its 'refounding'. (The account actually refers to Tyre's 'foundation', a statement which is clearly at odds with the historical record.) Yet, had such an encounter occurred, it is surprising that there is no earlier or more detailed tradition associated with the event.

Thus, based upon present evidence, the disruptions (if any) that may have occurred along the Phoenician coast appear to have had no lasting impact. The archaeological record, rather, bespeaks a continuity of occupation on the mainland, although at a clearly reduced level of economic prosperity.

How then do we explain the downturn in economic fortune experienced by the Phoenicians at this time? In the present author's opinion, one predominant factor led to such decline – the loss of foreign trade.

The decline of Egypt in the twelfth century

A combination of financial and environmental factors led to a significant decline in the economic fortune of one of Phoenicia's primary markets – Egypt. An extended period of drought that affected north-east Africa in the twelfth century led to a succession of poor harvests in the Nile valley. Fuelled by marked inflation and labour unrest, Egypt's economy foundered. Following the reign of Ramesses III (1194–1163 BC), the country suffered through a succession of weak and ineffectual rulers, who did little to alleviate its internal problems. The passing of Ramesses III, in fact, spelled the end of Egypt's western Asiatic empire. The resulting loss in foreign revenue base from war booty and annual taxes clearly exacerbated Egypt's already weakened economy.

The settlements of the Philistines and other Sea Peoples (Sherden, Tjekker) along the Palestinian coast doubtless had a disruptive, if not a catastrophic, affect upon Egypt's commerce with southern Anatolia and the Levant, depriving Egypt of access to the mineral resources of the former. An indication of a marked decline in trade may already be seen in the Papyrus Harris of Ramesses III, which records the construction of only two seagoing Mediterranean trading vessels. During the reign of that monarch's successor, Ramesses IV (1153–1147 BC), Egyptian maritime commerce with the Phoenician coast apparently came to an end.

The Phoenicians and inland trade

As with Egypt, Phoenician commerce within the continental Near East must have experienced a sharp downturn in the twelfth century, as existing markets declined and trade routes disappeared. This was clearly the case with the Mesopotamian realm. Crippled by poor agricultural yields, by political unrest, and by Elamite military aggression on its southern borders, both Assyria and Babylonia declined to one of their weakest states in a long history. In Babylonia, the gold standard (which seems already to have been defunct by the late thirteenth century) was temporarily replaced, in the middle years of the twelfth century, by a copper standard – a drastic move clearly triggered by a marked decline in long-distance trade with Egypt.

In Syria, the decline of Assyrian power and collapse of Hittite authority led to serious disruption of the trans-Euphratian caravan trade, which now fell vulnerable to interference from Aramaean nomadic bands. The dramatic reduction in overland trade is clearly reflected in the demise of key inland commercial centres such as Kamid el-Loz in the Beqa, which prospered as a transit station for Egyptian trade in the Late Bronze Age. The decline of Laish and Hazor, both flourishing mercantile centres in the Late Bronze Age, must have been particularly devastating to the Phoenician ports of Tyre and Sidon, in whose geographic orbit they were situated. Both Laish and Hazor had been active in in the Mediterranean trade that undoubtedly passed through the southern Phoenician harbour towns; indeed, the latter probably served as their primary commercial outlets.

The sudden disappearance of another major trading partner – northerly Ugarit – may, have opened the way for the development of future Phoenician trade. Of all the Levantine coastal ports, Ugarit was clearly the dominant participant in both inland and maritime trade in the Late Bronze Age. Ugarit's absence from the international scene clearly altered the balance of mercantile power in the eastern Mediterranean, creating new trade opportunities which the Phoenician cities were ideally positioned to capitalize on. With their inland markets severely curtailed, the Phoenicians turned increasingly toward overseas trade with Cyprus, which was now in the midst of its own economic renaissance.

The re-emergence of the Phoenicians in the twelfth century

The early years of Phoenicia's Iron Age renewal – the mid-twelfth century BC – remains an enigma, archaeologically and historically. The earliest textual source is an inscription of the Assyrian king Tiglath-Pileser I (1114–1076 BC), who launched an expedition to the Mediterranean coast in his fifth regnal year to obtain cedar wood for the renovation of the Anu-Adad temple at Ashur. In the process, the Assyrian monarch received tribute from Byblos, Sidon, and Arwad; the latter city was the terminus of Tiglath-Pileser's expedition and the probable collection site for the Phoenician tribute offerings.

Byblos alone is mentioned in a listing of Syro-Palestinian toponyms recorded in the Onomasticon (word list) of the Egyptian scribe Amenenope, a work datable to *c.*1100 BC.[18] The same city figures prominently in a remarkable Egyptian document of the early eleventh century that sheds invaluable light on the economic and political situation along

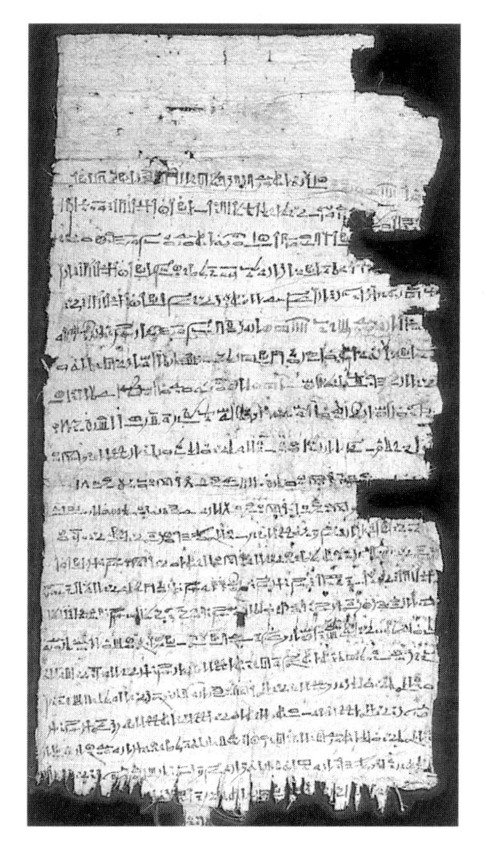

2 *Papyrus fragment from the Report of Wenamun. From El-Hibeh, Egypt.*

the Phoenician coast at this time.[19] (See fig. 2.) Written at the close of the Twentieth Dynasty in the fifth year of Ramesses XI, it recounts the journey of Wenamun, a senior official in the Theban temple of Amen-Ra who was sent by the High Priest Herihor to Byblos to fetch cedar wood for the construction of a new sacred barge to Amen. Wenamun embarks from the northern capital city of Tanis on a merchant ship commanded by a Levantine captain, Mengebet. He first lands at the port city of Dor, which, as the account records, was controlled by a contingent of Sea Peoples known as the Tjekker. Robbed (by one of his own crew) of the gold and silver he has brought in payment for the cedar shipment, Wenamun proceeds to Tyre (here the passage is unfortunately broken) and then to Byblos. Arriving penniless and without proper credentials, he is received in diffident fashion by the Byblian prince Zakarbaal, who demands that payment be sent from Egypt before the timber order can be filled. Wenamun complies. Upon receipt of partial payment, Zakarbaal orders the timber to be cut and delivered to the Egyptian envoy. As Wenamun prepares to depart, however, he is intercepted by a contingent of Tjekker ships which have been sent to arrest him. Zakarbaal intercedes on Wenamun's behalf; the Egyptian official manages to escape, but is then driven off course by a storm to Cyprus, where he is met at port by an unnamed Cypriot queen. Here the account breaks off.

The Wenamun account reveals much about maritime trade and politics in the Levant in the early eleventh century BC. The indifferent treatment that Wenamun receives at the hands of Zakarbaal reflects the changed political circumstances of the period. The Byblian royal house is no longer subservient to Egypt. On the contrary, Zakarbaal's confidence, which borders on the brash, reflects a spirit of economic independence.

The era of Wenamun is one in which international trade is conducted by joint enterprises between state-sponsored shipping firms. In the account, we learn of two such commercial lines, one under the control of King Smendes at Tanis, the other, under the Sidonian king or royal agent Werket-El (Warkat-Ili). In contrast to the Ramesside era, maritime trade initiative is clearly in Levantine hands. Wenamun travels to Byblos in a private vessel manned not by an Egyptian, but by a Phoenician crew. The conditions of the timber purchase are set by the Byblian royal house, which oversees the cutting and transport of the cedar logs. Such a dealing in cedar wood is no longer treated as a 'benevolence' or gift exchange between heads of state, but as a purely commercial 'for-profit' transaction. As in Wenamun's case, non-compliance on the part of the purchaser may result in a postponement or voiding of the agreement.

The Report of Wenamun underscores the commercial viability of the cedar trade, and offers a picture of the wealth and resources at the disposal of the Byblian royal house. For this large cedar consignment, involving three hundred men and oxen, Zakarbaal receives vessels of gold and silver, as well as numerous linen garments, rope, ox-hides, and five hundred rolls of finished papyrus. As we learn, a previous transaction involved six ships heavily laden with Egyptian merchandise. As the Wenamun account makes clear, such commercial exchange had gone on for some time; documented transactions date back at least to the time of Wenamun's grandfather, confirming that the port of Byblos was already active in the late twelfth century. Thus, within a relatively short period of time, from the incursions of the Sea Peoples in the first quarter of the twelfth century, the principal Phoenician ports (with the possible exception of Tyre) were able to re-establish themselves commercially. What factors lay behind this remarkable recovery?

Reduced to its essentials, the account of Wenamun provides an accurate indication of the key participants in maritime trade along the eastern Mediterranean during the early eleventh century: the Egyptians and the port cities of the coastal Levant under the control of the Phoenicians and various contingents of the Sea Peoples. (The Wenamun account makes specific reference to the Tjekker of Dor, Wenamun's first recorded stop.) As the report suggests, these various harbour towns were linked by commercial ties. It is perhaps not fortuitous that the story ends with an unscheduled landing of Wenamun's vessel at a port on the eastern coast of Cyprus. As copper merchants and commercial entrepreneurs, the Cypriots, like the Phoenicians, played an integral role in maritime exchange. The presence on Cyprus of a local inhabitant versed in Egyptian reminds us of the close cultural ties that bound the island and the Nile valley.

Wenamun's account includes the names of several other rulers who controlled the southern Palestinian coast. Although no details are given in the report, his early itinerary must have included a series of stops along the Philistine coast; at any rate, his passage clearly took him through that region. The Onomasticon of Amenope, which dates to *c.*1100 BC, the period immediately prior to Wenamun's account, specifically records the names of five cities along the Philistine coast, including Ashkelon, Ashdod, and Gaza, all of which were active at this time. In addition to the Philistines, the Onomasticon records the names of two other contingents of Sea Peoples: the Shardana and the Tjekker.

Archaeological investigation confirms the close cultural interrelationship between Palestine, Phoenicia, and Cyprus in the Early Iron Age. Shared elements in their material assemblages suggest that contact among the these regions was extensive.[20] All three emerged in a roughly parallel fashion during the course of the twelfth century, suggesting that their respective paths of development were intertwined. What is the implication?

CYPRUS, PALESTINE, AND PHOENICIA IN THE EARLY IRON AGE

Archaeological research has yielded vivid documentation for the vigorous economic recovery of the eastern Cypriot coastal ports of Enkomi and Kition in the twelfth century BC, following the incursions of the Sea Peoples. As excavations have revealed, both sites attained a high level of prosperity, which finds reflection in the ambitious programmes of architectural expansion undertaken by them.

Both sites were marked by intensive metallurgical activity centred on the smelting of copper. Such efforts, undertaken on an ambitious scale in the thirteenth century, reach a peak in the succeeding twelfth century. In all likelihood, copper from neighbouring mines in the region was exported at this time from the harbours of Kition and Hala Sultan Teke to Egypt and the Syro-Palestinian coast.[21]

Evidence for close cultural and commercial ties between Cyprus and the Levant may be found in the oriental influences evident in temple cult offerings and architecture at Enkomi and Kition and in the overwhelming dominance of Syro-Palestinian pottery among ceramic imports to Cyprus in the twelfth century.[22] The resurgence of the Cypriot state was thus probably linked to the renewal of trade with the Levant.

Like Cyprus, the major centres along the Palestinian coast from Ashkelon to Akko underwent rapid development in the second half of the twelfth century, following the Sea Peoples' incursions. By the century's end, the major Philistine cities (Ashkelon, Ashdod, Ekron, and Tell Qasile) had evolved into fortified urban centres. Their economic development was due, in large part, to emerging inland and maritime commerce.

Philistia's strong cultural ties to Cyprus and the Phoenician coast have long been noted. This cultural interrelationship spawned an evolving network of exchange that culminated, in the second half of the eleventh century, in a period of extensive trade between the Philistines and Phoenicians, as the pottery evidence at Tell Qasile clearly attests.[23] In this respect, the Phoenicians had stepped into the commercial void left by Ugarit, which had monopolized maritime trade with the major Palestinian ports in the Late Bronze Age.

THE ELEVENTH CENTURY: PHOENICIAN COMMERCIAL EXPANSION

By the second half of the eleventh century, as the archaeological record reveals, the Phoenicians had embarked upon a period of active trade and commercial expansion that would lay the groundwork for future developments in the first millennium BC. This period witnessed the introduction of many features of Phoenician material culture, among them bichrome (two-colour) pottery (see pp. 160–161).

The distribution of such bichrome pottery vessels bears witness to the emergence of wide-scale Phoenician trade within the Levant at this time. Documented all along the Phoenician coast from Tell Sukas in the north to the Mount Carmel peninsula in the south, their distribution extends well beyond the Phoenician zone – to Syria (the Amuq plain and Homs region), northern Palestine (the Galilee, Megiddo, and Beth Shemesh),

Philistia (Tell Qasile, Tell Masos), the northern Negev (Tell Esar), and the Nile Delta (Tell er-Retabeh).[24]

This same period of time is marked by incipient urban expansion within Phoenicia proper. At Tyre, signs of urban renewal may be seen in the rebuilding of destroyed walls and in the massive levelling ceramic deposit that extended over much of the excavation area. The architectural plans at both Tyre and Sarepta reveal major alterations in their layout, which involved the use of terracing and passageways, and the introduction of ashlar masonry. At Sarepta, the walls are built according to the 'pier-and-rubble' technique that would soon become a trademark of Phoenician construction. (See fig. 27.)

Marked urban expansion in the southern Phoenician realm is attested also at inland sites in the Galilee – at Tell Keisan and Tell Dan, where substantial town planning and domestic construction are attested. At Tell Dan, as excavations have revealed, the city underwent a major urban transformation in the eleventh century. The second phase of this renovation, which may be dated to the second half of the century, is accompanied by the introduction of Phoenician bichrome ware.[25] The archaeological record of the mid-eleventh century thus documents a pattern of active commercial expansion south from the region of Sidon into the Galilee and northern Palestine.

Such evidence has led to speculation that this expansion may have been achieved or accompanied by military force. The most dramatic evidence may be found at the coastal site of Dor, where a massive destruction layer datable to the mid-eleventh century immediately underlies the earliest level of Phoenician occupation at the site. This stratum, which yielded early Phoenician bichrome ware, produced a series of substantial mudbrick buildings of public character; renewed trade with Cyprus is attested by the presence of imported Cypriot White Painted ware.[26]

The site of Tell Dan (Bronze Age Laish) in the Upper Galilee presents a similar pattern. Around the mid-eleventh century, its urban community ends in violent destruction; the succeeding settlement, which was soon rebuilt, was marked by the introduction of Phoenician bichrome ware, once again signalling Phoenician presence.[27]

The interaction of both cities with the Phoenicians is clearly attested in contemporary historical records. The Report of Wenamun, which dates just before the period of the destructions, reveals the Tjekker-controlled city of Dor in maritime commercial competition with the Phoenician cities. The subplot of the story – the Tjekker theft of silver from Wenamun's ship at Dor, Wenamun's confiscation of silver from a Tjekker trader while en route from Tyre to Byblos, the subsequent arrival of a contingent of Tjekker ships to arrest Wenamun at Byblos, and the Byblian king Zakarbaal's veiled attempt to intercede with the Tjekker envoys on Wenamun's behalf – reveals the two participants in an uneasy, somewhat volatile trade relationship. Biblical Dan's close commercial association with the Phoenician coastal cities is clearly alluded to in the book of Judges, which is set precisely in this historical period. In it we learn that the tribe of Asher, to which Dan belonged, did not expel the inhabitants of Acco, Sidon, or Achziv, 'but dwelt among them'.[28] Elsewhere, the security of Dan and its inhabitants is compared with that of Sidon.

The Galilean city's close geographic proximity to both Tyre and Sidon – about 40 kilometres (25 miles) – is underscored in the later census of Israel undertaken by David: in it Sidon and Tyre are listed immediately after Dan.[29]

As the archaeological record suggests, the marked economic rise and urban growth of the Phoenician cities during the eleventh century clearly prompted a wave of Phoenician commercial expansion southwards – into the Galilee and along the coast of northern Israel. If the Phoenician context of the destruction levels at both Dan and Dor, and at other sites is correct, this commercial thrust may have been accompanied by military force.[30] At any rate, the spread of Phoenician commerce south beyond the Carmel peninsula into the Sharon coastal plain is clearly documented by the archaeological record.

As for the instigators of such action, the impetus may be securely placed in the southern Phoenician realm, namely the cities of Tyre and Sidon. In the absence of written documentation, it is difficult to assign primacy to one centre or the other. In a mid-eleventh century context, one is tempted to view Sidon as the primary initiator of such a land-based expansion, although it is entirely conceivable that both cities were involved.

At any rate, Sidon's dominant position among the Phoenician coastal cities in the late twelfth and eleventh centuries BC seems clear from the surviving historical record. In biblical accounts of the general period (Joshua, Judges, Samuel), it is Sidon, not Tyre, which appears as a powerful, territorially based city.[31] In the book of Genesis, Sidon is the first-born son of Canaan in the list of nations.[32] The term 'Sidonians' is, in fact, used throughout these texts (and the Old Testament in general) as a generic designation for Canaanites or Phoenicians. The few surviving extra-biblical texts, namely the Report of Wenamun and the Inscription of Tiglath-Pileser I, appear to confirm Sidon's pre-eminence at this time. In the Wenamun account, the city's harbour with its fifty commercial vessels receives prominent mention, while in the earlier Assyrian account Sidon appears second (after Byblos) in a list of three cities offering tribute to the Assyrian monarch.

A number of factors may have accounted for Sidon's primacy in the twelfth and eleventh centuries BC. In marked contrast to Tyre, Sidon possessed substantial territorial holdings. In addition to its own agriculturally rich coastal territory, the city held inland access through the Jezzine into the fertile southern Beqa, a critical access point for the strategic overland trade that ran southwards from Syria to the Upper Jordan valley.

As an island port, on the other hand, Tyre had no reliable access to mainland resources. This situation is well illustrated in the Late Bronze Age correspondence, where Tyre is harassed by a Sidonian military contingent posted on the mainland. (See fig. 1.) The Sidonian troops succeed in blockading the city and preventing its civilian inhabitants from securing access to mainland supplies, such as wood and fresh water. Abi-Milki, the Tyrian king, writes to the Egyptian pharaoh Akhenaten, begging for Egyptian reinforcements to protect the city from Sidonian aggression. His pleas apparently unanswered, Abi-Milki and the Tyrian townspeople subsequently evacuate the city by ship.[33]

The earlier Amarna correspondence vividly illustrates a major weakness of Tyre at this time – its economic dependence upon the mainland. Severed from its ties to the adjacent coastal town of Ushu, the Late Bronze Age city, despite its internal wealth and prosperity, falls vulnerable to outside attack; this situation could only have been exacerbated by the city's weakened circumstances in the Early Iron Age. From the Amarna letters it appears that Tyre's military support was negligible compared with that of Sidon and Arwad, each of which possessed naval fleets, chariots, and infantry.[34] By virtue of its mainland location, Sidon had a larger and more accessible hinterland upon which to draw; the extent of its suburban tombs and cemeteries in the Late Bronze Age reveal the substantial size of its surrounding population base.

The Amarna correspondence reveals another important distinction between Late Bronze Age Tyre and Sidon that clearly influenced the respective fortunes of these two cities in the succeeding centuries. As the southernmost of the mainland Phoenician ports, Tyre enjoyed a close commercial and political relationship with Egypt, its main trading partner. Sidon's commercial affinities, by contrast, appear to have been oriented more with the north. Its decision to side with the king of Amurru against Egypt in the late fourteenth century may, in fact, reflect the economic realities of its north-easterly trade orientation: in the face of a weakened Egypt, the city's decision to side with the Syrian coalition may have been a strategic one from a commercial standpoint.

Sidon's economic rise and Tyre's decline in the Early Iron Age were clearly influenced by their geographic circumstances. The decline of Egypt as a market and trading partner for Tyre must have been particularly devastating to the city's coastal maritime economy. The eleventh century saw Egypt in a state of marked military and economic decline under the politically fragmented 'Tanite' (Twenty-first) Dynasty. Egypt's western Asiatic empire had long since disappeared, and it is unlikely that foreign trade on any scale was conducted at this time. By the end of the century, even the cult precincts in the sacred capital of Thebes lay neglected and in ruin.

THE TENTH CENTURY BC: THE BIRTH OF THE TYRIAN MARITIME COMMERCIAL EMPIRE

Towards the end of the eleventh century BC, however, the balance of power between Tyre and Sidon began to shift in favour of the former. The presence of Phoenician pottery imports on Cyprus heralds the emergence of trade abroad.[35] Cypriot wares, too, begin to appear in quantity on the Phoenician mainland, at both Tyre and Sarepta, evincing an active bilateral trade between these two commercial centres.[36]

The distribution of early Phoenician pottery on Cyprus during the second half of the eleventh century – at Amathus, Episkopi, and Paphos on the island's southern and western coasts – clearly alludes to the existence of a much larger network of westerly Phoenician Mediterranean trade. The presence of early Greek Protogeometric-period pottery at Amathus and Tyre, together with the discovery of early Levantine imports at Euboean Lefkandi, indeed, points to active exchange between the island of Euboea and the Phoenician mainland via Cyprus in the tenth century BC.[37]

Further confirmation of early Phoenician trade in the Aegean may be found in the archaeological record at Kommos along Crete's southern coast, where Phoenician pottery, some of it dating as early as the mid-tenth century BC, has been found in quantity. The discovery of a tenth-century bronze bowl with the Phoenician inscription of its owner in a burial near Knossos datable to *c.*900 BC points to the possibility of a more permanent Phoenician presence on Crete by this time; archaeological finds from this time at Knossos and its vicinity clearly indicate that the island now functioned as an active centre for international trade.

Crete's strategic position as a commercial transit point for Aegean trade strongly suggests that Phoenician commerce in the tenth century may have proceeded further west into the Mediterranean. Indeed, the island of Sardinia, later colonized by the Phoenicians in the eighth century BC, offers itself as one such destination. To judge from the limited epigraphic and archaeological evidence at hand, this ore-rich island, a target of Cypriot trade in the Late Bronze Age, may already have been visited by Phoenician traders in the tenth and certainly by the ninth century BC.

There seems little doubt that the Phoenician initiative for this early Mediterranean trade rested with Tyre, the source of nearly all later Phoenician overseas foundations. Tyre's emergence in the tenth century under Hiram I and his successors, and the accompanying eclipse of neighbouring Sidon, may be attributed, in large part, to such maritime trade activity abroad, as the Bible itself makes clear. Much scholarly debate has centred on the extent and chronology of Tyre's early Mediterranean commercial ventures. While the bulk of its colonial activity does not appear to antedate the eighth century, Tyre's efforts at long-distance maritime trade clearly extended back several centuries before, as the early evidence for Phoenician commercial presence in the Aegean clearly demonstrates.

Such 'pre-colonial' trade, as it has been termed, could have been carried out effectively without the aid of permanent settlements; the only requisite was a temporary base of operations, which a neighbouring islet or coastal encampment could afford. Indeed, it has been argued that the Phoenicians' later efforts at colonization in the eighth and seventh centuries BC formed part of a concerted effort to safeguard long-established trade relationships in the face of emerging Greek colonial competition.[38]

As for Tyre itself, the historical record clearly attests to the city's burgeoning maritime trade interests in the early tenth century under Hiram I (971–939 BC). Among the Tyrian monarch's commercial ventures were a series of maritime expeditions undertaken with King Solomon (961–922 BC) to Ophir aboard ships of 'Tarshish'. (Such a joint commercial enterprise, or *hubur*, as we have seen, finds precedent at Byblos during the earlier epoch of the Wenamun report.) As the biblical account reveals,[39] these voyages, which were launched periodically from the port of Ezion-Geber (near modern Elat) at the mouth of the Gulf of Aqaba, were clearly initiated by Tyre, which furnished the officers and naval crews. As most scholars would now agree, Ophir, the geographic target of such trade, should be located along the north-eastern coast of Africa, either in the Sudan or, further south, along the Eretrian–Somalian coast. The primary object of these expeditions – gold – lends support to this supposition; it was this region, ancient Punt, that formed the primary gold source for the ancient Egyptians, beginning in the Eighteenth Dynasty.

Less clear is the meaning of the term 'Tarshish', which is employed in Old Testament accounts of the Ophir voyage to denote a type of Phoenician long-distance merchant vessel. The geographic identity of Tarshish has been the subject of great controversy among scholars, a number of whom favour its equation with historic Tartessos in the mineral-rich Guadalquivir region of southern Spain.[40] Based upon such an interpretation, the joint Tyrian-Israelite expeditions offer proof of early long-distance trade in metals with the western Mediterranean. Indeed, Phoenician foreign commerce in such commodities (especially silver, copper, and, later, iron) served the Tyrian economy by both yielding a highly exportable commodity on the open market (like Phoenicia's indigenous hardwoods) and by ensuring an ample supply of raw metal for its own active industrial needs. As the biblical account reveals, it was Tyrian knowhow that provided Solomon with the expertise to produce the bronze-work needed for completion of the temple in Jerusalem.[41]

TYRE AND THE UNITED KINGDOM OF ISRAEL

Construction of the Solomonic temple was the by-product of a commercial treaty entered into by Tyre and the newly emergent kingdom of Israel and Judah, the United Monarchy, founded by David (1000–961 BC). According to the biblical account, relations had been established already by the two principals during David's reign. As the Old Testament relates, the Tyrians, perhaps under Hiram's father, Abibaal, sent a delegation with gifts (including cedar wood) to the victorious Israelite monarch in an overture of peace and friendship. There seems little reason to doubt the historical veracity of this account. David's united Israelite kingdom encompassed the main cities and territories in the Akko coastal plain and the Galilee, i.e. the entire hinterland of southern Phoenicia extending right up to the borders of Tyre and Sidon. With the 'annexation' of these territories, Israel held effective control over Tyre's inland commercial routes. Thus, it was clearly in the Tyrians' commercial interests to initiate relations with their influential southern neighbour.

It is surely with the intention of perpetuating this relationship that Hiram sent an embassy to greet Solomon shortly after his accession in 961 BC.[42] At Solomon's behest, the two monarchs reached a commercial agreement over construction of the Israelite temple to Yahweh and royal palace in Jerusalem (see p. 129). In exchange for the required timber and technical expertise (carpentry, stone masonry, bronze casting), Solomon agreed to provide Hiram and his royal household with substantial annual provisions of wheat (20,000 kors, the rough equivalent of 4.2 million litres) and olive oil (20,000 bats, about 420,000 litres), together with a supplementary payment in silver.[43]

The initial pact, negotiated in Solomon's fourth regnal year, lasted about two decades (seven years for construction of the temple, thirteen for the palace). Upon its lapse, a second agreement, involving the sale of land on Israel's part, was reached. In exchange for a substantial payment in gold (120 talents according to the account in the Book of Kings), Solomon agreed to cede to Tyre twenty cities in the Galilee and Akko plain.[44] The region, termed 'Cabul' in the biblical account, was a production centre for grain and olive oil in antiquity, a fact that has been confirmed by archaeological research at sites such as Tell Keisan and Ḥorvat Rosh Zayit. The transaction was clearly motivated by economic concerns: by acquiring these rich farm lands the Tyrians could eliminate their dependence upon agricultural imports. That the city did, in fact, acquire and retain control over this territory is clear from the historical, epigraphical, and archaeological record.[45]

TYRE AND INLAND TRADE

Tyre's alliance with Israel in the tenth century clearly opened significant avenues for commerce within the continental Near East. Israelite control over the newly emergent Aramaean states in southern Syria, especially the kingdom of Maacah south of Mount Hermon, assured Tyrian overland communication with the eastern Galilee and the upper reaches of the River Jordan; through these means Tyre could tap into the lucrative Transjordanian trade network. Key to such commerce was the neighbouring northern Galilean city of Dan, which was strategically located, below Mount Hermon, at the crossroads of two major trade routes east–west and north–south. Tyrian commercial contact with Dan, now under Israelite control, and with the larger settlement of Hazor to the south is now clearly attested by the abundant presence of imported Phoenician pottery. The close ties between Dan and Tyre are apparent also from biblical references to intermarriage (Hiram, the Tyrian bronze caster, was the son of a Danite woman) and to the presence of Danite workers in the Phoenician ports.[46]

Israelite control of southern Judah and its conquest of Philistia and southern Transjordan (Moab and Edom) opened other avenues for Phoenician trade, especially with southern Arabia, a lucrative source of spices and precious minerals. As excavations at the Bersheeba valley site of Tell Masos confirm,[47] by the eleventh century Phoenician traders had already established a foothold in the southern Negev commercial corridor to the southern Arabah valley and Arabia. Moreover, the biblical account of the Ophir expedition reveals that the Tyrians were granted commercial access to the mouth of the Aqabah Gulf, the northern terminus for the south Arabian coastal trade controlled by the Midianites.

The defeat of the Philistines by the Israelites under David clearly empowered the Phoenicians commercially. By the eleventh century, the former had evolved into a powerful trading confederacy of five cities (Gaza, Ashdod, Ashkelon, Gath, and Ekron). Through them they controlled not only the inland commercial routes within southern Canaan itself but the coastal waters of the southern Levant. Their subjugation by Israel eliminated a formidable obstacle to Phoenician maritime trade with Egypt.

Israel itself and its capital, Jerusalem, represented a lucrative market for Phoenician trade and industry in the tenth century. Phoenician goods and commodities now entered the United Kingdom through its two major ports: Dor in the north and Joppa, Jerusalem's harbour, in the south. The precise location of the latter, the offloading point for Tyrian cedar shipments to Solomon, remains in question. An excavated inner harbour, or cothon, located east of Joppa on the ancient course of the River Ayalon, represents one likely possibility; its construction may have been effected with the help of Phoenician engineers.[48] The port city of Dor, however, clearly served as the main emporium for Phoenician trade, which, as archaeology has confirmed, was aimed largely at the northern Israelite realm. Heavily influenced by Phoenician culture, Dor itself, prior to this time, may have been under direct Phoenician political control.

Over the years, there has been considerable debate over the nature of the political and commercial relationship that Tyre sustained with Israel under the United Monarchy. While arguments have been made for political dominance on Israel's part, the existing evidence would suggest that the alliance was a reciprocal one undertaken between two powers on an equal footing. The agreements crafted appear to have been mutually advantageous; the Tyrians received needed agricultural assistance and trade protection, while Israel benefited from Tyrian commercial experience and technical knowhow. Indeed, as we have seen, Israel had far more to gain from Tyre as an independent commercial partner, especially in matters of maritime trade.

THE PHOENICIAN CITIES AND THE ARAMAEANS

In the absence of historical documentation, one can only speculate about the status of Sidon, Byblos, and Arwad at this time. It is probable, however, that their economies were now in decline, owing to the changed political environment in the surrounding Syrian region. During the tenth century, as the ancient sources clearly record, the general area fell under the control of the Aramaeans, an amalgam of West Semitic pastoralist tribes, who now occupied large tracts of Syria and central Mesopotamia. The massive eastward movement of these tribes severely affected neighbouring Assyria and Babylonia, obstructing internal communication and blocking traditional trade routes westward from the middle Euphrates to the Mediterranean. Plagued by administrative difficulties and grain shortages, the economies of both Mesopotamian states experienced a dramatic downturn, which at times reached crisis proportions. Such difficulties led to a rupture and perhaps even a cessation in commercial trade with the west.

The downturn in western trade had a negative economic impact upon the northern Phoenician coastal cities of Arwad and Byblos, which served traditionally as Mediterranean outlets for trans-Euphratian commerce. Trade with north-western Syria and southern Anatolia may have been disrupted also by the growing Aramaean presence in the Amuq plain and Sam'al (Zinçirli), trade corridors for Phoenician commerce with southern Anatolia. The economy of Byblos was further hampered by a loss of trade with Egypt, whose foreign economy suffered during the waning years of the politically troubled Twenty-first Dynasty.

THE RE-EMERGENCE OF EGYPT AND ASSYRIA

During the final decades of the tenth century BC, however, the economic and military fortunes of Egypt and Assyria would change dramatically, as both superpowers sought to reassert themselves militarily and politically. In northern Mesopotamia the Assyrians under Ashur-dan II (934–912 BC) undertook a series of aggressive military campaigns – the first in over a century – aimed at recapturing territory lost to the Aramaeans. Adad-nirari II (911–891 BC) capitalized on his predecessor's gains by thrusting deep into Aramaean territory along the upper Euphrates, thus setting the stage for the later ninth-century advances of Ashurnasirpal II and Shalmaneser III.

In Egypt, the accession of Sheshonq I (945–924 BC) ushered in the Twenty-second ('Libyan') dynasty. Under Sheshonq's strong leadership, Upper and Lower Egypt were quickly reunified and long-dormant trade re-established with Nubia. For the first time since the early years of the Twentieth Dynasty, Egypt showed signs of reviving its imperial aims in the southern Levant. From his headquarters at Tanis the Egyptian monarch launched a military attack on Judah and Israel, sacking Jerusalem and advancing as far as the Jezreel valley in northern Israel.

Under the looming threat of Assyria, and in the face of a militarily rejuvenated Nile kingdom, the Phoenician cities apparently undertook to ally themselves with Egypt. Evidence for the resumption of diplomatic ties between Byblos and the Nile valley may be found in a series of Egyptian royal statues reinscribed with royal Byblian dedications to Baalat Gubal. (See fig. 3.) Similar overtures may also have been made by the Sidonians and Tyrians, if the Egyptian royal-inscribed alabaster vessels apparently gifted to these two cities serve as any indication.

TYRIAN COMMERCIAL EXPANSION UNDER ITHOBAAL I

The ninth century witnessed the further expansion of Tyre's commercial empire under Ithobaal I (887–856 BC) and his successors. At this time, the city's growing mercantile needs were addressed by the construction of a southern artificial port, called the 'Egyptian', heralding the resumption of trade with the Nile valley. The Phoenician commercial network now appears to have encompassed the southern Anatolian realm. A particular focus of activity was the Gulf of Alexandretta and the Cilician coast, whose ports (Tarsus and Myriandros) served as outlets for Phoenician trade across the Taurus. Archaeological

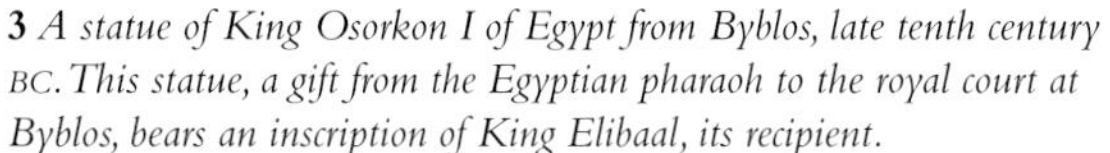

3 *A statue of King Osorkon I of Egypt from Byblos, late tenth century BC. This statue, a gift from the Egyptian pharaoh to the royal court at Byblos, bears an inscription of King Elibaal, its recipient.*

4 *A relief depicting a Phoenician tributary with a pair of monkeys, from the Palace of Ashurnasirpal II at Nimrud, Iraq, c. 865* BC.

evidence for Phoenician presence in inland north Syria, at the Neo-Hittite centres of Carchemish and Zinçirli, points equally to Phoenician involvement in the Taurus region and in nascent Syrian trade with the Euphrates river valley.[49]

Tyrian relations with Israel were renewed and strengthened by a marriage alliance between the two kingdoms.[50] In offering his daughter, Jezebel, to King Ahab (874–853 BC), Ithobaal sought to secure continued trade concessions with the flourishing Israelite kingdom and its newly established capital at Samaria. As the Old Testament sources clearly reveal, Jezebel later emerged as a powerful cultural and political influence in the Israelite court, both as queen to Ahab and queen mother to her son, Ahaziah, Ahab's successor.[51]

It is likely, although not proven, that the Tyrians, under Ithobaal, also sought an alliance with Aram-Damascus, now the most dominant of the central Syrian Aramaean states. Damascus' political and economic strength is evident from the fact that both Palestinian kingdoms, Israel and subsequently Judah, sought alliance with it; the latter offered up its remaining gold and silver reserves to persuade the Aramaean king Ben-Hadad I to side with it. Ben-Hadad's subsequent assault upon Dan and other northern Israelite cities in the Upper Galilee, in Tyre's immediate hinterland, must clearly have triggered a Tyrian move towards rapprochement with its Aramaean neighbour. As has been pointed out, the line of Israelite cities attacked by Ben-Hadad followed a vital communication route between Tyre and Damascus via the Beqa valley.[52]

It is within the reign of Ithobaal that the city of Sidon apparently fell within the political orbit of Tyre. Ithobaal is the first of Tyrian monarchs to call himself 'king of the Sidonians', a designation that remained in use until the end of the eighth century BC. The name of Sidon then disappears in Assyrian inscriptions from the time of Tiglath-Pileser III until that of Sennacherib. While the extent of Tyrian control over Sidon during this period remains unclear, the historical facts speak clearly for the existence of some form of multi-state confederation headed by the Tyrian royal house.[53]

Tyre's economic strength and commercial acumen under Ithobaal find clear expression in the city's initial efforts at colonization. According to Menander of Ephesus, the Tyrian king founded two colonies, the first (Auza) in Libya, the second (Batroun) along the Phoenician coast north of Byblos.[54] Through the foundation of Batroun, the city may have sought to gain a foothold in the profitable trans-Euphratian trade through the Akkar plain. The foundation in Libya (its location remains unknown) was almost certainly established as a coasting station for long-distance trade with the western Mediterranean. Two other early Tyrian colonies, Carthage and Utica, were founded further west along the Tunisian coast (see pp. 77 and 181). Closer to home, the Tyrians, perhaps under Ithobaal himself, established a colony at Kition on Cyprus. Tyrian activity there derived from its involvement in the island's lucrative copper trade.

The ninth century: Phoenicia and the Assyrians

Raw copper and copper vessels, in fact, figure prominently among the gifts offered by the Phoenicians to King Ashurnasirpal II (883–859 BC) on the occasion of his visit to the Mediterranean around 870 BC, the first by an Assyrian monarch in nearly 200 years. Although officially listed as 'tribute', the Phoenician goods presented to Ashurnasirpal were clearly gifts – voluntarily offered to secure trade concessions. The commercial nature of Ashurnasirpal's exploratory campaign to the Mediterranean coast is clear from its itinerary, which included the strategic Neo-Hittite trade capital of Carchemish on the Upper Euphrates. The Phoenician offerings – valued metals (gold, silver, copper, tin), fine linen garments, and precious materials (boxwood, ebony, and ivory) – were clearly intended to impress; so, too, was the exotic gift of monkeys, later represented in the possession of a Phoenician merchant on the walls of Ashurnasirpal's royal palace. (See fig. 4.) That

Phoenician diplomacy had earlier achieved its purpose may be seen in the inclusion of both Tyrians and Sidonians among the list of dignitaries invited to the inauguration of Ashurnasirpal's palace at the new capital of Kalhu (Nimrud) in 879 BC.[55]

The above-mentioned Mediterranean expedition represented Ashurnasirpal's only penetration across the Euphrates into Syrian territory. Political circumstances in the west changed dramatically under his son and successor, Shalmaneser III (858–824 BC). The latter launched an aggressive campaign in his accession year against north Syria and southern Anatolia, terminating at the Mediterranean, where the tribute of the (unnamed) 'kings of the sea coast', including presumably all of the Phoenician dynasts, was duly received. On the bronze gates decorating Shalmaneser's palace at Dur-sharrukin (Khorsabad) is a depiction of Tyrian tribute being transported by ship to the mainland; there it is carried by a long file of porters led by two suppliant Tyrian dignitaries into the presence of the Assyrian monarch and his entourage. (See fig. 5.) Silent witness to it all is the elderly Tyrian king, Ithobaal, who stands accompanied by his queen on the shore of the island city.

As his first and succeeding campaigns illustrate, Shalmaneser's primary objective was the subjugation of the Aramaean and Neo-Hittite kingdoms in the west. Of his thirty-four recorded campaigns, nineteen were conducted beyond the Euphrates in Syria. In his fifth regnal year, after securing control of the strategic western Euphrates crossing, Shalmaneser pushed south into Syria-Palestine; his advance was met at Qarqar by a united front headed by the powerful Aramaean states of Damascus and Hamath. Within the coalition, which included Israel, Ammon, and Egypt, were small contingents from the Syrian and northern Phoenician coastal cities, including Arwad and Arqa. Although Shalmaneser officially claimed victory, the battle of Qarqar appears to have ended in a standoff; over the next 15 years the Assyrian monarch would unsuccessfully confront Damascus (initially with and then without the support of Hamath) five more times. Under Ben-Hadad I and his successor Hazael, the powerful kingdom of Aram-Damascus was apparently more than a match for the Assyrian state.

The alignment of Arwad and the northern coastal cities with the Aramaean confederation is easily understood. The notable absence of Tyre, Sidon, and Byblos, however, requires explanation. The 'neutral' stance of these cities may be explained by the existence of a prior understanding that had been reached with Assyria under Ashurnasirpal II. Owing to their commercial importance, they appear already to have enjoyed a special 'protected' tributary status within the Assyrian realm.

AN ASSYRIAN INTERLUDE: THE RISE OF ARAM-DAMASCUS

The end of the ninth and first half of the succeeding eighth century BC marked a period of greater political freedom for the Phoenicians, during which time they were presumably free to conduct their commerce unhindered by outside powers. Preoccupied with the growing military presence of Urartu in southern Anatolia, the Assyrians, following Shalmaneser III, turned their attentions north, leaving the region of Syria–Palestine alone.

5 *King Ithobaal oversees the ferrying of Assyrian tribute from Tyre to the opposing mainland. The remainder of the frieze depicts a file of Phoenician tributaries being led into the presence of the Phoenician monarch. From the bronze gates erected at Balawat (Khorsabad), Iraq, by King Shalmaneser III, ninth century* BC.

Egypt, now plagued by political anarchy and internal rebellion under the disjunct Twenty-second Dynasty, had no energy for foreign affairs. The country, already divided between an independent Theban priesthood in the south and a local dynasty in competition with various Libyan tribal fiefdoms in the north, fell victim to a dynastic split in 818 BC, as a result of which the Delta kingship was now shared between two separate royal houses located in Leontopolis and Tanis.

Within this political vacuum, the regional influence of the already powerful state of Aram-Damascus grew greater still, peaking in the final quarter of the ninth century under Hazael. At this time, there are indications that the Phoenicians had strong commercial ties with the state of Damascus, whose Transjordanian possessions gave it control of the profitable southern Arabian incense trade through the Hijaz. As Ezekial relates,[56] Damascus supplied the Tyrians not only with their wines but with the wool required to sustain their lucrative dyed garment industry.

In the early eighth century BC, Tyrian inland commercial priorities may have shifted towards the kingdom of Israel, which profited at the expense of Damascus, now weakened by Assyrian intervention under Adad-Nirari III (810–783 BC). Under Jeroboam II (782–753 BC), Israel reached its maximum territorial extent since the days of the United Monarchy, regaining a portion of its Transjordanian possessions lost to Damascus. It would appear that Phoenician traders and artisans were now particularly active in the capital cities of Aram-Damascus and Israel. It is during this period that the earliest architectural evidence for Phoenician overseas colonization occurs – in Cyprus, North Africa, Sardinia, and southern Spain (see Chapter 7). Such colonial activity attests to an aggressive campaign of Tyrian-directed commercial expansion throughout the Mediterranean basin.

THE RETURN OF THE ASSYRIANS

This era of relative political independence for the Phoenicians came to an abrupt end with the ascension of Tiglath-Pileser III (744–727 BC) to the throne of Assyria in 744 BC. The new Assyrian monarch quickly launched an aggressive series of campaigns aimed at the total conquest of the Levant and the provincial annexation of its various independent states. With the conquest of the north Syrian coastal kingdom of Unqi around 738 BC, the whole of the Levant submitted to Assyrian authority. Unqi itself and the cities of the northern Phoenician coast above Byblos were directly annexed – into a newly created Assyrian province centred on the Phoenician city of Simyra. To the south, Tyre and Byblos, along with the kingdoms of Israel, Damascus, and Hamath, were accorded tributary status.

In the immediately succeeding years, with Tiglath-Pileser absent on campaign in the north and east, Tyre chose to ally itself in an anti-Assyrian coalition involving Damascus, Israel, and Philistine Ashkelon, aimed at creating a unified western front against Assyrian aggression. Assyrian reprisal was swift. In his advance upon Philistia, Tiglath-Pileser swept down the Phoenician coast, seizing Arwad (whose king Matan-Baal promptly submitted) and, soon thereafter, invading the town of Mahalab in Tyrian territory. Tyre's reigning monarch, King Hiram II, quickly submitted and offered tribute, obtaining Tiglath-Pileser's pardon; the city was spared Assyrian attack and the annexation of its territory.

The Assyrian king's ensuing defeat of the Syro-Palestinian confederacy dramatically changed the political landscape of the Levant. The kingdom of Aram-Damascus was vanquished and reduced to an Assyrian province. Israel, although left temporarily autonomous, was greatly reduced in size, its northern and Transjordanian holdings annexed by Assyria. Within 10 years, Israel, too would be reduced to provincial status, its capital, Samaria, conquered and destroyed. With Israel now effectively out of the picture as a political force, the Phoenicians turned further south towards Judah and Philistia for trade.

Tiglath-Pileser's leniency toward Tyre in 734 BC, i.e. his decision to leave the city intact and under independent rule, was based not upon Assyrian altruism but upon a recognition of the city's potential commercial importance to the empire. The Tyrians, however, were no longer autonomous in their commercial dealings. As two contemporary Assyrian documents reveal, the city was now placed under the authority of an Assyrian governor charged with overseeing internal security and the taxation of its lucrative timber trade. Tyre's great commercial prosperity at this time may be gauged from the enormous tribute exacted from Hiram's successor, King Mattan II, at the end of Tiglath-Pileser's reign. Mattan's payment of 150 gold talents was, in fact, the highest sum in gold ever assessed a tributary state in the Assyrian records.

Assyria's active commercial interest in Tyrian overseas trade is clearly underscored by the actions subsequently taken by Sargon II (721–705 BC) in securing the submission and tribute of the seven independent kings of Iatnana (Cyprus). Control of the Phoenician copper trade at Kition must have been a motivating factor in Sargon's unprecedented overseas venture. Indeed, the Phoenicians' overall involvement in the commercial metals trade throughout the Mediterranean could not have failed to attract Assyria's attentions.[57]

Up to the reign of Sargon II, the Phoenician cities and their territories were left alone, provided that they maintained a submissive posture to the Assyrian state. Such submission involved the payment of taxes and the offering of tribute (*tamartu*), which was exacted on a sporadic basis. This policy changed under Sargon's successor, Sennacherib (704–681 BC), who demanded regular annual tribute from the Phoenician cities and other dependencies in the empire as a sign of fealty to the state.

For various reasons, yet unclear (among them, perhaps, the non-payment of tribute), the Tyrians under King Luli (Greek Eloulaios) incurred the wrath of Sennacherib, who retaliated by invading its territory in 701 BC, prompting Luli's flight to Cyprus. (See fig. 6.). Sennacherib subsequently awarded the throne of Sidon and all of Tyre's continental holdings (including Ushu) to a Sidonian of pro-Assyrian bent named Tubalu (Ithobaal). There is no mention of an attack upon Tyre; bereft of its mainland territories, the island city apparently no longer posed an immediate threat to the Assyrians.

Sennacherib's actions were calculated. By isolating the city from its mainland dependencies, the Assyrian monarch cut off a crucial element of its power base. Although still autonomous, Tyre was now completely reliant upon its overseas possessions for economic support. The financial blow must have been devastating for the city, at least in the short term. For Sidon, however, the inheritance of Tyre's land empire (a coastal stretch of 160 kilometres (100 miles) extending southwards to the Mount Carmel peninsula) and the explicit support of Assyria gave it an economic boost over its rival southern neighbour.[58]

Sidon's territorial advantage over Tyre would not last long, however. Prospering from its territorial gains, and bolstered by an alliance with the Cilician king Sanduari, Sidon seized upon the opportunity afforded by Sennacherib's assassination to renounce Assyrian suzerainty. Once again, Assyria responded with a sure and heavy hand. In 677 BC, within 3 years of securing the throne, Esarhaddon (680–669 BC), Sennacherib's youngest son and successor, advanced upon Sidon, seizing the city and annexing its surrounding territory. The city and its town walls were demolished; the royal palace was ransacked and its contents carried off to Assyria. In the following year, Abdi-Milkuti, the royal perpetrator, was captured at sea and beheaded. The royal family and court, together with the city population, were deported, and foreign peoples resettled in their place; the city was rebuilt by the Assyrians and renamed Kar Esarhaddon ('Port Esarhaddon').

For reasons unstated, the southern portion of Sidon's kingdom (including the town of Sarepta) was now handed over to Tyre, which by now had regained its former southern coastal holdings in the Akko plain. Esarhaddon's gift to Tyre was probably awarded in recognition of the city's recent record of loyalty; under Luli's successor, Baal I, Tyre had been prompt and consistent in meeting its annual tributary quotas.

Tyre's posture of allegiance, it appears, was a purely public one. In reality, it had been actively involved in rebuilding its political and economic power base in an effort to free itself from Assyrian control. The island city now apparently stood at the head of a league of independent Levantine principalities, known in the Assyrian annals as the '22 kings of Hatti [i.e. Syria], the seashore and the islands'. Tyre's position of leadership in this confederation, which included the kingdom of Judah and ten cities each from 'Greater Syria' and Cyprus, gave it significant regional clout.

6 *An Assyrian relief depicting the flight of Luli, king of Tyre, to Cyprus. The tall edifice that appears above the city walls may represent the famed temple of Melqart, the entrance of which was marked by twin columns of gold and emerald. From the Palace of Sennacherib at Nineveh, Iraq. Early seventh century* BC.

THE PHOENICIANS AND KUSHITE EGYPT

Tyre's commercial partners also included Egypt, now under foreign, Nubian (Kushite) rule. For a period of years, Egypt and Tyre had already enjoyed a brisk trade relationship with the Kushites under Taharqa (*c.*690–664 BC).[59] In exchange for Phoenician imports (such as cedar and bronze), the Kushite king may have diverted some of the lucrative Nubian trade under his control to the Tyrian metropolis.

Egypt's re-emergence in the Near Eastern political sphere had already occurred some

years before, under Osorkon IV (*c.*730–715 BC), the last of the Tanite Twenty-second Dynasty kings. It was to the latter that appeal was made by Hosea of Israel in 726/5 BC. for military support of his anti-Assyrian coalition. During the final decades of the eighth century, in fact, Egypt skilfully manoeuvred behind the scenes, lending tacit support and encouragement to the rebellious activities of the southern Palestinian states.

Under the Kushites, however, Egypt assumed a more active and aggressive military stance in western Asia, joining forces, under its second king, Shabaka, with the

Judaean–Philistine confederacy against the Assyrians at Eltekeh in 702/1 BC. In the face of a growing Assyrian menace, the Kushite Taharqa, raised the political stakes. The Nubian monarch contracted an alliance with Tyre and its western coalition against Esarhaddon, hoping to shore up its Mediterranean line of defence against impending Assyrian aggression.

TYRE AND THE LATE ASSYRIAN KINGS: A CITY UNDER SIEGE

In 671 BC, Esarhaddon launched his second invasion attempt against Egypt, using the occasion to punish Tyre for its alliance with Taharqa. En route to Egypt, he laid preparations for the siege of the city before pressing southwards for the successful capture of Memphis, prompting Taharqa's flight to Nubia. Upon his return, Baal I, Tyre's sovereign, prudently capitulated to Assyria, agreeing to heavy tributary demands (including the settlement of payments in arrears) and suffering the temporary loss of his mainland territories. The victorious Assyrian sovereign commemorated his dual triumph over Egypt and Tyre with a series of victory stelae depicting Esarhaddon with the bound figures of Baal and Ushanahuru, Taharqa's captured son, the Nubian crown prince. (See fig. 7.) It was probably at this time that the city entered into a vassal treaty with Assyria that regulated its maritime trade.[60] Tyre had once again been humbled by its powerful Assyrian overlord.

Although seriously weakened, the island city, along with Byblos and Arwad, continued to function autonomously within the Assyrian realm. In 668 BC, the accession year of Ashurbanipal (668–631 BC), the kings of all three Phoenician cities offered tribute and naval assistance to the new Assyrian monarch during his first campaign against Egypt. Tyre's gesture, once again, seems to have been a political smokescreen, for within a few years, with Assyria again preoccupied with Egypt, the city rebelled, along with Arwad and other members of the Syrian confederation. In 662 BC, following the Assyrian capture and sack of Thebes, Assurbanipal instituted a land blockade of Tyre, ultimately prompting Baal's surrender and submission. While the city and its king were spared, Tyre's mainland possessions were ultimately stripped. By 640 BC, Tyre's continental empire had become an Assyrian province, its former possessions, Ushu and Akko, now under state control.

Assyrian suzerainty over the Levant was, however, slowly disintegrating. Plagued by civil unrest and a debilitating war with Elam, Assyria would return no more to the Phoenician coast. Within three short decades of its final campaign against the Tyrian mainland in 644/3 BC, the Assyrian empire would collapse, the victim of Babylonian aggression.

During the final quarter of the seventh century, the Phoenician coast, as Philistia to the south, appears to have fallen under Egyptian control. Capitalizing on the political vacuum now left in the Levant, Psamettichus I (664–610 BC), founder of the new native Saitic Twenty-sixth Dynasty, re-established Egyptian ties with the north. The historical documentation for Egyptian political presence in the Levant, while scant, is highly suggestive. According to an Egyptian document from 613 BC, the Phoenician coast had become an Egyptian dependency, governed by a provincial authority directly responsible to the

Pharaoh. In matters of commerce, Psamettichus himself boasts that his officers supervised Phoenician timber production and export.[61] The Tyrians themselves had by now established a commercial enclave in Memphis, Egypt's capital.

Proprietary concerns may thus have dictated Egypt's decision to ally itself with its arch-enemy Assyria against the Babylonians in the final decade of the seventh century. The ill-fated alliance between former political rivals was, however, short-lived. In 605 BC, the Babylonians, under their crown prince Nebuchadnezzar, succeeded in routing the combined forces of Egypt and Assyria at Carchemish. The seeds of Babylonian hegemony over the Levant had now been laid.

PHOENICIA UNDER THE BABYLONIANS

In his first year, Nebuchadnezzar II (604–562 BC), the new Babylonian monarch, marched to Syria, where he asserted his control over the kings of 'Hatti', who included the rulers of the Phoenician coastal cities, who duly submitted their tribute. Babylonian hegemony over the region, however, was far from secure. With encouragement from Egypt, the various Levantine states, including the kingdom of Judah and the Phoenician cities, soon put up resistance. In apparent response to a coalition organized earlier between Judah, Tyre, Sidon, and the Transjordanian states of Ammon, Moab, and Edom, Nebuchadnezzar took military action, besieging and destroying Jerusalem in 587 BC and launching a campaign aimed at securing the submission of the Phoenician coast in the following year. Around 585 BC, Nebuchadnezzar undertook his famous 13-year siege of Tyre, which had apparently resisted his advances in the previous campaign.[62] This long operation – in reality, a land blockade of the island city – should be understood as a strategem of containment rather than as a continuous, concerted attack. (Such an interpretation may explain why the event receives no mention in the official Babylonian Chronicles.) The historical

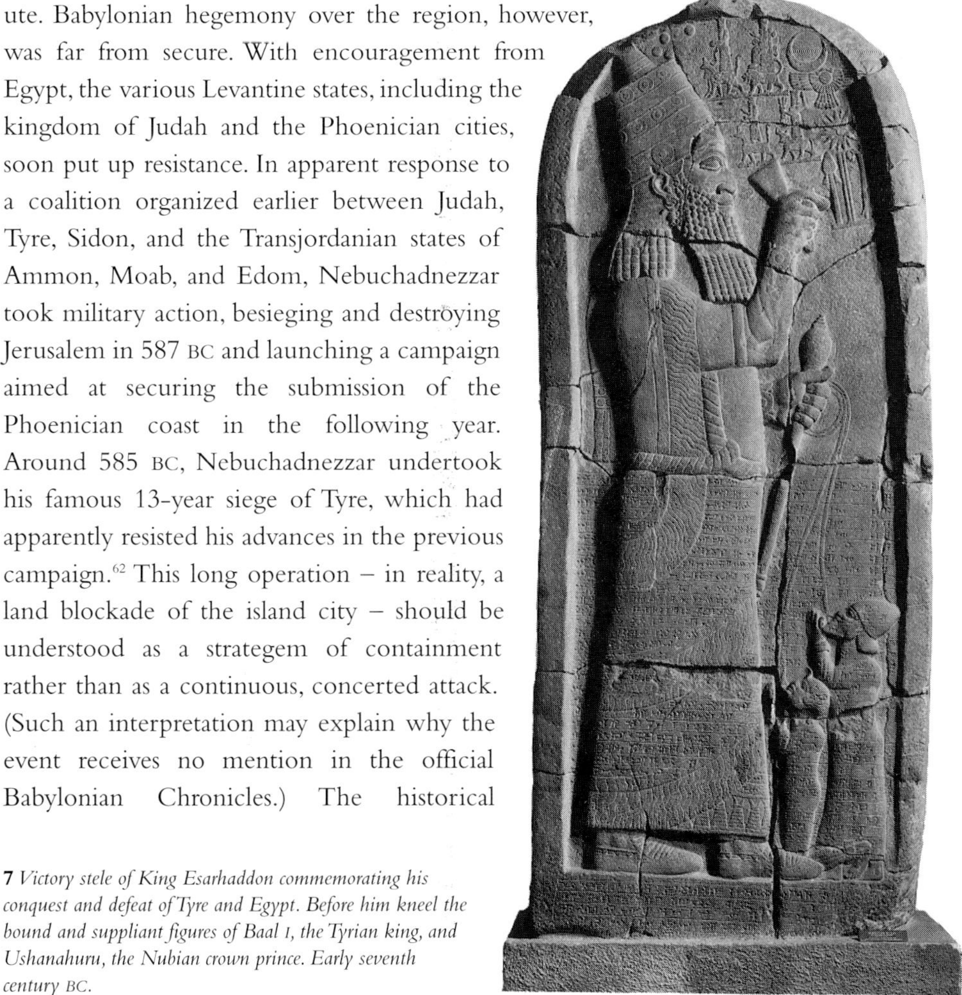

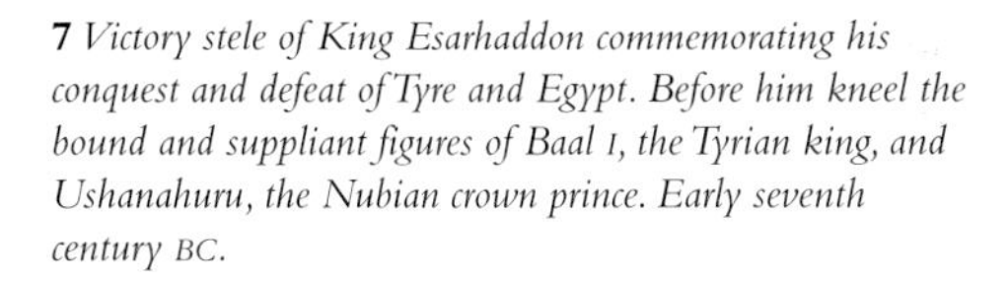

7 *Victory stele of King Esarhaddon commemorating his conquest and defeat of Tyre and Egypt. Before him kneel the bound and suppliant figures of Baal I, the Tyrian king, and Ushanahuru, the Nubian crown prince. Early seventh century BC.*

veracity of the siege is confirmed by a contemporary Babylonian document, which reveals that Nebuchadnezzar himself was personally involved in at least some aspects of its operation. While the outcome of the siege is unclear, the result, it appears, was not a clear-cut victory for the Babylonians; in all likelihood, a compromise was reached, in which Tyre was granted continued autonomy in recognition of Babylonian suzerainty.[63]

Indeed, the Tyrian dynastic line continued in power, as Josephus reveals in his list of succeeding Tyrian dynasts. As a consequence of Tyrian submission, its current ruler, Ithobaal III, was apparently replaced by Baal II. As had been the case previously with the rebellious Judaean king Zedekiah, Ithobaal may well have been deported to Nineveh at this time.

Following the reign of Baal II, Josephus records an interregnum of 7 years, during which the city was governed by a series of annually appointed judges, or suffetes. The circumstances surrounding this unprecedented constitutional change remain unclear. However, the two Tyrian kings (Maharbaal and Hiram III) who ultimately inherited the throne, upon resumption of the dynastic line, were each summoned, in turn, from the royal court at Babylon, indicating that both had suffered deportation years before at the hands of Nebuchadnezzar. When Tyre actually lost its autonomy is unclear; by Nebuchadnezzar's fortieth year (564 BC), however, the city had fallen under the jurisdiction of the Babylonian province of Kadesh.

Under the Babylonians, the Phoenician cities appear to have reached their commercial nadir. Babylonian annexation of southern Palestine (Philistia, Samaria, and Judah) and Transjordan (Ammon and Moab), on the one hand, and Cilicia, on the other, clearly curtailed Phoenician access to the lucrative south Arabian and southern Anatolian trade networks. Phoenician commerce with Babylonia itself is well attested in the numerous court records detailing Phoenician artisans in state employment, but it is unclear how much initiative the Phoenicians themselves were granted in this sphere. Under Nebuchadnezzar, the Babylonian state assumed control of Phoenicia's cherished cedar trade. On Nebuchadnezzar's rock-cut inscription at Wadi Brisa in northern Lebanon, the Babylonian monarch boasts of constructing a slip-way and roads through the mountains to facilitate transport of the timber overland to the Euphrates and thence to Babylon; contemporary building inscriptions reveal the extent to which cedar wood was utilized in state-sponsored construction projects, including Nebuchadnezzar's own palace.[64]

Little is known about the Phoenician cities and their relations with Babylonia following the death of Nebuchadnezzar in 562 BC. In the final years of the empire, under its last king, Nabonidus (556–539 BC), the Phoenician mainland centres may have enjoyed a period of relative independence, as the Babylonians turned their attentions away from the west towards more pressing matters at home. Such a loosening of administrative control may be envisaged from the mid-century onward, with Nabonidus occupied (on an extended campaign) in Arabia, and with the Medes threatening in the east. Babylon's decision under Nabonidus to reinstate the Tyrian dynastic line in 556 BC may indeed have been a gesture of political appeasement aimed at ensuring the city's continued allegiance during unstable times. While historical documentation is lacking, the same time period may have marked the reinstatement of the exiled ruling families of Sidon, Arwad, and Byblos, all of whom are attested in their home cities by the beginning of the fifth century.[65] Babylonian promotion of Phoenician autonomy under Nabonidus may help to explain why the Phoenicians remained faithful to the Crown in the empire's final years, despite mounting internal difficulties.

THE PHOENICIANS UNDER PERSIAN RULE

The end of Babylonian hegemony came swiftly in October of 539 BC with the Persian conquest of Sippar and Babylon under Cyrus the Great (559–530 BC). Nothing is recorded of the political status of the Phoenician cities in the early years of the empire. In all likelihood, they were included among the 'kings from the Upper Sea [Mediterranean] ... dwelling in royal palaces' who voluntarily offered their submission and tribute to Cyrus in Babylon.[66] Opinion is divided, however, on the precise date of their incorporation within the empire, whether in the early years of Cyrus or the reign of his successor Cambyses (530–522 BC), prior to the latter's Egyptian campaign.[67]

From the outset, the Phoenicians apparently enjoyed a very favourable position as a result of their strategic maritime importance to Persia and its westerly imperial aims. Indeed, throughout most of the Achaemenid period they served as the primary naval arm of Persia's maritime operations in the Mediterranean. This strategic role manifests itself in the very first stage of Persian westward expansion: the invasion and conquest of Egypt, undertaken by Cyrus' successor, Cambyses, in 525 BC. As Herodotus records, the Phoenician fleet from Tyre played a pivotal role in supporting the Persians' successful land attack upon the Nile Delta, laying the stage for the subsequent capture of Memphis, Egypt's capital.

As Herodotus notes, the Tyrians had volunteered their services to Cambyses, a clever move that quickly earned them the Persians' undying gratitude and trust. Throughout the sixth and succeeding fifth century, this strategem was consistently adhered to by the Phoenicians; indeed, their record of naval co-operation with the Persians, like that of the Cilicians (who were similarly rewarded by Cyrus for their unswerving loyalty), was exemplary.

The payoff for such active co-operation was significant. Circumstantial evidence would suggest that the Phoenician cities were treated generously from the very outset – almost as allies rather than vassal states. The extent of their political influence and autonomy may be gauged from Herodotus' account of Cambyses' planned attack upon Carthage following the successful Egyptian campaign. When ordered to sail against Carthage, the Tyrians refused, citing their treaty obligations to their daughter city. Rather than press his demands, the Persian monarch acceded to the Tyrians' wishes, and subsequently scrapped his invasion plans.

As with Phoenician Kition and the other Cypriot royal cities, all four mainland Phoenician centres – Tyre, Sidon, Byblos, and Arwad – were permitted to retain their dynastic autonomy. No explicit information exists regarding the Phoenicians' tributary obligations. Perhaps their active military co-operation – in placing their fleets at the disposal of the Persians – freed them from heavy monetary payments.

The Phoenician cities initially formed part of a wide-ranging administrative district, known as Athura ('Assyria'), which encompassed all of Mesopotamia and Syria–Palestine. In the early decades of the fifth century BC, under an administrative reorganization of the empire undertaken by Darius I (522–486 BC), this unwieldy region was subdivided, and a separate province, called Abarnahara ('Beyond the River') was created, which contained Cyprus and all of the Levantine mainland west of the Euphrates.

The Phoenicians clearly exploited their privileged position within the Achaemenid administrative hierarchy. Persian suzerainty and the empire's efficient communication network afforded them trade opportunities inland – with Mesopotamia and the Persian heartland itself. More importantly, Persian political control allowed them to capitalize on maritime trade with Egypt and the Mediterranean.

It was with such commercial objectives that the Phoenicians actively supported Persia's war efforts against Egypt and the western Greek realm. In the two preceding centuries, the Phoenicians had faced increasing competition from Greek traders in the Mediterranean; by the late sixth and early fifth centuries, such rivalry had struck dangerously close to home in traditional Phoenician markets, such as Egypt, Rhodes, and Cyprus. Greek trade had even penetrated the northern Levantine mainland, where Aegean imports witnessed a dramatic increase in the early years of the fifth century. It comes as little surprise, then, that the Phoenicians were, in Herodotus' words, 'the most zealous' of all of Persia's naval allies in attacking the Ionian Greeks and the city of Miletus at the battle of Lade in 494 BC. A prosperous Greek emporium, Miletus was a centre for East Greek coastal trade in the Aegean and, for this reason, received preferential treatment under the Persians, as it had earlier under the Lydians. (Cyrus himself had previously negotiated a separate treaty with the Milesians during his campaign against the region in 547 BC.) Miletus' subsequent destruction at the hands of the Persians thus eliminated a major commercial rival for the Phoenicians and opened up new avenues of trade in the Aegean. It was, no doubt, with the same hopes and expectations that the Phoenicians assisted Persia in its invasions of mainland Greece under Darius I and Xerxes (485–465 BC) in the following decade.

Similar commercial objectives fuelled Tyre's naval support of Cambyses in his advance upon Egypt in 525 BC. Here, too, during the previous 100 years, the Greeks had made serious inroads under the Saitic kings of the Twenty-sixth Dynasty. Already in the seventh century, under Psammetichus I, they had established a military base – the first of several on the eastern, Pelusiac branch of the Nile Delta, the Phoenician point of entry for Egyptian trade. In the last quarter of the sixth century, as archaeological investigation has revealed, the Ionian Greeks had established a substantial port settlement in the Nile Delta at Naukratis, in the vicinity of Sais, Egypt's Twenty-sixth Dynasty capital. In the decades prior to the Persian attack, the Greek trading town had reached its commercial apogee under the patronage of Amasis, Egypt's philhellene king. The Persian conquest of Egypt brought about a dramatic alteration in Egyptian foreign trade, which now once again favoured the Levant. The loss of Greek initiative is reflected at Naukratis itself, which underwent a rapid decline in the years following the Persian conquest.[68]

The Tyrians were well positioned to benefit from trade with Persian-controlled Egypt, recouping momentum lost in the earlier years of the sixth century, when the Nile kingdom, under Necho II, assumed the initiative in foreign trade with a newly created fleet of triremes. Necho himself utilized Phoenician sailors in an exploratory expedition from the Red Sea aimed at circumnavigating Africa.[69] Amasis' own political initiatives in the Mediterranean prior to the Persian conquest, which included alliances with Samos and perhaps Cyprus, must have raised some concern in Phoenician trade circles.[70]

Phoenician commercial activity in Egypt under the Persians is evidenced by the presence of a Tyrian commercial establishment at Memphis, known as the 'Camp of the Tyrians', which Herodotus himself visited.[71] Egypt's administrative capital, site of the naval dockyards, had long been the centre of Phoenician trade in the Nile Delta. It was in the eastern hinterland of Memphis that Darius I, in the final decades of the sixth century, completed construction of a canal begun by Necho, connecting the Nile with the Red Sea at the mouth of the Gulf of Suez. Its existence, noted in antiquity by Herodotus, has been confirmed by the discovery of a series of red granite commemorative stelae erected along its course by Darius.

Long reputed as maritime engineers, the Phoenicians may well have been instrumental in the canal's construction, as they were two decades later on a Persian-made channel of corresponding width across the Mount Athos peninsula in northern Greece.[72] At any rate, they must surely have benefited directly as intermediaries in the Egyptian Red Sea trade now facilitated by the canal. It is perhaps not far-fetched to imagine that, in return for their naval services, the Tyrians were granted a commercial concession in such transit trade by the Persians themselves. Phoenician commercial involvement at this time in the trade between the Mediterranean and the Red Sea is clearly attested by the presence of Phoenician inscriptions at Tell el-Kheleifeh at the mouth of the Gulf of Aqabah.

SIDONIAN HEGEMONY UNDER THE PERSIANS

Despite Tyre's efforts at rebuilding its commercial ties in the early decades of Persian dominance, it is Sidon, none the less, which emerges clearly as the pre-eminent Phoenician state by the early fifth century, a role which it occupied until the closing years of the Persian era. The indicators of Sidonian political ascendancy are clear and unequivocal. The city functioned as the regional headquarters and seat of a governor's residence throughout the Achaemenid era; a Persian garrison and royal park (*paradeisos*) were located there. Sidon's elevated status in the Achaemenid hierarchy is also evidenced by the fact that its coinage, alone among Phoenician cities, featured depictions of the Persian king, a privilege clearly bestowed upon it by the royal Crown. Moreover, it was the only city to issue the double stater, a heavy coin with considerable prestige as well as financial value.

Commercially, Sidon appears to have held the leading position among Phoenician cities. Diodorus comments on the wealth of the city, adding that 'its private citizens had amassed great riches from [its] shipping'.[73] The Aegean market was a lucrative one for Sidon, in contrast to Tyre, whose former colonial possessions were centred in the central and western Mediterranean. The city was the centre for the manufacture of carved marble anthropoid sarcophagi, which were widely traded throughout the eastern Mediterranean. (See fig. 61.) In the early fourth century, Sidonian trade with the Aegean may have peaked under Straton I (Abdashtart), its avid philhellene king, whose name is attested in inscriptions at the commercial centres of Delos and Athens; the latter city, in fact, issued a decree exempting Sidonian traders in Athens from taxation.[74] Of the Phoenician cities, Sidon's coinage was the most widely circulated. To judge from the numismatic evidence, Sidonian trade exceeded that of Tyre both in the Phoenician heartland and in the Plain of Sharon, now Sidonian territory by royal gift.[75] The archaeological evidence attests to Sidon's prosperity. The city's urban expansion to the south and east, the grand remodelling and extension of the Eshmun temple complex, and the lavish royal burials of the Sidonian kings themselves all bespeak an era of affluence. (See the frontispiece.)

A variety of explanations have been offered for Sidon's eclipse of Tyre in the Persian era; clearly, however, a single factor stands out among them all: Sidonian superiority in naval strength. From the reign of Darius onward, the Sidonian fleet was the most highly touted of Persia's naval contingents, its triremes the fastest and most effective in combat. During Xerxes' invasion of Greece in 480 BC, the Sidonian commander Tetamnestros occupied the highest rank among the Phoenician naval officers, and held the place of priority in the king's war council.[76] It was Sidon's naval strength that clearly dictated the city's choice as military headquarters for the Phoenician region; its strategic coastal position at the head of two main roads leading to the interior rendered it of further value as a garrison post.

PHOENICIAN CYPRUS UNDER THE PERSIANS

The Persian era marked a period of political and cultural expansion for the Phoenicians on Cyprus under the aegis of Kition, now independent from its mother-city Tyre. (See fig. 28.) Epigraphic and archaeological evidence from the classical period in Cyprus reveals the extent of Phoenician presence throughout the island – both along the coast as well as in the interior regions of the copper-rich Troodos Mountains (Golgoi, Tamassos, Idalion). During the Persian era, as it had before, Cyprus served as a strategic intermediary for Levantine coastal trade with the western Mediterranean; for this reason and for its copper resources, the island was of strategic commercial importance to the Phoenicians on the mainland, who sought to keep it under Persian control.

While the Cypriot Phoenicians were present in communities throughout the island, Cyprus' independent kingdoms fell largely under Greek dynastic rule, and their sympathies lay with the Aegean west. Consequently, the island, during the Achaemenid era, was the centre of a protracted 'tug-of-war' between Greek and Persian political interests. Conflict erupted at the turn of the fifth century, when the entire island, with the notable exception of Amathus, joined the Ionian Revolt of 499/8 BC. The Persian response was swift; with the aid of the mainland Phoenician fleet, an invasion was launched at Salamis, the rebellion's epicentre, and the confederate forces defeated on land. Within the year, the rebel cities, now besieged by the Persians, had capitulated, and the island fell once again under Achaemenid control. Amathus' refusal to join the revolt may be seen as a clear reflection of that city's political and commercial priorities. As the primary transit point for trade with the Levant and Egypt, it had a vested interest in remaining within the Achaemenid eastern Mediterranean trade network.

Following the Persian wars, the Athenian general Cimon attempted unsuccessfully, on three occasions, to seize control of Cyprus on behalf of the Greek Delian confederacy. Following the unsuccessful siege of Kition in 450 BC, a state of détente was reached between Greece and Persia under Artaxerxes I (464–424 BC), culminating in the Peace of Kallias in 449 BC. According to its terms, a north–south boundary was established at Phaselis along the Pamphylian coast of Anatolia, dividing the Mediterranean into Greek and Persian military spheres; Persian naval ships were thus prohibited from patrolling the Aegean (and the western coast of Asia Minor), while the Greek navy could no longer operate in the waters around Cyprus and along the eastern Mediterranean littoral. Cyprus remained under Persian control for the next four decades – until 412 BC, when the status quo was disrupted by another rebellion, again initiated by the city of Salamis.

In the decades following the Peace of Kallias, the political and economic power base of Phoenician Kition grew significantly, its control extending even to neighbouring Salamis, which now fell temporarily under Phoenician dynastic rule. The city expanded its territorial holdings to the north and west, annexing Idalion, around 450 BC, and extending its control to neighbouring Golgoi. A century later, around 350 BC, it acquired the kingdom of Tamassos in the Cypriot interior.

Kition's inland expansion was motivated by a single objective: the exploitation of copper. Both Idalion and Tamassos, along with a host of other Cypriot sites marked by Phoenician influence (Meniko-Litharkes, Golgoi, and Amathus), were located near the island's copper-rich deposits on the slopes of the Troodos Mountains, which had been mined since the Late Bronze Age.[77] With the island under Persian suzerainty, the bulk of the copper trade must surely have been directed to the eastern mainland. In all likelihood, the Phoenician ports, and the city of Tyre in particular, must have played a major role in facilitating such trade.

Recent excavations at Kition itself have uncovered a portion of the city's extensive dockyards erected at the end of the fifth or beginning of the fourth century BC. The newly developed harbour facilities and adjoining sanctuary complex formed part of an extensive programme of urban renovation in the Bamboula district, attesting to the city's current prosperity.[78] (See fig. 8.)

8 *View of ship sheds in the city dockyards (foreground); remains of archaic sanctuaries to Melqart and Astarte (background). Kition-Bamboula, Cyprus, fifth–fourth century* BC.

PHOENICIAN POLITICAL INDEPENDENCE IN THE WEST: THE RISE OF CARTHAGE UNDER THE MAGONIDS

By the late sixth century, as previously mentioned, Sidon stood as the dominant regional power in the Phoenician mainland. Its eclipse of Tyre was due, in large part, to the island city's loss of its overseas empire, of which Carthage formed a crucial part. What precipitated the split between mother-city and daughter-colony remains unclear; in all likelihood, the separation took root before the mid-sixth century BC, during Tyre's nadir under Neo-Babylonian suzerainty. The city's fall to Nebuchadnezzar in 573/2 BC and the ensuing interim period of political and economic instability may have occasioned the split. In its weakened state, Tyre was presumably no longer in a position to guarantee the safety and protection of its overseas colonies.

By the time of Cambyses' invasion of Egypt in 525 BC, Carthage had become a fully independent entity. According to Herodotus, the Persian monarch ordered the Tyrians to participate in a planned naval attack upon their sister city, a command which they refused to obey because of the strong oaths (*orkioi*) that bound them to their colonial descendants. (Herodotus uses the word 'children' in the text.) An attack upon Carthage would thus have constituted a serious breach of Tyre's treaty obligations to its former colony. The already considerable military strength of the North African city and the indispensability of the Phoenician fleet find reflection in Cambyses' decision to cancel his invasion plan; without Phoenician support, as Herodotus relates, the remaining fleets were no match for the Carthaginians.

Carthage's emergence as a political and military power is traditionally ascribed to the mid-sixth century BC, when the city, under the aegis of general Mago and his descendant-successors (known as the Magonids), embarked upon an aggressive campaign of conquest and colonial expansion. It is around this time, or shortly before, that Carthage first intervened militarily in both Sardinia and Sicily in an effort to safeguard Phoenician holdings there.[79] Undisputed evidence of Carthaginian military activity may be found in the events of 535 BC, when the city's naval forces, allied with the Etruscans, defeated the Greek Phocaeans in an encounter off the coast of Corsica.[80] Carthage's close commercial and political relationship with the Etruscans, then at the head of the Tyrrhenian confederation (comprising Tuscany, Latium, and Campania), finds dramatic confirmation in the discovery of three inscribed gold dedicatory plaques in Etruscan and Phoenician at Pyrgi, the commercial harbour of Etruscan Caere. Etruscan imports at Carthage confirm the close trade ties that existed between these two maritime powers. Archaeological research has, in fact, documented the extent of Carthaginian hegemony in the central Mediterranean at this time; as excavation has confirmed, the city's cultural presence and influence may be noted at Motya in Sicily, in Sardinia, and in Ibiza, Carthage's oldest overseas colony.

Carthage's conquests in Sicily and Sardinia underscore the strategic role that these two islands played in the formation and development of the Carthaginian maritime empire. As with Cyprus to the Levant, both Sicily and Sardinia lay in close proximity to the Carthaginian mainland, roughly 160 kilometres (100 miles) offshore. Both islands were strategically positioned for commercial trade within the Tyrrhenian basin. Sicily, as we have seen, was, moreover, a linchpin in Carthage's trade with the Aegean. Possession of Sardinia was critical to the protection of Carthaginian trade hegemony in the western Mediterranean.

The Greek colonial movement posed the greatest threat to Carthage in the pursuit of her Mediterranean commercial empire. As history records, a number of Greek colonial incursions in Punic territory prompted swift Carthaginian military intervention.[81] By the sixth century, the coast of Sicily, with the exception of its north-west sector, was dotted with Greek emporia. The largest and most prosperous of these were the cities of Syracuse and Acragas (Agrigento), both of them strategic harbours in the Aegean transit trade.

It was against the united armies of these two Greek cities, in fact, that Carthage launched its most ambitious expedition to date under the Magonid general Hamilcar, grandson of Mago, in 480 BC. The army of three hundred thousand men that landed at the Sicilian port of Panormus (Palermo) boasted contingents drawn from throughout the western Mediterranean – North Africa, Spain, Gaul, Liguria, and Sardinia – a sign of Carthage's economic strength and wide-ranging sphere of political influence. The pretext for the invasion was the restoration of Terillus to the throne of Himera, which had been usurped by the tyrant of Acragas; Hamilcar was bound by hospitality ties to Terillus' son-in-law, Anaxilas, tyrant of Rhegium.

In reality, a larger scheme underlay Hamilcar's actions – the incorporation of all of Sicily within the Carthaginian realm. Hamilcar's immediate opponents, Syracuse and Acragas (whom the city had faced some 40 years before in a Sicilian campaign aimed at neutralizing Spartan aggression), were the primary emporia for Aegean trade with Carthage. Possession of these two strategic harbour facilities would give Carthage complete control of the island's lucrative commercial trade.

An even broader, 'global' plan may have motivated Carthage's actions. According to the Greek historians Ephoros and Diodorus, the Persian king Xerxes, as part of his Greek invasion plans of 480 BC, had orchestrated an offensive pact with the Carthaginians that entailed the co-ordinated actions of the two powers;[82] as the Persians invaded, the Carthaginians would attack Greek Sicily and southern Italy. That such a pact had been concluded, probably through the intermediary of Tyre, is not at all improbable. Persia's aims at westward expansion into the Mediterranean had been clear since Cambyses' invasion of Egypt. For the Phoenicians on the mainland, a Carthaginian-controlled Sicily and an Aegean under Persian suzerainty would guarantee a direct and fully protected avenue of trade to the western Mediterranean. For the Persians, a Carthaginian offensive in Sicily would ensure the absence of Syracuse and the other Sicilian Greek cities from the Athenian war front. Such a Persian–Carthaginian coalition uniting the world's greatest land and sea powers may thus be considered likely on historical grounds.

The two offensives, whether jointly or independently conceived, ended in failure. Like the Persians at Salamis, the Carthaginians were soundly defeated at Himera and forced to pay war reparations in the amount of 20,000 silver talents. The defeat at Himera marked a turning point in Carthage's history under the Magonids, the quasi-dynasty of 'general-kings' that held sway over the city throughout the fifth century. The city now rejected its aggressive Mediterranean-based foreign policy and turned its attentions towards consolidating its territorial control in Africa. For the next 70 years, the Punic metropolis refrained from interfering in Greek affairs in Sicily, content with the status quo.

History has preserved little record of Carthage's early conquests in the Tunisian heartland under Hanno, Hamilcar's son and successor. By the end of the fifth century, however, the city appears to have gained control of a considerable portion of the Tunisian hinterland, including the fertile valleys of the lower Medjerda and Wadi Miliana, and the Sahelian coast of eastern Tunisia (Byzacenia) as far as Sfax.[83] (See fig. 9.)

The historical record is largely mute on the city's commercial activities during the period. As recent research on fifth-century imports at Carthage and its environs has revealed, the Punic defeat at Himera may not have resulted in a complete rupture in commercial ties with the Aegean.[84] Nevertheless, the temporary loss of access to the Greek Sicilian ports of Acragas and Syracuse, long primary outlets for Aegean goods into the city, must surely have been felt. The archaeological record, in fact, reveals a significant drop in imported commercial amphorae at Carthage during the middle years of the fifth century BC.[85]

At any rate, the city appears now to have concentrated its commercial activities in the western Mediterranean. The Carthaginian expeditions of Hanno and Himilco along the African and North Atlantic coasts (both of which may be situated in this general period) reveal a keen interest in exploring new avenues of trade beyond the Mediterranean straits. The archaeological record at Carthage documents a renewal of imports, especially from Cadiz and the far west, during the final decades of the fifth century. Evidence of the city's renewed prosperity may be seen in its urban expansion beyond the Byrsa hill region, manifest in the construction of a handsome coastal residential district and adjoining

9 *View of the Medjerda River Valley (Chemtou), Tunisia.*

maritime defensive system.[86] By 415 BC, Carthage had apparently accumulated large reserves of gold and silver.[87]

THE PHOENICIAN MAINLAND: THE LATE FIFTH AND FOURTH CENTURIES BC

The final years of the fifth century were a period of growing internal unrest and political weakness within the Achaemenid realm, particularly in the empire's western flank. The provinces of Lydia and Caria in western Asia Minor stood in open revolt; both insurrections were supported in part by the Athenians, who themselves were now involved in a protracted conflict with the Spartans, the so-called Peloponnesian war. In an effort to counter Athenian power, and to ensure the collection of tribute from the prosperous Greek cities of Asia Minor, Darius II (423–405/4 BC) entered into an alliance with the Spartans in 412 BC. In the conflict with Athens, the Persians promised the support of the Phoenician royal fleet, still the largest and most prestigious of the Persian naval contingents.

The final years of the fifth century witnessed a further blow to Persia's western imperial aims: the loss of Egypt. By *c*.405 BC, the Nile Delta region stood in open revolt under Amyrtaeus; within 5 years, the native Egyptian dynasty had consolidated control of Upper Egypt, putting an end to more than 100 years of Persian rule. Despite repeated attempts by Artaxerxes II (405/4–359/8 BC), the Persians failed to regain control of this crucial region until the empire's waning years – on the literal eve of its defeat by the Macedonians.

Such signs of declining Persian control in the west and the growing independence of Egypt, western Asia Minor, and mainland Greece were clearly of concern to the commercially oriented mainland Phoenician city-states. Throughout the fifth century, while the Persians remained firmly in control of their eastern Mediterranean empire, they had remained loyal. With the Achaemenid grip on the region unraveling, Phoenician commercial and political priorities now began to shift – away from the Persian epicentre towards the Mediterranean west.

On neighbouring Cyprus, the political situation was also in a state of flux. Since deposing the Phoenician dynast Abdemon in 411 BC, Evagoras, Greek tyrant of Salamis, had been laying the groundwork for independent Greek Cypriot control of the island. Evagoras' desire to wrest Cyprus from Persian control became evident in 389 BC, when an alliance was formed with Athens and Egypt. The anti-Persian coalition soon garnered support on the mainland; according to ancient Greek sources, both Tyre and the Arabian confederacy of southern Palestine joined the alliance.[88] Despite the inferences of the ancient Greek authors, it would appear, however, that the rest of the Phoenician mainland remained within the Persian fold. Tyre's independent decision to ally itself with the revolt may have been conditioned by its longstanding commercial ties with Egypt and Cyprus. Perhaps a Tyrian understanding had been reached with Evagoras over the future status of Phoenician Kition, once the island was securely under Salaminian control.

At the urging of Phoenician Kition and Amathus, who had resisted Evagoras' advances in the 390s,[89] the Persians responded decisively in 381 BC, defeating the confederate fleets of Cyprus, Egypt, and Tyre in a sea battle near Kition; although permitted to remain on the throne, the once-powerful Evagoras was now reduced to the status of a tributary, and forced to relinquish his Cypriot conquests. Strategic Cyprus was, once again, in Persian hands.

Achaemenid efforts to consolidate power along its Mediterranean flank, however, proved largely unsuccessful. In 373 BC, supported by a sizeable fleet drawn from Phoenicia, Cyprus, and Cilicia, the Persians launched a massive expedition to reconquer Egypt. Unlike Cambyses' successful campaign 150 years earlier, the Persian advance was slowed by an Egyptian blockade at the Pelusiac entrance to the Nile Delta; the resulting delay and the subsequent inundation of the Nile forced the Persian army to withdraw with heavy losses. Persia's failure to regain Egypt served as a catalyst for the rebellion that now brewed in the western provinces of Asia Minor; by the mid-360s, under the leadership of Ariobarzanes, satrap of Daskyleion, nearly all of Anatolia, with military and financial support from Egypt and the Greek west, stood in open revolt against Artaxerxes II and the Persian throne.

The role that the Phoenician cities played in the Great Satrapal Revolt of 363–361 BC is difficult to assess. Bolstered by military support from Athens, Sparta, and the western satrapies, Egypt, under Pharaoh Tachos (362–360 BC), launched an abortive campaign into Phoenician territory in 360 BC. According to Greek sources, the Egyptian monarch, victimized by internal revolt in the homeland, sought refuge with King Abdashtart (Straton) I in Sidon before defecting to the Persians, testifying to the Phoenician city's close ties with the rebellious Egyptian king.[90] Sidon's own seditious tendencies under Abdashtart are evident in the city's coinage, which now features the Phoenician monarch's crowned portrait in place of the conventional kneeling Persian king. A single surviving silver tetradrachm dated to Abdashtart's eighth year signals an attempt on the part of the phil-hellene monarch to adopt the Athenian weight standard for commercial exchange.[91] For his transgressions, Abdashtart I ultimately paid with his life – at his wife's hands.

Upon conclusion of the uprising in 362/1 BC, Sidon was occupied by Persian military forces and placed under the authority of Mazaeus (Mazday), satrap of Cilicia and Syria, in recognition of his assistance in suppressing the revolt. For a period of 4 years, the city's minting privileges were suspended, its coinage overstruck with Mazaeus' Aramaic imprint. The standard Sidonian royal coin type was retained, but with a subtle change: the image of the attendant Sidonian king who accompanies the royal Persian chariot on the reverse now wears an Asian rather than an Egyptian-style costume, signalling the disruption of Sidonian–Egyptian ties and the assertion of Persian political control. In 357/6 BC, the city was regranted autonomy; the kingship was reinstituted, its new monarch, Tennes (Tabnit II), hand-picked by the Achaemenid hierarchy, presumably for his pro-Persian tendencies. The city was again authorized by the Persian Crown to mint its prestigious silver double shekel, whose wide circulation bore witness to its importance within the Persian monetary system.

Nevertheless, under Tennes, Sidon erupted in full revolt some 6 years later, spearheading a rebellion that garnered the support of the other Phoenician cities. Sidon's disaffection stemmed from a number of factors, not the least of which was the increasingly invasive, high-handed policy of the Persians, now under the firm but belligerent hand of Artaxerxes III Ochus (359/8–338/7 BC). Intent upon re-establishing the Achaemenid military power base and securing its flanks, Artaxerxes III set about consolidating control of the western empire. As a garrison city and regional Persian headquarters, Sidon figured prominently in such plans, the ultimate objective of which was the reconquest of Egypt.

Persian–Sidonian relations apparently reached a breaking point in 351 BC, when the city was intensively garrisoned in preparation for a large-scale invasion of Egypt. The immensity of the operation clearly took its toll on Sidon's economy, diverting resources normally devoted to trade and cutting into commercial profits; as Diodorus relates, matters were greatly exacerbated by the insolent behaviour of the resident Persian officials, who taxed and requisitioned the city with arrogance.[92]

The defeat in the Nile Delta suffered by the Persians in the winter of 351/50 BC probably provided the catalyst for the Sidonian-led uprising, whose plans were laid in concert with Arwad and Tyre at Tripolis, political headquarters for the Phoenician confederacy. Following conclusion of an alliance with the Egyptian pharaoh Nectanebo II (359-341 BC), hostilities were initiated. The Persian royal game reserve near Sidon was ravaged, and the offending resident Persian officials in the city arrested and executed. Well provisioned and bolstered by Greek mercenary support from Egypt, the Sidonians succeeded in repelling a preliminary Persian satrapal advance subsequently sent by Artaxerxes III. Meanwhile, the Cypriot kingdoms, encouraged by these events, declared their independence.

The chronology and progression of the rebellion and its geographic extent remain unclear. Its probable origin in 351 BC following the Persian defeat in Egypt appears confirmed by the fact that Sidonian coinage under Tennes ends at this time; the disruption in minting activity may reflect unstable political circumstances and a shift to a wartime economy.[93] The rebellion's climax, however, clearly took several years to unfold, as Artaxerxes III recouped his forces and laid preparations for a final advance upon Egypt from Babylon. Such a time lapse, as Diodorus states, allowed the Sidonians ample time to prepare their war stocks, assemble a fleet, and construct an extensive fortification system with a triple line of defence.[94] The associated events on Cyprus equally presuppose a lengthy interval.

As the primary coastal base in the Levant, Sidon was Artaxerxes' first target. The city apparently fell without a fight; distraught by the size of the approaching Persian force (which numbered three hundred thousand men and held a combined fleet of eight hundred warships and cargo vessels), Tennes betrayed Sidon and its inhabitants, arranging secretly with the commander of the Egyptian Greek mercenaries to deliver the city over to Artaxerxes III in exchange for a guarantee of his own pardon and release. Tennes' treachery resulted in a devastating tragedy unprecedented in Phoenician history. Six hundred of Sidon's leading citizens were unwittingly ambushed and massacred outside the city's gates. Within, death and destruction ensued, as Artaxerxes' troops swarmed the city and its walls. According to Diodorus, many of Sidon's inhabitants chose to immolate themselves within their houses rather than submit to the Persians. In all, more than forty thousand people – men, women, children, and household slaves – met their deaths.

Artaxerxes, in his ruthless zeal, was determined to make an example of the rebellious city. The Sidonians' personal possessions, including the copious quantities of molten gold and silver found within the city's charred remains, were pilfered and sold. The city's surviving population was subsequently deported and enslaved. This event finds dramatic confirmation in a Babylonian text, dated in the month of Tishri in the fourteenth year of Artaxerxes Ochus (i.e. October 345 BC), recording the arrival of Sidonian captives in Babylon and Susa.[95]

Questions remain over Tennes' cowardly actions in the face of the Persian advance. Clearly, a retaliation on the part of Artaxerxes III had been anticipated; why, then, the duplicitous behaviour? The answer may lie, at least in part, in the collapse of outside support. Had Nectanebo reneged on a promise of Egyptian military help? There is no mention of Tyrian or Arwadite troop activity in Diodorus' account. Was Sidon effectively isolated in the struggle? Was the resolution reached at Tripolis truly an alliance of Phoenician confederate states or simply a paper tiger? The issue must remain open for now.

Sidon's demise spelled the end of the great revolt. Panic-stricken, the remaining Phoenician cities quickly submitted to the Persians; by 345/4 BC, all of Phoenicia and Cyprus were again in Persian hands. Despite Artaxerxes' assurances, Tennes himself was summarily executed, and the city, once again, placed under the authority of Mazaeus, satrap of Cilicia, who would control the city and its minting activity for the next 5 years.

Controversy persists over the extent of Sidon's destruction at the hands of Artaxerxes III. Was it as thoroughly devastated as Diodorus reports? Eye-witness accounts at the time of Alexander's conquest in 333 BC record that Sidon was again a wealthy and important city. Could it have regained its prosperity so quickly? The answer, in short, is yes. Sidon was too crucial an asset, militarily and commercially, for the Persians to allow it to lie in ruins. In all likelihood, the city already served as departure point for the Persian fleet in Artaxerxes' successful campaign against Egypt in 343 BC. The reconquest of the Nile valley in the following year clearly sealed its strategic indispensability as a Persian naval base of operation.

Sidon's commercial value to Persia must not be underestimated, Sidonian silver was essential to the Persian monetary economy. Hoard evidence, in fact, reveals that it remained in wide circulation, even throughout the interregnal years following Sidon's destruction.[96] The speed with which Mazaeus reissued Sidonian coinage in the first year of Persian occupation reveals such priorities. With the restoration of the monarchy under Abdashtart (Straton) II, its subservient, pro-Persian king, reconstruction must have proceeded afoot.

Nevertheless, the trauma suffered by Sidon was not easily forgotten. In 333 BC, as Alexander and his troops marched victorious along the Phoenician coast following the surrender of Arwad and Byblos and the defection of the Phoenician and Cypriot fleets, the Sidonian populace welcomed him with open arms; the wounds that they had suffered under Artaxerxes a decade before were clearly still etched in their memory.

The fate of Tyre was another story. Fiercely independent, and confident in its impregnability, the city and its populace ultimately resisted Alexander's advance. The protracted siege and subsequent capture of the city are well recorded by the ancient historians; the causeway that Alexander constructed to achieve his end survives today within the modern isthmus that now joins the island city to the mainland. Heavily fortified and armed with the latest siege weaponry, Tyre fought valiantly to the end against overwhelming odds, resisting not only the Macedonian assault but the blockade of the combined Phoenician and Cypriot fleets, now under Alexander's command. After seven months, in mid-July 332 BC, the city's walls were breached. Like Artaxerxes Ochus before him, Alexander dealt harshly with his conquered prize, determined to make an example of the rebellious city. Of Tyre's surviving population (many had already sought refuge at Carthage or with the Sidonians), six thousand were executed and another thirty thousand sold into slavery. As a reprisal for the death of Macedonian prisoners, two thousand young men were impaled along the coast, their crucified bodies left as a grisly reminder of Macedonian might and retribution.[97]

Tyre would soon recover commercially, and, under successive Greek overlords, regain its autonomy; yet it would never fully reclaim the pride of place that it had enjoyed under previous eastern regimes. Little by little, it became a truly Hellenized city, gradually exchanging its oriental customs for Greek ones. The conquest of Alexander, in fact, marked the beginning of the end for Tyre and Phoenicia as a Near Eastern entity.

THE PERSIAN PERIOD IN COASTAL PHOENICIA: TERRITORIAL EXPANSION AND URBAN DEVELOPMENT

The Achaemenid era as a whole represented a prosperous period of marked economic growth and urban development for the Phoenician cities. Sidon's wealth and prosperity, noted in the ancient sources, is confirmed by the numismatic and archaeological vidence; the lavish development of the Eshmun temple precinct is one such indicator. At Sidon, Byblos, and Beirut, as archaeology has shown, urban occupation spread outward well beyond the original settlement mounds. Recent excavations at Beirut document such urban development. (See fig. 27.) The new Persian-period settlement, in fact, laid the axial foundations for the later Hellenistic and Roman city. The prosperity of Tyre, Sidon, and Arwad in the Persian era finds further reflection in the prominence of northerly Tripolis, a joint foundation that now served as the political headquarters of the three metropolises.[98] Expanded harbour construction at the ports of Akko, Tyre, Sidon, and Kition attests to the burgeoning commerce and economy of these maritime centres.

As the Phoenician cities spread territorially, so, too, did Phoenician cultural and economic influence within the greater Levant itself, as population increase spawned emigration from major urban centres to peripheral areas. Recent excavations at numerous sites along the coast of northern Israel and the adjacent western Galilee confirm what is already known historically, i.e. that the entire Carmel coast from Tell Abu Hawam south to Jaffa flourished under Phoenician (Sidonian and Tyrian) control. Contemporary historical texts reveal that Phoenician hegemony extended even further south; according to the fourth-century *Periplus* of Pseudo-Skylax, the flourishing Phillistine port of Ashkelon now fell under Tyrian control, a fact confirmed by recent archaeological research.[99] As Joppa and Ashkelon demonstrate, the territory of an Achaemenid-period Phoenician city could be relatively diffuse and discontinuous in its extent.[100] Recent geographical studies have shown that Phoenician population growth and territorial expansion in the Persian period was accompanied by intense economic development of natural resources in neighbouring inland regions, such as the Homs corridor, Galilee, the southern Sharon plain, and the Ono region of central Palestine.[101] The exploitation of mineral and agricultural wealth in these areas served not only local domestic but greater regional and perhaps international needs.

While the central Phoenician states of Tyre, Sidon, and Byblos clearly prospered at this time, archaeological evidence from the northern mainland points equally to the growth of Arwad, which of all the Phoenician metropolises may have benefited most from Achaemenid patronage. During this time, Arwad controlled an extensive mainland territory dotted with numerous dependent towns, chief among them Marathus (Amrit), Antaradus (Tortose), and Simyra (Tell Kazel). The island city's hinterland penetrated far into the strategic Homs corridor, through which it held control of regional commerce inland to the Orontes river valley via the mountain sanctuary of Baetocece.

Although direct documentation about Arwad is largely lacking for the period, the city's affluence may be gauged, in part, by the prosperity of its dependencies, such as Amrit with its lavish Persian-period religious and funerary monuments. Contemporary levels at Tell Kazel document that town's regional importance as a production and distribution centre for agricultural produce and iron, rich deposits of which abound in the inland Mehta region.[102] Numismatic evidence suggests that Arwad's influence in the late Persian period extended north into coastal Syria, perhaps as far as Al Mina at the mouth of the Orontes. If Arwad was indeed responsible for the Phoenician resettlement at Tell Sukas in the early fourth century, the period may have marked the culmination of the city's power and prosperity.[103]

The southern Phoenician realm also experienced an urban renaissance. Archaeological research documents that a number of centres along Israel's northern coast (including Akko, Tell Abu Hawam, Shiqmona, Tell Megadim, and Dor) underwent a marked phase of urban expansion characterized by the institution of axial, 'hippodamic' street planning.[104] A hint of this may perhaps be found in the small excavated residential quarter at Sarepta, suggesting that Persian-period urban expansion at Sidon may have proceeded along similar lines. In the Punic west, as recent excavations have shown, such centralized axial planning characterized fifth-century residential development at Carthage and neighbouring Kerkouane.

The fourth century BC: the Hellenization of Phoenicia and the Punic west

While the age of Alexander marked the beginning of the Hellenistic period in the eastern Mediterranean, the process of Hellenization had begun in earnest a full century before, both on the Phoenician mainland and in the Punic west. Much of the impetus came from increased trade with the Greek realm. Along the coastal Levant, to the north (at sites such as Tell Sukas, Ras el-Bassit, and Al Mina) and south (at Akko and Dor), Attic pottery (Athenian black-glaze in particular) now appears in ever-increasing quantities, beginning at the end of the fifth century BC.

In the transmission of Hellenic culture to the Phoenician mainland, the island of Cyprus clearly played a focal role. Such Hellenizing influence intensified in the early fourth century under Evagoras I (411–374 BC), Salamis' pro-Athenian king. As the material record attests, Hellenism's imprint manifests itself increasingly within the Cypriot Phoenician realm.

As the historical and epigraphical record attests, the fourth century also marked a period of active Phoenician commercial activity in the Aegean. The primary initiator of such trade was Sidon. Hellenic cultural influence there may have reached a peak under Abdashtart I (376/70–360/58 BC), Sidon's avidly philhellenic king, who adopted the Greek name Straton. Its impact may be seen in the graecizing of personal names, the use of Greek coin types and weight standards, and the adoption of Greek military tactics and techniques. On an artistic level, Greek influence may be found on Sidonian funerary and religious sculpture (like the famous sculpted marble altar/podium of the Eshmun temple

10 *The so-called Sarcophagus of the Weepers. One of four such elaborately sculpted coffins uncovered in the royal necropoli of Sidon, this may have belonged to the fourth-century Sidonian king Straton I.*

complex at Bostan esh-Sheikh[105]), much of it imported or commissioned from Ionian Greek craftsmen. (See fig. 10.) Hellenism's imprint may also be found in the widespread adoption of Greek-style figured votive terracottas at sites such as Amrit and Umm el-Amed.

The fourth century also marked an era of Hellenic influence at Carthage, transmitted largely through neighbouring Sicily and its Greek colonial population. The impact of Greek Sicily upon Carthage grew appreciably toward the end of the fifth century, when the Punic metropolis asserted political control over much of the island's Greek population. Carthaginian military intervention came at the request of the Elymian city of Segesta, then involved in a protracted struggle with Greek Selinus and its powerful ally, Syracuse. In 409 BC, the Carthaginians, with a large expeditionary force under Hannibal, besieged and occupied Selinus, and then Himera, which had been abandoned by its inhabitants. In a public spectacle, three thousand Himeran men were tortured and executed on the spot where Hamilcar (grandfather of the present general) had perished in 480 BC. In reprisal for the earlier Carthaginian defeat, Himera was razed to the ground, and never occupied again.

The following years saw further Carthaginian military success and territorial gain in Sicily, including the capture and sack of the wealthy city of Acragas (Agrigento). By 406 BC, Carthage stood in control of the entire Greek portion of the island with the exception of Syracuse itself. This enviable situation would not last, however. Shortly after the Carthaginian withdrawal in 405 BC, Syracuse, under the initiative of its tyrant Dionysius I, set about fortifying the city's defences and strengthening its military in preparation for a western counter-offensive aimed at Motya, Carthage's Sicilian stronghold. In 397 BC, the Syracusan army invested the island city, eventually entering it by a mole constructed from the mainland; despite fierce resistance from its occupants, Motya was taken. The Carthaginians subsequently countered, under its general Himilco (another grandson of Hamilcar), with an advance upon Syracuse itself. The outbreak of an epidemic, however, ultimately forced the withdrawal of Punic forces encamped outside the heavily fortified city. As for Motya, although soon retaken by the Carthaginians, the city was not rebuilt; its surviving inhabitants were resettled in the new Carthaginian foundation of Lilybaeum on the opposing mainland.

The Carthaginian Sicilian campaigns of 410–405 BC marked the first in a series of engagements that would lock the Punic metropolis, over the ensuing fourth century, in an intermittent struggle with Syracuse over control of Sicily. Territorial limits between the two antagonists were ultimately established in 374 BC with the conclusion of a peace treaty that designated the River Halycus as boundary, giving Carthage a third of the island, including the cities of Selinus and Acragas. Carthage would effectively retain control of this territory over the next century, until the outbreak of war with Rome.

As history records, the Carthaginian sack of Acragas in 406 BC resulted in the seizure of a great many Greek works of art that were transported to Carthage and appropriated by the city and its aristocratic families. The incorporation of Greek Selinus and Acragas within the Carthaginian political sphere, too, led to an intensification of Hellenic influence, as commercial exchange between the Greek and Punic world was facilitated. It is during this time – a period marked by a dramatic increase in Greek imports – that the material culture of Carthage and its dependencies becomes thoroughly Hellenized in style and iconography. As period terracottas illustrate, classical imagery now permeates the pictorial repertoire, which includes Greek deities (such as Herakles and Hermes) and mythological creatures and monsters. At Carthage itself, influence from the Attic mainland may be documented increasingly throughout the fourth century, particularly in the realm of relief sculpture. (See fig. 11.)

The impact of Greek culture upon Carthage at this time is also clearly felt in the Punic religious sphere – with the institution of the cult of the Greek deities Demeter and Kore (Persephone). As Diodorus relates, the cult of the two grain goddesses, whose worship was widespread in Greek Sicily, was introduced in order to expiate the sacrilege committed by Himilco, who desecrated the goddess's sanctuary while encamped outside Syracuse in 396 BC. A votive deposit excavated on the Borj Jedid hill at Carthage may mark the ancient site of the temple.

External relations with the Sicilian Greek sphere were not the only concern for Carthage's trade expansionist, oligarchic regime, which was now increasingly dominated by a select body of leading aristocrats, known as the Council of One Hundred. In an

11 *detail from a marble sarcophagus from the St Monique cemetery, Carthage, Tunisia. Based upon its style and workmanship, the sculpted effigy on the lid of this late fourth-century Carthiginian sarcophagus may be attributed to an emigré Athenian craftsman.*

effort to stabilize relations within the Tyrrhenian basin (and out of concern for a treaty-alliance recently concluded between Syracuse and Tarentum), Carthage now sought to strengthen its ties to the north by concluding a series of treaties with Rome and the major Etruscan centres, including Caere, with which the Carthaginians had enjoyed close relations since the sixth century BC. These agreements presumably focused, to a large extent, on commercial rights and spheres of trading activity.[106] In its treaty with Rome in 348 BC, which augmented an earlier agreement reached in the late sixth century, Carthage forcefully reasserted its growing trade interests in Sardinia and along the eastern, 'Libyan' coast of North Africa. The document, in which Tyre appears as a separate but equal co-signatory, reveals Carthage to be the dominant power.

The treaty that followed in 306 BC, which banned the Romans from Sicily and the Carthaginians from Italy, reveals a markedly changed political situation, in which two equally matched maritime powers each anxiously safeguarded their respective commercial spheres. Four years earlier, Carthage had suffered the ignominy of an attack by the tyrant Agathocles of Syracuse upon its own shores – the first in its history – one that ultimately forced its populace to retreat within the city walls. In desperation, the city aristocracy sacrificed five hundred of its own children to Baal Hammon, convinced that religious neglect had brought them to such dire circumstances.

Agathocles' landing and march through Cape Bon encountered mile upon mile of well-irrigated, prosperous Carthaginian estates planted with vines, olives, and fruit-bearing trees – testimony to the city's agricultural wealth.[107] After centuries of dependence upon outside support, the city, now more than self-sufficient agriculturally, was able to export surplus crop yields. Carthage's maritime empire was rapidly being transformed into a territorial one.

Barely a generation before the signing of the Romano-Punic treaty of 306 BC, Carthage's mother-city, Tyre, had fallen to another emerging European power, the Macedonians. Carthaginian envoys, there to present their annual offerings to Melqart, witnessed the event. The winds were changing; with the advent of Rome and Macedon, the political landscape within the Mediterranean had altered forever.

Chapter Two

THE CITY

Situation and topography

Whether trading posts, industrial towns, or true urban centres, nearly all Phoenician establishments in the homeland and abroad shared a number of common characteristics. With few exceptions, they were compact, geographically defined settlements situated on or near the coast in navigable, easily defensible positions. Offshore islets, peninsulas, and headlands formed favoured locations. As trading establishments, nearly all were located near sheltered anchorage – in natural bays or harbours, lagoons, or riverine estuaries. The Phoenician mainland cities were generally situated within narrow, agriculturally fertile stretches of coastal plain, the settlements abroad within access of a hinterland rich in raw materials (especially ores and minerals).

The urban characteristics of the Phoenician city

By comparison with other urban centres within the continental Near East (i.e. Syria, Mesopotamia), the Phoenician cities were relatively small in size, ranging from an average of 2–6 hectares (5–15 acres) for the smaller towns (Beirut, Sarepta, Tell Keisan) to 40-plus hectares (100-plus acres) for the larger urban establishments. Of the mainland cities, Arwad and Sidon – at roughly 40 and 60 hectares (100 and 150 acres), respectively, were the largest physically (see figs 74 and 75). Analysis of bedrock at Tyre suggests that the pre-Roman city, even after Hiram's expansion projects, probably covered no more than 16 hectares (40 acres). (See fig. 12.) As recent excavations have shown, the town of Beirut prior to the Persian period totalled no more than 2 hectares (5 acres). The extent of Iron Age Byblos has yet to be determined.

The typical Phoenician settlement was composed of two districts: a 'lower town', which housed the business area and residential quarters of the city populace, and an 'upper city', which accommodated its major temples, administrative buildings, and the residences of the well-to-do. The latter also served as a defensive citadel and was often separately walled. The commercial life of the Phoenician city was invariably organized around its port facilities, wharves, and warehouses. The focus of activity was the broad market square or plaza, which was generally located in proximity to the main harbour and city entrance. Heavy industrial activity (metal-working, purple dye production) tended to be segregated in the periphery of the lower town – often near the harbour itself or at the rear of the settlement. Such activity could also be attached to a major sanctuary precinct (as at Sarepta and Kition). Cottage industries, such as textile weaving, faience manufacture, and pottery production, were typically spread throughout the urban landscape.

In most instances, fresh water was secured from local sources, such as rivers or springs. Where local supply was insufficient for population needs, as at Tyre, water was piped in or otherwise physically imported. When necessary, existing supply was augmented by excavated wells, or built, lime-plastered cisterns (*cf.* Tyre and Arwad). Urban facilities for the drainage of run-off water and rain consisted of flat open gutters.

As for the dead, public cemeteries (including ritual burial precincts, i.e. *tophets*) were located outside the city walls, often in physically isolated or demarcated zones – on opposite river banks, along sandy shore lines, or on adjacent ridges or foothills (see pp. 132–133 and 138–142).

The Phoenician port

Central to every Phoenician emporium were its harbours, which formed the commercial focus and economic heart of the city. The latter were often situated behind a line of sandstone reefs abutting the coast, which offered protection against swells and prevailing winds. In some instances, as at Tyre, a primary natural harbour was supplemented by a separate, artificially constructed port facility.

With its two built breakwaters constructed upon submerged offshore reefs, Tyre's artificial southern harbour typified a Phoenician port installation. Its moles were constructed in standard fashion. A bedding was first prepared by levelling the reef, creating a table upon which the mole's ashlar foundations were fixed. These, in turn, supported a stone superstructure composed of multiple rows of large, cubical blocks. When vertically faced, such an artificial breakwater (which ranged from 10 to 15 metres (33 to 49 feet) in width) could be used as both a quay and a pier. Offshore islets or detached quays could also be used as 'floating' ports for foreign trading vessels.

In configuration, Phoenician harbours were either 'open' or 'closed', depending upon the width of the harbour entrances and the amount of offshore protection they afforded from outside attack. As literary sources reveal, an open harbour could be closed off by a chain in times of military crisis. With its closed, artificially constructed inner basin and adjoining open harbour, the northern port facility of Sidon offers a typical example of a Phoenician 'double harbour'. A slightly different configuration characterized the island emporium of Arwad with its adjacent twin coves facing out on to the mainland. (See fig. 75.) The two bays were sheltered from prevailing winds by an artificially augmented finger of rock, which served as a central jetty for both harbours. At both Sidon and Tyre, communication between port facilities was facilitated by means of an artificial channel.

The city of Atlit on Israel's northern coast offers the earliest and most complete example of a Phoenician harbour installation of the Iron Age. (See fig. 13.) Situated on the north-eastern side of a coastal promontory, the port, in active operation from the seventh to the fifth centuries BC, was composed of two separate mooring areas equipped with a mole and quay, one anchored to the coast, the other extending from an offshore islet. A second neighbouring island was utilized as a warehouse facility. The harbour entrance,

12 *An aerial view of Tyre.*

defined by the two perpendicularly aligned moles, was more than 200 metres (650 feet) wide, making it an 'open' port. To the east of the harbour, a twin-towered gate (marking the terminus of the city precinct wall) divided the port from the city proper, which was located inland along the shore.

The port of Atlit reveals the Phoenicians' technical sophistication in methods of harbour construction: the ability to build vertical ashlar walls underwater with an accuracy and precision of fitting that eliminated any need for mortar or clamps. A proper bedding for the jetty's foundation walls was secured by levelling the bedrock or paving the soft sea bottom with a wide pillow of rubble and pebbles. Its superstructure was then composed of finely cut ashlar blocks that were laid as headers to provide maximum resistance from the destructive action of the waves. Effective maintenance of the port was ensured by the emplacement of a narrow secondary sea exit, which served as a flushing conduit for sediments that accumulated in the harbour basin.[1]

An innovation of the Punic period was the cothon: a rock-cut rectangular basin accessed by a narrow canal or entry channel, which served as a holding area for ships. Examples have been found at Punic sites around the Mediterranean: at Motya on Sicily, at Madhya and Rachgoun in North Africa, and, most recently, at Phalasarna on western Crete. The largest and best known of these cothons are the two rock-cut port installations at Carthage: the square commercial harbour built in the third century BC, and the later, adjoining circular naval port. The latter, equipped with a central islet (the site of the Carthaginian 'admiralty', according to Appian), was ringed in antiquity by a series of dry docks and ship-sheds that could accommodate two hundred and twenty warships together with their furnishings and tackle.[2]

Domestic architecture

THE PHOENICIAN HOUSE

Recent excavations at Carthage and a number of sites in the southern Phoenician realm (Dor, Tell Keisan, and Tell Abu Hawam) have added to our knowledge of Phoenician domestic architecture. As the archaeological evidence reveals, a typical Phoenician Early Iron Age house consisted of three or four modestly sized rooms arranged in varying configurations. Often, a large horizontally aligned hall provided access to two (and sometimes three) smaller adjacent rooms of equal size in the rear. The three- or four-room dwelling was the dominant house form in ancient Israel, and its appearance at sites along the southern Phoenician coast must be understood in the context of this southern, Palestinian tradition.

Archaeological investigation at two widely disparate sites have shed new light on aspects of Phoenician house design and construction. At Ḥorvat Rosh Zayit in the Lower Galilee, excavations have uncovered an early fortified Phoenician trader's residence. In ground plan, the building consisted of a central hall surrounded by eight variously sized rooms, which served as commercial storage facilities. (The entire complex contained some three hundred plain-ware storage jars.) (See fig. 14.) The complex, which was originally two-storeyed (the level of the upper floor is marked by stone thresholds), was enclosed by a massive wall with four corner towers. This unique structure, which may be firmly dated to a period spanning the mid-tenth to the mid-ninth centuries BC, affords a rare view of an early Iron Age Phoenician manor.[3]

Recent excavations on the Byrsa hill at Carthage have uncovered a Phoenician residence in its entirety, documenting its architectural evolution over a period spanning 200 years – from the eighth to the sixth centuries BC.[4] (See fig. 15.) In its second construction phase, the house consisted of a long rectangular building with a large enclosed courtyard (with a built well) in front and a series of four rooms arranged in longitudinal pairs at the back. In its general characteristics and construction (mudbrick walls on a high stone base), this courtyard dwelling

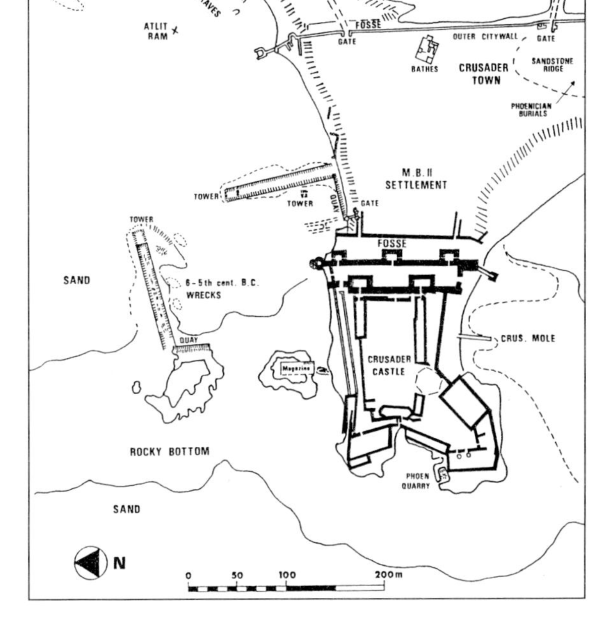

13 *Plan of the city and harbour at Atlit, Israel.*

compares closely with earlier houses of the Late Bronze Age from the northern Levant, underscoring the continuity in architectural tradition that bridged these two periods.[5] Since Carthage was a Tyrian foundation, the house probably represents the type of urban dwelling found at the Phoenician mother-city itself.

In its third building phase, the interior of the house at Carthage was reconfigured as a courtless four-room dwelling with three long parallel chambers in front and a large room (spanning the width of the house) at the back. The models for this house type may again be found in the Syro-Palestinian region, once again reflecting the cultural influence of the homeland. In the second half of the seventh century BC, the house was again remodelled, utilizing a new wall construction technique known as *opus Africanum*, marked by the use of monolithic piers (orthostats) in alternation with zones of mudbrick and stone rubble. (See figs 16 and 17.) This technique, now attested in Carthage, is a simple variant of the earlier 'pier-and-rubble' construction method utilized by the Phoenicians in the Iron Age. (See fig. 27.) The major difference between the mainland technique and its African counterpart concerns the manner in which the upright piers are constructed. In the west, they are monolithic, while in the east (*cf.* Dor, Sarepta, and now Beirut), they are built up from individual ashlar blocks laid in 'header' and 'stretcher' fashion.

As for the Byrsa dwelling's superstructure, it was probably two-storeyed, with upper-floor access provided by an inner, rear staircase, as in later Punic houses from North Africa and Sardinia (see below). Based upon parallels from the Levantine mainland, the upper storey was probably spanned by wooden beams supported by internal pillars. The house was capped by a shed- or saddle-shaped roof of baked clay tiles.

The Byrsa house excavation produced evidence for the adoption at Carthage of an age-old oriental practice: the foundation offering, by which the dedicant consecrated a building by placing a deposit within the structure's foundations. This practice is documented twice in the Byrsa house, during two different phases of its construction. In the first (Phase IIB), a clay oil lamp and a handmade pottery bowl were deposited during renovation of the dwelling's central courtyard well; subsequently, during construction of the four-room house (Phase III), a ceramic bottle, its mouth intentionally broken and capped by a flat stone, was placed beneath the floor. The remains of plant ash found in the bowl of the first deposit indicate that a burnt offering had probably taken place. The Byrsa dwelling thus reveals much about the close relationship of a colony, in its early stages, to its mother-city.

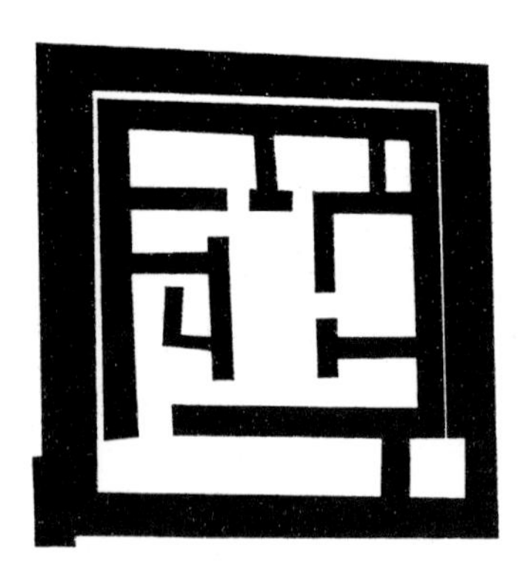

14 *Plan of a fortified trader's residence at Ḥorvat Rosh Zayit, Israel.*

THE PUNIC HOUSE

Thanks to archaeological research in recent decades, we are now better informed about the layout and appearance of houses in the Punic west. For the present study, attention may be drawn to urban dwellings in three excavated residential areas: a district of Carthage located on the southern slope of the Byrsa Hill (see fig. 17); the town of Kerkouane on Cape Bon to the north-east of the city (see fig. 22); and the Sardinian hill town of Monte Sirai (see figs 18 and 21).[6]

All three sites, ranging in date from the fourth to the second century BC, have revealed entire residential complexes compactly arranged in blocks, or insulae. Although unstandardized in their format, they share a single architectural focus: the central courtyard, around which the house is oriented in an axial or radial fashion. (See figs 15, 17 and 18.)

The courtyard, the primary source of light and air, formed the heart of domestic activity in the Punic household; it also furnished a private, secluded setting. Its colonnaded porticoes provided direct access to the principal chambers of the house, including its main salon, bedrooms, and storerooms. Nearly all courtyards were marked by a central feature – an excavated well or an impluvium for the receipt of rainwater, which was collected and stored in an underground, plastered cistern. Most Punic houses were equipped with some form of basic plumbing – in the form of a stone channel that carried sewage and overflow out into the street gutters. (Unlike later Roman cities, Punic towns had no central sewerage system.) The more affluent homes had private, plumbed bathrooms outfitted with plastered tubs. (Toilets were generally located in separate public facilities.) Beginning in the third century BC, bathroom floors often carried mosaic pavements in a variety of styles, chief among them *opus tessellatum*, with its cut mosaic cube decoration, and *opus signinum* ('chip pavement'), with its random, sprinkled decoration of white marble chips set into a reddish cement bedding. The stone and mudbrick walls of the house were often plastered and painted.

All Punic houses, large and small, were equipped with some form of kitchen facility, often recognizable by the stone or terracotta ring hearth set into its corner. A long narrow room, it was often situated on the main axis of the house opposite the entry corridor. Unlike the Greek or Roman house, there was generally no separate dining facility;

15 *Plan of a house at Carthage, Phases 2 and 3. University of Hamburg excavations.*

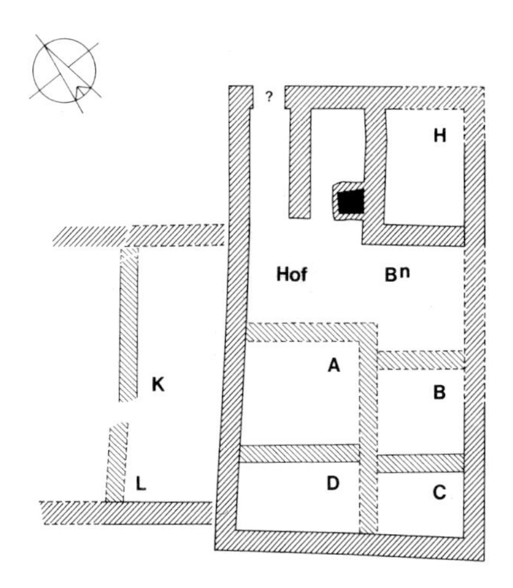

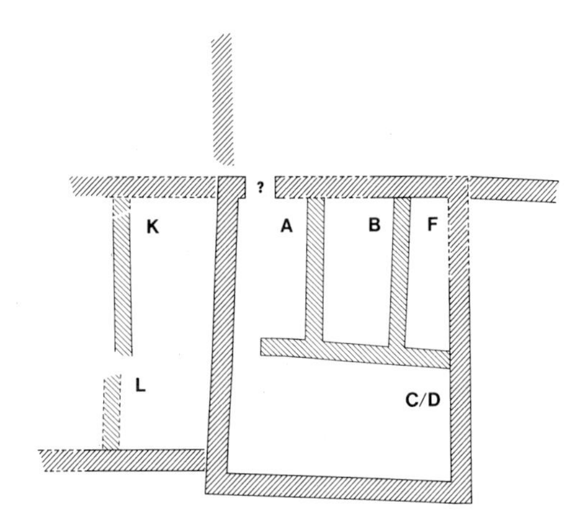

16 *View of the archaic settlement at Carthage, Tunisia. University of Hamburg excavations.*

17 *View of the late Punic settlement on the Byrsa hill, Carthage, Tunisia.*

meals were presumably taken in the courtyard, weather permitting. Bedrooms, which were normally accessed off the courtyard or located on an upper floor, were typically small and windowless. In addition to closets and storerooms, larger houses were often equipped with rear service quarters. Rooms located at the entrance to the house may have functioned as shops or commercial quarters.

The dwellings in the late Punic quarter on the Byrsa hill (see fig. 17) illustrate another notable aspect of Punic urbanism: the use of multi-storeyed housing. The probable existence of tall apartment complexes in this district can be deduced from, first, the presence of mosaic pavements that come from at least two upper storeys; second, the thickness of the houses' main walls; and, third, the number and capacity of underground cisterns located in each housing block. In all probability, they represent the six-storeyed structures at Carthage noted by Appian[7] in his account of the Third Punic War (149–146 BC).

Motya: a study in the urban evolution of a western Phoenician city

Largely abandoned since antiquity, the island emporium of Motya in north-western Sicily provides a unique opportunity to study a Phoenician city in its totality. (See fig. 19.) Its urban history is marked by a fixed terminal date of 397 BC, when the city was besieged and destroyed by Dionysius I of Syracuse. Although the island saw renewed settlement in the fourth and succeeding centuries, occupation became increasingly limited, and the city never fully regained its urban stature.

The Phoenician island settlement, which covers roughly 40 hectares (100 acres), was founded some time in the second half of the eighth century BC. By the sixth century, the city was already well established as an urban centre. Focal to Motya's orientation were its two port facilities, located in the north-east and south-west of the island. The northern harbour and adjoining city gate marked the primary point of entry. It abutted a built causeway, erected around the mid-sixth century, that connected Motya to the mainland. From the northern gate, a thoroughfare lead directly to a public market square and an unidentified sanctuary precinct known today as the 'Cappiddazzu'. This area, situated on one of two regions of relative high ground on the island, represented the city's civic centre. The southern port, with its dry dock, or *cothon*, marked the emplacement of a second, later, entry gate into the city. In its vicinity stood a large tripartite building, which probably served as a warehouse for the inventorying and storage of commodities.[8] Motya's most dominant topographical feature is the sharply rising hillock in its south-eastern sector. This high ground, which reveals extensive traces of ancient walls and artificial terracing, probably marked the city's 'upper district', where the residences of the affluent were located.

The archaeological remains at Motya afford the unique opportunity to trace the

A. Vestibule, perhaps of commercial function (shop)
B. Kitchen
C. Master bedroom
D. Bedroom
E. Storeroom
F. Courtyard

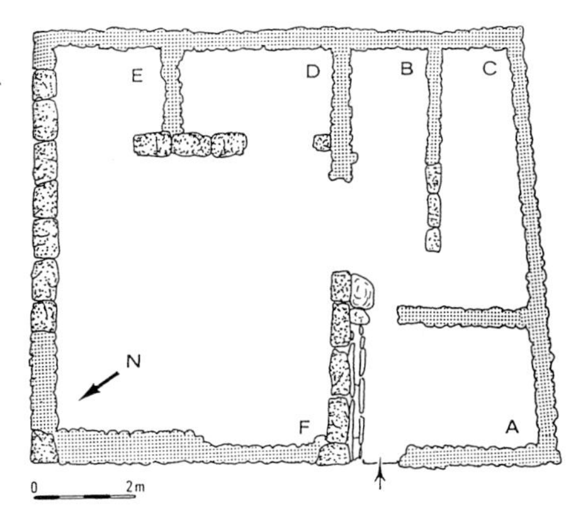

18 *Plan of a Punic residence (Fantar House), Monte Sirai, Sardinia.*

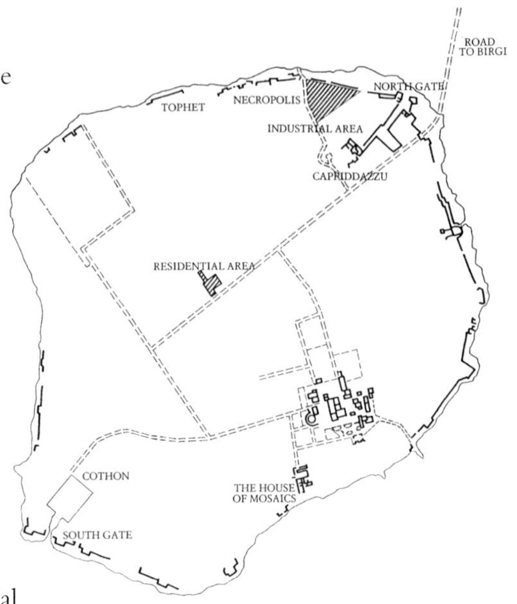

19 *Plan of Motya, Sicily.*

urban evolution of a Phoenician city. The early settlement (of the late eighth and early seventh century BC) appears to have been a relatively small one, with habitation concentrated on the high ground and adjoining harbour region in the north-east. The city expanded southwards in the second half of the seventh century, when the area of the later southern gate was first utilized for commercial purposes. The succeeding sixth century saw the beginning of true urban development at Motya involving large-scale defensive, mercantile and industrial construction. At this time, residential growth spread inland; the city's south-eastern 'upper district' also saw initial development. Increased commercial activity prompted the construction of a causeway linking Motya to the mainland. Around the mid-sixth century, population pressures led to the abandonment of the northern necropolis and the transfer of the city's burial grounds to Birgi on the opposite mainland. Before the end of the century, a central zoning plan organized along the main north-east/south-west axis of the city was introduced; this zoning scheme was further developed in the succeeding fifth century, as residential construction continued to spread. Motya's growth ended abruptly with the devastating siege of 397 BC and the exodus of its population to mainland Lilybaeum. Thereafter, the city witnessed a sharp economic decline, marked by deteriorating living conditions and a dramatic reduction in urban development.

The urban development of the Phoenician cities: an overview

The fourteenth century BC effectively marked the beginning of urban architectural history on the Phoenician mainland. As archaeological research at both Tyre and Sarepta reveals, the Phoenician cities now embarked upon a relatively long period of stable architectural development.[9] In correspondence dating to the reign of Akhenaten (1353–1335 BC), Tyre is described as a great city, comparable in wealth to metropolitan Ugarit.[10] Contemporary urban growth at Byblos is likewise evidenced by the city's expansion from the original promontory settlement into the surrounding plains.

Following the political upheavals triggered by the Sea Peoples' incursions in the early twelfth century, the Phoenician coastal cities underwent a period of economic decline. Urban recovery soon followed, however. By the early eleventh century, as the Report of

Wenamun reveals, the Phoenician ports of Byblos and Sidon had become flourishing commercial entities once again.

The expansion of Tyre under King Hiram I in the mid-tenth century BC offers the first detailed account of the urban development of a Phoenician centre (see 'Tyre' in Appendix). The ensuing Middle Iron Age (900–550 BC) – the period of Assyrian and Babylonian hegemony – appears to have been a time of steady urban growth for Phoenicia's cities. Although data are lacking for the primary coastal centres, recent archaeological research at a number of secondary sites provides us with a glimpse at such development. At ninth-century Sarepta, for example, excavations have revealed a portion of the city's newly conceived residential quarter, consisting of two complexes of well-built houses divided by a narrow street and an open square. Urban development at Sarepta in the succeeding century is attested by the construction of a large public building with a series of adjoining halls or corridors.[11] Recent excavations at Beirut have revealed that the ancient town was equipped with a massive new fortification wall and glacis, some time before the tenth century BC. (See fig. 25.) At this time, settlement may have spread outward from the tell, which may now have assumed the function of a fortified citadel.[12]

Urban growth in southern Phoenicia is evidenced by the spread of Phoenician settlements southwards into the Akko plain and adjoining Lower Galilee. Excavations at Tell Keisan have revealed a prosperous agricultural community with multi-roomed houses organized into discrete blocks. In the north, the towns of the Akkar plain, Tell Arqa and Tell Kazel in particular, reveal evidence of renewed settlement in the eighth and seventh centuries BC.

Perhaps the most dramatic sign of urban development in this period may be found in Phoenician expansion overseas, which was well established by the mid-eighth century. Evidence of Phoenician colonial initiative may be found throughout the Mediterranean – in Cyprus (Kition, Amathus), North Africa (Carthage, Utica), Sicily (Motya), Sardinia (Sulcis, Tharros), and southern Spain (Almuñecar, Toscanos, Moro de Mezquitilla, and Cadiz).

At Carthage (after Kition the most important of early Phoenician foundations), recent excavations on the eastern slopes of the Byrsa hill have yielded dramatic evidence for intensive urban settlement by the end of the eighth century BC. (See fig. 16.) The dense wall-to-wall arrangement of houses in this district suggests that an urban plan, based upon residential city blocks, may already have been implemented. The archaeological findings thus fit an emerging pattern of a city planned right from the start.

Based upon the results of stratigraphic soundings within Carthage's settlement area and the topographical evidence of extramural burials surrounding it, it is now possible to get an accurate sense of the physical extent of the early city. (See fig. 20.) Using such data, an occupied settlement of more than 24 hectares (60 acres) can be reconstructed, extending at least 800 metres (875 yards) along the ancient coastline.[13] As for Carthage's inicipient urban plan, there are archaeological indications that the upper settlement was based upon a semicircular system of streets fanning out from the Byrsa hill.[14] By the fifth

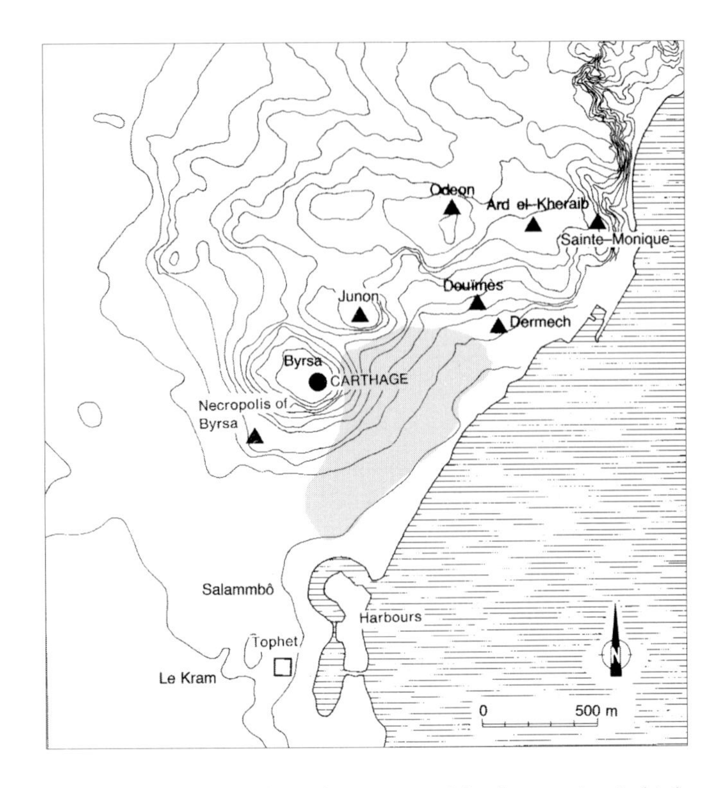

20 *Map of Carthage with the outline of the archaic settlement.*

century BC, as excavations have revealed, the residential quarters of the lower city (which was oriented parallel to the coast) were built according to an orthogonal plan defined by a network of streets intersecting at right angles.

This axial grid plan, known as 'Hippodamic' (after the Greek sixth-century architect from Miletus who first wrote about it), was widely adopted in the Phoenician world, beginning in the fifth century BC. This period marked a revolutionary change in the urban fabric of the Phoenician city. In the west, aside from Carthage, the Hippodamic plan is attested in Sicily – at the Phoenician cities of Motya and Soluntum, and in Greek Selinus in its later Punic phase. In the Levantine mainland, orthogonal town planning is clearly documented, beginning in the fifth century BC, at a variety of sites along the southern Phoenician coast – from Dor northward to Akko.[15] At the northern extreme of the Phoenician littoral, axial planning is documented at Tell Sukas and Al Mina. Although undocumented, it can be assumed that the major centres in the Phoenician heartland, Sidon and Byblos in particular, incorporated axial planning in their urban development. (Both cities appear to have undergone major urban expansion during the Persian period.) As excavations have revealed, Sarepta underwent a period of urbanization, manifest in an aggressive programme of levelling and filling that affected both of its excavated districts.[16] Sarepta's industrial sector was replaced by a residential quarter marked by an axial street arrangement. Recent excavations at Beirut have also revealed that the Persian-period lower town settlement followed an orthogonal plan, the directional axes of which served as the basis for the orientation of the later Hellenistic and Roman city.[17] (See fig. 27.)

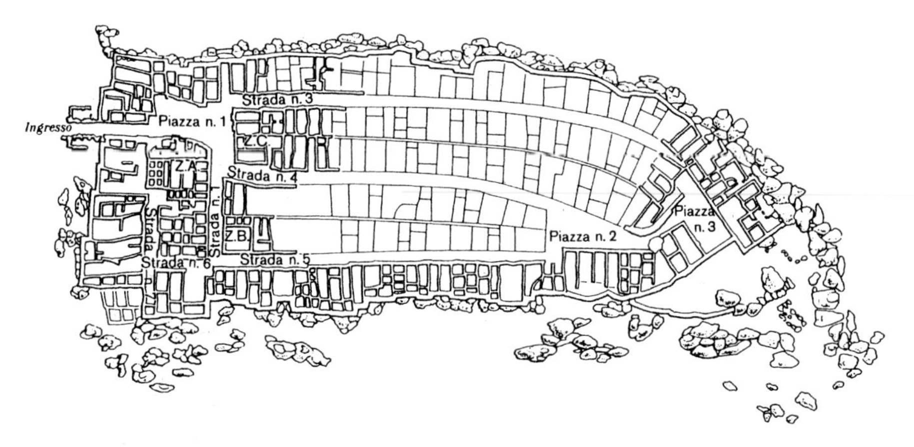

21 *Plan of the Punic settlement on the acropolis of Monte Sirai, Sardinia.*

22 *Aerial view of a Punic settlement at Kerkouane, Tunisia.*

While adopted widely in the mainland, Hippodamic city planning was only selectively utilized in the Punic realm. The urban fabric of the major towns in Sardinia, notably Monte Sirai and Tharros, was based upon the traditional manner of 'contour-planning', in which construction followed the natural topography of the site; the result was a communication system that was wandering rather than direct.[18] (See fig. 21.) Such flexibility in urban arrangement is also in evidence at Kerkouane. (See fig. 22.) Despite the absence of topographical constraints (the city was situated on a flat stretch of sandy coast), the newly established city precinct was marked by a system of intersecting roads of variable width and orientation, defining insulae of equally varying dimensions. Such non-standardized planning, which runs counter to the rigid structure of the Hippodamic system, points to indigenous preferences. Contour-planning is very much in evidence at Punic Carthage, which maintained a radial street alignment in its upper district even after rectilinear planning was instituted in areas of newer construction along the coast.[19]

The defence of the Phoenician city

PHOENICIAN ARMED FORCES

Little is known about the size and composition of the armies at the disposal of the Phoenician cities. Their land forces, it would appear, consisted primarily of light infantry, augmented by chariotry and archers. (See fig. 23.) From the seventh century BC onwards, iron arms (spear-points, spear-butts, short daggers, and lances) appear frequently in Phoenician graves, suggesting that such troops, under normal circumstances, were composed of native regulars, who served as volunteers or conscripts.

Of the various components of the military, the best known was the Phoenician navy, which was highly respected in antiquity for its speed and agility. The prominent role played by the Phoenician war fleets in the Persian wars is well known; according to Herodotus, the naval squadrons of Tyre, Sidon, and Arwad were indispensable to the Persian war effort. The most powerful of these fleets apparently belonged to Sidon; its fourth-century coinage, in fact, features a depiction of a Phoenician war galley before the city's turreted walls. (See fig. 29 i.)

At the heart of the Phoenician military fleet stood its war galleys. In the early first millennium BC, the standard craft were the triaconter and penteconter, single-banked vessels with thirty and fifty rowers, respectively. Some time in the eighth century, the invention of the raised deck made possible the creation of a double-banked galley, with two superimposed, staggered lines of rowers working their oars from inside the vessel, the upper on the gunwale itself, the lower through ports in the hull. (See fig. 24.) The two-level galley (whose invention may perhaps be attributed to the Phoenicians) enjoyed a distinct advantage over the one-level: it was a far more compact, shock-resistant vessel – literally half the length of its single-banked precursor (perhaps 20 versus 38 metres (65 versus 125 feet)). In the seventh and sixth centuries BC, the two-banked galley served as the Phoenician warship *par excellence*. Like all war galleys, the brow at the waterline extended into a point which was shod with bronze for ramming and disabling enemy vessels.

Its successor, the Phoenician mainstay of the Persian fleet, was the versatile three-banked trireme. Like the two-banked vessel, it was equipped with a ram and a single square sail set amidships on a retractable mast. When sprinting, the trireme could achieve a top speed of almost 9 knots. The Phoenician version differed from its Greek contemporary by having a higher deck, a longer and cone-shaped ram, and a figurehead at its prow. It perhaps had the same number of rowers as the Greek version: twenty-seven in the upper row, twenty-five in the other two on each side. It had no outrigger; the rowers were accommodated inside the hull.[20]

23 *Armed terracotta horseman, from Byblos, Lebanon, eighth–sixth century BC.*

24 *Relief depicting a double-banked Phoenician war galley. From the Palace of Sennacherib at Nineveh, Iraq, early seventh century* BC.

PHOENICIAN FORTIFICATIONS

Archaeological documentation for the fortification of the Phoenician cities on the mainland during the early Iron Age remains scant. Of the primary coastal establishments, only Byblos has preserved any evidence of its early defensive works; those of Tyre, Sidon, and Arwad remain a complete unknown. Recent archaeological research at Beirut, however, has helped to fill this gap, providing valuable information on the development of that city's successive defensive systems and their construction. As excavations reveal, the Late Bronze Age settlement was protected by a pilaster wall (the third in a series of ramparts dating back to the Middle Bronze Age) buttressed by a glacis of pebble stones and large limestone rubble angled at a slope of 20 degrees. This structure was replaced before the Early Iron Age by a massive new stone fortification wall with a large glacis of steeper angle (33 degrees) contoured to the curved perimeter of the settlement mound. (See fig. 25.) This rampart was ultimately supplanted, in successive order, by a casemate wall of well-dressed limestone blocks (in the seventh to sixth century BC) and by a massive circuit wall faced with rubble stones (some time in the Persian period).[21]

The defensive architecture of northern Israel, well documented at sites such as Megiddo and Hazor, provides important additional information about the probable appearance and construction of the contemporary Phoenician fortifications. At both sites, the city ramparts consist of relatively narrow, towerless curtain walls of casemate construction, a feature documented also in early Iron Age Phoenician military construction in Sardinia (Sulcis, Tharros). Recent excavations at the southern Phoenician port of Dor provide perhaps the best parallels. Dor's ninth-century ramparts consist of a solid massive brick wall, some 3 metres (10 feet) wide, reinforced at its base by a plaster-faced clay glacis, and constructed upon foundations built partly of brick and partly of stone.

25 *View of the defensive fortifications and glacis of the settlement mound at Beirut, Lebanon, tenth–early ninth century* BC.

The city's defences, which served Dor until the mid-fourth century BC, were punctuated by a main city-gate with flanking mudbrick towers set upon a foundation of huge limestone blocks. With their regular alternation of salients and recesses, Dor's fortifications, in all likelihood, typified the type of defensive construction utilized on the Phoenician mainland during the early Iron Age.[22]

Attention may be drawn to a defensive outpost of seventh- to sixth-century date constructed on the Baniyas river north of Arwad. Situated on a ridge dominating a bend in the river, this fortress, an irregular trapezoid some 500 by 250 metres (550 by 275 yards), utilized the natural defences afforded by its setting; only its exposed northern flank was artificially fortified – with a massive wall of large rough-cut stone blocks laid in irregular rows, the whole punctuated by three gates preceded by entry ramps.[23]

An idea of the superstructure of Tyre's city walls in the Assyro-Babylonian period (ninth to sixth centuries BC) may be gained from the early sixth-century ramparts at Motya and from contemporary depictions in Assyrian and Phoenician art. At Motya, the city defences, which follow the shoreline, consist of a single narrow wall provided with alternating towers (traces of twenty of which are preserved) and sally-ports. On the Assyrian reliefs we see, variously depicted, the battlemented ramparts of a city, consisting of multi-storeyed curtain walls (provided with wall-walks) punctuated at regular intervals by lofty, turreted towers with crenellated parapets. Although largely conventionalized, some of these depictions reveal interesting and archaeologically verifiable architectural details.

The depiction of Tyre on the bronze Balawat gate reliefs of Shalmaneser III shows two monumental arched portals with double-leafed entrance gates of wood or bronze. (See fig. 5.) Another representation of the city on a wall relief (now lost) from the palace of Sennacherib (704–681 BC) at Nineveh shows a series of round shields hung from the city battlements, as described by the prophet Ezekial.[24] (See fig. 6.)

A Phoenician silver bowl from Cypriot Amathus depicts a citadel with stone masonry towers equipped with crenellated parapets of rounded form, an architectural feature documented at Motya. (See fig. 26.)

Efforts at Phoenician Iron Age defensive construction intensified in the late sixth to fourth centuries BC, when a number of coastal centres, Sidon and Byblos prominent among them, served as regional defensive outposts within the Achaemenid realm. At this time, the fortifications of Sidon expanded southwards into undeveloped territory. The ashlar limestone foundations of a well-articulated wall mark Sidon's new southern city boundary.[25] The city's turreted ramparts are proudly depicted on early fourth-century coinage. (See fig. 29 i.) At Byblos, the north-eastern flank of the acropolis was extended by a defensive outwork in the form of a rectangular fortress with seven large, closely set straddle towers.[26]

Phoenician techniques of defensive construction are well attested in the Persian period. The cities of the southern Phoenician coast (and northern Israel) employed a standard wall construction involving upright ashlar piers in alternation with zones of fieldstone rubble infill. This 'pier-and-rubble' technique, which was also widely employed in domestic architecture, represents a hallmark of Phoenician construction in the Persian and ensuing Hellenistic periods.[27] (See fig. 27.)

The defensive walls of Byblos, and almost certainly those of Tyre, Sidon, and Arwad, also employed a more labour-intensive technique involving double-faced, dressed ashlar walls enclosing an infill of earth and stone chips. These structures were further strengthened by the use of gypsum cement, a feature noted by Arrian in his description of Tyre's ramparts on the eve of Alexander's conquest. The strength and solidity afforded by this technique allowed the construction of truly massive fortifications. According to Arrian,[28] Tyre's city walls stood in excess of 16 metres (17.5 yards) in the fourth century BC.

The Persian period witnessed not only an increase in the height and thickness of wall construction but a more elaborate use of advance fortifications; according to Diodorus,[29] Sidon's lofty ramparts were protected by a triple defensive ditch. The rock-cut trench often formed the primary line of defence in Phoenician cities at home and abroad.

The Persian and ensuing Hellenistic periods reveal the earliest evidence for the elaborate fortification of Phoenician harbours, which required protection from local piracy as well as external attack. One foolproof method of securing a harbour was to place it physically within the city's defensive fortifications, creating a 'closed port'. Tyre's original northern harbour is one such example; its inclusion within the city's walls may have been the direct result of Hiram's expansion efforts in the tenth century BC.[30]

More commonly, as in the case of Sidon's artificial northern port, stone-built towers and bastions were erected on or adjacent to moles and harbour entrances. Such an advance defensive installation may have stood on the small islet of Kalaat el-Bahar ('Castle of the Sea') overlooking Sidon's port facility. At the southern port of Atlit, a series of square ashlar towers were built against the city's breakwaters in an effort to safeguard the harbour entrance.

26 *Gold-plated silver bowl, depicting the siege of a city, from Amathus, Cyprus, late eighth–early seventh century BC. On the outer register, a walled city is beset by converging trains of horsemen, hopolites and archers; in the register below, two royal figures in Assyrian dress pluck flowers from a stylized palmette.*

PUNIC ARMED FORCES

The history of the Carthaginian military is a long and complex one, extending over more than six centuries – from the city's foundation in the early eighth century to its final defeat at the hands of Rome in 146 BC. Little is known of the army and its activities during Carthage's evolving years; prior to the city's early efforts at colonization in the sixth century BC, its size and movements were presumably limited to the immediate protection of the city and its environs.

The first historically verifiable reference to Carthaginian military activity occurs in 535 BC, when city forces, in alliance with the Etruscans, met the Greeks of Phocaea in a sea battle off Alalia in Corsica.[31] It is around this time, in historical accounts concerning General Mago and his descendants, that we have the first concrete documentation of the Carthaginian army and its make-up. Under the Magonids, who held sway from *c.*550 to 400 BC, the city's armed forces were composed primarily of foreign contingents drawn from the various subject states within the Carthaginian realm. (Before then, the army is thought to have been largely a citizen levy, backed up by tributary allies.) By the fifth century BC, Carthaginian involvement in the military, aside from the ranks of senior officers, appears to have been restricted to an élite reserve corps of two thousand five hundred individuals known as the 'Sacred Battalion', which served directly under the head of state.

By far the largest foreign contingent in the Carthaginian army was the Libyans – the modern Berbers of Tunisia – who filled the ranks of the light infantry that composed the army's core. Other primary contingents from the subject states included the Sardinians and the Spanish (Iberians). A number of allies also contributed; chief among these were the Libyan Phoenicians (Punic citizens resident in Carthage's North African colonies), and the Numidians and Mauri, who made up the most important part of the cavalry. A

27 *Pier-and-rubble construction from the Persian-period district at Beirut, Lebanon. Lebanon University excavations.*

host of other foreign troops – Celts, Ligurians, Etruscans, Campanians, Corsicans, and native Sicilians (both Elymians and Sicules) – rounded out the army's ranks. Greek soldiers, primarily from Sicily, also served. Scythed war chariots, an inheritance from the Near East, saw continued usage until the period of the Punic Wars, when they appear to have been supplanted by the tactical use of native North African elephants, which were more effective at disrupting the enemy in close combat. Through time, the Carthaginian army was increasingly influenced by Greek military practice, particularly in the use of siege weaponry. By the fourth century BC, if not before, it had adopted the Greek hoplite formation and, perhaps later, the Macedonian phalanx.

While the Carthaginian army drew heavily upon native conscripts from subject territories such as Libya and Sardinia, hired mercenaries played an increasingly important role. By the battle of Himera in 480 BC, they are clearly present in substantial numbers.[32] As the ancient sources reveal, these mercenaries were often recruited from peoples, such as the Gauls and Campanians, who were known for their aggressive, war-like character. The initial decision for their employment was almost certainly a practical one, dictated by logistical and financial concerns. The use of foreign soldiers freed the city's skilled population from military service and allowed them to devote their full energies to commerce, the primary source of the city's revenue.[33]

Carthage's use of mercenary troops and their relative importance to the army has been a subject of much debate. Did the city, as has been argued, grow increasingly reliant upon the use of hired soldiers? Or did it have ample enough reserves from North Africa to meet its growing military needs? By the fourth century BC, at any rate, the latter appears to have been the case.[34] As for the structure and organization of the Carthaginian armed forces, only the basic outlines are known. Its generals and ranking officers were drawn from among the Carthaginian aristocracy; the former were elected by the Peoples' Assembly, a body to which they were strictly accountable. Subalterns came from the various nationalities that composed the army's ranks. The native contingents, which served according to their indigenous military training (as sling throwers, in the case of the Balearic islanders; or as horsemen, in the case of the Numidians), were given a fair degree of autonomy. Each was allowed to retain its native dress and fighting equipment (the Iberians, their native sabres; the Celts, their long slashing swords). In size, the army ranged from twenty-five thousand to as many as a hundred thousand men or more. As in the later Roman empire, the primary unit of command appears to have been the century; squads of infantry were organized in groups of five hundred.

In sharp contrast to the army, whose heterogeneous ranks were filled with foreigners, the Carthaginian navy was largely recruited from its citizen body. Its fleets ranged in size from several dozen ships to armadas of one hundred and twenty or more. The Phoenician three-banked trireme formed the predominant vessel type from the seventh into the fourth century BC. Toward the end of the fifth century, a war galley manned by sets of four rowers, the quadrireme (in later Roman terminology), was introduced by Carthage. Some versions, at least, may have been single-banked, like the earlier penteconter, accommodating a crew of perhaps two hundred oarsmen, with four men working each of twenty-five oars a side. Continuing a trend toward use of larger vessels, both the mainland Phoenician and the Carthaginian fleets subsequently added a type with sets of five rowers. The quinquereme, as the Romans later called it, became the ship of the line in the Punic Wars. If single-banked, with five rowers per oar, it would have measured roughly 40 metres (130 feet) in length, and could have accommodated a total crew (including deckhands and auxiliary marines) of over three hundred men.

PUNIC FORTIFICATIONS

Most Punic cities were fortified; Carthage was no exception. According to literary sources, by the Hellenistic period the entire city was completely surrounded by walls. Recent excavations in Carthage's 'Magonid' quarter have uncovered the ashlar foundations of the city's maritime ramparts erected at the end of the fifth century. By the third century BC, Carthage's inland fortifications were composed of three separate lines of defence: a thick inner wall (17 metres [56 feet] in height, according to Diodorus) with towers and casemates; an intermediate rampart; and, beyond, a pair of trenches divided by a central wooden palisade. The line of this double moat, which ran the length of the isthmus joining Carthage to the North African mainland, has been traced and verified through aerial photography and archaeological research.[35]

Excavations at Kerkouane on Cape Bon have uncovered the intact fortifications of a typical Punic suburban settlement of the fifth to fourth centuries BC. In conformance with the Carthaginian principle of in-depth defence, the town was protected on its inland side by two curtain walls divided by an interior moat 10 metres (33 feet) wide.

Carthage's North African empire was protected by a series of forts and military outposts positioned to safeguard both dependent settlements and the outlying frontier. A substantial number of these have been identified. Built in various configurations – square, oval, polygonal, and elliptical – these defensive installations were protected by a system of outer fortification walls and advance bastions that secured the main entrance.

A crucial base of defensive operation within the Carthaginian empire, Sardinia and its cities exemplify Punic military architecture at its finest. The most impressive fortifications may be found at Tharros, the island's major urban centre. The city was equipped with a triple line of massively constructed defensive walls, the outermost measuring over 6 metres (20 feet) high and 2.5 metres (8 feet) thick. The island city of Sulcis, Sardinia's primary emporium, was also protected by a defensive complex of casemate walls erected on the crest of hills behind it. At the centre of this complex was a massive stone tower overlaying an earlier nuraghic (native Sardinian) fortification; this tower complex, situated on the highest bluffs of the city, provided an excellent vantage point from which to survey the plains below.

Each of Sardinia's major centres was protected by an advance line of military outposts situated strategically in the surrounding hinterlands. One such installation was the fortified hilltop town of Monte Sirai. Founded by Sulcis in the seventh century BC, this acropolis settlement housed a military garrison manned by some six hundred soldiers. As at Sulcis, its central element of defence was a massive stone keep built upon the ruins of an older nuraghic defensive tower. In a fashion characteristic of Punic settlements on Sardinia, the citadel's entrance was protected by a series of advance fortifications erected outside the main gate.

The administration of the city

THE PHOENICIAN HOMELAND

The governance of the Phoenician city and its political infrastructure remains a difficult and elusive topic. Unfortunately, there are no surviving Phoenician documents that deal with political affairs; the sources at our disposal are generally late and derive from a non-oriental, classical context.

Structurally, the Phoenician towns functioned as true city-states, each operating independently under the aegis of a local dynast. At Byblos, Phoenicia's oldest documented city, the names of royal rulers appear already in the third millennium. By the mid-fourteenth century BC, the Phoenician coastal cities of Tyre, Sidon, Byblos, Beirut, and Arwad appear as established, independent entities under the control of native ruling houses.

Within scholarly circles, much debate has centred on the question of the powers and prerogatives of the Phoenician king (Punic *mlk*). According to one point of view, his decision-making abilities in the civic sphere were circumscribed by the powers of the local city élite, or 'merchant aristocracy'. Our earliest historical documents – the Late Bronze Age Amarna correspondence and the eleventh-century Report of Wenamun – paint a very different picture, however. In the Wenamun report, the local Byblian dynast Zakarbaal appears as an aggressive and vigorous monarch directly involved in matters of state. In his commercial dealings with the Egyptian envoy Wenamun, Zakarbaal effectively manages all aspects of the cedar wood transaction – from the initial terms of the sale to the appointment of work crews assigned to carry out the operation. In the succeeding tenth century, the Tyrian monarch Hiram appears no less authoritative a figure. Both contexts suggest that political initiative resided ultimately with the king, who served as functioning head of state.

As in other Near Eastern monarchies, the power and authority of the Phoenician king was closely tied to his sacred function as intermediary between the divine and mortal spheres. As royal inscriptions record, one of the king's primary roles was that of chief priest and religious functionary. Royal piety is expressed in the theophoric structure of various Phoenician kings' names, which typically incorporate the names of principal divinities such as Baal, Eshmun, Melqart, and Astarte. The popular royal names Adonibaal ('My lord is Baal') and Abibaal ('My father is Baal') are two such examples. King Hiram's sons Baalbazer ('Servant of Baal') and Abdastratus ('Servant of Astarte') also illustrate such practice.

Regarding the other organs of the Phoenician body politic, the Report of Wenamun refers to an 'assembly' of Byblians with which King Zakarbaal confers regarding a pressing matter of state (i.e. the demand of the Tjekker for Wenamun's extradition). The political body here referred to is the Council of Elders, an ancient Phoenician institution documented in the Amarna correspondence.[36] A more explicit reference to it can be found in the later seventh-century treaty between the Assyrian monarch Esarhaddon and King Baal I of Tyre; here, the members of the council, a consultative body that governs alongside the king, are referred to as 'elders' of the city.

Alongside this select council of elder city statesmen and aristocrats, the ancient texts refer to a larger, more encompassing body known as the 'Peoples' Assembly'. Documented in the mainland Phoenician realm at Tyre and Sidon, this institution was apparently composed of the 'enfranchised' population of the city, i.e. its free male citizenry. As with the Council of Elders, little is known of its function or authority. Did it have the power to propose or initiate legislation or did it simply affirm decisions taken by the king in deliberation with the city elders? In the absence of textual evidence, no firm conclusions can be drawn.

In studying their governance, one should not lose sight of the fact that, during much of their history, the Phoenician cities served as client- or vassal states under a variety of political overlords – Egyptian, Assyrian, Babylonian, Persian, and Macedonian. Given the paucity of surviving documents, the specific nature of these relationships, which varied significantly from period to period, is often difficult to assess. In general, however, foreign overlordship appears to have been relatively non-invasive from a political standpoint, geared primarily at ensuring the timely payment of taxes and tribute and the contribution of services. Political oversight rested in the hands of a resident foreign governor (or, occasionally, a sympathetic native ruler), who served as a representative of the ruling dynasty. Under the Assyrian, Babylonian, and Persian regimes, the city of Sidon served as the official seat of such a residence.

THE WESTERN COLONIES

Virtually nothing is known about the administration of the early overseas establishments founded by the Phoenicians. Initially, governance may have been held collectively by members of the 'founding party' under the aegis of its expedition leaders. Over time, such an ad hoc arrangement would have been replaced by a true colonial administration, headed by a prefect or governor appointed by the mother-city. Phoenician inscriptions on a pair of fragmentary bronze bowls from Cyprus testify to the existence of two such resident Tyrian governors under King Hiram II in the mid-eighth century BC.[37]

Especially in its early stages, economic ties between the financially dependent colony and its mother-city must have been extremely close. As has been cogently argued, a single institution, the temple, was instrumental in perpetuating this relationship.[38] A visible symbol of the king and founding state, it served not only as a mediator of political conflict but as a conduit for financial exchange. This phenomenon is apparent in the relationship between Tyre and its primary early foundations: Kition, Carthage, and Cadiz. At all three, the establishment of a local sanctuary to Melqart, Tyre's national deity, accompanied the colonial foundation. In the case of Carthage, the colony sent a tithe of its public treasury annually to the mainland Tyrian sanctuary of Melqart, a practice that continued down to the Hellenistic period.

From the fifth century BC onwards, a new republican form of municipal administration, headed by two chief magistrates, or 'suffetes', is attested at Carthage and other western Phoenician colonies in North Africa and the Mediterranean. The office of suffete (from Latin *sufes* and Punic *spt* ('judge' or 'governor')), held conjointly by two officials, was an elected rather than an appointed position with an annually renewable term. As the ancient sources reveal, the suffetes' authority as heads of state was supreme. Their executive functions and prerogatives (still poorly understood) were broad, and encompassed a wide range of legislative and judicial responsibilities. While they were chosen ostensibly on the basis of merit and experience, personal wealth and social prestige no doubt figured largely in the selection process; like the later consuls of the Roman empire, the suffetes demonstrated their largess to the populace by erecting public monuments or sponsoring banquets and festivals.

Punic texts and Latin sources confirm that suffete magistracies were common throughout the Punic realm – in North Africa, Sicily, and Sardinia – right up until Roman times. The origins of this municipal institution remain the subject of debate. While some would trace its beginnings to the very emergence of the western colonies, others, more plausibly, would see it in an evolutionary context – as an offshoot or expression of the Punic states' emerging economic and political independence from the homeland. If this assumption is correct, the beginnings of suffete administration in the west should not be placed much before the sixth century BC.[39]

The suffetes presided over two other primary institutions in the Punic realm: the Senate and the Peoples' Assembly. The former was responsible for the review of both internal and external affairs. Matters of foreign policy (the declaration of war, the resolution of external conflict, and the receipt of foreign embassies) were of particular concern to it. Within the Carthaginian Senate, a commission of thirty-plus members was entrusted with the responsibility of preparing and reviewing projects for submission to the larger body. From the Senate as well came an elected judicial tribunal (of one hundred or one hundred and four Carthaginians), which served as a high court of justice responsible for overseeing state security.

As in the Phoenician homeland, the Peoples' Assembly was composed of individuals drawn from the free male citizenry. It appears that membership in this body (known in Punic and Neo-Punic inscriptions as the *'am*, or 'people') was elective; the criteria for selection (age, status, personal wealth) is not known. The Peoples' Assembly held the right to review decisions and debate them publicly; the election of generals was also their prerogative.

A few brief remarks may be made about Carthage's own empire in North Africa and the Mediterranean and its method of administration. Like their Roman successors, the Carthaginians, in managing both conquered and inherited colonial territory, allowed their subjects a great deal of local, domestic autonomy, limiting centralized control to fiscal matters, such as the collection of taxes and tribute. The governance of Carthage's African empire, which ultimately stretched from Algeria to the border of Cyrenaica, was based on a subdivision into administrative districts (called 'lands' in Punic) that were controlled by officials appointed from the capital. The most harshly governed were the native Libyans, for whom military conscription and the payment of annual rents and taxes was mandatory. Carthaginians and Libyan Phoenicians (Punic citizens resident in Carthage's North African colonies) were normally exempt from both.

Local administrative autonomy was granted to former Phoenician establishments in North Africa (Utica), Sardinia, and Sicily, which maintained their own suffete magistracies. Both Greek and native (Elymian and Sican) communities in Sicily were accorded political autonomy as well. Carthaginian administrative control was more direct in Sardinia and (later on) in Spain, where patterns of governance – a centralized military command, mandatory conscription among native tribes, and state intervention in the economic sector – paralleled that in effect in North Africa.

This overview of Phoenician and Punic governance may be concluded with an archaeological footnote on matters of civic administration. To date, no public buildings of administrative function have been identified at any Phoenician or Punic site. As others have observed, this phenomenon may not be entirely fortuitous; in contrast to the Greek and Roman world, where such public buildings (council and assembly halls, courts of justice) were commonplace, business in the Semitic world was often conducted in the open – in public squares or at the entrances to city gates. Such practice may help to explain the apparent absence of such structures in a Phoenician context.

The social fabric of the Phoenician and Punic city

Of all aspects of the Phoenician city perhaps the most elusive is its societal structure. As in other ancient Near Eastern cultures, the populations of the various Phoenician and Punic centres were marked by social stratification, a fact that may be inferred from the range in quality of burials. Yet, it is difficult to gauge the extent of disparity between the 'haves' and 'have-nots' in Phoenician and later Punic society. In contrast to the classical world, there are few texts that speak of unrest or rivalry among citizens of various social grades.

Nevertheless, the ancient sources (both biblical and classical) allude to the wealth and power of the merchant aristocracy in cities like Tyre and Carthage. Such references clearly point to the existence of a class of powerful men, whose fortunes and social reputations were founded upon their success in the commercial trade. Such individuals – the shipping magnates and heads of trade syndicates – must surely have comprised the majority of the 'city elders', in whom municipal power and authority resided.

For the cities of the Phoenician mainland, the bulk of wealth thus appears to have been concentrated in the hands of a select group of individuals, whom we may call a merchant oligarchy. The picture, however, is less clear for Carthage and the western Phoenician colonies. Was Carthaginian wealth, indeed, concentrated in the hands of the city élite? Or was it more broadly distributed among a middle-class sector of shop owners, merchant dealers, and artisans?

The problem is especially vexing when one confronts Carthage's emerging North African empire. Was the agricultural wealth of the interior in the hands of huge landed estates administered by the 'rural nobility', or was it more equitably distributed among individual farms operated by the Carthaginian citizenry? Scholarly opinion is divided on the question. The answer awaits more definitive archaeological data.

Another unanswered question concerns the relative status enjoyed by various sectors of the city population in Phoenician and Punic society. If one imagines a spectrum with the mercantile aristocracy at one end and the city's servile population at the other, what occupied the middle? What was the status of the numerous artisans, craftsmen, merchants, and vendors that filled the cities' rosters? How extensive were the citizenship rolls of Carthage and Tyre, and who was entitled to legal and political representation? Along what lines did Phoenician and later Punic society divide?

In assessing the societal make-up of the Phoenician cities, one must factor in the existence of a substantial non-native population, which included resident foreigners (merchants, artisans), imported seasonal labourers (especially in the ports), and slaves. As the ancient sources reveal, the latter formed a significant component of the work force.[40] Under the Carthaginians, slaves (especially prisoners-of-war) were enrolled in state industrial facilities, such as mines and naval shipyards. They were also enlisted, in times of war, in defence of the city; in such instances, they were often enticed with the promise of liberty in the event of military victory. In an agricultural context, slaves were heavily employed as field hands, together with semi-dependent rural workers. In the urban sector, they served in a variety of professional capacities – as industrial workers and artisans, and as servants on large estates; some of the latter undoubtedly performed in an administrative or managerial capacity. Within Carthaginian society, at least some slaves were accorded limited legal and civic rights: to marry, to worship publicly and offer sacrifice, and to purchase their own freedom.[41] Doubtless, social distinctions existed within this heterogeneous population unit, whose ranks included not only captives, prisoners-of-war, and convicts but also chattel slaves acquired on the open market. Between the free wage labourers and the slave population stood another social class in Carthaginian society – 'freemen', former slaves who were able to purchase back their freedom. This sector of enfranchised slaves was apparently a significant one, indicating that at least some types of slave could, in fact, earn wages with an eye towards redeeming their liberty, and that Carthaginian society not only condoned but institutionalized the process; from Punic legal decrees we know that enfranchisement, in fact, required the approval of the Peoples' Assembly. Within the servile population, attention may be drawn to the existence of debt-bondsmen: tenant labourers who were tied to the land through debt obligations.

As a result of their commercial focus, the Phoenician cities fostered a highly mobile, transient population, which included not only professional 'travellers' (merchants, shippers, sailors, prospectors) but also those who, by choice or necessity, worked abroad (emigré artisans and craftsmen, miners, export traders, colonists). It also included a mobile foreign population (of seasonal workers, professional traders, and imported slaves), some of whom established temporary residence in the city. Such economic activity clearly encouraged social intermingling (and, in some instances, intermarriage) among diverse population groups, contributing to a heterogeneous, racially and ethnically mixed population. As surviving depictions on terracottas and sculptural reliefs reveal, such was clearly the case at Carthage.

The existence of a culturally mixed population raises some interesting questions. How did Carthage's ethnic diversity affect the definition of the *'am*, or citizen body? What was the political status of the many Carthaginian (or Tyrian) émigrés who established permanent residence abroad? Did their political roots and cultural identity remain with the homeland, or did they gradually assimilate within their adopted communities? How did the home port regard such foreign transplants?

Special consideration must also be given to the role that women played in Phoenician and Punic society. Beyond their priestly involvement in the religious sphere, we know very little of the professional capacities in which they served. Within the former, women could occupy the highest of positions – as head priest or even president of a priestly board.[42] As contemporary texts reveal, such a prerogative was limited to women of the highest social rank.

As elsewhere in the ancient Near East, Phoenician women contributed significantly to the local economy, especially in cottage industries such as weaving and textile manufacture. Funerary inscriptions from the Carthaginian *tophet* provide tantalizing bits of information about their professional status. On one votive stela, a woman named Shiboulet is identified by profession as a 'city merchant'.[43]

Surviving texts, unfortunately, shed little light on the legal or civic rights of women. As in all Semitic societies, they were able to own, inherit, and bequeath property. Their legal rights (in matters such as property ownership) were almost certainly protected by written codes. Could women, in select instances, acquire citizenship rights? The surviving epigraphic evidence, while suggestive, is not conclusive.[44]

Chapter Three

ECONOMY: COMMERCE AND INDUSTRY

THE PHOENICIAN CITIES were rooted in a maritime economy. Not only did the sea provide their primary channel for trade but it also furnished the basis for their major industries, such as shipbuilding, fishing, and purple-dye production.It also defined their commercial outlook. It was by the waterways that the Phoenicians, working both as primary shippers and as commercial entrepreneurs, traded with Egypt, the Aegean, and the central and western Mediterranean.The sea, moreover, offered the Phoenicians a lucrative avenue for commercial exploration, enabling them to procure and transport quantities of valued raw materials over long distances.

The Phoenician pre-monetary economy

Prior to the adoption of money in the fifth century BC, Phoenician commerce with the outside world was governed largely by financial pacts or trade agreements that established fixed terms of exchange. Such treaties, which standardized equivalencies in raw materials, were especially needed in trade with large complex economies like those of Egypt, Babylonia, or Cyprus. Such fixed pricing agreements clearly underlay Phoenicia's foreign commerce from an early period. It was on such a basis, for example, that the Phoenicians conducted their profitable cedar trade with Egypt. The Report of Wenamun, set in the early eleventh century BC, provides a detailed account of the goods and raw materials furnished by the Egyptian court as payment to the Byblian royal house for a large shipment of Phoenician timber. As one would expect, precious metalwork in gold and silver topped the list, followed by quantities of valued goods and materials, such as linen, papyrus rolls, cow-hides, and rope. The relative amount of each commodity paid was clearly based upon a predetermined exchange rate set against the price of cedar wood.

Although one-sided transactions, Phoenician tribute payments to Assyria were similarly calculated on fixed equivalencies of raw materials. The primary sums were set in prescribed weights of valued metals (gold and silver, followed by lead, copper, and, later, iron), livestock, and precious raw materials, including ivory, exotic woods, linen and wool fabric, and elephant hides. As the Assyrian tribute lists and pictorial reliefs reveal, metals – the primary medium of exchange in the ancient Near East – were often presented as tableware, which could be hoarded, and quickly and easily converted to bullion. Their relative values fluctuated according to availability and demand. The aforementioned trade agreements also fixed equivalencies of goods for services. Such terms of exchange were particularly pertinent to the Phoenician economy, which was based, in large part, on the service industry. The financial agreement reached between kings Solomon and Hiram of Tyre over construction of the Jerusalem temple illustrates such an exchange. Hiram's contribution included not only the required building materials (cedar and fir), but the services and expertise of his own men, both in cutting and transporting the timber, and preparing, on site, the wooden beams required for the temple's construction.[1]

In return for his services, the Tyrian king received a large annual contribution of agricultural produce (wheat and oil) from Solomon. The final agreement was thus based upon an equation of raw materials (timber) and services on Hiram's part – for agricultural commodities, issued on an extended basis (20 years) by Solomon. The transaction was a fairly complex one, involving not only exchanged materials, but promised services, on the one side, and a protracted annual payment, on the other.

The nature of Hiram's request from Solomon – food staples for the palace's domestic needs – underscores what must have been a recurrent factor in Phoenicia's commercially driven economy: a shortage of agricultural produce. The country's narrow alluvial coastal plain clearly limited potential for agricultural development, especially the cultivation of cereals; within Phoenicia itself, extensive exploitation of grain was possible only in the northerly Akkar plain and in the fertile Beqa valley to the south.[2] Access to new agricultural resources was clearly a factor in Tyre's expansion into the fertile Sharon plain and adjacent Galilee plateau in the early first millennium; in antiquity, both ranked among the most productive of wheat-growing districts in the southern Levant. Nevertheless, in the late seventh and sixth centuries BC, the city continued to import both wheat and oil from its southern neighbours, Israel and Judah.[3]

Two agricultural commodities vital to its domestic economy, the vine and the olive, were extensively cultivated in Phoenicia itself, especially in the foothills and plateaux of the Lebanon range. The country's soil and climate were ideally suited for their cultivation. By the fifth to fourth centuries BC, both Phoenician commodities, greatly admired in antiquity,[4] were exported widely throughout the Mediterranean, especially to Egypt, a primary market for Phoenician agricultural produce.[5] The Mediterranean find-distribution of Phoenician transport amphorae, in fact, bears witness to an extensive Levantine transit trade in these goods. It appears that the Phoenicians shipped both domestic and foreign wines and oils in their amphorae, which were also apparently marketed independently as containers. Recent study has confirmed that these commercial vessels were produced in standard capacities for export.[6]

Ezekial's famed prophecy, 'The Ship Tyre', provides an interesting glimpse into the city's far-flung trade network in the seventh century BC.[7] Tyre's past maritime prowess is extolled, its commercial movements compared with those of a huge seagoing vessel. The city's Mediterranean trading partners include the islands of Cyprus and Rhodes, the southern and western coasts of Anatolia, and the elusive kingdom of 'Tarshish' in southern Spain. Ezekial's text also enumerates Tyre's extensive *inland* trading connections – with partners such as Israel and Judah, Damascus, Edom, Arabia, and the cities of Mesopotamia.

Ezekial's inventory of Tyrian imports reveals an important shift that occurred in the city's commercial objectives since Hiram's day. In sharp contrast to Phoenician Early Iron Age commerce, which was geared towards meeting domestic needs, Tyre's trade is now clearly aimed at an international market. The primary commodities that Tyre acquires – precious metals and minerals, ivory, dyed and embroidered garments and fabrics, spices, wines, and livestock – are obtained not only for internal use but for redistribution abroad. The goal is to enrich the economy through an influx of foreign revenue.

Specific attention may be drawn to several categories of trade item mentioned by Ezekial. The first and foremost is that of raw metals and precious minerals. The acquisition of ores and metals was undoubtedly the catalyst for Phoenician commercial exploration abroad, prompting the earliest efforts at island colonization in the Mediterranean (on Cyprus and Sardinia) and leading ultimately to the foundation of Phoenicia's two greatest overseas emporia: Carthage and Cadiz. Ezekial's inventory elucidates an important stage in the evolution of the Phoenician metals trade. Of all commodities mentioned, iron is the only one to appear twice. From the tenth century BC onwards, the market for this durable metal witnessed extraordinary growth, reaching a peak in the eighth and seventh centuries under Assyrian demand.

The second category – the most frequently mentioned in Ezekial's inventory – is that of embroidered and dyed fabrics: fine linen from Egypt, and blue- and purple-dyed garments from Cyprus, Edom, and Mesopotamia. The latter were also a Phoenician speciality, their rich colour produced from purple dye, the famous 'Tyrian blue' extracted from the murex shell. The Phoenician garments were produced primarily from wool, which the Phoenicians imported from Syria via Damascus, as Ezekial's list reveals. Both the garment trade and the production of purple dye formed mainstays of the Phoenician economy (see pp. 163–164).

The structure of the Phoenician economy

While the ancient sources tell us a great deal about the Phoenicians' commercial network, they are largely mute on the subject of the economy and its inner workings. We have little information, for example, about the primary mechanisms of economic control or the institutions responsible for administering them. In the Late Bronze and Early Iron Age, the king and palace appear to have been both the primary initiator and the recipient of most trade-related activity. In many respects, the palace-based economies of the Phoenician cities were characteristic of those found throughout the Near East and Mediterranean area (e.g. Aegean, Cyprus, northern Syria) in the second millennium BC. In the Amarna correspondence, King Rib-addi of Byblos refers to the wealth of the 'house of Tyre', which he compares with that of northerly Ugarit. While clearly exaggerated, Rib-addi's comparison with the larger, more prosperous north Syrian port is revealing, and hints at the broader economic relationship that Ugarit enjoyed with the Phoenician cities. The economies of both had much in common. Among other things, they were based primarily upon foreign commerce and revenues generated by maritime-based industries, such as fishing, shipbuilding, and purple-dye manufacture. The Late Bronze Age archives at Ugarit, in fact, reveal evidence of the close, reciprocal commercial ties that existed between these two maritime entities.[8]

As at Ugarit, Phoenician shipping was carried out through commercial syndicates or trading partnerships, known as *hubur*s. Within the Phoenician realm, this institution is first attested in the early eleventh century BC in the Report of Wenamun. Here we learn of a *hubur* involving twenty ships jointly managed by the king of Byblos and the Egyptian ruler Smendes.[9] As the Old Testament relates, Kings Hiram and Solomon entered into such a maritime business association when they launched their famous Red Sea trading expedition to Ophir.[10] In the Phoenician realm, the *hubur* appears to have been a prerogative reserved for heads of state in conducting international trade. Scholarly opinions are divided on the role that the private sector may have played in the early Phoenician economy.[11] The historical record, however, strongly suggests that the primary economic initiative resided with the king and palace, which retained the exclusive right to trade directly with foreign powers. It was only later, beginning in the eighth century BC, that a strong mercantile aristocracy developed as a result of trade opportunities afforded by Phoenician overseas commercial expansion. At this time, a diversified market, spurred on by Assyrian demand and by expanded colonial activity, encouraged private entrepreneurship on a significant scale (see Chapter 7).

In the Late Bronze and Early Iron Age, Phoenician trade thus appears to have been controlled largely by the state. Phoenician merchants, serving in foreign ports like Ugarit, effectively functioned as agents or representatives of the palace; as the Wenamun report indicates, mercantile activity in the home ports was strictly supervised by the king through local maritime officials, such as the harbour master. It was through such a port authority that the activities of resident foreign traders were monitored.

The ongoing pursuit of international trade led ultimately to the establishment of Phoenician commercial bases, or enclaves (known in Greek as *enoikismoi*) on foreign soil. The Egyptian port of Memphis was the site of one such trading community, whose existence may be traced back to Ramesside times. Such ports-of-trade, run by Phoenician merchant-agents, were regularly equipped with warehouse facilities in which raw materials could be accumulated and stored prior to shipment. By agreement with the host country, the residents of such trading establishments were granted special commercial and legal privileges, such as political immunity and the right to erect local sanctuaries (as attested at Memphis). No doubt, similar enclaves of resident foreigners must have existed in the harbour districts of the Phoenician mainland ports. In this connection, we may note the presence at several Phoenician harbours (e.g. Akko, Atlit) of offshore islets or wharves that may have served as open emporia for foreign merchant vessels.

As for the size of the merchant fleets at the disposal of the Phoenician cities, we have little direct data. In the Report of Wenamun, the king of Byblos makes reference to seventy vessels under his authority: twenty cargo ships (*mnš*) situated in his own harbour, and fifty coastal vessels (*br*) anchored in the port of Sidon. Assyrian palace reliefs from the

I *Gold pectoral of King Ip Abi Shermu. From Byblos, Lebanon, eighteenth century* BC. *The shape and falcon iconography of this pectoral reflect the strong influence of Egyptian artistic models.*

II *Stand of cedar trees, from the Barouk, Lebanon. Due to extensive deforestation in antiquity, only small tracts of once-abundant cedar survive today in the Lebanese mountains.*

III (right) *Bronze statuette of male priest or deity with gold overlay. From Cadiz, Spain, eighth–seventh century* BC.

IV (above) *Gold funerary mask, from the region of Sidon, Lebanon, fifth–fourth century* BC.

V *Limestone sarcophagus of Ahiram, King of Byblos. From Byblos, Lebanon, first half of the twelfth century or later.*

VII (right) *A group of gold jewellery from Tharros, Sardinia, seventh and sixth centuries* BC: *A gold earrings in the form of an ankh; B gold earrings with figure of Horus falcon over a basket; C earring with bulla-shaped pendant; D gold amulet case; E diadem with decoration of palmettes. Phoenician bracelets or diadems, such as this, were made of embossed and granulated plaques of gold and gilt-silver joined by cylindrical hinges.*

VI (below) *Ivory furniture plaque depicting a lioness attacking an African. From the palace of Ashurnasirpal II at Nimrud, Iraq, eighth century* BC. *This exquisitely carved ivory demonstrates the delicate use of applied gold leaf and coloured stone (carnelian) and paste (lapis lazuli) inlays for which the Phoenicians were renowned.*

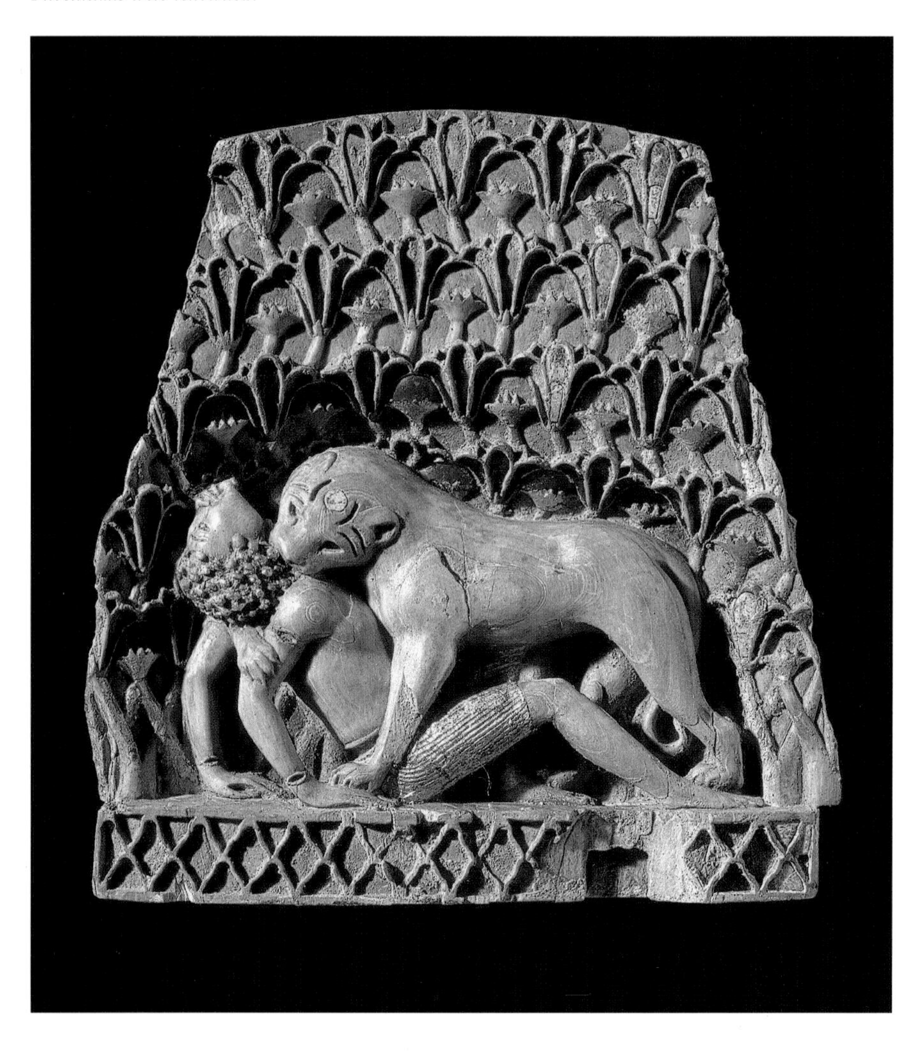

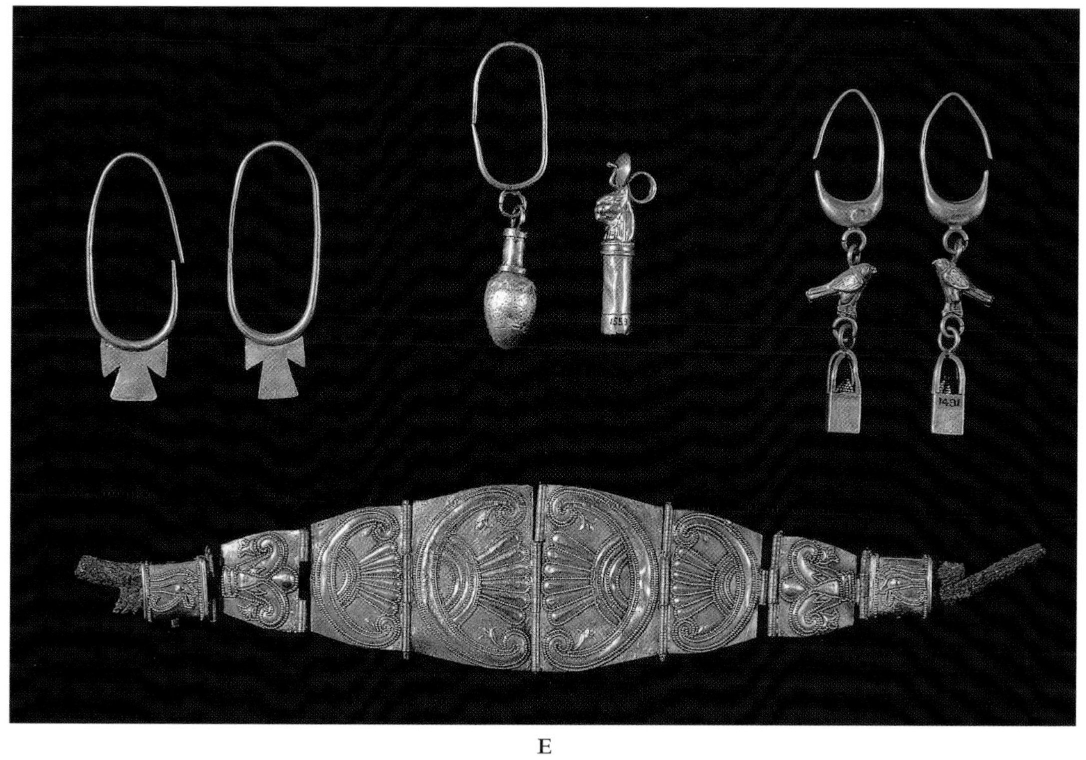

VIII (above) *Cast glass bowl from Praeneste, Etruria, Italy, seventh century* BC.

IX *Rod-formed glass pendant in the form of a bearded male head from Carthage, fourth–third century* BC.

X *Mask of bearded male, from the mainland cremation cemetery at Tyre, Lebanon, seventh century* BC.

XI *Red-slip mushroom-lip jug from Amathus, Cyprus, eighth century* BC.

XII *Red-slip pitcher with trefoil spout from Amathus, Cyprus, eighth century* BC.

ninth century onwards depict several varieties of Phoenician commercial craft: a small merchant galley with upturned prow and stern; and a larger, round-bottomed sailing ship with symmetrical upright stem- and sternposts. (See fig. 28.) The former, called *hippoi* ('horses') from their equine-headed prow ornaments, served primarily for local coastal or riverine transport. The latter class of vessel was known in antiquity as the *gaulos* ('tub'). Its deep, rounded hull could accommodate large cargoes. Averaging between 20 and 30 metres (65 and 100 feet) in length, the *gaulos* bore a sturdy mast amidships, rigged with a single fore- and backstay, that supported a broad rectangular sail. The latter was secured along the head to a single long yard. Towards the stern stood a quarterdeck, which provided shelter for the crew, and also the ship's galley. Wide-hulled and sturdy in construction, the Phoenician *gaulos* was well suited for deep-water, long-distance commerce (*cf.* the biblical ships of 'Tarshish').[12] Recent discoveries of underwater wrecks in the Mediterranean have enhanced our knowledge of Phoenician and Punic commercial craft and their construction.[13]

External relations: the Phoenician cities and their colonies; the Phoenicians under foreign suzerainty

Few data are available about the financial impact of the Phoenician colony upon its mother-city. Aside from the initial outlay of capital (ships, manpower, and supplies) involved in its foundation, ongoing maintenance costs for the metropolis must have been considerable, especially in the settlement's formative years. Once established, however, colonial income could provide a substantial source of outside revenue. As Diodorus records, the city of Carthage sent a tithe of its annual profits to the Tyrian temple of Melqart;[14] other foundations must have had similar treaty obligations toward their mother-cities. The colonial foundation could also benefit the metropolis in assuring a strategic open line of trade communication; the foundation of Kition, for example, must

28 *Relief depicting Phoenician* hippoi *transporting logs. From the Palace of Sargon II at Khorsabad, Iraq, late eighth century* BC. *The two citadels in the background probably represent Sidon and Tyre.*

have provided a tremendous economic boost to Tyre in its pursuit of Cypriot copper.

Equally difficult to quantify is the economic impact exerted upon the Phoenician cities by their Iron Age political overlords – the Assyrians, Babylonians, and Persians.[15] Financial obligations varied considerably through time, as changing political circumstances dictated. Under the Assyrians, tribute appears to have been imposed only on an occasional basis down until the reign of Sargon II (722–705 BC) and his successors. Around this time, Assyrian commercial and tributary demand for metals – silver and iron in particular – exerted considerable financial pressure on the Phoenician cities, fuelling maritime exploration in search of ore sources in the late eighth and seventh centuries BC. In addition to their tribute obligations, it is probable that the Phoenicians benefited commercially from the booming trade in metals now triggered by growing Assyrian market demand.[16]

Under Persian suzerainty, beginning with King Darius I (522–486 BC), royal tribute was assessed annually. As under the Assyrians and Babylonians, the Phoenician cities were taxed on their natural resources, especially their timber reserves. Another form of tax (*miksu* in Akkadian) was assessed on local industries (e.g. purple-dye production, shipbuilding, or metal-working). Tolls and customs duties were equally imposed on Phoenician land and sea trade; maritime commerce was strictly regulated and probably administered, as in Assyrian times, by foreign harbour officials. The economies of the Phoenician cities were affected also by taxation on human labour (*ilku* in Akkadian) in the form of military conscription and corvée duty. Both probably targeted Phoenicia's skilled sailors and craftsmen (especially its carpenters and shipwrights) upon whom the Persians relied heavily for the manning and construction of their naval fleets.

Phoenician coinage

The Phoenicians were late in adopting the practice of minting coins. The first mainland issues appeared around 450 BC – more than 150 years after coinage first circulated in western Asia Minor. The reason for the delay is easily understood: with an economy based upon a long tradition of fixed exchange involving raw goods and metals, there was no practical incentive to coin. By the fifth century BC, the Phoenicians traded primarily within the Achaemenid commercial realm, which itself was based upon a similar economy of exchange. (The Persians' own decision to issue coinage was, in fact, motivated chiefly by an interest in facilitating exchange with the minting cities of Greek western Asia Minor.) Moreover, the Phoenicians were no longer trading extensively within the Aegean, where coinage was largely utilized.

In spite of these circumstances, within a span of two decades (*c*.455–435 BC) all four of Phoenicia's coastal centres (Byblos and Tyre at first, followed by Sidon and Arwad) successively adopted coinage. In the absence of compelling economic incentives, what inspired this move? Aside from its financial value, coinage served as an instrument of political expression; cities minted coins in order to express their autonomy and enhance their civic prestige. This certainly appears to have been a motivating factor in the Phoenician cities' initial decision to mint. By the mid-fifth century BC, Tyre, Sidon, and Arwad had all suffered the indignity of military defeat at the hands of the Greeks; their once invincible naval fleets, long a source of national pride and prestige, lay decimated. Political détente between the Persians and Greeks had now been reached, opening the door to greater commercial and cultural exchange with the Mediterranean world. The situation was thus ripe for the mainland Phoenician cities to reassert themselves politically and economically. What better way than through the minting of coinage? Under the circumstances, it is not surprising that three of Phoenicia's four mainland centres (Sidon, Byblos, and Arwad) adopted the war galley as a primary numismatic motif. A potent symbol of Phoenician military might and maritime power, the galley served not only as a reminder of past greatness but perhaps as a harbinger of success to come.

Historically, another factor must be taken into consideration. The mainland cities were not the first Phoenician emporia in the east to mint coinage. That honour fell to the city of Kition on Cyprus, which adopted the practice under King Baalmilk I (479–449 BC) a full generation before the mainland. (See fig. 29 a, b.) Nor was Kition's move a unilateral

29 *Phoenician coins:*
Kition, Baalmilk I. (a) Obv. Herakles-Melqart. (b) Rev. Seated lion.
Tyre, Stater. (c) Obv. Flying dolphin and murex shell. (d) Rev. Owl with crook and flail.
Arwad, Tetrobol. (e) Obv. Marine deity.
Arwad, Tetrobol. (f) Rev. War galley with shields.
Byblos, Adarmilk. (g) Obv. War galley with hippocamp. (h) Rev. Lion/stag combat.
Sidon, Double stater. (i) Rev. War galley before city walls. (j) Obv. King in chariot.
Byblos, Macrinus, Bronze. (k) Rev. Temple of Baalat Gubal with betyl.

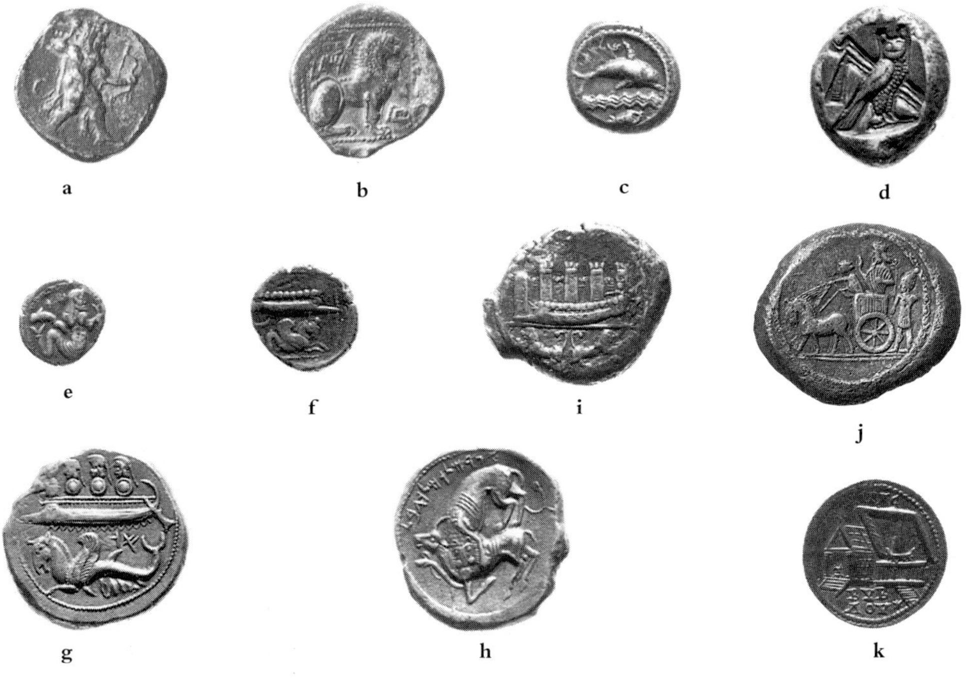

a b c d

e f i j

g h k

one; its decision was clearly triggered by its Greek commercial and political rival, Salamis, which had already made the decision (under King Evelthon) to issue coinage toward the end of the sixth century BC. Other Cypriot cities, including the Phoenician-influenced port of Lapithos, soon followed suit. The coinages of both Lapithos and Kition were integrated within the greater monetary system (based upon the Persian weight standard) adopted by Cyprus under Achaemenid rule. The Phoenicians' move toward coinage may thus be understood within the context of an historical sequence of events that began on Cyprus a half century earlier. It is no coincidence that Tyre and Byblos assumed the initiative in this regard; both cities (especially Tyre, the mother-city of Kition) had close commercial ties to the island. Kition's earliest issues featured the figure of its national deity Herakles-Melkart and that of a seated lion, long a potent symbol of empire and monarchy in the ancient Near East. (See fig. 29 a, b.)[17] Combined, the two images proclaimed Kition's civic and royal identity, a message reinforced by the placement of a royal inscription ('of Baalmilk') above the lion's back.

On its earliest issues, datable *c.*450 BC, Tyre chose, for its obverse, a flying dolphin and a murex shell, both obvious references to the city's maritime greatness. (See fig. 29 c.)(The latter was subsequently replaced by the figure of a marine deity riding on a winged sea horse (hippocamp).) Equally revealing is the motif chosen by the city as reverse emblem: an owl with a crook and flail. (See fig. 29 d.)These implements, venerable symbols of Egyptian royal power and authority, were closely associated with the falcon god Horus, a subject widely adopted in Phoenician art. The Tyrian diemaker, however, chose to replace the falcon with an owl, an image unattested in the ancient Near East, but closely connected with the city of Athens.[18] As the symbol of its tutelary goddess Athena, the owl appears prominently on the reverse of Athenian coinage, beginning in the late sixth century BC. Like its Athenian precursor, the Tyrian owl exhibits the same frontal head pose with staring eyes.

Tyre's decision to adopt the owl as reverse emblem (as it appears on Athenian coinage) can be no coincidence. Its Greek commercial rival, Athens, now occupied an enviable position. As head of the Delian league, it stood at the very pinnacle of its political and economic power. The city's silver tetradrachms, minted primarily for foreign trade, circulated widely in the Near East and in Phoenicia. By combining the image of the Athenian owl with the royal trappings of the Egyptian Horus falcon, the Tyrians strove to create their own distinct coin type that could stand alongside (and perhaps compete with) that of Athens. (Tyre ultimately went on, shortly before the mid-fourth century, to adopt the Attic standard.[19])

Like Tyre, Arwad adopted the figure of a marine deity – half-human, half-fish – on its obverse, and a war galley with a row of shields along its bulwark on the reverse. (See fig. 29 e, f.) Byblos utilized a variety of symbols denoting royal power on its early coinage. A recumbent sphinx wearing the double crown of Egypt was the first device to occupy its obverse, followed by a war galley with horse-headed prow and three military occupants. (See fig. 29 g.) Its reverse showed a variety of animal combat scenes: a vulture with wings outspread landing on a ram, and a series of lion attacks involving a bovine victim. (See fig. 29 h.) From its outset, Sidon's coinage featured the war galley – riding with sail unfurled on the open seas, or anchored before the battlemented walls of the city. (See fig. 29 i.) Its reverse displayed a series of royal images: the Persian monarch shooting a bow or slaying a lion; or a four-horse chariot with crowned occupant, identifiable either as the Persian king or, perhaps more plausibly, as the cult statue of a local Baal. (See fig. 29 j.) The latter interpretation finds support in the presence of a second figure – that of the Sidonian king in priestly garb – who later accompanies the chariot on foot. The coinage of mainland Phoenicia, with the exception of Arwad, employed the Phoenician weight standard, based upon the shekel. Early issues were minted exclusively in silver. As a mark of its premier status among Phoenicia's cities, Sidon alone issued the double shekel, a coin of considerable value and prestige.

The economic role played by Phoenician coinage remains an open question. Initially, it probably circulated as measured bullion. By the beginning of the fourth century BC, however, it appears to have been produced in quantities large enough to have functioned effectively in commercial exchange. In the excavated shops of Al Mina and in the ancient port district of Byblos, large quantities of small denominations in both silver and bronze have been uncovered, clearly attesting to their commercial use in local trade. Moreover, the emergence of bronze coinage in the second quarter of the fourth century BC clearly affirms that Phoenician currency was now circulating in a monetary economy.[20]

As one would expect, the commercial theatre for such currency was the Mediterranean coastal route extending from Cilicia south to Gaza and the Nile Delta. Patterns of distribution within the four coin series, however, varied considerably. The moneys of Tyre and Sidon were most heavily exported beyond Phoenicia's borders, while that of Arwad enjoyed a fairly limited, regional distribution. The coinage of Byblos, on the other hand, was almost entirely reserved for internal city use.

In contrast to its mainland Phoenician counterparts, Arwad, like the Cypriot cities, issued its coinage on the Persian standard. As the major outlet for trans-Euphratian trade via the Akkar plain, it probably served under the Achaemenids as the primary Mediterranean port for commerce with Cyprus and the west. Aside from Tyre, Sidon, Byblos, and Arwad, none of the other mainland Phoenician cities struck coinage prior to the Hellenistic period. The town of Beirut, as perhaps others, probably used the double shekels of Sidon, then commercially dominant.

The weight standards on which the various city coinages were based is poorly understood. Cast lead weights of triangular and cubical shape dating from the final centuries of the first millennium BC and bearing various symbols (including the Tanit sign) and letters (denoting the minting authority, i.e. Marathus, Arwad) reveal that various standards were used by different cities, based upon a shekel ranging in weight from 6 to as many as 13 grams. A classification system for the measurement of liquid capacities is also attested.

The western Phoenician emporia: economic considerations

Like their eastern precursors, the economies of the early western Phoenician colonies were tied directly to maritime commerce and trade. Many, like Carthage and Utica on North Africa's coast, were strategically situated as commercial ports-of-call along an axis leading east–west from the homeland to the western Mediterranean. Others, like Sulcis on Sardinia and Cadiz in southern Spain, were located at the source of important trade routes leading to a material-rich hinterland. Although established initially as emporia for mainland Phoenician long-distance trade, the western Phoenician colonies ultimately evolved into independent economic entities with their own regional networks of exchange. Such was the case with Carthage, the most enduring and commercially successful of the early western Phoenician colonies.

The economy of Carthage

Like its mother-city Tyre, the geographic situation of Carthage determined its maritime orientation. Beside a natural harbour of exceptional quality, the city was situated almost midway along the main Phoenician trade route between the Levant and the Atlantic straits. Carthage's foundation, the work of Tyrian aristocrats, was established with an eye towards long-distance commerce; throughout most of its history, the city, in fact, served as an active intermediary in the Mediterranean transit trade. Aside from its early commercial ties to Tyre, however, the historical record is largely mute on the subject of the city's early economy. The earliest archaeological evidence for trade – in the form of commercial amphorae and imported pottery of seventh century date – underscores the early importance of the Tyrrhenian basin to the Carthaginian economy.[21] This region, encompassing Sicily, Sardinia, and the western coast of Italy, remained central to Carthage's trade network throughout its history. The north-western corner of Sicily, with the mainland cities of Panormus (modern Palermo) and Soluntum, and the offshore island of Motya, formed its closest overseas territory; through the narrow intervening straits, Carthage monitored access through the central Mediterranean. Etruria (modern-day Tuscany) was the city's oldest foreign ally and trading partner; from an early date, commercial relations between the two sea-trading entities were regulated by commercial agreements.[22]

Carthage's maritime economy, in fact, was based upon a system of treaty trade, which set commercial parameters and offered trade protection for its respective participants. The terms of two such treaties, enacted between Carthage and Rome in 509 and 348 BC, have come down to us.[23] Both clearly underscore Carthage's commercial priority: the unhindered pursuit of trade in the central Mediterranean. According to the terms of the treaty (which were clearly favourable to Carthage), Rome was prohibited from trading in Sicily and Sardinia and along the eastern coast of North Africa, two regions critical to Carthage's emerging economy. By restricting trade east along the African coast, the Punic emporium protected its commercial ties with the coastal regions of Byzacena (in eastern Tunisia) and Tripolitania (in modern Libya), both of which served as important outlets for trans-Saharan commerce with tropical Africa.

The central Mediterranean islands of Sardinia and Sicily played an even more crucial role in Carthaginian trade. With its abundant metal resources and agricultural wealth, Sardinia had long attracted Phoenician commercial interest. As a result of its strategic location along the east–west Mediterranean trade axis, neighbouring Sicily also played a pivotal role in the Carthaginian commercial network. In addition to its Punic settlements, the island was home to some of the most prosperous Greek emporia in the Mediterranean world. With an overall population estimated at a quarter of a million, the fifth-century port of Syracuse was the economic rival of Athens; both Syracuse, Acragas (modern Agrigento), and the Carthaginian-controlled city of Greek Selinus all probably held substantial resident communities of Punic merchants.

As with mainland Phoenicia, the Carthaginian economy was fuelled by a dominant commercial interest: the acquisition of metals – especially silver and gold, but also tin, copper, iron, and lead. For both the eastern Phoenicians and Carthaginians, southern Spain represented one of the primary sources for silver. As history records, the mines of south-eastern Spain around Carthago Nova furnished enormous revenues to the city in late Punic times.[24] Direct Carthaginian control of this area, however, was not initiated until the late third century BC. Earlier Carthaginian efforts were probably concentrated, via Cadiz, on the Spanish mines of the Guadalquivir valley in upper Anadalusia – at Cerro Salomon (Rio Tinto) or Castulo. (See fig. 72.) The rich silver-bearing lead deposits of south-western Sardinia and northern Etruria may also have been tapped.

According to the Greek historian Thucydides,[25] by the fifth century BC the city possessed an abundance of precious metals (both gold and silver). The extensive gold coinage issued by Carthage in the succeeding fourth century attests to the vast stocks by then accumulated by the city. In all likelihood, this gold was obtained, in part (by direct or indirect trade) from west Africa; other sources (in Spain, Morocco, and the western Sudan) may have been utilized as well.[26]

As for the lesser-valued metals, deposits of both copper and iron were available in North Africa; local supply was probably augmented by imports from regions such as southern Spain, Sardinia, and Etruria. Archaeological investigation at Carthage itself has shown that iron was worked extensively in the city.[27] Tin, the indispensible ingredient in the production of bronze, may have been acquired from Galicia by way of the Atlantic coast or southern Spain; alternatively, it may have come from northern Europe (Cornwall or Brittany) via the Rhone valley and coastal Massalia. Carthaginian interest in the Atlantic coastal route is evidenced by the voyage of Himilco, whose journey was prompted, at least in part, by the city's interest in opening up the tin route.[28]

Although the acquisition of metals dominated Carthage's trade strategy, other commercial pursuits contributed to the city's economic prosperity. One very lucrative avenue was the wholesale export trade, an activity with which Carthage was closely associated (and sometimes parodied[29]) in antiquity. The city served as a clearing house not only for its own goods but for a variety of foreign commodities, many of which were imported expressly for redistribution abroad. Archaeology has shown, for example, that, in the fourth century, Carthage was a major outlet for distributing Attic black-glazed pottery and Corinthian commercial amphorae. Many imported agricultural products, like wine and silphium (a grass native to the Libyan Cyrenaica, whose stalk and juice were valued as a condiment and medicine), were probably recirculated on the open market as well.

As history records, textile weaving and dyeing were clearly a major Carthaginian industry; recent excavations at the district of Le Kram in modern Carthage's southern suburbs have, in fact, revealed evidence for an active purple-dye industry in antiquity (one attested also at neighbouring Kerkouane).[30] With the notable exception of textiles, however, the Carthaginians did not actively export their manufactured goods abroad. In fact, many of the city's archaeologically documented industries (faience, pottery, metal-work) appear to have been aimed primarily at a local, North African market. According to the fourth-century authority Pseudo-Skylax, the Carthaginians traded faience and foreign pottery with the Libyan natives, or Berbers, in exchange for exportable precious raw materials – gold, gems, exotic woods, and ivory; although not specifically mentioned, local Carthaginian metal-work must have figured prominently in such exchange.

Within the Carthaginian economy, attention may be drawn to several major industries that served the Punic state and furnished a livelihood to its population. Notable among these were shipbuilding and armament production (in bronze and iron); both flourished in times of war. For ship construction and related woodworking industries, adequate sources of timber (oak, pine, and juniper) were available in the greater vicinity of Carthage, both at Utica and in the region of Cap Bon.

Another lucrative Punic industry was fishing. Carthage itself was involved in the export of fish, including tuna, stocks of which are still exploited off the Tunisian coast. The heart of this industry lay, however, in the Atlantic coastal waters of southern Spain and Morocco, where numerous industrial establishments for the salting and processing of blue fish (tuna, mackerel, and sardines) had been established in antiquity. Through Cadiz in southern Spain, the Atlantic export trade in salted fish passed to Carthage and other locations in the Mediterranean. Attention may be drawn to the discovery, at Greek Corinth, of a large deposit of fifth-century Punic commercial amphorae containing filleted fish exported from the Spanish or Moroccan coasts near the Straits of Gibraltar.[31]

Attention may be drawn to another industry that played a vital role in the Carthaginian economy: the slave trade. Such commerce in human labour was a commercial pursuit that the Carthaginians had inherited from their Phoenician precursors. The latter were renowned in antiquity for their involvement in such trade, which was active from the Late Bronze Age to the Hellenistic period.[32] According to the classical sources, the Carthaginian domestic market for slaves was an enormous one, especially in the sphere of agriculture and state industry. According to Polybius, as many as forty thousand slaves were employed in the Iberian silver mines of Cartagena alone.[33]

The sources for such commercial trade varied. War served as one extremely lucrative channel. It is by such means that the Carthaginians acquired the bulk of their slaves; prisoners-of-war were conscripted especially for use in state industry (mines, shipyards, military). The spoils of war often included entire city populations of women and children sold into slavery. As the ancient sources reveal, moreover, beleaguered cities were sometimes compelled, under economic duress, to sell off their inhabitants.

Piracy formed another lucrative commercial avenue for the slave trade. The Phoenicians were notorious kidnappers.[34] As the ancient sources reveal, the targets were often hapless women and children. Carthage's second treaty with Rome clearly enumerates the rules of conduct regarding captive-taking, as well as the recourse available to victims of piracy. Slaves were also acquired through commercial trade, both for domestic use and for resale abroad. The ancient classical authors offer a small glimpse at such commerce in chattel slavery, the bulk of which may have come via trans-Saharan trade with tropical Africa. Black slaves may also have been obtained from the Sudan, and from the southern edge of the Berbery, via west Africa, where the Carthaginians are known to have traded. The Mediterranean basin itself was another potential source. According to Timaeus, the Carthaginians traded women to the Balearic islanders in exchange for male slaves.[35]

The above represents an overview of the Carthaginian economy as it existed prior to the fourth century BC, when the city embarked upon an aggressive campaign of African territorial expansion.[36] By the end of that century, Carthage controlled a hinterland some 65 kilometres (40 miles) deep that extended westwards as far as Hippo Acra (Bizerte) and eastwards to Hadrumetum and Thapsus. Its acquisition engendered the emergence of an agrarian-based empire that was administered by an affluent Carthaginian landed aristocracy. The farms and estates of this growing hinterland, which encompassed the fertile, wheat-producing plains of the Medjerda valley (see fig. 9), and the fruit orchards and vineyards of the Tunisian coastal lands east of Carthage, produced increasing agricultural yields, which enabled the city – once dependent upon food imports – to export its agricultural bounty (especially wheat) abroad in the late fourth century BC.[37] Carthage's eventual loss of its overseas empire (Sicily and Sardinia first, followed by Spain) in the succeeding third century led it to intensify its political and economic grip over the African interior, spawning the creation of a tightly controlled, colonial administrative system that the Romans eventually inherited. The land and its wealth had now replaced the sea as the pillar of Carthage's economy.

Coinage

THE WESTERN PHOENICIAN CITIES

The history of coinage among the Phoenician colonies of the western Mediterranean developed independently from the cities of the eastern mainland. Like them, the western colonies adopted the practice at a relatively late date – well after the Greeks struck their first issues. The first of the western Phoenician cities to mint were the Punic centres of western Sicily, Motya and Panormus chief among them.[38] As with the Phoenician emporia on Cyprus, precedent had been set by the Greek Sicilian cities (Himera, Selinus, Acragas, Gela, and Syracuse), which had all begun to mint over the course of the second half of the sixth century BC.

For ease of commerce with the Greeks and Sicels on the island, the Phoenicians of Sicily adopted the Attic–Euboean weight standard, now already well established in the main Greek Sicilian centres. The first denomination to appear was the didrachm, the basic coin of Sicily's western Greek zone. Phoenician assimilation with the Greek monetary system in use on the island may be seen also in the adoption of Greek-language inscriptions and in the choice of numismatic motifs, which closely mirrored those of their Greek counterparts, Syracuse in particular.[39] That all of the Sicilian Phoenician cities undertook to mint under their own name prior to Carthage's first coinage may be taken as a measure of their political autonomy.

CARTHAGE

The earliest coinage struck by Carthage, around 410 BC, was minted for use in Sicily – as payment to the Carthaginian troops stationed on the island during that city's war with the Sicilian Greeks. This early issue, which was clearly intended for large payments, consisted of silver tetradrachms of Attic weight bearing the legend *Qart-hadasht* (Punic for Carthage, 'New city'). (See fig. 30 a.) Following conclusion of the war (after a hiatus in the early fourth century BC lasting from *c*.390 to 350 BC), Carthage resumed the minting of silver coinage in Sicily, again presumably to meet military expenditures. Throughout the duration of the fourth century, the city relied upon a group of Sicilian Punic mints (including Panormus and, probably, Lilybaeum) for the production of currency; in the early third century BC, two minting authorities, identified by Punic legends as 'the people of the army' and 'the financial controllers', are attested. The city's late entry into the sphere of coinage has been interpreted as a sign that its commercial orientation continued to be focused on underdeveloped regions in the western Mediterranean and Atlantic coastal region, where commercial barter was practised.

As with the western Phoenician cities, the iconography of the Siculo-Punic silver series was, to a large extent, modelled on the earlier Greek coinage of Syracuse. A recurrent obverse and reverse type is the classicizing head of the Syracusan nymph Arethusa surrounded by dolphins. (See fig. 30 c.) (Several issues also bear another prominent Syracusan coin type: a four-horse chariot surmounted by the flying figure of Nike, the winged goddess of victory.) Another ubiquitous image, featured on the reverse, is the horse (see fig. 30 b, c, d); represented head-and-neck or full figure, it appears in standing, walking, or galloping pose before a palm tree. All three motifs – goddess head, horse, and palm – formed the numismatic trademarks of the coinage produced by the metropolitan mint. The palm, which is featured alone as reverse image on Carthage's first silver issue (see fig. 30 a) and, later, on smaller gold and electrum denominations minted by the city, may be understood as a universal symbol of 'Phoenician' and 'Punic' civic identity. (The modern term actually derives from the Greek word *phoinix*, meaning 'palm tree'.) After *c*.390 BC, the minting of silver coinage at Carthage may have been discontinued for a period of more than 100 years – until shortly before the beginning of the First Punic War (264–241 BC). It may well be that the city had reached a state of financial exhaustion following its

30 *Punic coins:*
(a) Carthaginian, 410 BC. *Obv. Nike with wreath above forepart of horse. Rev. palm tree.*
(b) Carthaginian, c. 325 BC. *Obv. Head of Arethusa/Kore. Rev. Horse galloping before palm.*
(c) Siculo-Punic tetradrachm, c. 315 BC. *Obv. Head of Arethus. Rev. Horse head and palm tree.*
(d) Carthaginian gold stater, c. 320–310 BC. *Head of goddess. Rev. Standing horse.*

protracted war efforts in Sicily in the early fourth century BC. Such circumstances may have underlayed Carthage's decision, some time before *c.*350 BC, to begin minting bronze coinage on a Greek model.[40] The economic importance of this new system of small bronze units and fractions can be seen in its widespread circulation, not only in the Carthaginian homeland but across the Punic empire, pointing to the emergence of a monetary economy at Carthage and its overseas territories.

It was not until the second half of the fourth century BC that Carthage itself began minting currency, including fractional denominations, on a regular basis. The city's first substantial issue in precious metal was a series of gold (and, later, electrum) staters and fractions minted on the Phoenician weight standard. The remarkable size of the gold issue finds dramatic illustration in the number of dies (88 obverse and 104 reverse) attested over a 10-year period – between 320 and 310 BC; the issue was probably motivated by an increase in military expenditures at a time of renewed conflict with Syracuse.

The coin types adopted for the Carthaginian gold and electrum series remain standard throughout: the diademed head of a goddess (obverse) and a standing, walking, or galloping horse (reverse). (See fig. 30 d.) The meaning of both types, which, as already noted, predominate in the Siculo-Punic series, is unclear. The diademed female head, which derives stylistically from the image of Arethusa on Syracusan coinage, is clearly meant to depict a deity. Possibilities include Tanit, tutelary goddess of Carthage, and Kore, daughter of the Greek grain goddess Demeter, whose worship was adopted at Carthage in 396 BC. The horse represents even more of an enigma. Is it a nationalistic emblem (of greater Libya) or, perhaps, a symbol of one of Carthage's two primary deities: Baal Hamon or Tanit? Or is it an allusion to the horse's head uncovered by Carthage's Tyrian colonists, according to the city's foundation myth? No one can say for sure.

In the early third century BC, following the conclusion of war against the Syracusan tyrant Agathocles, the city introduced a new series of bronze coins of larger format and heavier weight, which achieved a wide circulation throughout the Carthaginian empire. The central minting source appears to have been Sardinia, the last of Carthage's central Mediterranean holdings to adopt the use of coinage. The Sardinian mint continued in operation throughout the third century, until the Roman conquest of the island in 238 BC.

Chapter Four

LANGUAGE AND LITERATURE

Phoenician language and literature

PHOENICIAN BELONGS to a family of languages known as North-west Semitic, which is customarily subdivided into two groups, Canaanite and Aramaic. Phoenician is a member of the Canaanite group, to which Hebrew and the various languages of Transjordan (Ammonite, Moabite, and Edomite) belong. Linguistically, it may be divided into two main phases: an archaic (tenth to seventh centuries BC) and a classical one (sixth to first centuries BC). The classical phase may be further subdivided into Middle (sixth to fourth centuries BC) and Late Phoenician (third to first centuries BC). (The latter subdivision falls beyond the scope of this study.)

At its height, the Phoenician tongue enjoyed a widespread diffusion within its homeland: the Levantine coast from the region of Dor in northern Israel up to the former territory of Ugarit in north Syria. Through trade and cultural influence, its usage spread far beyond such limits – to the Nile Delta and Upper Egypt, to southern Anatolia (Cilicia and Cappadocia), and westward to the Aegean.

Following its overseas expansion, the language passed, through colonial settlement, to Cyprus and to the areas further west in the Mediterranean: North Africa, Malta, Sicily, Sardinia, and southern Spain. The name *Punic* describes the phase of language and type of script developed in Carthage and its colonial possessions, beginning in the sixth century.

The Phoenician tongue's prominent occurrence in monumental royal inscriptions from southern Anatolia underscores the early prestige that it enjoyed as a language of diplomacy. (See fig. 31.) The symbiosis of Phoenician with other languages, in fact, finds reflection in the relatively large number of extant bilingual inscriptions (in Hittite, Greek, Cypriot, and, later, Latin).

In many respects, Phoenician was the most developed of languages in the North-west Semitic Canaanite group. In contrast to Hebrew and the Transjordanian tongues, which were somewhat isolated geographically, it evolved rapidly as a language, undergoing many innovations in grammatical development, especially in the area of phonology. Phoenician innovation may be seen clearly in the number of vowel and consonantal shifts that it experienced, such as the contraction of diphthongs (*ay* to *ē* and *a*; *aw* to *ō* and *ū*).

With respect to orthography or spelling, on the other hand, the Phoenician language was quite conservative in its development. In contrast to Aramaic, its writing system was strictly consonantal: it employed no vowel letters. The nature of its vocalization is only

31 *Phoenician inscription of Kilamuwa, king of Sam'al. From Zinçirli, Turkey, c. 825 BC.*

partially understood; what little is known may be gleaned from Akkadian and later Punic and classical texts.[1] Its script, too, evolved slowly, as tenth-century royal texts from Byblos and subsequent inscriptions from the early colonies reveal. (See fig. 4.) The letter-forms themselves underwent a minimum of change, retaining their compact and upright posture (although, beginning in the late tenth century, the letter stems exhibit a general tendency to elongate).[2]

As may be expected in a language so long-lived and widely diffused, the Phoenician tongue is marked by dialectical differences on both a diachronic and a geographic level. Such dialects may be isolated early on in the region of Byblos and, to a lesser extent, on Cyprus and in northern Syria and southern Anatolia. The Byblian dialect tends to be more archaizing compared with the others. Elsewhere, both in the colonies and in the homeland (especially at Sidon and Tyre), a homogeneous language known as Standard Phoenician was employed. As one would expect, the dialect of Tyre and Sidon is the dominant linguistic form attested abroad, reflecting the region's primary role in westward expansion. In their use of formal and cursive features, the Byblian, Cypriot, and Sidonian dialects also exhibit regional peculiarities in the style of their script.[3]

The legacy of Phoenician as a language has been clouded by the almost complete loss of a literary record. Of the various Phoenician and Punic compositions alluded to by the ancient classical authors, not a single work or even a fragment has survived in its original idiom. An explanation may be sought in the dramatic transformation in writing medium that accompanied the introduction of the cursive alphabetic script. Perishable materials such as wood, ivory, papyrus, and parchment now replaced the durable baked clay medium of the cuneiform tradition. Very few have survived the humid environment of the coastal Levant; a few papyrus fragments from Egypt alone testify to the large corpus of texts in that material which once existed. (See fig. 2.)

Nevertheless, as the classical sources reveal, a wide range of Phoenician works – on subjects ranging from history and law to religion and philosophy – did once exist. The references, by and large, are Roman in date and refer primarily to Carthage and its later literary tradition. The Phoenician cities in the east, however, also possessed extensive archives of an historical and economic nature that were housed and maintained by the palaces and temples. In the Report of Wenamun, King Zakarbaal of Byblos consults such ancestral records, written upon papyrus scrolls; Zakarbaal's order from the Egyptian agent, in fact, included five hundred rolls of this writing material. Tyre, too, possessed extensive and very ancient archives; the historian Menander of Ephesus claims to have translated them into Greek.

Unfortunately, the surviving Phoenician texts consist largely of commemorative, votive, and funerary dedications recorded on stelae, statues, and sarcophagi. (See the frontispiece and figs 3, 33, 34, 35, 37, 41 and 71, and plate V.) While a handful of royal inscriptions from Byblos and Sidon are of historical importance (see figs 31 and 34), the great majority of extant documents are brief, stereotyped and formulaic in nature; as such, they are of interest primarily for the study of personal names and their ethnic affiliations. Other inscriptions – markings on ostraca (inscribed potsherds), seals, and vessels (see figs 36 and 70) – record little more than owners' names and contents. In total, the entire Phoenician corpus from the eastern mainland and colonies (excluding Carthage and its environs) numbers only several hundred texts.

The origin and development of the Phoenician alphabet

There is general agreement among scholars that that the modern linear alphabet arose somewhere in the Levant during the second millennium BC. The precise date and point of origin, however, remain highly debated. Where in the Syro-Palestinian realm did the alphabet originate and how was it transmitted to the Phoenicians?

The modern story begins in the early twentieth century with the discovery of a series of pictographic inscriptions at Serabit el-Khadem, an Egyptian mining community of the Middle and early New Kingdoms in the Sinai peninsula. Study undertaken on this 'proto-Sinaitic' script, which probably dates to the Middle Kingdom (see note on page 114) and is attested by roughly twenty-five texts uncovered at the site, has led to some interesting conclusions. The individual pictographs each marked a discrete sound, the phonetic value of which appears to have been determined by the initial value of the Semitic word represented, according to the acrophonic principle. (The picture of a house, for example, denoted the letter 'b' – from the Semitic word (*bayt*) for 'house'.) Proto-Sinaitic's pictographic character, combined with the use of the acrophonic principle, suggeststhat it may have been inspired by Egyptian writing recorded on hieroglyphic stelae at the site.

While attempts at decipherment of the script have proved only partly successful, enough of the individual signs have been identified to support the conclusion that the proto-Sinaitic inscriptions represent a rudimentary form of alphabetic writing, in use by the early centuries of the second millenium BC. Scattered inscriptions of a similar character subsequently found in the Palestinian realm have complemented the picture and offer evidence for the perpetuation and development of such pictographic alphabetic writing down into the twelfth century BC. Like their Sinaitic counterparts, these 'proto-Canaanite' inscriptions were initially written both vertically and horizontally (the latter in either direction: right-to-left or left-to-right); through time the horizontal orientation prevailed. The characters themselves were gradually simplified and abstracted, setting the stage for the emergence of the Phoenician linear alphabetic script at the close of the second millennium BC.[4]

Around the mid-fourteenth century or shortly before, the Canaanite linear alphabet was adapted to the prevailing cuneiform writing system at Ugarit in north Syria. Spelling-books of the period reveal that the order of its characters, originally totalling thirty in number, corresponded roughly with that of the later Phoenician system. In the course of the succeeding centuries, the Canaanite linear alphabet underwent a process of simplification, leading ultimately to a reduced system of twenty-two characters or graphemes. The latter formed the direct antecedent of the Phoenician alphabet of the late eleventh century BC.

At Byblos itself, a pseudo-hieroglyphic syllabic writing system of about one hundred and twenty signs was employed in the second millennium. Its exact chronology remains unclear. While an early dating in the eighteenth or seventeenth century BC has long been proposed, there are indications that its use may have developed, or at least persisted, in the second half of the second millenium, perhaps right up until the adoption of the alphabet.[5] Despite several efforts, the Byblian pseudo-hieroglyphic script remains undeciphered.[6]

The spread of the Phoenician alphabet

With its twenty-two consonants, the Phoenician alphabet is well documented on early Byblian monuments, such as the sarcophagus of Ahiram. (See figs 3 and 32, and plate V.) Already by this time, the stance and form of its letters had become fixed. So, too, had the horizontal direction of its script, which read uniformly in sinistrograde fashion (i.e. from right to left). In the early Byblian texts, words within sentences were delineated by short vertical strokes; in later Phoenician and Punic texts, however, the words were presented in unbroken sequence, often dividing arbitrarily at the end of lines.

As the inscriptional evidence reveals, the Phoenician alphabet spread quickly beyond the borders of the homeland. By the ninth century, it had been adopted by a variety of neighbouring tongues, including Aramaic, Hebrew, Ammonite, Moabite, and Edomite. In each of these languages, the alphabet soon evolved along its own lines; a clear distinction from the Phoenician may be seen in the use of certain letters (*'aleph*, *waw*, *yod*) to denote vowel sounds. The Phoenician script itself, as previously stated, remained unvocalized.

Phoenician commercial expansion abroad within the Mediterranean led to the export of the alphabet – at first to Cyprus and the Aegean (Crete), by 900 BC (see figs 36 and 70), and a century later, to the western Mediterranean (Sardinia and southern Spain) (see figs 41 and 71). Its impact was most clearly felt in the Aegean realm. As ancient classical tradition underscores,[7] the Phoenicians were responsible for the introduction and adoption of the Greek alphabet, a fact confirmed by the names, shapes, values, and order of the letters attested in early Greek scripts.

As for the date of the Greek alphabet's adoption, past estimates have ranged from the mid-second millennium to the eighth century BC.[8] An initial date of around 800 BC, or perhaps slightly earlier, may be reasonably postulated for its emergence, based upon correspondences in letter form between the early Greek scripts and the Phoenician mother tongue. Greek alphabetic writing is attested early on in the form of graffiti on pottery sherds; the earliest date to the second quarter of the eighth century.

Regarding the process, it was probably the product of a direct exchange between two individuals – a Greek recipient and a literate or semi-literate Phoenician (priest, scribe, merchant, or artisan). The innovative use of vowels by the Greek initiator (using 'left-over' Phoenician signs such as *'aleph*, *he*, and *'ayin* which had no consonantal equivalent in ancient Greek) lends support to this assumption.

As for the place of transmission, a variety of locations present themselves, ranging from the Greek mainland and Euboea to Crete, Rhodes, western Asia Minor, Cyprus, and the Levant; all are sites of direct interchange between Greeks and easterners. According to Herodotus,[9] the alphabet was imported to the Boeotian city of Thebes by the legendary Phoenician Kadmos. The Euboeans have been recently proposed as transmittors. As archaeology has shown, the island was an early and active recipient of eastern trade; the Euboeans themselves may be linked commercially with both Al Mina and Pithekoussai, both find-sites (along with Euboea itself) of early Greek alphabetic graffiti. However, other scenarios are equally possible.[10]

32 (right) *Chart of the Phoenician alphabet.*

	Ahirom c.1000 BC	Bronze plaque tenth century BC	Spearhead tenth century BC	Yehimilk c. 950 BC	Abibaal c. 925 BC	Elibaal late tenth century BC	Shipitbaal I and Abdo c. 900 BC	Ancient Cypriot inscription early ninth century BC	Nora ninth century BC	Kilamuwa I and II c. 825 BC	Limassol eighth century BC	Karatepe eighth century BC	Casket from Ur seventh century BC.	Hassanbeyli seventh century BC	Abu-Simbel c. 590 BC	Abydus c. fourth century BC	Yehawmilk c. fifth-fourth century BC
ʾ																	
b																	
g																	
d																	
h																	
w																	
z																	
ḥ																	
ṭ																	
j																	
k																	
l																	
m																	
n																	
s																	
ʿ																	
p																	
ṣ																	
q																	
r																	
š																	
t																	

Punic language and literature

The Phoenician language utilized in Carthage and North Africa evolved independently to the point that a distinct dialect had evolved by the sixth century BC. Under Carthaginian influence, Punic usage spread widely in northern Tunisia, the Carthaginian heartland. Elsewhere, until the final years of the empire, the spread of Punic dialect in North Africa was largely restricted to the Carthaginian emporia along the Libyan, Algerian, and Moroccan coasts. Under the influence of its mother-city, Punic usage became standard in other regions of the Carthaginian empire – in Sicily, Sardinia, Malta, the Balearics, and southern Spain.

Over time, differences arose between Punic and its mother tongue. For example, the language began to incorporate signs representing vowel sounds in its alphabet by at least the fourth century BC – much earlier time than the mainland. It is within the development of the script itself, however, that the Punic variant, with its elegant cursive style and elongated vertical stroke, is most easily identified. In its interplay of cursive and formal features, the Punic dialect relates more closely to the antecedent local scripts of Byblos and Cyprus than to the southern Phoenician mainland (the region of Tyre and Sidon).[11]

The study of the evolution of Punic is complicated by the paucity of data from the early period (eighth to fifth centuries BC). With a few notable exceptions, the textual record at Carthage (which totals well over six thousand inscriptions) begins effectively in the fourth century BC. As in the east, the inscriptions – on votive and commemorative stelae – are brief and formulaic in nature (see fig. 45). A handful of more elaborate inscriptions (relating to temple construction and the administration of sacrificial taxes) do, however, provide a glimpse at the evolved literary tradition which held sway in the city.[12] Indeed, from at least the fourth century BC, the literacy level at Carthage must have been quite high, judging from the number of surviving private commemorative stelae.

Little record survives of the many books that filled the city's libraries at the time of Carthage's destruction in 146 BC. Classical references attest to the existence of Punic historical works; from the Greek author Plutarch we learn of the 'sacred books' in Punic safeguarded by the city's temples. Few Punic texts survive, however; none in the original. The *Periplus* of Hanno, the Carthaginian navigator's account of his famous African voyage, survives in a late Greek version, while the *Poenulus* of Plautus includes actual passages in Punic rendered into Latin. Given the close interplay between Carthage and the Greek and later Roman realms, it is regrettable that more original works in Punic have not survived in classical translation.

NOTE

Similar rock-cut inscriptions, at least as early as the proto-Sinaitic texts, have recently been found at Wadi el-Hol in the desert north of Thebes; for their discovery, see John and Deborah Darnell in University of Chicago Oriental Institute *Annual Report*, 1994-1995; and J.N. Wilford, *NY. Times*, 14 November 1999, 1,10. New information became public as this book was going to press.

Chapter Five

RELIGION

Phoenician religion

THE PANTHEON

AS ONE WOULD EXPECT over a long history, the Phoenicians underwent a marked evolution in religious practice. As a growing body of evidence suggests, however, the entire period (including the transition from the Late Bronze to the Early Iron Age) was characterized by relative continuity rather than abrupt or dramatic change. Much has been written in recent years about the revolutionary changes that transformed Phoenician religion at the beginning of the first millennium BC. While change clearly occurred, especially at Tyre under Hiram I, it should be understood as a modification of existing practice rather than as outright innovation. Hiram did not, in fact, introduce the cult of Melqart at Tyre, but promoted and institutionalized it. As Herodotus (who purports to have spoken directly with the Tyrian clergy) records, the cult was an ancient one, dating back to the city's origins in the third millennium BC.[1] In fact, as Josephus relates, all three of Tyre's main sanctuaries were well-established in Hiram's own day. Of the temples to Melqart and Astarte, we are informed that the Tyrian monarch simply rebuilt or enlarged them, supplying newly cut cedar for their roofs.[2] Although the name Melqart is not attested before the first millennium BC, there is compelling reason to believe that the god's dynastic cult existed at Tyre long before. The incorporation of the divine element *mlk* in fourteenth-century Tyrian royal titulature strongly suggests this.[3] As with the public institution of an annual celebration of Melqart's 'awakening', Hiram aimed at elevating the city god's cult as an instrument of state policy.[4]

Elsewhere in Phoenicia, the overall picture in the first millennium is one of continuity. At Byblos, the cult of Baalat Gubal ('Lady of Byblos'), attested since the period of the Egyptian Old Kingdom, persists. Baalat's consort Baal Shamem ('Lord of the Heavens'), documented in the tenth-century royal inscription of Yehimilk, is already well known from Egyptian texts of the New Kingdom; he is mentioned in Amarna correspondence from both Byblos and Tyre.[5] Baal Shamem may, in fact, be equated with the Bronze Age Semitic storm deity Haddu, attested at Ugarit and Byblos in the second millennium BC.[6]

Astarte and Eshmun, Sidon's chief deities, have roots extending back into the second millennium BC; both occur in ritual texts from Ugarit. The two appear together in a North-west Semitic incantation from an Egyptian medical papyrus of the fourteenth century BC; as has been suggested, its context may originally have been Sidonian.[7] Astarte's Ugaritic associations may also be seen in the epithet *ḥr* found on a seventh-century

Phoenician bronze statuette from El Carambolo near Seville (see fig. 41).[8]

Yet other deities, well attested in a Late Bronze Age Ugaritic context, maintain a presence in the succeeding Iron Age. The god El, the supreme being and father of the gods in Ugaritic mythology, appears in an eighth-century Phoenician inscription from Karatepe and perhaps also in the seventh-century treaty between Esarhaddon and Baal I of Tyre.[9] Baal Saphon, whose worship was widespread in the second millennium BC, is later attested at Tyre and Carthage.[10] Venerable Reshef reappears in the Karatepe inscriptions and, later on, at Sidon and in Cyprus, where his worship appears to have enjoyed widespread popularity. (See fig. 33.) His attestation at Kition, *Ršp ḥṣ* ('Reshef of the Arrow'), finds an antecedent in Late Bronze Ugarit; the Semitic god Shed, too, is attested in the late second millennium.[11] As has been suggested, the Byblian goddess Baalat may be equated with the Ugaritic Anat, consort of Baal.[12] It was at Byblos, in the Late Bronze Age, that the Egyptian cults of Osiris, Isis, and Amen, well documented within Iron Age Phoenicia, were apparently first introduced.[13] The Late Bronze Age religious tradition within Phoenicia thus shares much in common with that of the later Iron Age.[14]

Such evidence for continuity notwithstanding, the city cults of the Phoenician Iron Age reveal a strong autonomous development. During this time, the gods Melqart, Eshmun, and Astarte, in particular, assume new and increased importance and emphasis, as the presence of divine elements in personal names, such as Germelqart ('client of Melqart') and Abdashtart ('servant of Astarte'), suggests. The cults of all three divinities enjoyed enormous growth and diffusion at this time. At the start of the first millennium, Baal Shamem, too, re-emerged as a vital, independent deity. The cultic development of these divinities in the Iron Age may be understood as a reflection of the growing autonomy of the various independent city centres which promoted their worship.

Scholarship in recent years has led to a reinterpretation of the nature of the Phoenician Iron Age religious pantheon. As was formerly maintained, each city was governed by a family triad, consisting of a mother- and father-deity and their male offspring, a young god of vegetation, whose death and rebirth marked the annual agricultural cycle. This notion has now been dispelled in favour of the model of a dual city hierarchy composed of a supreme male and female deity – a Baal and Baalat. This divine coupling is attested at each of the three major Phoenician centres: Melqart and Astarte at Tyre; Eshmun and Astarte at Sidon; and Baal and Baalat at Byblos.

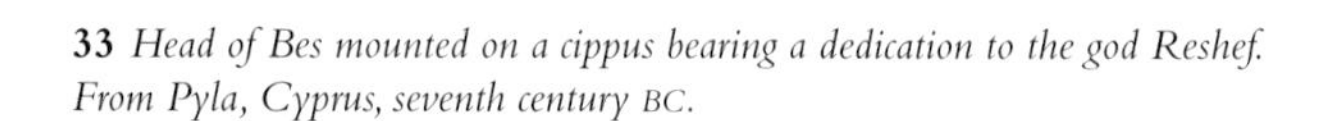

33 *Head of Bes mounted on a cippus bearing a dedication to the god Reshef. From Pyla, Cyprus, seventh century BC.*

In each instance, the chief male deity is associated with the notion of death and rebirth. Josephus records that King Hiram of Tyre instituted the public celebration of Melqart's 'awakening', a spring ritual reenacting the resurrection of the god following his death and ritual cremation. A similar enactment took place at Byblos; the Greek author Lucian describes an annual celebration commemorating the god Adonis.[15] According to Greek mythology, the young hunter, victimized by a wild boar, was compelled to divide the year between the world of the living and the dead. The figure of Adonis (whose name is derived from Semitic *'adōn*, 'lord', or *adōnai*, 'my lord') may be equated with the Byblian Baal, whose cultic memory is preserved in the names of numerous Byblian kings (e.g. Abibaal, Elibaal, Shipitbaal).[16] The Sidonian god Eshmun was equally venerated as a dying and rising divinity. In each case, particularly that of Tyrian Melqart, the goddess (i.e. Astarte) may have played a role in the god's resurrection, perhaps through the enactment of a 'sacred marriage' (involving the king and either the queen or a priestess) similar to that celebrated in the Mesopotamian Akitu festival marking the New Year; the absence of documentation for this rite in Phoenicia proper precludes any firm judgement.

Unfortunately, the varying traditions associated with Phoenician deities are, on the whole, poorly understood. Their godly titles are often generic and draw their identity only by association with a specific city or locale. The chief male deity at Byblos, for example, is known simply by his title Baal (Phoenician for 'lord' or 'master'). As with other aspects of Phoenician civilization, an understanding of Phoenician religion is severely hampered by the limited nature of the available sources, which consist primarily of the Hebrew bible and various classical and early Christian writers; all of them present limited and often biased perspectives.

Baal's consort at Byblos is referred to in the texts simply as Baalat Gubal ('Mistress of Byblos'); her personal name remains unknown. Baalat's pre-eminence is manifest in the many surviving royal inscriptions dedicated to her, which underscore her status as patron and protectress of the reigning dynasty. (See fig. 34.) Equated by the Egyptians with the goddess Hathor, her Phoenician identity, which remains unclear, appears distinct from that of the

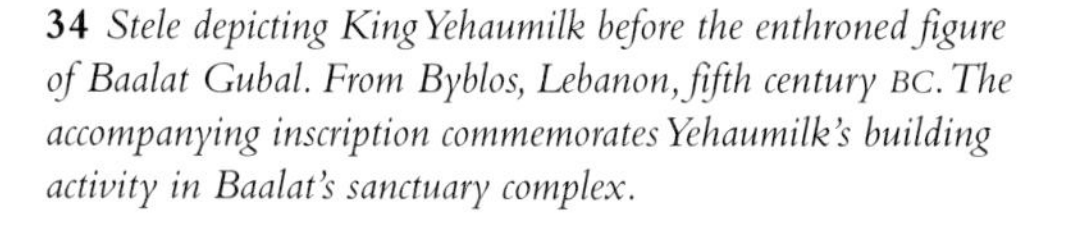

34 *Stele depicting King Yehaumilk before the enthroned figure of Baalat Gubal. From Byblos, Lebanon, fifth century* BC. *The accompanying inscription commemorates Yehaumilk's building activity in Baalat's sanctuary complex.*

goddess Astarte venerated at Tyre and Sidon. Baalat's maternal and fertility functions are attested by her later association with the Greek goddess Aphrodite.

The chief god of Sidon was Eshmun, a local variant of Baal. As his name reveals (the root *šmn* means 'oil'), Eshmun was revered in Sidon as a god of healing. His extramural sanctuary at Bostan esh-Sheikh is closely associated with the Yidlal spring and its beneficial waters. Later associated by the Greeks with Aesklepios, god of medicine, Eshmun's widespread popularity is manifest in the diffusion of his cult to Tyre and Arwad. The primary goddess of Sidon was Astarte, a multi-faceted deity whose functions included that of dynastic patron, celestial and marine deity, and goddess of fecundity. Astarte's close association with Eshmun is manifest in her epithet *šm bʿl* ('name of Baal'); twin or adjacent temples to the two divinities were erected by King Eshmunazar in the city proper.

Astarte was equally venerated as chief goddess at Tyre, where she appears paired with Melqart, the Tyrian Baal. Her aggressive, warrior aspect is clear from her citation in the seventh-century treaty agreement between Tyre and Assyria, where she is called upon to smash the bows of potential violators.[17] According to Josephus, the goddess's temple already stood in the tenth century, when Hiram elected to rebuild it along with that of Melqart. A similar pairing is attested archaeologically at neighbouring Umm el-Amed to the south, where twin sanctuaries were apparently erected to Astarte and Milkashtart (a local manifestation of Astarte and Melqart) in the Hellenistic period. The middle years of the first millennium, in fact, saw the emergence and diffusion of numerous cults devoted to deities with compound names (Eshmun-Melqart, Milkashtart, Shed-Horon, Reshef-Shed). The discovery at Sarepta of an inscribed ivory plaque dedicated to Tanit-Astarte testifies to the close association between these two deities, affirming the mainland origin of the former goddess, whose cult achieved enormous popularity at Carthage and the Punic west, beginning in the fifth century BC. (See figs 35, 45 and 48.)

The primary male deity at Tyre was Melqart, whose name (*Milk-qart*, 'King of the City') reveals his primary function as the city's dynastic deity. Melqart appears to have been the divinized personification, or hypostasis, of the ideal Phoenician king; as such, he was regarded as the archetypal founder of the city and the protector of its far-flung colonial interests. In this connection, he played an integral role in the foundation of Tyre's primary western colonies (Kition, Carthage, and Cadiz). Like Astarte, Melqart's persona has been broadly interpreted, his divine characteristics encompassing aspects of agricultural, maritime, civic, dynastic, and even netherworld activity. Such functional flexibility may indeed have characterized many of Phoenicia's primary deities during an era when divine power appears to have been concentrated increasingly in a narrowing pantheon of deities.

The many textual references to the regional manifestations of Baal underscore his character both as supreme storm deity and as functional head of the Phoenician hierarchy. Epigraphically, he rarely appears without an epithet (i.e. Marqod, Malagê, Addir ('Mighty')) or toponymic qualifier (e.g. Baal Sidon). As one would expect, many local manifestations of Baal are associated with sacred high places and promontories, such as the Amanus range (Hamon (*ḥmn*)), Mount Saphon-Casius (Saphon (*ṣpn*)), the Lebanon range

(Lebanon (*lbnn*)), and Mounts Hermon, Tabor, and Carmel. Most prominently, Baal appears in various manifestations as a storm deity (such as Baal Saphon and Baal Shamem). Mount Saphon (modern Djebel el-Aqra in northern Syria) formed the locus for the storm god's domain; in Ugaritic mythology, Baal had already established his palatial residence there. This mountain, which dominates the Syrian coast at a peak altitude of over 1700 metres (5600 feet), clearly served as a navigational landmark, as did Mount Carmel and the promontory of Ras en-Naqura (probable location of Baal Rôsh (*r'š*), 'Lord of the Cape') south of Tyre. As storm deities, Baal Shamem and Baal Saphon posed threats to coastal navigation; in the maritime treaty between Tyre and Assyria both are invoked as sources capable of shipwrecking potential violators: 'May [they] let loose an evil wind on your ships, tear their riggings, and carry away their masts.'[18]

Cosmogony

There is little direct evidence for the Phoenicians' own view of the world's origins. The only extant source is a Roman-period account by Philo of Byblos (preserved in excerpts by the fourth-century church father Eusebius of Casearea), which records a series of cosmogonies purportedly drawn from the writings of Sanchuniathon, an ancient Phoenician priest from Beirut.[19] While much of Philo's account is heavily corrupted by inferences from Greek mythology, some of the basic elements appear verified by parallels in mythological texts from Late Bronze Age Ugarit. In Philo's divine genealogy, the gods El (Cronos) and Dagon (Greek Siton, 'grain') figure prominently; both are well attested in the Ugaritic literature. In the god-lists from Ugarit, El (Semitic for 'god') is styled 'father of humankind'. His role as creator-god is further confirmed by the phrase *'l qn 'rṣ* ('El, creator of the earth') preserved in an eighth-century Phoenician inscription from Cilicia.[20] The cult of Dagon, too, is attested in the Phoenician realm.[21] According to Philo's account of the world's origins, the universe originated from primordial chaos; a dark and windy gas spurred the creation process, which emanated from a mud or slime called Mot. In Philo's account of the origins of culture, the craftsman god Chusor (Ugaritic Kothar ('the skilled one')) is credited with the invention of iron technology, a fitting achievement for a Phoenician divine entrepreneur.

Cultic practices

The cultic calendars of the various Phoenician cities were governed by a prescribed series of feasts and celebrations that revolved around the agricultural cycle. Sacrifices were offered in celebration of the New Year and the advent of ploughing and harvesting; as various texts suggest, solar and lunar worship played a prominent role in the Phoenician calendar, which was calculated on observation of the new moon. Integral to the cycle was the spring awakening or resurrection of various vegetation deities, such as Melqart of Tyre or Eshmun of Sidon. In the Tyrian Melqart festival (which took place in February/March), the god was burned in effigy on a ritual pyre, and later resurrected through a ritual marriage with his spouse, Astarte. The ritual celebrated not only the cyclical rebirth of nature but the restoration of the cosmic order over which Melqart and the Tyrian king ruled.

A central element of Phoenician cult was the *marzeḥ* (Punic *mrzḥ*, 'place of reunion'), a religious association centred on a particular god or temple complex. The institution, which regularly celebrated religious feasts or funerary banquets, was of great antiquity; the term appears in Late Bronze Age texts from Ugarit to denote ritual meals held in honour of deified ancestors, or *rephaim*. The Phoenician *marzeḥ* (the term denotes both the religious body and the festival) appears to have been an élite societal grouping. Like its Greek counterpart, the *thiasos*, its celebrations, which involved memorial offerings and sacrifices, were marked by heavy drinking; its earliest reference from the mainland may, in fact, be found on a bronze wine cup.[22]

Sacred prostitution formed another long-established Phoenician institution, associated particularly with the cult of Astarte.[23] A fifth-century inscription from Kition on Cyprus lists both male and female prostitutes among Astarte's temple personnel. The Greek historian Herodotus alludes to the Cypriot practice, in which native women proffered themselves in fulfilment of a religious vow or obligation.[24] The custom (which presumably involved young, unmarried virgins) may well have characterized Cypriot Astarte's cult at Kition, Amathus, and Paphos. The literary evidence for ritual prostitution on the Phoenician mainland, although dating to the Roman period, is equally compelling; its very prominence at Astarte cults at Byblos, Heliopolis/Baalbek, and Afqa argues strongly for its priority in the homeland.

As inscriptions attest, public worship in urban sanctuaries was administered by professional clergy. At the head of the religious hierarchy stood the chief priest or priestess, who presided over the city's cultic affairs. As the evidence at Byblos and Sidon suggests, these positions were closely linked with the royal house; during the Persian period at least, the king himself or a member of his immediate family (including the queen mother) often served as priest(ess) of the reigning deity: Baalat Gubal at Byblos, Astarte at Sidon. In general, the priesthood appears to have been an hereditary institution drawn from the ranks of the city aristocracy. On Hellenistic-period stelae from Umm el-Amed, members of the male priestly class appear barefoot and clean-shaven, dressed in a turban-like bonnet and a long, pleated linen tunic with wide sleeves; a folded stole of thin cloth, a priestly attribute, is suspended from the left shoulder. (See fig. 35.) According to the Latin author Silius Italicus, the priests of the Temple of Melqart at Gades (Cadiz) wore white vestments, shaved their heads, and practised sexual abstinence.[25]

An inscription from the sanctuary of Astarte at Kition offers a unique insight into the variety of personnel employed in the service of a Phoenician temple. The list includes scribes, choristers, butchers, bakers, barbers, servants, a 'water master', and a 'sacrificer'. A pottery bowl from the sanctuary reveals the importance of the ritual cutting of hair; its inscription, engraved by a man named Moula from the neighbouring town of Tamassos, records how he had shaved his head in worship of the goddess, who 'listened to his prayer'. In gratitude, he presented the bowl, filled with his hair, as a votive thank-offering

35 *Limestone stele depicting priestly figure, from Umm el-Amed, Lebanon, fourth–third century BC.*

on his own behalf and that of his family.[26] (See fig. 36.)

The office of 'sacrificer' on the Kition inventory presents a tantalizing reference to an important, but poorly documented, facet of Phoenician ritual. Contemporary parallels from the Old Testament suggest that the offering of blood and burnt sacrifices must have been a common practice among Phoenician worshippers. The remains of carbonized bones recovered from the ashes of altars at the Kition temple complex attest to the ritual sacrifice of lambs and sheep; both animals were offered to Astarte by Moula.[27] As other texts attest, the sacrifice and consumption of pig was taboo.

Unfortunately, little survives of the Phoenician liturgy apart from a few formulaic expressions: 'may [the divinity] bless you', 'may he hear your voice'. In marked contrast to Ugarit and the Mesopotamian realm, there are no surviving hymns, prayers, or oracles that shed light on the ceremonies of worship. The absence of written texts forces a greater reliance upon the study of votive scenes for a reconstruction of Phoenician cultic practice. Illustrated seals and dedicatory stelae depict the worshipper in varying gestures of prayer – with the right hand raised to the level of the mouth, with both hands uplifted, or with hands clasped at the waist. Phoenician metal bowls and ivories depict female cultic dancers and musicians in votive procession before an enthroned divinity or priestess; the latter appears, with lotus flower, pomegranate, or shallow bowl in hand, before a tripodic altar or offering table.[28] The members of the musical ensemble traditionally play a double-pipe, lyre, and tambourine; the last is often held by female votaries in terracotta. As in ancient Egypt, singing or chanting accompanied such ritual enactment;

36 *Red-slip pottery bowl with thank-offering of hair to the goddess Astarte, from the Great Temple at Kition, Cyprus, ninth century BC.*

cultic singers (*šrm*) appear in the Kition temple account. The wearing of ritual masks may also have played an important role in processional rites.[29]

As dedications and pictorial reliefs reveal, oblations in the form of incense, perfume, milk, oil, wine, honey, fruit, cakes, and bread were regularly dedicated as thank-offerings to the divinity. Shallow bowls (*phialai*) were frequently used in acts of libation; according to classical sources, they were ritually thrown into cultic pools or basins. A Phoenician silver bowl from Etrurian Caere depicts a scene of ritual libation involving a procession of female *hydrophoroi*, or water bearers, dressed in diaphanous gowns.[30] As pictorial scenes reveal, the offering and burning of incense was considered a major act of piety by the Phoenicians; the petalled candelabrum or incense stand itself may have functioned as a symbol of divine presence.[31] (See fig. 62 f, h.)

Other forms of aniconic (non-figural) symbol marked the site or presence of the divinity in the Phoenician realm. One such was the *asherah*,[32] a small votive column or post of wood meant to evoke the sacred groves or wooded temple precincts of the same name that adjoined Phoenician fertility cults, such as that of Astarte at Afqa. More widely attested in ancient art and literature were the monolithic standing stones dressed in the form of a cone or tapering pillar, known as betyls. Their Semitic name, which means 'home of the god', clearly explains their function – as symbols marking the presence and locus of the divinity; as such, they stood in the centre of the sanctuary proper before the altar or offering table.

The betyl, or *maṣṣebah* (*mṣbh*, 'dressed stone') as it is otherwise called in the Old Testament, stood singly or in groups of two or three, the whole set directly into the ground or elevated upon a stone socle. (See fig. 37.) Excavations at the eighth-century shrine at Sarepta have revealed the actual emplacement of a betyl, set before an altar at the sanctuary's western end. (See fig. 38.) Recent archaeological work at Kommos on Crete has uncovered a triadic installation of such standing stones intact within its temple setting.[33] Actual betyls, measuring up to 1.5 metres (5 feet) in height, have been found at various western Phoenician sites, including Motya and Mogador.[34] The classical sources document the perseverance of Phoenician betyl worship, which lasted well into Roman times. Two famous settings – that of Byblos (Temple of Baalat Gubal) and Paphos (Astarte sanctuary) – occur on imperial coinage (see fig. 29 k); the appearance of the latter is described by the Latin historian Tacitus on the occasion of an official visit to the Paphian shrine by the Emperor Titus (AD 79–81).[35]

37 *Inscribed marble obelisk, from Kition, Cyprus, fourth–third century BC. The Phoenician inscription on the base of this stele records a dedication to Eshmun-Adonis. In the inscription, the monument is referred to as a maṣṣebah.*

38 *View of Tantit-Astarte shrine at Sarepta, Lebanon, showing emplacement of betyl and altar/offering table.*

As in many ancient Near Eastern religions, divination appears to have played an important role in Phoenician cult. Signs and omens were variously interpreted through the study of dreams, animal entrails, and supernatural phenomena. Belomancy (the study of the flight of arrows) may also have figured prominently, if a series of early inscribed Phoenician arrowheads may be ritually interpreted.[36] Prophecy, often delivered through a temple oracle, played an important role as well; here, the divinity communicated through the intermediary of a priest or cultic medium, who revealed the divine message in a trance or ecstasy.[37] The biblical account of the contest between the Israelite prophet Elijah and the prophets of Baal on Mount Carmel offers some insight into the prophetic techniques utilized by the Phoenician priesthood. Here, in connection with a burnt sacrifice, the prophets of Baal lacerate themselves, dance feverishly, and exhort the deity with a drone of ritual cries.[38]

As the archaeological record amply attests, Phoenician votive offerings assumed a wide variety of shapes and forms, ranging from metal arms, utensils, and vessels to terracotta and stone dedicatory plaques and stelae. Votive models of thrones and miniature shrines formed popular offerings. The image of an empty throne supported by winged sphinxes marked the symbolic emplacement of the deity; large-scale representations in stone, such as that uncovered in the temple of Eshmun at Sidon, appear associated with the goddess Astarte. By far the most common form of votive offering was the bronze or terracotta image of a worshipper or deity. (See plate III and and figs 39, 40 and 64.) Mould-made and mass-produced, such terracotta plaques and statuettes filled the open-air precincts of Phoenician sanctuaries. The votive clutter that accumulated was periodically swept clean, its contents redeposited in special pits or trenches known as *favissae*. The recovery of this votive material has added substantially to the archaeological record documenting Phoenician cultic worship.[39]

Such votive offerings offer an insight into another important facet of Phoenician religion – that of private, domestic cult. Practised within the home and in local or rural

39 *Terracotta statuette of a pregnant mother-goddess, eighth–sixth century BC, provenance unknown. Such figurines, rendered in seated pose with hand drawn above the abdomen, were offered by women for a safe pregnancy and a successful childbirth.*

shrines, popular religion tended to focus on issues of vital concern to the family, often revolving around the health and safety of women and children.[40] Female fertility and the protection of infants figured prominently, as numerous mould-made terracottas of veiled pregnant females attest. (See fig. 39.) Iconographically, these figurines may be associated with the great mother-goddess Astarte, whose worship is documented by other forms of seated and standing nude female figure. Within the Phoenician realm, Astarte was also venerated in natural caves or caverns. A grotto to the goddess at Wasta, south of Adlun, bears witness to this popular form of worship; its walls were decorated with graffiti depicting female genitalia. A number of caves sacred to Astarte later evolved into sanctuaries of the Virgin Mary. Another aspect of popular cult involved the worship of imported Egyptian deities, including Amen, Bes, Bastet, Osiris, Isis, and the child-god Horus.[41] Scattered inscriptions and the evidence of private names reveal the extent to which such worship permeated the Phoenician realm. The cultic influence of the Egyptian god Amen, head of the Theban divine hierarchy, is attested early on in royal circles. With the exception of Amen and Osiris, however, the other Egyptian divinities that entered the Phoenician domain were all closely associated with the protection of women and children. The popularity of the mother-goddess Isis and the leonine dwarf-god Bes amply attests to the growing importance of Egyptian-influenced Phoenician cults associated with healing, fertility, and magical protection, beginning in the mid-first millennium BC. (See figs 33, 40 and 62 d–f, h.) The divine recipients included gods such as Shed, Shadrapha, Ptah-patek, and Horon.

One of the frustrations in piecing together the mosaic of Phoenician religion stems from the difficulties in identifying images of deities. The problem is complicated by the scarcity of inscribed votive figurines. There are few clearly identifiable images of Eshmun or Melqart, for example.[42] The latter seems to have been associated, from the sixth century onwards, with Herakles; depictions from Cyprus, in particular, portray him with the Greek hero's club and lion-skin, but the extent of this association outside the island remains unclear. (See fig. 29.) Numerous Levantine bronze figurines depicting an armed warrior-god in smiting pose have been identified with Reshef. None of these statuettes, however, derives from a secure Phoenician mainland context; the figurine type, in fact, appears to have been a Late Bronze Age creation of north Syria or southern Anatolia.

40 *Terracotta vase in the form of the Egyptian god Bes. From Kition, Cyprus, sixth–fourth century* BC.

The same vagaries of interpretation apply to Phoenician Astarte. The image of the standing nude goddess with hands clasping her breasts is, once again, of northern Syrian rather than Phoenician origin. While Phoenician depictions of the type *may* represent Astarte, this assignation is not entirely clear; the same problems apply to the identification of the seated, nude pregnant female figurine type within the Phoenician realm.[43] Of all such depictions, only the bronze seated female from El Carambolo in Spain (see fig. 41) may be securely identified by inscription with Astarte, who is elsewhere associated with a sphinx-support throne. (See also figs 42a and 60.)

What lies behind the ambiguity in the depiction of Phoenician votive images? The answer may perhaps be sought in the underlying aspect of aniconism in Phoenician religion. As has been noted elsewhere, this tendency towards non-figural representation is a striking feature of the Eshmun sanctuary at Sidon. No cult statues of either Eshmun or Astarte have been recovered from the precinct; the surviving cultic images consist of empty sphinx-support thrones, a series of undecorated stone urns, and a pyramidal cippus (a pillar-shaped stone marker).[44] (See fig. 42a.) This reluctance to personify the deity may be understood within a long cultic tradition of non-figural representation, manifest already in the Early Bronze Age sanctuaries of Byblos.

The tradition that gave rise to the betyl, or standing stone, as a divine marker was a potent and an enduring one in the Phoenician realm. As we shall see, this same tendency toward aniconism manifests itself in the western, Punic, world.

RELIGIOUS ARCHITECTURE

As with other aspects of Phoenician culture, the study of temple architecture is complicated by the paucity of

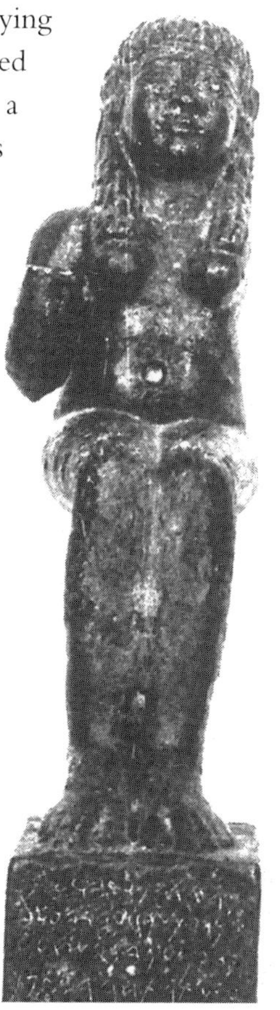

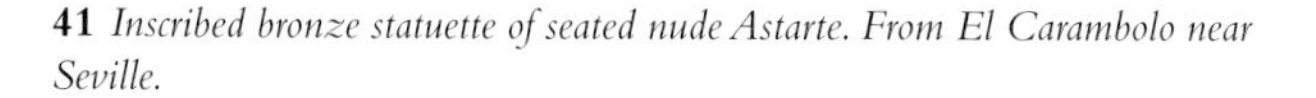

41 *Inscribed bronze statuette of seated nude Astarte. From El Carambolo near Seville.*

42 *Astarte chapel with sphinx-support throne and adjoining pool. Eshmun sanctuary complex, Bostan esh-Sheikh, Sidon, Lebanon, fourth century* BC.

archaeological data. No early Phoenician cultic installation dating either to the Late Bronze or early Iron Age has yet been recovered from the mainland. Indeed, most of the sanctuary complexes that have been found date to the Hellenistic and Roman periods, when pre-existing structures were radically transformed or rebuilt.

Nevertheless, one can identify two essential aspects of the Phoenician temple: the open-air precinct (typically associated with the *bamah*, or 'high place', of the Old Testament); and the built, enclosed temple. The former typically consisted of a paved, open, elevated courtyard or *temenos*, enclosing a cultic installation of some sort (i.e. a betyl, altar, or shrine (*naiskos*)). Where feasible, it was located on high ground – on a mountain peak or ridge, or on the summit of a neighbouring hill. When set in a level, low-lying area or in an urban context, the open-air complex was raised above ground by means of a built platform or elevated terrace.

A classic example of a hillside precinct is the so-called Ma'abed at Amrit, a large open enclosure cut into the slope of a hill overlooking the valley of the Nahr Amrit. In its centre stood a built, cube-shaped chapel set upon a monolithic stone socle roughly 5 metres (17 feet) square. The rock-cut basin (which was originally filled with water, as erosion marks on the monument's base attest) measures 47 by 39 metres (51 by 43 yards), with a depth of over 3 metres (10 feet).

It was originally enclosed on three sides by a covered portico with square pillars. Its initial construction may be traced back to the end of the sixth century BC, based upon the evidence of a votive trench that contained earlier statuettes and two Phoenician dedications; as the associated finds suggest, the cult appears to have been devoted to the god Eshmun.

At neighbouring Ain el-Hayat, two opposing chapels grace an open-air sanctuary of comparable type and date, set within a shallow natural pond. The western chapel, which is the better preserved of the two chapels, is a monolithic structure resting on a cubic block that is 3 metres (10 feet) square. In a fashion that is typical of Phoenician *naiskoi*, its doorway is capped by an entablature of Egyptianizing variety with a flaring architrave and an upper frieze bearing a row of *uraei*, or sacred serpents, surmounted by solar disks. The dual nature of the sanctuary and its natural water source distinguish it from the Ma'abed.[45]

The most monumental example of a Phoenician open-air sanctuary may be found in the Temple of Eshmun at Bostan esh-Sheikh near Sidon.[46] The original complex, which may be dated to the early sixth century BC, was marked by a massive, truncated pyramidal structure (60 by 37 metres, 65 by 40 yards) resembling a ziggurat. This structure was subsequently supplanted, in the early Persian period, by a monumental, quadrangular ashlar podium (70 by 50 metres, 77 by 55 yards) terraced against the slope and rising some 22 metres (24 yards) above the valley floor. Its upper terrace, an elevated open-air precinct, held a central prismatic altar of dressed stones with a large staircase on its western face. Subsequent additions to the sanctuary included a marble altar (the 'Tribune of Eshmun') decorated in bas-relief with Hellenic divinities and dancers, and a large chapel to Astarte with central sphinx throne opening on to a paved pool; both structures were erected at the base of the podium in the fourth century BC. (See fig. 42.)

The Sidonian sanctuary possessed an elaborate system of water channels and basins which connected the Nahr el-Awwali with the 'Ydlal spring'. The latter, which is mentioned in an inscription dated to the fourteenth year of the Sidonian king Bodashtart, apparently served as a site of ritual ablutions. Such hydraulic installations testify to the important role that water rites played in Phoenician therapeutic cults. The recently excavated sanctuary complex at the Kition Bamboula quarter clearly attests to this fact.[47] (See fig. 8.)

Attention may also be drawn to the site of Umm el-Amed, a large, naturally elevated, open-air precinct composed of two adjacent temple complexes situated south of Tyre. Although its present configuration dates to the Hellenistic period, the overall layout, which consists of two narrow elevated shrines set within enclosed open courtyards, probably reflects an earlier antecedent dating to the Persian period.[48] Like the porticoed, open-air temple enclosure with central betyl illustrated on a third-century Roman coin of Byblos (see fig. 29 k), it documents the perseverance of the open precinct plan in Phoenicia over successive periods of remodelling and rebuilding.

As for the famed Phoenician roofed temples attested in antiquity, the archaeological record is extremely sparse. No traces have yet been found of any of the great mainland urban sanctuaries of the Iron Age. Temple I of the Kathari precinct at Kition on Cyprus remains the only excavated example of a monumental sanctuary complex from the

Phoenician east. Over its three phases of construction ranging from *c.*850 to 400 BC, the building, which was constructed upon the foundations of an earlier Late Bronze Age sanctuary, maintained a spacious, semi-roofed courtyard with flanking porticoes and central unroofed aisle. The whole led up to a shallow, elevated rear chamber, or holy-of-holies, whose entrance was marked by two rectangular, freestanding pillars built of ashlar blocks.

Neither archaeology nor the ancient sources have preserved any indication of the size of the urban sanctuaries of the Phoenician mainland. Yet, if surviving chapels, like those at Amrit, are any indication, they were probably not of monumental size. Here, attention may be drawn to an actual plinth with flanking pillar bases from the precinct of Baalat Gubal at Byblos, which marks the emplacement of the large-scale portico erected there by King Yehaumilk in honour of the goddess.[49]

As has been recently suggested, the appearance of this portico (and the stele which it housed) is accurately mirrored in a terracotta plaque from the site, which depicts a tall temple façade with Ionic columns, an entablature with winged sun disk, and recumbent lion acroteria (pedimental ornaments).[50] (See fig. 43.) If the proportions represented on the plaque may be taken as a guide, Yehaumilk's construction, which measured 6.5 metres (21 feet) in width, stood at slightly under 10 metres (32 feet) in height.

The archaeological evidence from the mainland, although limited, would support the supposition that Phoenician roofed temples were of modest size and dimensions. The excavated Iron Age shrines at Tell Sukas, Sarepta, and Tell Arqa are all simple rectangular structures of modest scale. The two excavated Hellenistic-period temples at Umm el-Amed and Kharayeb are also of relatively modest proportions.

Even assuming that the main temples at Tyre, Sidon, and Arwad were more monumental than these, their respective sizes must still have fallen far short of the larger temple complexes known to have existed in Syria–Palestine in the Late Bronze and Early Iron Age.

According to Josephus, Hiram's reconstruction programme at Tyre included the rebuilding and refurbishing of the city's existing sanctuaries to Melqart and Astarte. Although no specifics are given, one may posit that, in a burgeoning city where real estate was already

43 *On this terracotta plaque, the king of Byblos appears before Baalat Gubal within a shrine-like setting. From Byblos, Lebanon, fifth century* BC.

at a premium, such expansion efforts *may* have concentrated on rebuilding upward rather than outward for purposes of external visibility. The tall edifice that towers above Tyre's urban landscape on a late eighth-century Assyrian relief depiction of the city, if correctly identified as the Temple of Melqart, would lend support to this assumption. (See fig. 6.) If the island temple of Herakles (Baal Shamem), which Hiram joined to the main island, had served as a beacon or navigational marker for ships approaching the city, it, too, must have been a structure of imposing elevation.

The three newly renovated Tyrian sanctuaries could hardly have failed to attract King Solomon's attention, and his appeal to Hiram for Phoenician help in building his own monumental temple must have been motivated, at least in part, by the sight of them. In realizing plans for his own lofty sanctuary with its multi-storeyed side chambers, Solomon may have targeted the Phoenicians for their engineering skills. The question remains: to what extent was the Israelite temple influenced, in design and conception, by Phoenician architectural models? In the present author's opinion, the lack of architectural precedent on the Phoenician mainland and the Old Testament account itself would suggest that such influence was minimal. According to the Bible, the Phoenicians were commissioned specifically to produce bronze cultic furnishings for the temple and to work on its interior ornamentation.[51] As for the temple's construction, they were to provide the raw cedar wood and to assist Israelite workmen in the preparation of the timber and ashlar stonework.[52]

Their input, thus, was on a technical rather than a conceptual level. The brazen pillars (Jachin and Boaz) that Solomon commissioned from the Phoenicians may well have been modelled after the monumental twin columns that Hiram had erected in the Tyrian Baal Shamem sanctuary. But the design for the temple's massive tripartite structure must have come from elsewhere, probably from Syria or Mesopotamia, where a tradition of axially aligned, multi-chambered temples existed.

Punic religion

THE PANTHEON

The roots of Punic religion are to be sought in the east. The city of Carthage, as one would expect, preserved the cults of its mother-colony, Tyre. The oldest surviving inscriptions from the city mention the goddess Astarte and a male divinity Pumay (Pygmalion), a god of Cypriot origin who is also recorded in an early Phoenician inscription from Sardinia. Written documents from Carthage attest to the worship of other mainland Phoenician deities, among them Reshef, Baal Saphon, and Shadrapha.

Pride of place among early Carthaginian deities must, however, have fallen to Melqart. The great god, patron of Tyrian colonial enterprise, played a crucial role in the Punic city's legendary foundation. Elissa, Carthage's foundress, was, in fact, the wife of the Tyrian High Priest of Melqart; according to legend, she brought with her the god's sacred relics as an assurance of his protection. While the surviving documentation for Melqart's worship at Carthage is late, the god's early primacy in the city hierarchy reveals itself in his popularity: Melqart's name is, in fact, attested more than fifteen hundred times in twenty-five different Carthaginian personal names that express the individual's personal piety (e.g. Abdmelqart, 'Servant of Melqart'; Bomilcar (Bodmelqart), 'In the hand of Melqart'). As history records, the Punic metropolis sent yearly delegations to Tyre for the spring celebration of Melqart's 'awakening'. Interestingly, the cult title 'resuscitator of the divinity' is attested at Carthage, not Tyre; its prominent association with high-ranking Carthaginian dignitaries suggests that Melqart's annual festival in the city was an important one.[53]

From an early period, however, Melqart's worship at Carthage and other cities in the Punic west was rivalled and ultimately surpassed by the cult of another mainland male divinity, Baal Hammon, 'Lord of the Amanus', a mountain range north of Ugarit. Like Phoenician Dagon, Baal Hammon was a god of agriculture; in this capacity, he often appears enthroned with a sceptre tipped with ears of wheat. A fifth-century stele from Hadrumetum offers the earliest pictorial depiction of the god – in a high tiara and long robe, seated with lance in hand on a throne flanked by sphinxes; with his raised right hand, he blesses a bonnet-clad worshipper.[54] Baal Hammon's power over the land and its fertility rendered him of great appeal to the inhabitants of Tunisia, a land of fertile wheat- and fruit-bearing plains. It propelled his worship not only throughout the Tunisian heartland, but through all of coastal North Africa. The cult of Hammon is also attested early on in the Mediterranean colonies of Malta, Sicily, and Sardinia; his appearance there is probably the result of diffusion from the east.

Beginning in the fifth century BC, Baal Hammon's authority at Carthage was shared increasingly with Tanit (Punic *tnt*), a female divinity who is invoked on dedicatory stelae from the *tophet* precinct. Tanit's name appears before that of Baal Hammon with the epithet *pene baal* ('face of Baal'). Like the title *shem baal* ('name of Baal') accorded to Phoenician Astarte, the expression reveals her initial dependence upon the god. Tanit's title *rabat* (the feminized form of *rab* ('chief')), however, underscores her position as sovereign mistress. The two deities remain largely inseparable as coupled entities at Carthage.

Tanit's functional identity has engendered a good deal of debate about her relationship to Astarte, with whom she was closely associated both in the east and at Carthage itself; an inscription from the Carthaginian *tophet* refers to the presence of a sanctuary to the two goddesses.[55] Like Astarte, Tanit's personality was complex. Many of her divine aspects, including the etymology of her name, remain unclear. From Carthage, her worship spread within Tunisia itself and abroad to the Mediterranean colonies, Sardinia in particular. At Ibiza, a cult was dedicated to her at the cavern of Es Cuieram, where she is depicted in a winged form reminiscent of the Egyptian mother-goddess Isis.

As on the Phoenician mainland, Astarte and Melqart figured prominently in Punic cults of the central and western Mediterranean. The chief god of Tyre was worshipped on Malta, at Lixus in Morocco, and at Cadiz. Melqart's temple at Cadiz, renowned for its oracle, was second only to that of Tyre in wealth and importance. Astarte's role as goddess of fecundity is expressed in a variety of manifestations, many of them clearly influenced by pre-existing native cultic traditions. On Malta, her worship is attested at Tas Silg in a Punic temple complex built upon the remains of an indigenous megalithic sanctuary dating from the Chalcolithic period. The goddess's worship at Mount Eryx in western Sicily was also the product of symbiosis with a native Sicilian deity.

Astarte's procreative powers manifest themselves in her association with cults of ritual prostitution. Her celebrated sanctuary at Eryx was renowned for it; surviving inscriptions reveal the spread of its cult both to Sardinia and to North Africa. A text from the former records the names of two sacred prostitutes in the service of Erycine Astarte: a mother and daughter named Amotmelqart ('Servant of Melqart') and Arishutbaal ('Of the divine spouse').[56] Astarte's sanctuary at Sicca Veneria on the Tunisian mainland was equally renowned for its rites of sacred prostitution;[57] recent excavations at Etruscan Pyrgi document a similar practice in honour of the goddess.

As on the Phoenician mainland, Punic worship at Carthage was heavily influenced by foreign cults, like that of the Egyptian goddess Isis. A Carthaginian inscription reveals that a temple to her stood in the third to second century BC.[58] As amulets attest, Isis' infant son Horus (Harpocrates) was equally venerated in private worship; the latter was assimilated with the Punic god Shed, whose cult as a healing divinity was widespread in Sardinia. Sicilian Hellenic influence at Carthage is dramatically attested by the introduction, in the early fourth century BC, of the cult of the mother-and-daughter grain-goddesses Demeter and Kore; as inscriptions relate, their sacred rites were celebrated annually by a professional priesthood attached to their temple. Certain texts document aspects of popular, magical religious practice influenced by foreign cults. In a third-century spell from Carthage, the dedicator calls on the goddess Hawwat, a supernatural being, to act on her behalf against a woman with whom she had a financial dispute.[59]

The aniconic nature of Punic worship is well attested in the sacred images recorded on the thousands of dedicatory monuments preserved at Carthage and other Punic sites in North Africa and the Mediterranean. These include a variety of symbols, both lozenge- and bottle-shaped, enshrined within small *naiskoi*. The most dominant form is the betyl, the tapering upright stone attested in Phoenician worship. (See fig. 44.) Represented singly, it is often depicted in

44 *Shrine-shaped stele with twin betyls, from Burj al-Chemal near Tyre, Lebanon, fifth century* BC.

45 *Votive stele with sign of Tanit. From the tophet at Carthage, Tunisia, fourth century* BC. *The stele bears a four-line inscription with a dedication to Tanit and Baal Hammon.*

multiples of two, three, or four; the most popular is the triple cluster with dominant central element. Other aniconic images, largely associated with the goddess Tanit, include the crescent moon, the open hand (a symbol of prayer), and the so-called 'sign of Tanit', a triangle surmounted by a horizontal arm and disk. (See fig. 45.) The votive stelae, together with surviving records of sacrificial tariffs, provide a wealth of information regarding the widespread practice of animal sacrifice in the Punic world. As the the reliefs depict, the victim (most often a lamb or sheep) was led in solemn procession to the altar by a priest or officiant, accompanied by the offerant and porters of ritual implements (axes, knives). The animal was then immolated and drained of blood, its decapitated head placed upon the altar. While the victim burned, the officiant, equipped with an incensarium, recited a prayer of offering. After the victim's fat and entrails had been consumed, its flesh was cut up and divided between the sacrificer and the offerant, the former receiving the breast and right thigh, the latter the remaining flesh and the skin. The victim's ashes were then buried and the dedicatory stele erected.[60]

THE *TOPHET* PRECINCT AND CHILD SACRIFICE

The Punic world was famous (indeed infamous) for another form of sacrificial rite involving human beings, more precisely young children. The classical sources are filled with references to this practice, which is generally ascribed to the Phoenicians, but specifically associated with the Carthaginians. The Greek historian Cleitarchus, writing in the early third century BC, is most explicit: as he relates, the Carthaginians promised one of their children in sacrifice to Cronos (the Greek equivalent of Baal Hammon) in order to obtain 'a great favour'. He goes on to describe how the child was cremated in the arms of a bronze cult statue, whose hands extended over a brazier into which the victim fell, its limbs contracted and face distorted in a kind of smiling grimace.[61] Other, later, authors provide additional, sometimes lurid, details. Plutarch tells of childless couples who bought children from the poor to offer in sacrifice; as he relates, their throats were cut to the sound of flutes and drums, which drowned out the cries and wails of grieving family members. According to the Latin authors Pliny and Silius Italicus, child sacrifices were performed annually by the Carthaginians. The Greek historian Diodorus, on the other hand, relates that they were enacted publicly in response to a military crisis. According to his account, the Carthaginian aristocracy, under siege by the tyrant Agathocles, offered up two hundred of their noble born in an effort to appease a Carthaginian deity whom they had offended through neglect and ritual abuse: in place of their own offspring they had wrongfully substituted children surreptitiously purchased from commoners.[62]

Archaeological investigation over the past century has, in fact, revealed widespread evidence of the Punic practice. Excavations throughout the central Mediterranean – in Sicily, Sardinia, and North Africa – have uncovered a series of extramural, open-air enclosures housing the charred remains of young children buried in terracotta urns deposited in natural cavities or in small stone-built pits cut into the virgin bedrock.[63] As osteological analysis has shown, the deceased were young infants up to 3 years in age, some of them apparently born prematurely.[64] Their gender remains a mystery: their calcined remains typically consist of little more than teeth or the digital bones of a hand or foot. The occupants are usually buried alone, although in some instances (e.g. at Tharros on Sardinia) they may be accompanied by offerings of young animals – lambs, kids, and small birds.

One of the largest of such burial precincts has been located at Carthage itself, near the shore and area of the later port facility. Excavations conducted there since the early 1920s have revealed a sequence of densely packed burials layered one on top of another, extending in unbroken sequence from the end of the eighth century to 146 BC, when the city fell to Rome. Only a portion of the entire grounds, which once covered an extensive area of undetermined dimensions, has yet been identified and excavated.[65] (See fig. 46.)

The Carthaginian sacred precinct, or '*tophet*', has long been the subject of controversy.[66] Debate persists over the significance of the myriad of infant cremations deposited within its confines. Do they offer grim testimony to the ritual practice of child sacrifice described in the ancient sources? Argument persists over the very use of the term *tophet*, which derives from a Hebrew Bible reference to a roasting area in the valley of Ben-Hinnom, where Israelite children were sacrificed by fire. This heinous practice was

46 *View of the tophet precinct at Carthage under excavation in 1979. ASOR Punic Project.*

condemned by the prophet Jeremiah, who lived at the end of the seventh and early sixth century BC, the period of usage of the Punic cremation grounds.[67]

The debate over the *tophet*'s interpretation has been rekindled in recent years.[68] Sceptics have drawn attention to the high percentage of apparently premature and new-born babies among its occupants. Given the high mortality rate that existed in antiquity, are these not more likely to have been burials of still-born children and young infants deceased from natural causes? The great rarity of infant burials in adult Punic cemeteries suggests that children were interred separately. What more appropriate way of honouring the deceased infant than by placing him in an enclosed burial precinct sanctified by Baal Hammon himself? In so doing, the family could ensure the future well-being both of young survivors and of those not yet born.

Such an interpretation, however, meets with serious obstacles. To begin with, there are the classical authors themselves, who testify to the institutionalized sacrificial practice. While the Greek and Latin sources display an admittedly anti-Carthaginian bias, can we justifiably dismiss their accounts as mere distortion or diatribe? Second, there is the evidence of the burials themselves and their accompanying votive markers. (See figs 45 and 47.) From the late seventh or early sixth century BC onward, the latter speak of *molk* offerings – human and animal – to Baal Hammon and Tanit. (The term *'mr* signifies the offering of a lamb, while the qualifier *b'l*, although its precise nuance is debated, clearly denotes a human deposit.) Etymologically, the term *molk* may convey the notion of 'offering', underscoring the votive significance of the ritual act, evident in the recurrent use of the Punic word *ndr* ('vow') on the stelae themselves. In character, the *tophet* stelae thus stand apart clearly from the normal gravestones found in traditional cemeteries.

The immutability of the *tophet* precinct itself points to its sacred, ritual status. Unlike a conventional cemetery (which is typically unwalled), it may not be relocated (contrast the case of the Motya necropolis, which was ultimately transferred from the island to the adjoining mainland). Such strict adherence to sacred grounds explains the often chaotic layering of urn burials resulting from the periodic re-landscaping of the *tophet* grounds. The high premium assigned to sacred real estate may explain why older burials are frequently cut into or supplanted by later ones, a phenomenon particularly apparent at Carthage itself.

In interpreting the *tophet*, a great number of problems and issues remain unresolved. These concern the various processes underlying the sacrificial rite. The classical sources tend to emphasize collective offerings undertaken by the state in

47 *Votive stele depicting a priest with child, from the tophet at Carthage, fourth century BC.*

response to external crises (war, pestilence, famine). The archaeological evidence (both the votive inscriptions and the burials themselves), however, suggests that sacrifices were initiated primarily by families or individuals. The occurrence of multiple offerings within a single urn and of stelae dedications by members of the same family point to this fact.

Questions remain about the offerants themselves. How widespread was the practice among the general Punic population? The votive inscriptions from Carthage reveal that the sacrificial rite was practised by the upper classes – the merchants, priests, and magistrates of the city. The stelae bearing written dedications, however, represent only a small fraction of the surviving gravestones (only forty of a thousand at Motya, for example). Who were the other dedicants and from what stratum of society did they come?

Other questions surround the emergence and evolution of the sacrificial rite. The *tophet*'s early occurrence at Carthage (in the late eighth century) would suggest that the institution was an inherited one. According to Quintus Curtius, the practice had been imported from the mother-country by its Tyrian founders.[69] That child sacrifice was current in the Levant may be inferred from the widespread and early appearances of *tophets* in the west as well as from the numerous invectives directed against the rite by the Biblical prophets. A late eighth-century Phoenician inscription of the king of Cilicia, recently discovered at Inçirli, provides dramatic testimony of the practice. In it, a Tyrian priest advises the king to perform a *molk* sacrifice of a lamb as well as an expiatory holocaust of his son or grandson in apparent response to a plague which had broken out in the Cilician camp.[70] The Tyrian priest's recommendation and the ensuing dialogue that it engenders clearly underscores the currency of such sacrificial practice within the Phoenician realm. At present, however, no firm archaeological evidence for a *tophet* has been found in the Phoenician homeland; it may well be that such sacrifices were not segregated within specific precincts in the east as they were later in the Punic west.

An understanding of the internal history of the *tophet* is complicated by the problems involved in dating and sequencing the urn deposits themselves. The precinct's complex, often jumbled stratigraphy, moreover, frustrates any serious efforts at correlating burials. Little is known about the configuration and appearance of the *tophet* in its initial stages. The very earliest deposits appear to have been largely unmarked above ground. The use of grave monuments – in the form of plain L-shaped or cubic blocks (known as *cippi*) – began sometime in the seventh century BC. The tall, richly ornamented, gabled stelae so characteristic of the *tophet* in its later stages were not introduced until some time in the late fifth century BC.

At Carthage itself, the *tophet* witnessed a dramatic rise in usage, beginning in the fourth century BC, underscoring the city's rapid urban growth at this time. Based upon the density of extant burials, it has been estimated that as many as twenty thousand urns were deposited in the fourth to third centuries BC. Preliminary analysis of the urn remains suggests that there may have been a greater incidence of infant sacrifice now, compared with the earlier seventh century, when young animals were more commonly offered in substitution for children. Such information has engendered speculation about the use of child sacrifice as a mechanism of population control.[71] The data, at presence, are far too limited to draw any definite conclusions.

In summary, the archaeological and literary evidence would support the interpretation of Punic child sacrifice as a votive, institutional practice organized around the worship of Baal Hammon and Tanit. Perhaps the most compelling witness to its deep-seated ritual significance may be found in the tenacity of the cult itself, which persisted long after its abolition by the Romans. Excavations at Tunisian Hadrumetum, site of the second largest *tophet* complex in North Africa after Carthage, revealed evidence for its continued use well into the first century AD, if not beyond. The early church father Tertullian claims that infant sacrifices were still being offered, in secrecy, as late as AD 200.[72]

The entire phenomenon, needless to say, is imperfectly documented and even less perfectly understood. No single model may ever adequately explain its function in Punic society; in all likelihood, it had many different levels of meaning, which answered the diverse needs of a heterogeneous population. We are completely ignorant of the various processes and ritual timetables that may have governed the sacrificial practice. Analysis of wild grasses recovered from urns at Tharros suggests that sacrifices there may have been seasonal in character, with cultic activity culminating in late summer; according to other theories, based upon the offerings of lambs and kids born in spring litters, the *molk* sacrifice may have been connected with fertility rites celebrated in March.[73] The classical sources emphasize sacrifices that address exceptional circumstances – military and environmental crises. The *tophet* stelae, on the other hand, record offerings made in answer to personal prayers or vows. Hopefully, further study of the inscriptions themselves, along with comprehensive statistical analyses of the *tophet* deposits, will lead to a fuller understanding of the processes underlying this intriguing practice.

RELIGIOUS ARCHITECTURE

The documentary evidence for early Punic, pre-Hellenistic temple architecture is surprisingly slim. At Carthage, the great temples on the city acropolis have long since vanished, obliterated by a massive Roman rebuilding campaign that levelled the hilltop. Recent excavation, however, has uncovered the remains of a late Punic temple complex in the city's coastal district dating to the late third or early second century BC. The sanctuary, probably dedicated to Baal Hammon, is of great interest for its temple archives, consisting of more than three thousand Greek and Egyptian clay papyrus seals, spanning the seventh to fourth centuries BC, that accompanied papyrus documents burnt in the Roman destruction of the city in 146 BC.[74] The neighbouring excavations of Hamburg University have uncovered the remains of an early Punic domestic shrine of *c.*500 BC, consisting of a large cult basin used for ritual bathing and libation. The sacred symbols set as tesserae into its pavement reveal its religious function: these included the sign of Tanit and a circle enclosing a cross, the symbol for Baal Hammon.[75] (See fig. 48.)

Of the many other Punic temple complexes found throughout North Africa, none, to date, has revealed architectural vestiges clearly predating the Hellenistic period. In Sicily,

48 *View of a cultic basin found within a house at Carthage. c.500 BC. The religious function of this bathing facility is evinced by the symbols of Tanit and Baal Hammon inset into its paved floor. University of Hamburg Excavations.*

the only major early complex known is the 'Cappiddazzu' at Motya, which saw usage from the seventh century BC onwards; the identity of the deity worshipped there remains unclear. Excavations on Mount Eryx have failed to uncover any pre-Roman traces of the famed sanctuary of Astarte, which was completely demolished during construction of the Norman castle that currently occupies the site. Only a few Punic temple structures have been uncovered on Sardinia; all of them (including the 'monolithic temple' at Tharros and the temple of Sardus Pater at Antas) were heavily altered or rebuilt during the Roman period. As its architectural vestiges reveal, the Antas temple, which was dedicated around 500 BC to the god Sid, consisted originally of a small rectangular *cella* (with an altar enclosing a sacred rock) set within a large open *temenos* 68 metres (75 yards) square. No early temples have been found in either Spain or Morocco. (As recent investigation has shown, the sanctuaries at Lixus apparently date to the Roman period.) The general emplacement of the temple of Melqart at Cadiz – on the islet of Santi Petri – is now indicated by the discovery of submerged monumental ruins.

Phoenician funerary practice

Although the texts themselves are largely mute on the subject, the burial practices and funerary iconography of the Phoenicians point to a firm belief in an afterlife. Inscriptions on several royal sarcophagi reveal that the Phoenicians called their dead *rephaim*, the same term used in Late Bronze Age Ugarit to refer to the divine ancestors, or deified deceased. While there is no explicit evidence in Phoenician texts for the practice of ancestor worship, the term *rephaim* (whose very root means 'to heal') implies a positive belief in the life beyond. According to Philo of Byblos, the Phoenicians identified the notion of death with the god Mouth. If this is true, Phoenician belief in this primordial, otherworldly being would lend further credence to the notion of a spiritual concept of the hereafter.

Iconographic evidence from funerary settings would, in fact, suggest that the Phoenicians entertained the notion of spiritual rebirth in the next life. The adoption of Egyptian motifs, such as the *ankh* (the symbol of life) and the lotus flower, potent symbol of regeneration, points to this conclusion. The iconography of the lotus figures prominently on the sarcophagus of Ahiram. There the flower appears three times: once on the side wall, in the hand of the king who sits enthroned before a procession of votaries; and twice on the sarcophagus lid, held by Ahiram himself and his son Ithobaal; the latter lifts the upright flower to his face as though to inhale its fragrance. By contrast, the lotus held by Ahiram in the processional scene droops distinctly. As the lotus's vital, life-giving powers are embodied in the living flower, the wilted plant should signify that the king is deceased.

In Egyptian tomb depictions, the lotus flower is sniffed by the deceased and his family members in a gesture aimed at ensuring the symbolic rebirth of his soul in the afterlife. On the Byblian sarcophagus lid, Ithobaal's lotus-smelling gesture should embody the same meaning; as the ritual dedicant of the sarcophagus, his symbolic actions are meant to ensure the safe passage of his father's soul to the afterlife. The iconography of the lotus, in fact, permeates Phoenician and Punic religious art, where it appears in a variety of divine contexts clearly associated with the protection and renewal of the deceased. With their long cultural ties with the Nile valley, the Phoenicians were strongly influenced by Egyptian funerary beliefs. Direct proof of such cultic exposure may be found in an Egyptian bronze funerary situla of the sixth century BC, which bears a Phoenician dedication to the goddess Isis; its dedicant, Abdi-Ptah, was a Phoenician worshipper of the Egyptian god of Memphis. A similar vessel with Astarte dedication from Har Miṣpe Yamim in northern Israel reveals the spread of Egyptian cultic influence to the Phoenician mainland.[76]

Archaeology has been enormously helpful in reconstructing Phoenician burial rituals, which are poorly documented in the texts. As the Bible attests, ceremonial leave-taking was typically accompanied by ritual acts of lamentation, such as the wearing of sackcloth, the tearing of hair, and the beating of breasts; such gestures are performed by the female mourners on the Ahiram sarcophagus. (See plate V.) At Carthage, archaeological traces (in the form of carbonized remains of food and broken tableware found in burial fill) suggest that a ceremonial meal or banquet was enacted over the grave to inaugurate its closure. A burial's completion may have been ceremonially marked by the pouring of libations or the burning of incense. The latter practice is attested at Trayamar in Spain, where incensaria were deposited, along with numerous red-slip plates, on the roof of a chamber tomb. As their highly fragmentary state reveals, the latter were ritually broken at the time of burial according to a practice well documented elsewhere in the Near East, most recently at the early cremation cemetery at Tyre.

The ritual preparation of the deceased for interment varied according to social class. The body was washed, doused with perfumed oils, and wrapped in cloth bandages. As surviving fibulae (ancient clothing pins) and jewellery (see plate VII) attest, the affluent were more elaborately dressed – in one or more tunics. For the upper classes, purificatory rites may often have involved the use of imported aromatics; a funerary inscription from Byblos notes that the deceased was 'swathed in myrrh and bdellium' (a gum extracted from certain palms). The practice of embalming was rare, and probably reserved only for royalty and aristocracy; the body of the Sidonian king Tabnit was thus prepared. Members of royalty were also buried with gold death masks (see plate IV), or with their eyes and fingernails covered with gold or silver foil in the Egyptian fashion. According to her sarcophagus inscription, Batnoam, the mother of the Byblian king Ozbaal, was buried with a gold mouth band.

As burials attest, the deceased was provided with all the requirements for the afterlife. The most essential of utilitarian items were pottery vessels, which could range from a simple jug (for a young child) to a whole complement of shapes – oil bottles, plates, cups, dippers, cooking pots, and tripod-bowls. (The mushroom-lipped jug and trefoil-mouthed oinochoe (wine pitcher) were the stock-in-trade of Phoenician Early Iron Age tombs. (See fig. 65 and plates XI and XII.) Luxury ceramic items included Greek, Cypriot, and Etruscan imports, and specialty vessels shaped in the form of animals (*askoi*). Items of jewellery – earrings, bracelets, rings, and beads – formed common elements of personal adornment. The affluent wore ornaments of gold and silver; bronze, stone, and bone formed economical substitutes. Tomb inventories often included magical items, such as ritual razors, masks (see fig. 68 and plate X), and painted ostrich eggs, which protected the deceased and safeguarded his or her passage to the life beyond. Egyptian amulets – figurines, scarabs, and *udjat* ('eye of Horus') plaques – formed common talismans. Age- and gender-related burial items included dolls and toys (for children), cosmetic containers and weaving implements (for women), and iron weapons and armour (for men).

The interments of the upper class were often placed in coffins, rangeing from simple rectangular wooden boxes with flat or gabled lids to decorated anthropoid sarcophagi in terracotta or imported marble. From the mid-first millennium BC onwards, the latter formed the preferred burial receptacle for the well-to-do. (See fig. 61 a, b.) Royal stone sarcophagi often carried stern warnings to potential violators, underscoring the tomb's inviolability as an eternal resting place. (See the frontispiece.) In his burial epitaph, King Tabnit of Sidon proclaims: 'Whosoever thou be, each man who finds this coffin, open not the lid and disturb me not, because with me there is no money, no gold, nor anything worth plundering, except myself who lie in this coffin. Open not my lid and disturb me not, because this is an abuse of Astarte. And if thou dost open my lid and disturb me, there will be no descendants for thee in thy life under the sun, nor rest with the dead.'[77]

Among the mainland Phoenicians, the predominant burial practice during the Late Bronze Age was inhumation, the interment of the deceased. Some time early in the first millennium BC, a new method of burial disposal – cremation – appeared in the coastal Levant, both along the Phoenician mainland and in neighbouring Syria and Palestine.[78] The chronology and geographic priority of its introduction remain the subject of controversy. The recent excavations at Tyre document its usage as early as the tenth century BC, suggesting that the practice may have originated in Phoenicia itself. The succeeding centuries witnessed the contemporary usage of both burial practices on the continent.[79]

From the eastern mainland, beginning in the eighth century BC, the process of cremation was introduced to the Phoenician colonies of the central and western

Mediterranean. There it formed the dominant burial practice for three centuries until it was gradually supplanted by inhumation, beginning in the sixth century BC. Both in the east and in the region of Carthage, inhumation remained the predominant method of disposal, especially among the upper classes. No adequate explanations have been offered for the fluctuations in usage which marked these two burial practices. In the Phoenician west at least, there seems to have been no ethnic underpinning to the use of either method. Both occur in the same types of graves, within the same cemeteries and even, upon occasion, within the same burial complex. The differing regional variations in patterns of usage remain unexplained.

As archaeological research has shown, the cremation process took place on a ritual pyre, which was erected either in the tomb itself or in a location outside. When the pyre was lit within the grave, the burnt bones were simply left in place. A plate or amphora was then deposited over the cranial remains, and additional pottery scattered around the lower extremity of the deceased; the burial was then covered with stones. When the pyre was set outside (the preferred method), the charred remains of the deceased were collected (together with some charcoal) and wrapped in a cloth, or deposited in an urn or amphora which was then lowered into the grave. The unguent containers used in ritually preparing the deceased were transferred to the grave, while the libation vessels (which had been thrown on to the pyre during cremation) were left behind.[80]

The recent excavations at Tyre have afforded a first glimpse of the cremation rites practised by the city population during the early centuries of the first millennium BC.[81] The burials themselves were placed in urns set within shallow pit graves excavated into the sandy shoreline. These urns, which contained an assortment of personal items (primarily jewellery and amulets), were accompanied by one or two unguent vessels. Upon their deposition, a series of plates were smashed against the tomb in a ritual of closure. Large tombstones were then erected alongside individual graves or groups of burials.

Crudely carved in a variety of shapes from the local sandstone, or 'beach-rock', these grave markers, which are typically inscribed, often bear a religious symbol or motif (*ankh*, crescent-disk, shrine, flower).[82] The inscriptions, or epitaphs, consist of simple personal names, with or without patronymic; nearly all incorporate the names of popular Phoenician deities: Melqart, Baal, Astarte, El, and Eshmun. Both Hammon and Tanit, the primary deities at Carthage, appear. Tanit's occurrence is the earliest from the mainland outside of the Sarepta votive plaque. In contrast to the later Punic votive stelae, the Tyrian tombstones are cursorily executed in both carving and script; their sketchiness and irregularity suggest that they were carved on site by amateur craftsmen unaccustomed to working in stone. The prominent use of ritual symbols, such as the *ankh*, the sun disk, and lotus, evince a common concern for the prosperity of the deceased and his or her continued existence in the hereafter.

As stated above, various types of tomb were utilized equally for both cremation and inhumation, both on the mainland and in the west. A broad distinction, however, may be drawn between tombs designed for individuals and those intended for collective use, either by families or by professional groupings. The first and simplest variety, which was fashioned for single, exclusive use, was the *fossa* grave, a shallow oblong pit excavated in the soil or rock. This type was widely employed throughout the Phoenician realm by the lower classes. A second variety, the shaft grave, consisted of a narrow vertical well or rectangular shaft, which was typically enlarged at the base to accommodate the burial. In the Punic west, beginning at Carthage in the seventh century BC, such tombs were equipped with increasingly deeper shafts capable of accommodating multiple, laterally cut burial cells. A third variety of burial, found at nearly all sites and in all periods, consisted of a simple rectangular pit of human dimensions. From the sixth century onwards, it assumed a number of variant types, ranging from simple to elaborate built-stone construction; the latter type, when completely lined and covered by stone slabs, is known as a cist tomb. In some instances, a stone sarcophagus was placed in the pit.

The final category of grave was the built or rock-cut underground chamber tomb, or hypogeum. Examples from the eastern mainland were accessed by a shaft or a stepped, open-air ramp, known as a *dromos*. The hypogea themselves, which were designed for single or multiple burials, were either excavated (as at Tell Rachidiyeh and Tambourit) or built (as at Kition and Amathus). The two Early Iron Age tombs at Achziv held the remains of 200 and 350 individuals, respectively. In the Punic west, such hypogea could also be equipped with an entry shaft (as at Carthage, Utica, and Trayamar) or a flat or stepped access ramp (as at Monte Sirai and Sulcis) (see figs 49 and 50); both varieties of tomb could be excavated or built. As in Cyprus, the built chambers tombs were typically constructed of large, well-cut ashlar blocks and covered by a flat ceiling with a pitched roof; their interiors often bore ornate architectural decoration. The use of monumental, above-ground tomb structures was a relatively late development in both the Phoenician east and the Punic west. The most notable grave monuments from the homeland are four pyramidal- and cube-shaped funerary towers found at Amrit, the

49 (right) *Dromos entrance to chamber tomb at Monte Sirai, Sardinia.*
50 (below) *Cut-away views of excavated Punic tombs. Shaft grave, Tuvixeddu cemetery, Cagliari, Sardinia. Dromos tomb, necropolis at Sulcis, Sardinia.*

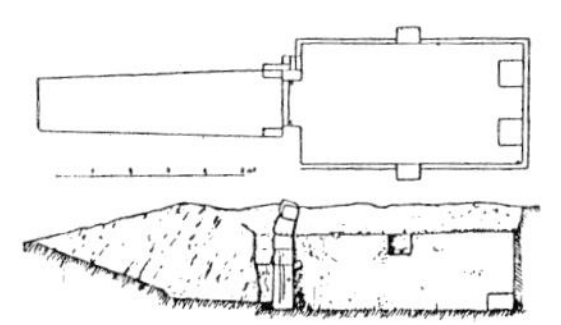

earliest of which dates to the fourth century BC. The Punic-influenced mausolea from North Africa (as at Dougga and Sabratha) date to the Hellenistic period.

The Phoenician cemeteries were normally isolated from their settlements by physical distance and, where feasible, by a natural barrier, such as water. For riverine establishments, necropoli were typically situated on the bank opposite. Island cities, like Tyre, Arwad, and Cadiz, located their urban cemeteries on the mainland. Most larger centres appear to have had multiple burial grounds. Their differentiation was sometimes chronological (the cemeteries of Carthage, for example, spread outward as the city grew), but more often societal. The burials of children (normally placed in amphorae) appear to have been isolated in their own precincts or buried under the floors of houses; their graves are conspicuously absent from the adult cemeteries. Class distinctions also figured in the distribution of cemeteries; as the elaborate built chamber tombs of Sainte Monique at Carthage attest, the well-to-do buried their dead in their own precincts.

The larger cemetery complexes contain a wealth of information about the ethnic and social make-up of the Phoenician communities. The newly discovered cremation cemetery at Tyre offers some important insights in this regard. (See fig. 73.) The distribution of the burials themselves and their associated tomb goods bear witness to social stratification within the city. In contrast to the simpler, unmarked burials, the more elaborate graves or tomb groupings are identified by monumental stelae; their elaborate furnishings contain a variety of luxury items, including gold jewellery and imported goods such as Egyptian scarabs and Greek and Cypriot pottery. In one, a large stone-rimmed pit grave dating to the seventh century, the deceased was buried in a large painted Cypriot urn and accompanied by an extensive pottery inventory, including imported Greek cups. The grave, moreover, was marked by a dedicatory offering consisting of a wooden case containing four terracottas: a horseman with shield, a male bearded funerary mask (see plate X), and two miniature model shrines or altars. The burial also contained evidence of a ritual fire that had been set in honour of the deceased; its occupant was clearly a man of some social standing. Concerning the Tyrian cremation cemetery, many questions remain. Do the distribution of burials – in clusters of two or more funerary urns marked by grave stelae – correspond to discrete family units or other lineal groupings within the city? The vast extent of this cemetery (estimated at 40,000 square metres) and its prolonged use (spanning some 400 years) underscore the spread and longevity of the cremation practice within the funerary life of the city. What segment of the population buried themselves in this manner? What, if any, were the societal distinctions between the practitioners of cremation and inhumation? Did the two maintain their own distinct and separate cemeteries at Tyre, as at the Dermech (cremation) and Juno (inhumation) precincts at Carthage? Inscribed and uninscribed tomb stelae appear side by side within the cemetery itself. Does this reflect a distinction in literacy level and social stratification? Or is the use of a simple uninscribed icon (*ankh*, crescent-disk) or human representation a mark of religious preference? These are questions that only future archaeological research can hope to answer.

Chapter Six

MATERIAL CULTURE

Phoenician material culture

TOWARDS AN UNDERSTANDING OF PHOENICIAN ART

OF ALL THEIR CULTURAL ASPECTS, the artistic heritage of the Phoenicians may represent the greatest enigma. Very few of their early works have survived, a fact that may be partly explained by archaeological happenstance: with the exception of Byblos and, now, Beruit, none of the major Phoenician coastal centres has been systematically excavated below Roman-period occupation levels. The surviving material record, moreover, provides only a partial picture of Phoenician output, as its two most valued commodities, decorated textiles and carved woodwork, have not withstood the passage of time. For the most part, fragile precious metals, especially silver, have also disappeared, the victim of human and environmental intervention. Commercial factors have altered the equation as well. As the literary and archaeological records underscore, the Phoenicians were great traffickers and, as such, marketed their goods at a foreign clientele. Our definition of Phoenician art is thus based, in large part, on finds from outlying regions that formed distant markets for Phoenician traders.

In spite of such limitations, the development of the Phoenician artistic tradition may, nonetheless, be traced with a 'broad brush' from the Late Bronze Age through the early first millennium BC. The Late Bronze Age finds from ancient Ugarit (modern-day Ras Shamra) are of particular relevance in this regard. Metal-work and carved ivories from the site present numerous parallels with Phoenician work of the early first millennium BC. Such correspondences provide evidence for direct continuity between the Late Bronze Age coastal Syrian tradition and its Phoenician counterpart in the Iron Age. Scattered finds of this period from the Levantine mainland further suggest that local Phoenician metal-work and ivory carving were strongly influenced by the surrounding Syrian and Canaanite artistic milieu.[1] (See figs 51 and 52.)

The literary testimonies from the Bible and from contemporary Assyrian sources[2] support the existence of a strong and flourishing craft tradition in the Phoenician Levant at the close of the second millennium BC. Solomon's request to King Hiram for Phoenician assistance in constructing and decorating his palace and temple presupposes that a well-developed and highly respected craft industry existed at Tyre by the mid-tenth century BC. Indeed, Hiram's emissary is said to have been 'skilled in the use of gold, silver, bronze, iron, stone, wood, scarlet, violet, fine linen, crimson, in engraving of all kinds, and in the execution of any design suggested to him'.[3] As the Report of Wenamun reveals, Byblos,

51 *Bronze repoussé plaque with fanciful animal combat scenes. From Tyre, Lebanon, fourteenth century BC*

too, was a prosperous and commercially active port in the first half of the eleventh century BC; there is every reason to believe that a royal craft industry in bronze- and wood-working was already in existence at that time.

Ironically, the literary evidence for a flourishing Phoenician craft tradition in the Early Iron Age is not supported by the material record. With the notable exception of the Ahiram sarcophagus, whose date remains the subject of controversy, no Iron Age Phoenician artistic monument may be securely dated before the ninth century BC. The stone coffin of the Byblian king Ahiram is of critical importance to an understanding of the development of Early Iron Age Phoenician art. (See plate V.) While its inscription may be securely assigned to the early tenth century BC, the sarcophagus itself, if it derives from the tomb's initial burial context, may be considerably earlier. Here, a date in the first half of the twelfth century is indicated by the latest find – a fragmentary ivory plaque in a hybrid Canaanite-Mycenaean style depicting a bull attacked by a lion and griffin. Proponents of the earlier dating compare the coffin's royal processional scene with a very similar rendering on an ivory inlay from Megiddo. As the latter comes from a building context assignable to the period of Ramesses III (1184–1153 BC), the Ahiram sarcophagus should date to the same period.[4]

Significantly, the Byblian coffin, like the Megiddo ivory inlay, exhibits comparatively little Egyptian influence in its style and composition. The majority of its figural details, including the modelling of the lions that decorate its base and lid, reflect a northerly Syrian artistic tradition. The reduced emphasis on Egyptian models apparent both on the Ahiram sarcophagus and on other twelfth-century works from Cyprus and Palestine contrasts sharply with the strongly Egyptianizing character of earlier Levantine art from the fourteenth century BC. The reversal in trend finds explanation in the historical record of the Early Iron Age. The twelfth

52 *Ivory statutette of seated deity, from Kamid el-Loz, Lebanon, fourteenth century BC.*

and succeeding eleventh centuries marked a period of economic and political decline for Egypt, during which time the Phoenicians redirected their attentions towards other, more influential, neighbours, among them the Assyrians. It is within such a context of reduced economic dependence on Egypt that King Hiram's commercial ties with Israel in the early tenth century may be understood.

While Phoenician artisanry clearly flourished at Tyre in the tenth century, it is only later – in the second half of the ninth and the eighth century BC – that archaeology has substantiated such activity with actual finds of Phoenician luxury goods, such as the metal bowls and carved ivories. Indeed, the eighth century was the true era of Phoenician internationalism, when Tyrian ships plied the Mediterranean from Cyprus to the Straits of Gibraltar and beyond in search of precious goods and raw materials. Such a commercial scenario creates serious problems for the art historian. The Phoenicians' wide-ranging trade contacts and their interest in catering for foreign markets resulted in the creation of a truly eclectic art style, perhaps the most outward-looking of all contemporary Near Eastern cultures. How do we set about defining the parameters of this unique and geographically encompassing art style?

Faced with a lacuna in the archaeological record from the mainland, one has been forced to rely heavily upon stylistic criteria in formulating a definition of Phoenician art. While such a classification process is valid, the danger of overextrapolating is a very real one, particularly in an artistic milieu such as the Phoenician, which is characterized by a unique and often unprecedented combination of contrasting styles and motifs.[5] By definition, Phoenician art is an amalgam of many different cultural elements – Aegean, north Syrian, Cypriot, Assyrian, and Egyptian – and it is this strongly eclectic quality that complicates any attempt to categorize strictly on the basis of style.

In fact, the relative influence of the various ethnic elements in Phoenician art depends upon a variety of geographical and chronological factors. Over its long duration, Phoenician culture experienced many evolutionary changes. Locale, too, played an important role. Phoenician society was a transient one, in which merchants and artists travelled freely. The literary sources hint at the role that the itinerant craftsman played in antiquity. As we shall see, a growing body of archaeological evidence would suggest that many of the Phoenician objects found abroad were actually manufactured in situ by resident foreign craftsmen.

Past studies have tended to focus on the prominent Egyptian element in Phoenician art, which has been isolated as its major identifying characteristic. In truth, Egyptian cultural influence within the Phoenician realm varied greatly through time, as the Nile kingdom's own political and economic fortunes evolved. The Egyptian Eighteenth Dynasty (fifteenth to fourteenth centuries BC) marked a period of great artistic impact on Phoenicia and the greater Levant. The succeeding Early Iron Age (twelfth to tenth centuries BC) did not. Egyptian influence peaked again in the eighth and in the late sixth to early fifth centuries during the renascent Egyptian Twenty-second Dynasty and under Persian rule; thereafter, it was eclipsed by Hellenism. The picture was a constantly evolving one. All of these trends, it should be noted, affected artistic production in official circles; local craft traditions were more idiosyncratic and regional in their focus. With such observations in mind, we may review some of the major categories of Phoenician artistic production.

IVORYWORK

The marked Egyptian character of Phoenician art beginning in the ninth century may thus be understood within the context of renewed Egyptian influence in the Levant under the Twenty-second Dynasty (945–712 BC). Such influence is manifest on the Phoenician ivories, which show a strong dependence, formally and stylistically, on Egyptian art of this period; the models may be sought in metalwork from Tanis, Egypt's capital.[6]

Decorated ivorywork seems to have been a particular speciality of the Phoenicians; extensive groups of carved ivories in Phoenician style have long been identified at a number of locations outside of Phoenicia proper – in Assyria (at Khorsabad), northern Syria (at Arslan Tash and Zinçirli), and in northern Palestine (Samaria). The Assyrian capital of Nimrud (ancient Kalhu) in northern Iraq has yielded the largest collection of such ivories, which have been divided into two stylistic groups: Phoenician and northern Syrian. The Phoenician group, the core of which was discovered in a storeroom of the North-west Palace of King Ashurnasirpal II, exhibits strong Egyptian influence in its style, technique, and iconography. Among other subjects, the Phoenician-style ivories include a variety of genre themes borrowed from Egyptian art: the birth of Horus, a cow suckling a calf, youths binding a papyrus, a lioness in a papyrus thicket, a griffin trampling a fallen Asiatic. The ivories also feature a variety of winged deities and animals: humans, snakes, falcons, and sphinxes, to name a few. They are typically shown in symmetrical pose, often flanking Egyptian symbols and cult objects, such as the *ankh*, scarab beetle, or djed pillar, symbol of stability.

The Phoenician-style ivories employ a variety of techniques, including ajouré (perforated openwork) and champlevé, a form of deep relief carving in which the background is cut away to reveal the primary decoration. The designs are further ornamented by cloisonné work inset with coloured glass paste and semi-precious stones. (See fig. 53 and plate VI.) The ivories themselves consist primarily of rectangular plaques designed as inlays for wood panelling or furniture: beds, couches, tables, thrones, and chests;[7] in all likelihood, the majority of these inlays travelled with their furniture settings. Ivory- and wood-working were closely associated activities for the Phoenician craftsman. Both employed the same joinery techniques, involving the use of mortice tenons and pins. The individual parts of larger pieces of ivory furniture were often marked by Phoenician letters to indicate their correct arrangement, and to assist in the assembly of the complete object. Ezekial's 'ship of Tyre' is said to have possessed a cedar cabin with an ivory pavilion within. The Phoenician ivory furniture inlays from Samaria may, indeed, have come from the famous 'ivory house' of Ahab, whose lavish interior was probably executed by Phoenician craftsmen. The initiative for its construction may have come from Ahab's wife, Jezebel, who was a Phoenician princess. p

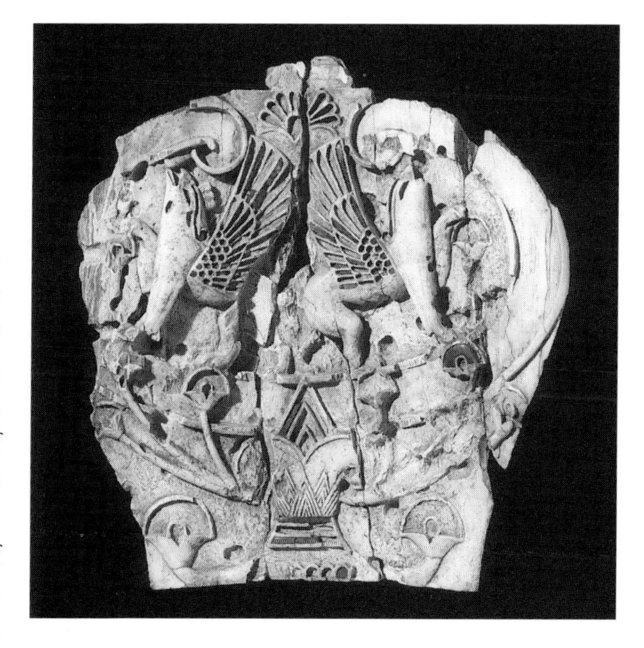

53 *Ivory plaque depicting paired griffins perched within a palmette. From Nimrud, Iraq, eighth century* BC. *The griffins, poised with upraised paws, are shown nibbling at the delicate tendrils of the sacred plant.*

As the biblical texts underscore, the Phoenician ivory carver's art was clearly intended for an élite clientele, consisting primarily of foreign aristocracy. As its high level of quality reveals, production was a palace-controlled industry, its practitioners, members of professional guilds. As in bronzecasting, the skill was probably passed, by arduous apprenticeship, from father to son. Ivory, obtained from elephant tusks, was itself a precious material. By the eighth century, the elephant, indigenous to northern Syria, appears to have become extinct, the victim of overhunting. Thereafter, the ivory utilized by Phoenician artisans was drawn exclusively from tusks imported from North Africa and, perhaps, India. The bronze gates of Shalmaneser III at Balawat depict the raw material being offered as tribute by Sidonians and Tyrians.

Scholarly research in recent years has focused on defining the differences between the Phoenician and northern Syrian styles within the Nimrud ivory corpus. While much progress has been achieved, many questions remain. The problem of origins is a particularly thorny one, especially for the Phoenician-style ivories, since very few examples have been recovered from the Phoenician homeland. Unlike their Syrian-style counterparts, moreover, there are no sculpted stone monuments from the Phoenician mainland with which they can be compared. In truth, there is little hard evidence to associate them with any of the major Phoenician production centres; such attributions are based entirely on stylistic supposition.

It has long been assumed that the Phoenician ivories and bronzes found at Nimrud and other Assyrian cities were Levantine transplants – either tribute or war booty taken from Phoenicia itself. The possibility remains, however, that these ivories, or at least a portion of them, were carved in situ by resident Phoenician artisans recruited from the coast. The latter possibility is suggested by the discovery at Nimrud of an unworked quantity of Egyptian blue, a form of faience paste that the Phoenicians used as an ivory inlay. Indeed, Phoenician artisans may well have worked at a variety of neighbouring commercial centres outside of Phoenicia proper.

METAL-WORK

The reputation of the Phoenicians as highly skilled metal-workers is well established in the Old Testament. The Greek poet Homer, writing in the eighth century, records the gift of a large ornamented silver vessel fashioned by skilled Sidonian craftsmen. Of impressive size and beauty, it was awarded by Achilles as the first prize the funeral games of Patroclus.[8]

Throughout the Aegean and the Near East – from Italy in the west to Mesopotamia in the east, decorated metal bowls in both bronze and silver have been recovered from a variety of archaeological contexts dating from the ninth to the seventh century BC. Compared with the ivories, the bowls are an extremely eclectic lot; both iconographically and stylistically, they are a true amalgam of different cultural elements: Aegean, northern Syrian, Assyrian, and Egyptian. Yet despite their stylistic diversity, they exhibit an underlying uniformity in scheme and composition, which betrays a common artistic heritage and justifies the assignation Phoenician.[9] All display a round central medallion (ornamented with a rosette or scene) and one or more concentric bands of decoration. The themes vary greatly – from alternating plants, animals, and genre motifs (heroic combat, smiting pharaoh, lion attack) (see fig. 54) to continuous figured friezes (military and animal files, votive processions) which, on occasion, depict a narrative in sequential episodes. (See figs 26 and 56.) The great majority are simple shallow, hammered bowls 'raised' from a single piece of sheet metal; their distinctive quality lies in the various decorative techniques employed, which consist of a combination of chasing, engraving, and shallow repoussé

54 *Gilt-silver bowl with medallion scene depicting a four-winged daemon dispatching a rampant lion. From Kourion, Cyprus, late eighth or early seventh century BC. In characteristic fashion, the bowl's surrounding registers depict an amalgam of isolated scenes or vignettes.*

55 *Bronze bowl depicting paired griffins within shrines. From the palace of Ashurnasirpal II at Nimrud, Iraq, eighth century BC. This vessel belongs to a subgroup of bowls with a distinctive four-part arrangement.*

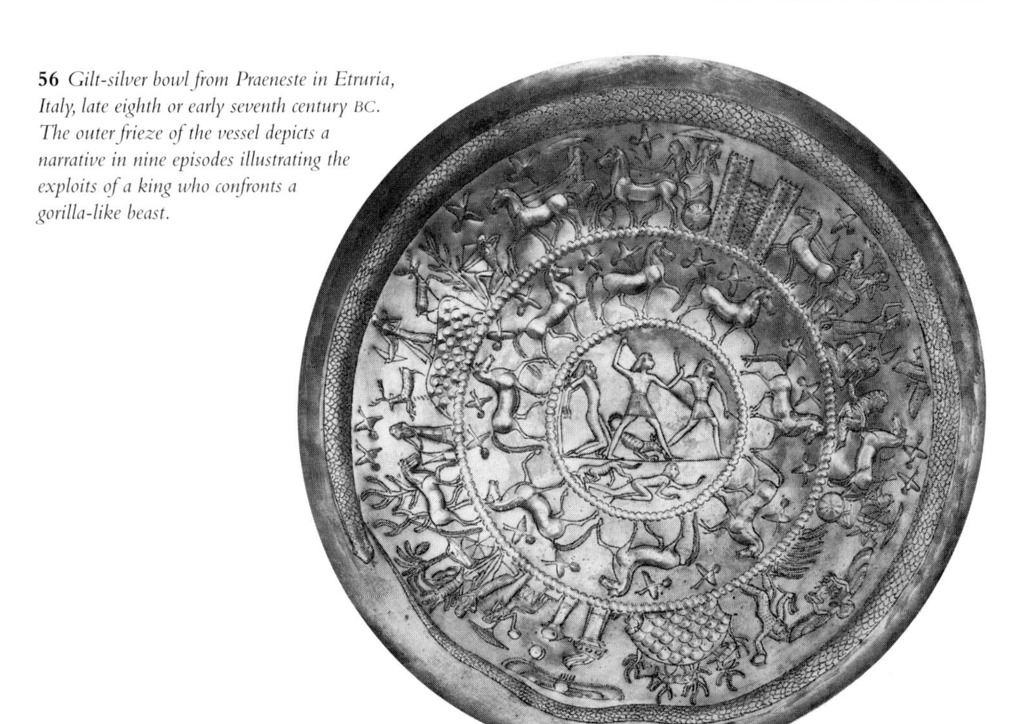

56 *Gilt-silver bowl from Praeneste in Etruria, Italy, late eighth or early seventh century BC. The outer frieze of the vessel depicts a narrative in nine episodes illustrating the exploits of a king who confronts a gorilla-like beast.*

work (the method of producing a relief design by hammering from the reverse side).

As with the ivories, the metal bowls have engendered much discussion over their origin. Clearly, a number of stylistic groupings can be discerned: certain of the bowls from Crete and Italy display a markedly Egyptianizing style, while others from Greece and Assyria show a blend of Syrian and Egyptian artistic features. (See fig. 56.) Certain series may be grouped by subject matter: military files, votive processions, and rows of animals (bulls and sphinxes). With a few notable exceptions, however, it is impossible to associate them geographically with known production centres. The almost complete lack of excavated sheet-metal finds from the Levant precludes any discussion about the location of workshops.[10]

From a chronological standpoint, the bowls reveal some interesting trends. The examples in bronze precede those in silver. (Production of the latter does not begin until about 700 BC.) Of the bronze examples, the bowls with rosette medallion form the earliest grouping, datable to the ninth century BC. The recent discovery of several examples of this variety from datable tomb contexts at Lefkandi on Euboea reveals that the series originated in the tenth century BC.[11] Such an early production date accounts for the absence of Egyptian influence and the popularity of the votive procession genre, which is rooted in earlier Levantine work of the late second millennium BC.

The Phoenician bowl corpus sheds some interesting light on the question of regional production centres. A homogeneous group of vessels may be assigned to a Phoenician workshop on Cyprus, which was active at the end of the eighth and early seventh

57 *Bronze jug with palmette-terminal handle, late eighth–seventh century BC. Provenance unknown.*

centuries BC.[12] (See figs 26 and 54.) Iconographically, the series, which also includes seals, bronze horse trappings, and ivories, shows a strong predilection for Assyrian motifs. (See fig. 62 c.) Such influence accords perfectly with the political status of the island, which was then tributary to Assyria. Several of the bowls (which are of gold-plated silver) bear the Cypriot inscriptions of their aristocratic owners, including one 'Akestor, King of Paphos'. (See fig. 54.)

The gilt-silver bowls from Etruria, which form another distinctive group, also appear to have been the work of an atelier of resident Phoenician craftsmen. As their excavated contexts reveal, their recipients were members of the local aristocracy. In all likelihood, these bowls were manufactured as diplomatic gifts of exchange from locally mined silver.[13] Phoenician metalsmiths also produced a distinctive variety of jug with vertical handle terminating below in a plate with repoussé palmette ornament; examples in bronze and silver have been found throughout the Mediterranean from Spain to Cyprus.[14] (See fig. 57.)

Phoenician artisans created a variety of small cast bronze figurines, which were manufactured primarily as votive offerings for temples and domestic shrines. (See fig. 41 and plate III.) The subjects consist largely of seated or standing male and female deities in Egyptianizing dress, often poised with hand extended, palm out, in a gesture of blessing. Surprisingly few have so far been recovered from Phoenicia proper, but a number of examples found abroad appear to have been exported from the mainland. The finer examples have inlaid eyes and faces overlaid with gold or silver foil.

Stone sculpture

The Phoenicians appear never to have developed a coherent tradition in large-scale stone statuary, a fact perhaps not surprising for a culture specializing in portable art. As scattered finds reveal, however, they did produce fine carved relief sculpture, primarily for funerary purposes. Notable are a series of round-topped stelae that depict deities and scenes of worship. (See figs 35 and 58.) Primary production of these sculptural reliefs, carved from local limestone (*ramleh*), does not appear to predate the Persian period, when large-scale stone sculpture in other media (sarcophagi, statuary, architectural reliefs) is first attested on Cyprus and the mainland.

It was at this time that Phoenician sculptors began producing statuary in the round. As one might expect, Egyptian models furnished the prototypes. The bulk of the early statuary portrays a common subject: a male youth in Egyptian dress advancing with one arm held at the side and the other bent and drawn across the chest. Clad in a skin-tight, short-sleeved tunic, he wears a pleated kilt, or *shenti*, and an elaborate floral collar, or *ousekh*. Interestingly, this dress style, which is well attested in Cypriot sculpture of the sixth to fifth centuries BC, finds its inspiration not in contemporary Egyptian sculpture of the Saitic period (Twenty-sixth Dynasty), but in earlier models of the New Kingdom. The latter period features the skirt type employed by the Phoenician sculptor – a flowing, full-length garment with central pendent flap decorated below with a pair of serpents with solar disks. It was through art of the Twenty-second Dynasty, in the ninth century BC, that the Phoenician artist acquired the stylistic models for his sculptural creations; from the mainland, the style influenced Phoenician fashion on Cyprus.[15]

Of early monumental sculpture, very little exists; attention may be drawn to an unfinished male colossus in limestone from Byblos, whose Egyptian antecedents may be clearly seen in its sculptural stance, Egyptian wig, and supporting back pillar.[16] In addition to local limestone, the Phoenicians also worked in alabaster; workshops specializing in this material produced both relief sculpture and a variety of cosmetic vessels, including bottles in female form. (See figs 59 and 60.)

SARCOPHAGI

Among Phoenician crafts, the production of sarcophagi must have been a thriving industry. The extant record, however, is only a partial one: of the countless wooden coffins that were carved in antiquity, only scattered remnants survive. Aside from the Ahiram sarcophagus (see plate V), all surviving Phoenician stone examples date to the Persian period, when the carving of anthropoid (human-form) coffins apparently originated in Phoenicia. The roots of the tradition may be sought in Egypt; the two earliest Phoenician mummiform sarcophagi, those of the Sidonian kings Tabnit I and Eshmunazar II, were, in fact, Egyptian imports. (See the frontispiece.) To date, more than a hundred stone anthropoid sarcophagi dating from the mid-fifth to fourth century BC have been recovered from tombs in the Phoenician mainland. (See fig. 61.) The subjects are both male and female. (The latter predominate.) Their gender is indicated by the headpiece, which is carefully coiffed and sculpted. With a few notable exceptions, the rest of the body is summarily rendered in a mummiform shape that tapers to a flattened ledge representing the feet. As one would expect, the earliest examples in the series are most strongly Egyptianizing in style, mimicking their southern prototypes, both in the shape of the box and lid and in the stylistic rendering of the head. Beginning in the later fifth century, through influence from the Cypriot, East Greek, and Attic spheres, the sarcophagi become increasingly Hellenized

58 *Stele depicting the striding figure of a storm god atop a lion. From Amrit or Tell Kazel, Syria, ninth or eighth century* BC.

in style. The variety of hairstyles depicted (which evolve from a snail-curled to a wavy and then tussled coiffure) reflect Greek fashion. Through time, the coffin becomes progressively more flattened and less human in form, the latest examples consisting of a neckless head-mask appended to a rigid, elongated box.[17]

The authorship of the Phoenician sarcophagi has been the subject of much debate. Arguments for their Greek workmanship have been based upon their strongly Hellenizing style and their primary material: imported marble. Yet, idionsyncrasies in style and carving technique and the occasional presence of Phoenician letters (representing sculptors' signatures or manufacturers' marks) suggest that their makers were indigenous. As for their source of manufacture, the city of Sidon, whose royal necropoli have yielded the majority of examples, represents a logical possibility. Arwad, too, may have been a regional centre of manufacture, judging from the local basalt of which its coffins are made. The Aegean island of Paros was the primary source of the imported marble; the presence of an unfinished sarcophagus on the island, moreover, suggests the likely existence of a Phoenician enterprise there, which not only marketed but actually produced and exported sarcophagi to the mainland.[18]

JEWELLERY

The Phoenicians also specialized in the production of jewellery in precious metals, following a tradition dating back to the Bronze Age. (See plate I.) Their skill may be seen, above all, in the delicate use of granulation and filigree-work, often rendered in a painstakingly minute scale. The Phoenician jeweller was fond of embellishing his work with insets of coloured glass or semi-precious stone, such as lapis lazuli and carnelian. Gold and plated silver were the preferred materials; for the less affluent, bronze was enhanced with gold or silver foil overlay.

Owing to the paucity of excavations in the homeland, the greater part of surviving Phoenician jewellery has so far been found in the Punic west, especially at Carthage and Tharros (see plate VII); both were regional centres of production, beginning in the seventh to sixth centuries BC. It is clear, however, that many of the early Punic finds were patterned after mainland models. Excavated finds of jewellery from Cyprus help to supplement the picture. The importance of Sidon as a centre of manufacture may be gleaned from the lavish gold and silver jewellery recovered from later Persian burial contexts there.[19]

59 (above left) *Alabaster relief depicting a recumbent sphinx on a pedestal. From Arwad, Syria, sixth–fifth century* BC.
60 (above right) *Alabaster vessel in the form of a goddess seated on a throne flanked by sphinxes. From Tutugi (Galera) near Granada, Spain, seventh or sixth century* BC. *This ritual vessel was designed to hold a liquid, which, when poured into a hollow in the goddess' head, flowed from her pierced breasts into a large bowl.*

As its iconography and its funerary context suggest, much of Phoenician jewellery served a magical, protective function. Symbols, such as the Egyptian *ankh*, eye of Horus, scarab beetle, winged solar disk, and the crescent-and-disk, appear regularly on pendants, amulets, and rings. The Phoenician jeweller was fond of embellishing necklaces, earrings, and ornamental plaquettes with miniature pendants in hammered gold; these were fashioned in a variety of shapes, including collared vessels (*bullae*) (see plate VIIC), U-shaped 'purses', falcons (see plate VIIB), pomegranates, and wire circlets. Another common type, known as the 'ball-and-cage', consisted of a solid square box surmounted by a small granulated pyramid. (See plate VIIB.) Other types of pendant included repoussé sheet-metal plaques in the form of female figures, lotus flowers, and eyes of Horus, as well as medallion- and shrine-shaped disks with elaborately embossed or granulated decoration. Another popular item of Phoenician jewellery was the finger-ring, which frequently carried an oval or cartouche-shaped bezel or a scarab setting in a swivel mount. (See fig. 62 e, g, h.) Earrings were typically leech-shaped; a popular variety featured a pendent cross which, when seen together with the attachment ring, formed an *ankh* sign. (See plate VIIA.) In addition to the above repertory, Punic jewellers specialized in the production of gold amulet cases with animal-headed terminals. (See plate VIID.)

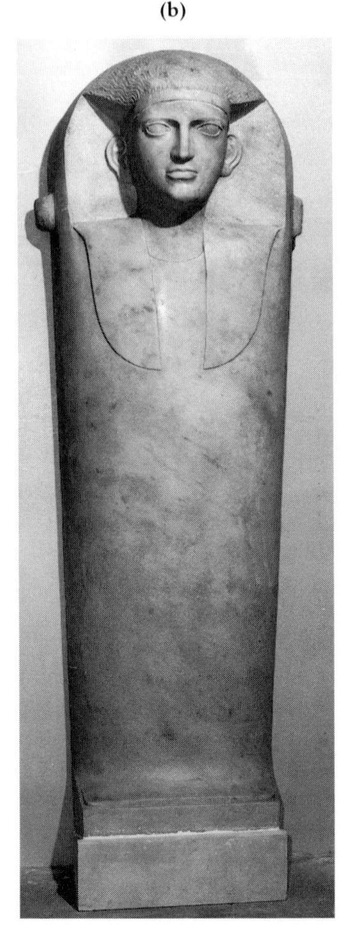

61 (a) *Marble female anthropoid sarcophagus, from Magharat Ablun, Sidon, Lebanon, fifth century BC.*
(b) *Marble male anthropoid sarcophagus, fifth century BC. Provenance unknown.*

SEAL ENGRAVING

As it was throughout the Near East, the cylinder seal was utilized early on in Phoenicia. With the advent of the alphabetic script and the introduction of papyrus, however, it was gradually supplanted, towards the end of the second millennium BC, by the stamp seal. The earliest varieties were cone-shaped, carved in a soft stone with stylized linear representations of animals and hunting scenes.

Some time around the beginning of the first millennium BC, the Phoenician seal engraver adopted the use of the scarab, its form patterned after the coleopteryx beetle, a sacred Egyptian symbol of regeneration. The earliest examples from the Phoenician mainland, datable to the ninth century BC, display an assortment of fragmented Egyptian symbols – the *ankh*, falcon, uraeus serpent, and eye of Horus – presented within a series of horizontal registers, often subdivided into panels. (See fig. 62 a.) In Phoenician fashion, the Egyptian motifs are juxtaposed out of context, with non-Egyptian animal subjects thrown in; several display cartouches with false hieroglyphs. The more elaborate examples bear images with possible royal associations, such as the four-winged scarab and the robed

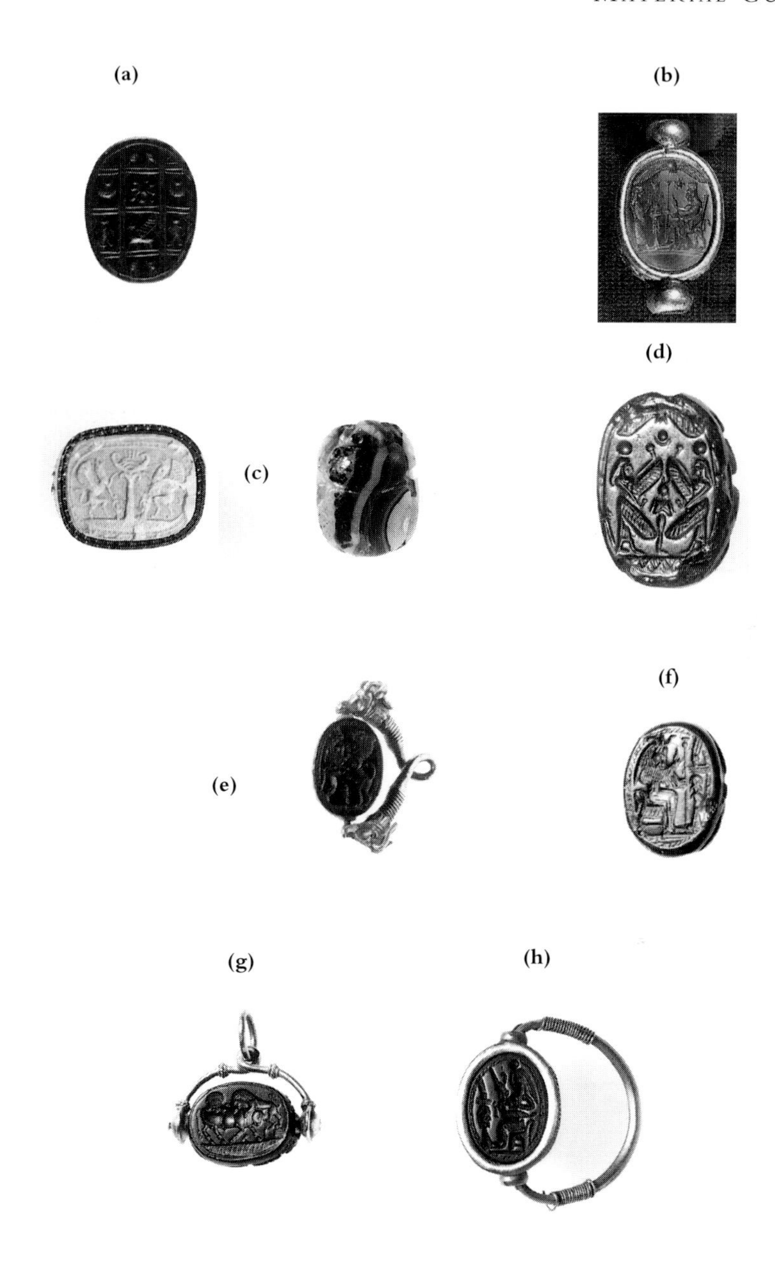

62 *(a) Lapis lazuli scaraboid with compartmentalized decoration, from Byblos, Lebanon; (b) amethyst scarab, worshipper before enthroned goddess. From Helalieh, Lebanon; (c) banded agate scarab, griffins flanking sacred tree, provenance unknown; (d) carnelian scarab: Isis and Nephthys flanking Horus, provenance unknow; (e) green jasper scarab in gold setting: Bes wrestling with rampant lions, from Byblos, Lebanon; (f) green jasper scarab: enthroned bull-headed deity before incense burner, from Tharros, Sardinia; (g) green jasper scaraboid in gold hoop setting: lion-bull combat, from Tharros, Sardinia; green jasper scarab in gold swivel setting; (h) Isis suckling Horus before an incense burner, provenance unknown.*

figure with *ankh* and upraised hand. An early ninth-century example, recently discovered at Ḥorvat Rosh Zayit, is cast in bronze with lead inlays.[20]

The multi-registered composition of the Early Iron Age seals was ultimately reduced to a simplified format with a primary scene framed above and below by a winged sun disk and the Egyptian *nub* sign (signifying heaven). (See fig. 62 b, d, e, f.) The scarab form itself was often streamlined, its anatomical structure abbreviated or omitted altogether to yield a simplified oval, known as a scaraboid. (See fig. 62 a, g.) The latter served to showcase the variegated, polished hard stones utilized by the Phoenician lapidary – amethyst, chalcedony, carnelian, agate, serpentine, quartzite, onyx, and jasper.

The iconography of the Phoenician seal engraver reflects a strong interest in Egyptian religious and magical themes concerned with regeneration. Popular subjects included the birth of Horus from the lotus flower and scenes of Isis nursing the infant Horus (often symbolized by the suckling cow and calf). (See fig. 62 d, h.) The seal-carver's repertoire also included a host of winged, protective deities and genies shown individually or paired around a sacred plant; a popular character was the four-winged daemon. The simpler seals, produced in soft stone and glass paste, often featured individual animals and floral motifs, such as sphinxes, griffins, falcons, and palmettes. Iconographically, the seals of the eighth to seventh centuries BC reveal a close dependence upon the repertoire of the Phoenician bowls and ivories; in many instances, the seal-carver seems to have quoted or excerpted directly from them. (See figs 54 and 62 c.)

Phoenician seal engraving reached a peak in the fifth to fourth centuries BC, when production spread throughout the Punic Mediterranean. The city of Tharros on Sardinia served as a primary centre of production and redistribution for scaraboids carved from a variety of locally mined hard stones, including green jasper (see fig. 62 f, g). Such seals display a diversified repertoire of the themes drawn not only from the Egyptian, but from the Etruscan and western Greek (Ionian) cultural spheres. Among divine figures represented, Isis (see fig. 62 h), Bes (see fig. 62 e), Herakles, and a form of bull-headed Baal (see fig. 62 f) were especially popular. Scenes depicting animal combat were also favoured. (See fig. 62 g.)

FAIENCE AND GLASS

Phoenician glass was celebrated in antiquity. According to the Latin author Pliny, Sidon was renowned for its workshops. Strabo reports that the southern Phoenician coastal dunes between Tyre and Akko furnished the best sand for glassmaking.[21] In all likelihood, the technique of glassblowing, which revolutionized the glass industry, originated in the region in the late first century BC.

Long before this time, the Phoenicians had been actively involved in glass manufacture. The literary and archaeological evidence suggest that, in the Late Bronze Age, the Phoenician mainland and perhaps also Cyprus were manufacturing and trading in raw glass and finished products. The correspondence from Tell el-Amarna in Egypt refers to imported shipments of raw glass from Tyre and its neighbours; the Ulu Burun wreck carried a consignment of cylindrical glass ingots and a Canaanite jar full of glass beads.[22]

By the late eighth century BC, following an extended lapse in the Early Iron Age, glass production is again attested in Mesopotamia, which now served as a manufacturing centre for vessels in the core-formed technique. The process, which employed heated rods of coloured glass that were wrapped around a sand or clay core, was utilized earlier in both Egypt and Assyria during the Late Bronze Age. Its westward spread within the Mediterranean in the seventh century BC has been attributed to migrant glassworkers from Mesopotamia, who may have established a local industry on the island of Rhodes.

Several early groups of core-formed vessels, however, appear to have originated in workshops outside of the Mesopotamian sphere. One is a class of juglets with white-threaded decoration; its Mediterranean distribution (Rhodes, Crete, Etruria) and its association with related vessels found in the Levant (at Achziv and Lachish) suggest an eastern Mediterranean origin, perhaps within the Phoenician sphere. Phoenician traders may also have been responsible for the export of a transitional group of sixth-century glass alabastra with a widespread Mediterranean distribution (Egypt, Cyprus, Carthage, Tharros in Sardinia, and Praeneste in Etruria).[23] The absence of mainland Phoenician documentation for both groups, however, precludes any definitive attribution.

The vigorous Mediterranean industry in core-formed bottles that arose toward the end of the sixth century and flourished in the succeeding fifth and fourth centuries, however, was clearly a Greek and not a Phoenician prerogative. As has been observed, the Hellenic character of their shapes (alabastron, amphoriskos, oinochoe, aryballos) and their pronounced Aegean concentration point to an East Greek centre of production – on Rhodes itself or one or more of the Greek communities along the Ionian coast of Asia Minor.[24]

More directly associated with the Phoenicians are a group of cast vessels – alabastra and hemispherical cups and bowls – in a thick, translucent glass, that were moulded in the lost-wax technique and subsequently polished (and occasionally wheel-cut) in a hardened state. (See plate VIII.) Such luxury vessels in cold-cut glass have been found in Spain, Etruria, Crete, and Assyria (Nimrud); all of their shapes (which include phialai, hemispherical bowls, alabastra, and handled jugs) consciously imitate forms in other media (metal, alabaster, pottery), once again underscoring the close interrelationship that existed between separate workshops. In this regard, attention may be drawn to a cold-cut glass imitation of a Phoenician metal bowl from Nimrud; the same site also yielded a series of painted glass plaques in Egyptianizing Phoenician style.[25]

Phoenician craftsmen also appear to have been responsible for the manufacture of cast coloured glass inlays for ivorywork. Many of the Phoenician-style ivory furniture panels from Nimrud were decorated in this manner; such plaques were formed from sections of preformed canes or segments of sheet glass that were cut and assembled (and then fused) into geometric or floral designs.

In the late seventh century BC, Phoenician workshops in the eastern Mediterranean began producing a series of rod-formed polychrome glass pendants in the shape of demon masks, animals, and male and female heads. The production sources for these head beads, which served as talismans on necklaces, are difficult to pinpoint; the Phoenician coast, Cyprus, and the Egyptian Delta all represent viable possibilities; in all likelihood, they were produced in a number of diverse locations, including Carthage in the Punic west. The earliest examples, depicting mouthless grotesques and ram heads, were small (less than 3 centimetres (1 inch)) and unostentatious. The later pendants grew progressively larger and more elaborate; the Punic male head beads with curly beard and coiffure measured up to 8 centimetres (3 inches) in height. (See plate IX.) Found throughout the Mediterranean and beyond – in Anatolia, south Russia, and even transalpine Europe – such portable trinkets travelled widely through primary and secondary trade.[26] Phoenician workshops on the mainland and on Cyprus also produced a variety of glass seals and beads (including a version in ribbed blue glass), which were exported to the Aegean. Of the seals, attention may be drawn to a distinctive class of Egyptianizing scaraboids in blue and green glass.

The Phoenicians also worked extensively in glass paste and faience, a self-glazing, silica-based frit invented earlier by the Egyptians. Such frit-like materials were moulded to form a seemingly infinite variety of charms, including scarabs and amulets in the form of Egyptian symbols and deities. Such trinkets, produced in local ateliers on the mainland, Cyprus, and Rhodes, were the stock-in-trade of Phoenician merchants. (The Greek poet Homer refers to them as *athyrmata*, 'baubles' or 'playthings'.) The very best of Phoenician faience work was admirably done (see fig. 63); the bulk, however, was careless hackwork produced to satisfy popular market demand. Phoenician craftsmen on the island of Rhodes produced a series of handsome faience perfume or unguent vessels, including a group of anthropomorphic vases in the form of kneeling women and monkeys.[27]

63 *Some Phoenician attempts at imitation of Egyptian faience could be quite convincing. A case in point is the famous 'Bocchoris' vase from Etruscan Tarquinia, which bears the royal cartouche of a twenty-fourth-Dynasty Egyptian king of the late eighth century. A similar vessel was found at Motya on Sicily.*

TERRACOTTAS

The Phoenician coroplast, the modeller of terracotta figurines, stands apart from the other forms of artisan so far considered. By and large, his products were aimed at a local market. His style and approach were often idiosyncratic, his work modest and unpretentious – the product of a 'folk art' tradition. The regional character of mainland Phoenician terracottas may be seen in their general absence abroad and in the association of particular types with specific locales (e.g. the miniature shrines with southern Phoenicia, the equestrian figurines with the region of Amrit [see fig. 23]). In marked contrast to other categories of Phoenician art, their production may be firmly tied with the homeland, as numerous archaeological finds from Sidon, Achziv, Sarepta, and now Beirut attest. In the case of Kition, the discovery of terracottas and associated moulds points to the existence of a local workshop.[28]

The terracottas themselves may be divided on technical grounds into three broad groupings: those made by hand, those thrown on the potter's wheel, and those reproduced in a mould. All three techniques are well attested in the Near East. The purely handmade figures are often crude and naive in conception, the idiosyncratic products of amateur craftsmen. With their tapering conical torsos, moulded heads, and handmade arms of rolled clay, the wheel-made terracottas evince a more uniform tradition. Like the handmade varieties, they show little awareness of foreign stylistic conventions. It is within the moulded figurines and plaques that outside influence is most apparent. Such figurines, generally produced in open moulds, have been found throughout the southern Phoenician coastal realm – as ex-votos in sanctuaries, as funerary offerings in cemeteries, and, occasionally, as cargo in sunken transport ships. As their subjects clearly reflect, they are primarily votive in character. A common type is the standing nude female with hands cupping or supporting the breasts. Another ubiquitous variety is the veiled pregnant goddess (the so-called *Dea gravida*) seated with right hand placed above the abdomen. (See fig. 39.) Both types were potent symbols of fertility and fecundity. The pregnant female figurine is sometimes found in association with the statuette of a bearded male deity wearing an Osirian *atef* (ostrich-feathered) crown. The two formed part of a divine couple, whose identity remains unclear.[29] Another popular category of terracotta votive was a miniature shrine with a pillared architectural façade and a central cult image (see fig. 43).[30] The representation of a deity seated upon a sphinx-support throne was also a widespread cultic image. On a more secular level, the Phoenician coroplast produced animal-shaped vessels, early examples of which have been found at Carthage.

While the Punic coroplastic tradition paralleled that of the east in the basic techniques employed, the absence of several widespread terracotta types, such as the seated pregnant goddess and bearded male deity, underscores the independent nature of its development, which was largely shaped by the mediating influence of Cyprus and Sicily. It was through Cyprus that the Punic realm inherited several basic types, such as the lamp-bearing figurine and the votive statuette with wheel-turned body and separately modelled head; the latter type is abundantly represented throughout the Punic west. (See fig. 64.)

Through the Greek colonial foundations in southern Sicily, the Punic terracotta tradition was impregnated by Hellenic influence at an early date. Greek forms and styles emerged in the west around 600 BC, a full century before their appearance in the homeland. The Balearic island of Ibiza was home to one of the most active and innovative centres of western, Punic terracotta production. From the end of the sixth to the mid-second century BC, coroplasts from Ibiza produced a vast number of terracottas in a variety of styles, including moulded female statuettes in Hellenic style and dress, and an extensive series of bell- and egg-shaped votive statuettes in the Cypriot tradition.[31] (See fig. 64.)

One of the oldest and richest of Phoenician coroplastic arts was that of mask-making, a tradition whose roots extended back to the Late Bronze Age. Wheel-made and slightly under-life-size, with cut-out eyes and mouth, such masks form a frequent offering in Phoenician mainland burials, beginning in the eighth century BC; a stunning example has been uncovered recently at Tyre's mainland necropolis. (See plate X.) The decorative techniques employed by the Phoenician artisan – the application of red and black paint and the use of impressed circlets for the hair and beard – point to the influence of earlier Cypriot models. It was from Cyprus via the eastern mainland that the Punic masking tradition originated in the seventh century BC.[32]

POTTERY

In contrast to other areas of creative endeavour, the Phoenicians were extremely conservative in their ceramic tradition, which shows little of the creativity and flair that mark so many of their artistic pursuits. In fact, Phoenician pottery as a whole is rather mediocre in character, both in its decoration and in the quality of its potting. Its commercial value derived primarily, if not exclusively, from its utilitarian function as tableware or as containers for other more marketable commodities.

The pottery we now associate with the Phoenicians (and which serves as a marker of their cultural identity) is first attested in the Early Iron Age (*c.* mid-eleventh century BC).[33] At this time the distinctive bichrome (two-colour) technique appeared. (See fig. 65.) The decorative scheme uses a series of broad red or reddish-purple bands outlined by narrow grey or black lines; these encircle the vase horizontally or appear vertically, on opposing sides, as filled circles or 'bull's eyes'. The latter ornamental scheme also decorates the interior surface of shallow bowls (fig. 65 c–h). Aside from the concentric banding itself, the decorative repertoire of the bichrome potter was limited to a few geometric patterns: combinations of straight and wavy lines, pendent triangles, vertical lozenges, six- or eight-pointed stars, and hatched banding. (See fig. 65 f, i)[34]

64 *Bell-shaped terracotta statuette with a lamp on its head. From Ibiza, fifth century BC.*

Some time around the mid-ninth century BC, the bichrome style gave way to a new technique involving the overall application of a burnished red (or occasionally black) engobe or slip. (See plates XI and XII.) Such polished red-slip ware remained fashionable for some three centuries until the advent of the Persian period (*c.*550 BC), when imported Greek wares (especially Athenian black- and red-slip) came into vogue.

The Phoenician potter employed a repertoire of shapes (including bowls, plates, flasks, jugs, pitchers, and storage jars) that remained fairly standard throughout the Iron Age (see fig. 65). Three classes of vessel may be singled out: the strainer-spouted jar, the neck-ridge jug, and the trefoil-mouth pitcher. The strainer-spouted jar is attested early on; its trough-shaped, upward-tilting sidespout held a strainer at its base, which filtered sediments from heavy liquids. The neck-ridge jug underwent a long development – from a simple pilgrim flask to a spherical jug to a ring-based vessel with flaring, ultimately mushroom-shaped, rim. (See fig. 65.) The mushroom-lipped jug formed the recurrent type of the Phoenician colonies in the seventh and early sixth centuries BC. (See plate XI.) The third shape – the pitcher with trefoil (three-lobed) spout – was the most elegant of the three; its tapering form and carinated shoulder reveal a derivation from metal-work. (See plate XII and figs 57 and 65 o, p, q.)

Among the varieties of Phoenician monochrome pottery, attention may be drawn to a type of ceramic ware known as black-on-red, which bore a distinctive banded decoration of finely drawn black-painted lines on a polished red slip. The technique was widely employed in Cyprus on a series of juglets, which traditionally had been identified as Phoenician, based upon a resemblance to similar wares from the mainland. As clay analysis has shown, however, the Cypriot juglets in this technique are not of Phoenician, but native Cypriot manufacture, and should be distinguished from their mainland counterparts in Philistia and Phoenicia proper; all three are products of distinct traditions.[35]

At Carthage and in the Punic west, the early ceramic repertoire of the eighth and seventh centuries adheres closely to the mainland Phoenician tradition, adopting many of the same shapes, including the mushroom-lipped jug, the trefoil-mouth pitcher, and the flaring-lipped plate. (See fig. 65 m, n.) In the late seventh century BC, however, Punic pottery began to diverge regionally through interaction with surrounding ceramic traditions, both foreign (Greek and Etruscan) and indigenous (Iberian and Sardinian). This independent development came to an end around 500 BC with the emergence of Carthage as the dominant regional political power.

The excavations at Sarepta have yielded a great deal of information about the firing and preparation processes employed by the Phoenician potter. His kiln, made of fieldstone walls with a clay coating, was two-levelled, consisting of an upper chamber in which pottery was stacked, and a lower one, subdivided into two kidney-shaped lobes, for stoking and firing. (See fig. 66.) Pottery preparation was done in an adjoining courtyard, which was equipped with a potter's wheel and a circular basin; the latter held the slip that was applied as decoration to the vessel's surface when leather-hard. The excavations at Sarepta have also yielded the remains of a cemented basin used for washing and storing clay.[36]

65 *Chart showing the evolution of Phoenician pottery shapes.*

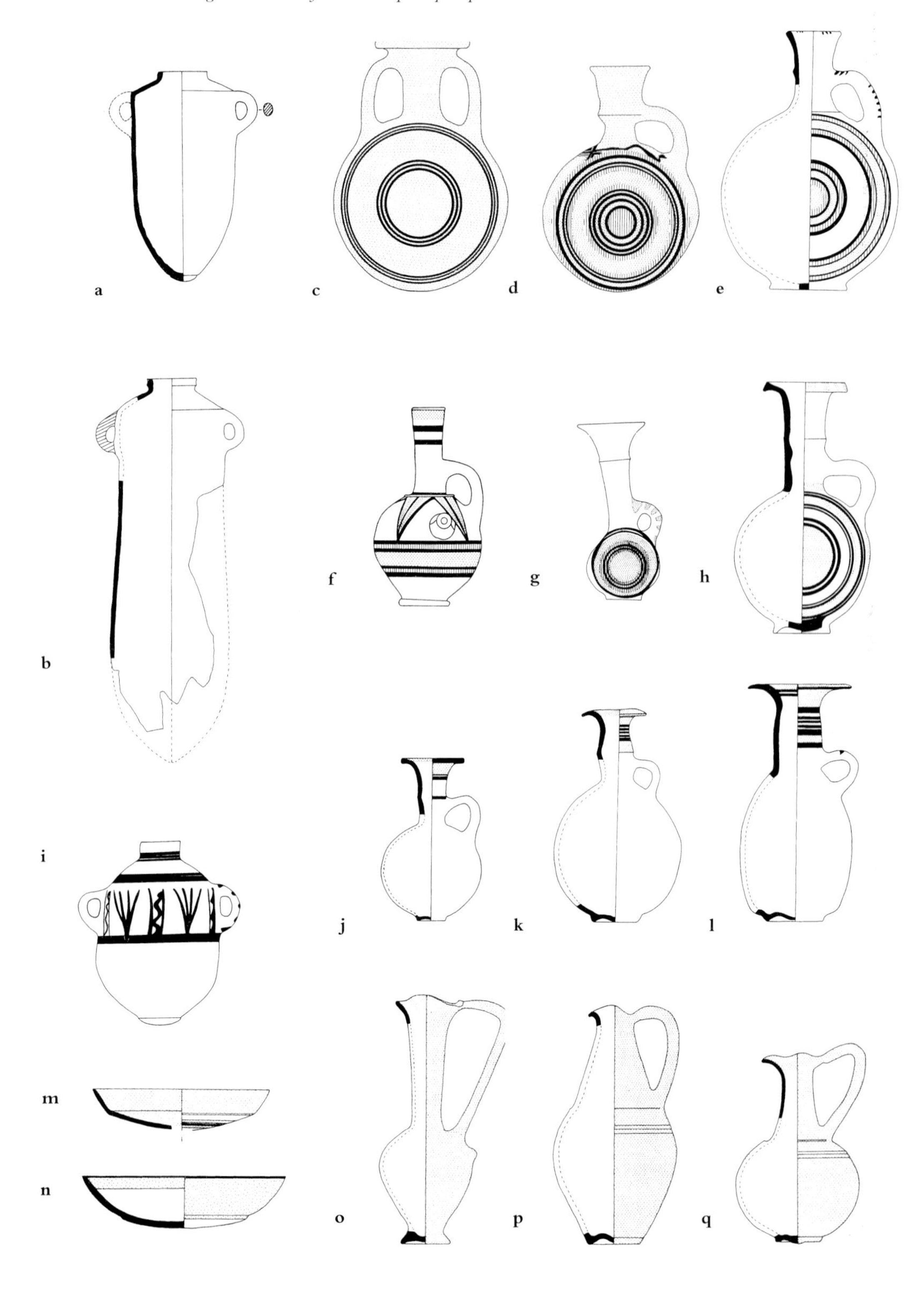

Present-day investigation at the Lebanese village of Beit Shehab offers some indication of the lengthy processes involved in Phoenician pottery manufacture. In the modern method, the clay, excavated from nearby terraces, is levigated for four to five months in a series of settling basins, and then stored in a cellar. Once fashioned, the jars are allowed to dry for several weeks. During the actual firing process, the kiln is kept burning for eight days at a maximum temperature of about 800 degrees centigrade; after a gradual cooling period of 24 hours, the kiln is then emptied of its contents.[37] In all likelihood, the ancient Phoenician potter adhered to a roughly similar schedule.

TEXTILE WEAVING AND DYEING

The Phoenicians were renowned in antiquity for the production of decorated fabrics. Homer, writing in the eighth century BC, tells of the colourful woven textiles for which the Sidonian women were famous. Garments of brightly coloured fabric figured prominently among the Phoenician tribute recorded by the Assyrians. The prophet Ezekial, too, speaks of the Tyrian trade in choice garments and in clothes of embroidered purple.

Tragically, however, not a shred of Phoenician fabric has survived to inform us about the appearance or construction of these coveted textiles. Their embroidered designs and decorative techniques remain a mystery. The ancient texts do, however, provide us with detailed information about the celebrated dye – Tyrian purple – that gave them their vaunted reputation.[38] The dye's ancient association with the Phoenicians and Tyre is clear. The modern name 'Phoenician' stems from the Greek word *phoinix*, which, among other things, denotes the colour purple or crimson. According to Greek legend, the Tyrian dye was discovered by Melqart himself, while strolling along the Mediterranean shore with his dog and the nymph Tyros. As the myth relates, the canine bit into a large sea-snail and stained its mouth purple; the god promptly dyed a gown with the extract and presented it to his consort. The mollusc type, the *murex*, was featured by the Tyrians on their fourth-century coinage. (See fig. 29 c.)

66 *Firing chamber of pottery kiln uncovered at Sarepta, Lebanon. University of Pennsylvania excavations.*

Archaeological research both in the homeland and abroad has verified the Phoenicians' association with the *murex* and dye production. At Sidon, exploration in the early twentieth century documented the remains of two massive heaps of broken and discarded *murex*, the remnants of an extensive dyeing installation that utilized both major types of the Mediterranean mollusc species (*Murex trunculus* and *Murex brandaris*). Excavations at Sarepta have uncovered a similar pile of crushed shells, along with pottery sherds covered with a purple deposit, which chemical analysis has verified to be molluscan purple. The Sareptan pottery fragments came from Canaanite storage jars dating to the thirteenth century BC, providing the earliest scientifically datable evidence for large-scale production of the purple dye.

The Latin authority Pliny, writing in the first century AD, provides an account of the actual dyeing process. He describes how the *murex* shells were broken and their glands extracted and heated for ten days in a large tin vat containing salt water.[39] The dye gradually liquified out, producing a colourless compound that yielded the colour-fast purple dye, when re-exposed to the air. The intensity of the colour, which ranged from rose to dark violet, varied according to the dye strength used; according to Pliny, the coveted Tyrian purple was produced by double-dipping the wool. Modern experiments have reproduced and verified the ancient process, confirming that *Murex trunculus* was utilized in rendering the dye. The fullest results were obtained by plunging the wool into the reduced compound prior to oxidation, enabling the dye to permeate the textile's fibres.

The process itself, as the ancients reveal, was both painstaking and excruciating, as the secreted *murex* glands produced a nauseating stench. This explains why the refuse heaps marking the ancient dye production were located downwind – on the lee side of town. However, the results more than justified the effort. The dye produced (a single ounce of which required thousands of molluscs) was worth more than its weight in gold. An early mark of royalty, its production was ultimately controlled, in Roman Imperial times, by the state; the Emperor Nero even issued an edict permitting only the emperor to wear the purple fabric.

EXOTICA: *TRIDACNA* SHELLS

Among the exotica produced by Phoenician artisans, particular attention may be drawn to one specialty item carved from the shell of the giant Indo-Pacific clam *tridacna*. More than a hundred examples have now been found, ranging in location from Italy to the continental Near East (Jordan, Iraq, Iran). (See fig. 67.) Judging from their homogeneous style and technique, it appears that all were produced in a single or closely related group of workshops around the mid-seventh century BC, as evidenced by their standardized decorative format. The entire back of the shell and the interior perimeter bear incised decoration depicting animals and human figures paired around floral motifs. The interior, more simply decorated, typically features recumbent sphinxes. The exterior, the main field, depicts a variety of male figures (deities, archers, horsemen) set against an elaborate backdrop of stylized lotus plants. The umbo of the bivalve shell itself is carved in the shape of a human female or bird's head.

Stylistically, the *tridacna* shells display many correspondences with late Assyrian art, evident especially in the rendering of the umbo head with its broad features and fleshy lip; the latter is delicately carved with drilled features (pupils, nostrils, ears) and carefully incised coiffure. The style as a whole is marked by the use of cross-hatching.

The concave centre of the *tridacna* shell is left undecorated, suggesting that it was used (as shells often were in antiquity) as a container for eye cosmetics. The style of the umbo head relates closely to a group of cosmetic palettes in alabaster and limestone from Jordan, the handles of which are formed as heads. Both types appear to have derived from the same workshop. As for the production centre, a location along the southern Phoenician coast remains the best guess.[40] The shell's broad inland distribution, along with the evidence of recent finds from northern Israel, would support such a Phoenician coastal production centre.[41]

PHOENICIAN ARTISTIC INFLUENCE ABROAD

As the archaeological record clearly attests, the Phoenicians' westward commercial forays within the Mediterranean clearly exerted a strong cultural impact upon the surrounding indigenous cultures in the basin. From Cyprus to Spain, along the path of Phoenician trade,

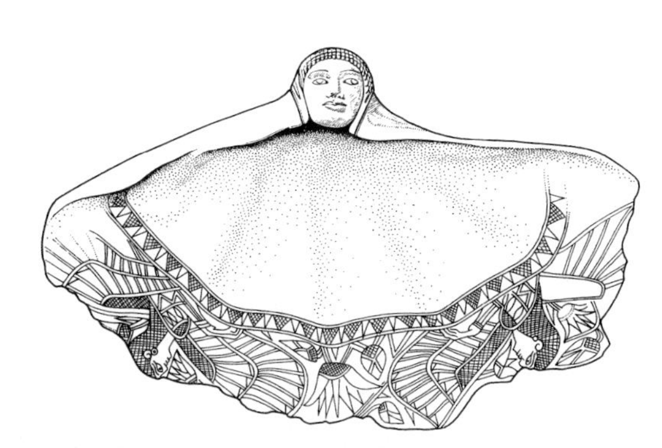

67 *Engraved tridacna shell from Vulci in Etruria, Italy, seventh century* BC.

evidence of Near Eastern influence may be found in the artistic traditions of Crete, Greece, central Italy, Sicily, Sardinia, and the Iberian peninsula. This 'orientalizing' phenomenon, which is marked by the regional adoption or imitation of eastern artistic models and techniques, originated in the late eighth century BC and flourished in the succeeding seventh.

The term 'orientalizing' itself is a broad one, and encompasses a variety of manifestations, each resulting from varying levels of interaction between visitor and host tradition. The strongly Near Eastern character of the indigenous art of Crete and Etruria, for example, was the product of direct influence exerted by resident Phoenician craftsmen. In both regions, such influence is most apparent in metal-work and ivorywork, two media in which the Phoenicians themselves actively traded. Needless to say, oriental artistic impact is clearest and most apparent in the period following initial contact, when eastern models were often copied or imitated directly. This initial imitative stage soon led to a period of synthesis and adaptation, in which the native artist developed his own distinct style blending foreign and native elements. This process of independent development may be traced in both Etruscan and Cretan metal-work.[42]

Within a given tradition, the extent of oriental cultural impact mirrors the intensity of Phoenician trade contact in that region. It is not surprising, then, that dynamic orientalizing artistic traditions arose not only in Etruria, but in Sardinia and southern Spain, where the Phoenicians concentrated their mining efforts. The strongly orientalizing character of native Tartessian art found inland along the Guadalquivir valley clearly reflects such commercial activity, which was generated, in all likelihood, by Phoenician merchants and artisans based at Cadiz.[43] As in Etruria, the orientalizing character of the sumptuary arts (i.e. precious metal-work) from princely burials in the region clearly betokens an active level of diplomatic exchange between Phoenician entrepreneurs and local rulers.

In other areas less directly affected by trade, artistic influence from the Levantine mainland tended to be more dilute. Such appears to have been the case in the Attic Greek mainland, where early oriental influence, apparent in the Late Geometric pottery tradition, arrived indirectly via Crete. Eastern influence there first manifests itself in Athenian hammered metal-work, again signalling the priority of that medium in the receipt and transmission of Near Eastern motifs. In other parts of Greece and the Aegean realm – in the Corinthiad, the Argolid, Laconia, Euboea, and the Cyclades – eastern cultural influence came by different routes, mirroring the complexity of commercial interchange that shaped the region in the late eighth and seventh centuries BC.[44]

Punic material culture

In many respects, the early Punic artistic tradition attested at Carthage and in the Mediterranean colonies represents an inheritance from the east. In the eighth and seventh centuries, many aspects of the minor arts (including the ceramic and coroplastic arts, terracotta production, ivorywork, and faience and rod-formed glass manufacture) remain close to their oriental precursors; the island of Cyprus, it would appear, played a seminal role as transmitter.[45] Such a relationship is to be expected from a series of colonial dependencies founded from the mainland.

Yet, at an early stage, significant differences begin to emerge. While finds from early Carthage clearly point to connections with the eastern mainland, they also reflect close cultural ties with the central Mediterranean and Aegean realm. The very earliest pottery from the Carthaginian *tophet* (from the so-called Cintas Chapel) is closely allied with the ceramic wares of Greek western Italy (Campania) and Ionian Ithaca; Corinthian pottery, too, is attested early on.[46] Indeed, Hellenic influence, largely disseminated through Greek Sicily, permeates the Punic cultural tradition at a much earlier date than in the mainland.

In marked contrast to the Levant, there is little evidence for the production of luxury goods in precious materials, such as silver and ivory. No Phoenician metal bowls have been found in North Africa or, indeed, in any other part of the Punic Mediterranean realm outside of Sicily. Apart from small amulets, carved ivorywork, too, is largely absent, with the notable exception of southern Spain (in the region of the lower Guadalquivir), where an active local Phoenician bone industry in incised combs, plaquettes, and vessels flourished in the seventh to sixth centuries BC.[47]

Attention may be drawn to several categories of Punic artistic production in the west that stand apart, in type or medium, from the eastern mainland. The first and most numerous are the carved stone votive monuments from the *tophet* precincts. The earliest (*cippi*) are of rough cubic shape and carved from sandstone. Beginning in the late fifth century BC, Punic workshops began manufacturing tall, gabled limestone stelae in the Greek fashion; those bearing carved decoration share a common repertory of motifs, prominent among them the sign of Tanit, the raised hand, the crescent-disk, and, less frequently, representations of humans and animals. (See figs 44, 45, 46 and 47.) Greek iconographic influence is manifest in the adoption of the caduceus motif (modelled after Hermes' serpentine staff), Ionic architectural façades, and the use of Greek border patterns (bead-and-reel, egg-and-dart, triglyph-metope). Among the Mediterranean stelae, distinct regional differences emerge. Those from Sicily and Sardinia feature the human image in a variety of poses, while the Carthaginian, by contrast, remain largely figureless. From the fifth century BC onwards, the Carthaginian artisans move away from depicting pillared shrines, while the Italian carvers continue to reproduce them. The variety of motifs and carving styles employed on the stelae suggest that many hands were at work in their production, the majority of them relatively unskilled. The repetition of single and grouped motifs suggest that the craftsmen utilized common models or pattern books. Surprisingly few of the stelae, however, represent duplicates or exact copies. That at least some of the monuments were prefabricated is indicated by existence of stelae with blank inscriptions panels reserved for the purchaser.[48]

In the coroplastic arts, Punic funerary masks and protomes (molded plaques in the form of a human visage) represent a cohesive and distinct tradition. Unlike their counterparts in the east, which represent the individual products of local craftsmen, the Punic examples conform to groups or series, which were mass-produced in cosmopolitan

68 *Terracotta male mask of grimacing type. From Carthage, Tunisia, seventh–sixth century* BC. *This mask type, characterized by a caricatured male face with wrinkled features, enjoyed a long floruit in the Punic west.*

workshops. Of the Punic protomes, the female variety clearly predominates. The earliest in the series, dating to the second half of the sixth century BC, sport a striated Egyptian wig or a veil in the Greek tradition; their features (oval face, almond eyes, faint smile) reflect the influence of Sicilian or Ionian Greek models. The Punic male masks are mainly of the 'grotesque' variety, depicting a grinning or grimacing man with wrinkled ('old') or, less frequently, unlined ('youthful') features. (See fig. 68.) Another popular variety was the Greek satyr or silen.

Alongside the mask, the Punic craftsman specialized in the production of several other categories of funerary art. One was the decorated egg of the ostrich, a bird indigenous to the deserts of Egypt and the North African Maghreb. A recurrent tomb good at Carthage, the ostrich egg's popularity as a burial offering is evidenced by its long history and its widespread find-distribution throughout the Mediterranean. Curiously, the egg remains undocumented in the Phoenician homeland; the bird, originally an inhabitant of the northern Syrian steppe, may well have been hunted to extinction by the Early Iron Age. Large and thick-shelled, with a polished surface resembling ivory, the ostrich egg lent itself well to decoration; in the hands of the Punic artist, it was alternatively trimmed as a bowl or vase, or cut into a disk or mask bearing a stylized face with evil-averting eyes. As a decorated vessel, the egg was typically ornamented with painted bands or panels filled with geometric or floral decoration.[49]

Another unique category of Punic funerary offering was the copper razor, a small ritual axe with a crescent-shaped blade and an oblique stem, which was frequently shaped as the head and neck of a bird (swan or ibis). Found in tombs at Carthage as well as in Sardinia and Ibiza, such implements, which occur in relatively limited numbers (about two hundred in total), probably served a magical, purificatory function associated with ritual shaving. Originally undecorated, they bore stippled and, later, incised designs, beginning in the fifth century BC. From the late fourth century onward, elaborate depictions of deities (Egyptian and, later, Greek), animals, and plants predominated. Among the Egyptian gods, Isis and Horus figured prominently; of the Greek divinities, Herakles and Hermes, the latter in his role as conductor of the deceased.[50]

Chapter Seven

Commercial Expansion Abroad

Phoenician overseas settlement and trade in the Mediterranean

Cyprus

As discoveries of Phoenician pottery along the island's southern and western coasts clearly reveal, from the eleventh century onwards Cyprus served a strategic role as an entrepot for Phoenician westward trade within the Mediterranean. The archaeological and epigraphical record from Kition confirms a date around the mid-ninth century BC for the earliest Phoenician settlement on the island. Evidence so far produced for earlier Iron Age occupation remains inconclusive.

As the historical record confirms, Kition (Punic *Kt*(*y*)) formed the urban nucleus and epicentre for Phoenician settlement on Cyprus, which was confined elsewhere to small commercial communities or trading posts within existing towns. Originally a Tyrian foundation, Kition became a self-governing entity, perhaps as early as the late eighth century BC. The city's early coinage bears witness to the existence of an independent Phoenician city dynastic line by the early fifth century BC. (See fig. 29 a, b.) An important Cypriot settlement in the Late Bronze Age, Kition (situated at present-day Larnaka) was occupied by the Phoenicians (after a period of abandonment lasting some 150 years) in the ninth century. The ancient Phoenician walled city remains largely unexcavated, with the exception of the Kathari sanctuary complex situated in its northern periphery; the latter was erected upon an earlier, thirteenth-century *temenos* precinct. Recent excavations on the Bamboula hill, Kition's southerly harbour district, have yielded remains of the city's port facilities built during the classical period. (See fig. 8.)

One of the largest and most active of Phoenician communities on Cyprus outside of Kition was situated at the southerly coastal port of Amathus, a native Cypriot foundation. Phoenician commercial presence there is evident from the quantity of early imported Phoenician ware found in the city's numerous chamber tombs. (See plates XI and XII.) The recent discovery of what appears to be a local Phoenician cremation cemetery along the city's southern shore reveals that a substantial and prosperous resident community of Phoenician traders was established there by the sixth and fifth centuries BC.[1]

Debate persists over the identification of Qart-hadasht (Punic for Carthage, or 'New City'), a Phoenician foundation mentioned in the Assyrian sources. The purported discovery in the Limassol region of two fragmentary bronze bowls of mid-eighth century date inscribed for the Tyrian governor of Qart-hadasht (under King Hiram II) has led to speculation that neighbouring Amathus may have been the site of this Phoenician colony. The balance of evidence, however, favours Kition.

The growing number of Phoenician inscriptions found on Cyprus affords an accurate indication of the extent of Phoenician settlement there, much of it tied directly to transit trade (Amathus, Paphos, Lapithos) and the copper industry. Phoenician involvement in the copper trade is affirmed by the number of Phoenician-influenced sites (Tamassos, Golgoi, Idalion, Meniko, Alassa) located inland on the spurs of the copper-rich Troodos range. Phoenician presence there is often manifest in the strongly oriental character of the local Cypriot cult. (See fig. 69.) As the archaeological evidence suggests, the Phoenicians at Kition were involved in their own commercial initiatives, particularly in the Tyrrhenian basin (Sardinia, Etruria), where Cyprus had traded earlier in the Late Bronze Age.[2]

Rhodes

Like Cyprus, Rhode's strategic position on the coasting route from the Levant to the Aegean made it an ideal transit station and secondary point of departure for Phoenician commerce. Finds of Phoenician luxury items (ivories, *tridacna* shells, gold and silver jewellery) of the late eighth and seventh centuries attest to such trade. The discovery on neighbouring Cos of black-on-red ware unguent flasks reveals that the Cypriot Phoenician export trade in such vessels to Rhodes and the Dodecanese was well established by the mid-ninth century BC. According to Ezekial, the Rhodians numbered among Tyre's chief trading partners.[3] Besides this role, Rhodes served as a regional production centre for Phoenician goods, among them trinkets and luxury items in faience (including scarabs, incised vessels with low-relief decoration, and anthropomorphic unguent vases). Beginning in the late eighth century BC, Rhodian Phoenician factories also exported ceramic unguent flasks in a local fabric imitating Cypriot and mainland pottery types.[4]

Evidence for Phoenician settlement on the island prior to the Hellenistic period remains ephemeral. The presence of infant burials in amphorae at the archaic necropoli of Kameiros and Ialysos points to the existence of resident Phoenician communities in these localities. Recollection of early Phoenician presence on Rhodes may also be inferred from the various Greek 'Cadmian' myths concerning Phoenician colonization of the island.[5]

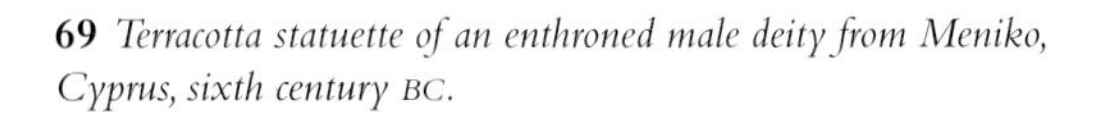

69 *Terracotta statuette of an enthroned male deity from Meniko, Cyprus, sixth century* BC.

CRETE

Phoenician presence on Crete was first intimated by the discovery, in 1884, of a cache of orientalizing bronzes on Mount Ida (Zeus Cave). Subsequent finds have corroborated this fact. The discovery of a bronze bowl with a Phoenician rim inscription at Teke near Knossos provides the earliest and most dramatic evidence thus far. (See fig. 70.) The vessel, datable on archaeological grounds to *c*.900 BC, probably belonged to a Phoenician resident, or *metoikos*. Recent excavations at Eleutherna and in the region of Knossos have yielded luxury goods of oriental and orientalizing workmanship equal in quality to the Idaean finds.[6]

Phoenician presence along Crete's southern coast has been documented by recent excavations at Kommos, which have uncovered a Phoenician-style three-pillared shrine as well as quantities of imported Phoenician pottery datable to the ninth century. Such evidence underscores the primacy of Crete as a transit point for Phoenician Mediterranean trade. Homer intimates this in Book 13 of the *Odyssey*, when he describes the hero's westward passage from Crete to Ithaca aboard a Phoenician trading vessel. The Mediterranean distribution of Phoenician luxury goods in glass, metal, and ivory allows us to trace this commercial route.[7]

As elsewhere in the Mediterranean, metal prospecting served as a catalyst for Phoenician involvement on Crete. The island is rich in phosphorus-bearing iron ore, deposits of which were undoubtedly worked in antiquity; recent excavations at Kommos have revealed the presence of one such iron-working centre. The island's pivotal importance in the iron trade is reflected in the ancient name Cape Sideros ('Iron Cape') assigned to its north-eastern promontory, the first landfall for a vessel sailing west to Crete from Rhodes. Immediately south of Cape Sideros lies Itanos, a port of reputed Phoenician foundation, whose early coinage suggests possible trade ties with the mainland Phoenician port of Arwad. As archaeological and textual evidence has shown, market demand for iron under the Assyrians and their successors rendered it a profitable trade commodity for the Phoenicians and other Mediterranean commercial entrepreneurs.[8]

As the literary and archaeological evidence reveals, the island of Crete stood on a southern Aegean Phoenician commercial route (skirting the Greek mainland) that was aimed at the central and western Mediterranean. Focal to such transit trade was Phalasarna, Crete's westernmost harbour, the direct departure point for ships travelling north to the island of Cythera and the south-eastern Peloponnese. Recent excavations have shown that the Cretan port facility contained a rock-cut holding basin, or *cothon*, of Phoenician variety.

Revealingly, Cythera's eastern port, the most immediate destination for westward maritime commerce from Crete, bears the ancient name *Phoinikous*.[9] Cythera itself was associated in antiquity with the Phoenicians; according to Herodotus,[10] the island's chief sanctuary of Aphrodite Ourania was founded by them. Like western Crete, both Cythera and the opposing Laconian mainland represent rich sources of iron ore. Southern Laconia, in particular, possesses iron-rich hematite deposits of high purity, which may well

70 *Detail of Phoenician inscription on the rim of a bronze bowl. From Teke, Crete, c.900 BC.*

have attracted the Phoenicians in antiquity. Both Cythera and Gytheion, Laconia's main harbour, formed early centres of purple-dye production in the Minoan period. No firm evidence of Phoenician occupation has yet been found at either port location, where Iron Age habitation levels remain largely unexplored.[11]

THE NORTHERN AEGEAN

As on Cyprus and Crete, Phoenician trade with the northern Aegean was propelled largely by mining interests and the metals trade. Herodotus informs us that the Phoenicians had settled on the island of Thasos with this objective. The Greek historian claims to have seen their extensive mining operations along the south-eastern side of the island, were a Phoenician temple to Herakles was sited; excavations conducted by the French have exposed the location of these mines.[12] From Thasos, the Phoenicians, in all likelihood, prospected on the opposing Thracian mainland – in the area of Mount Pangaeum and the River Strymon, where rich gold and silver deposits were later tapped by the Thasians themselves and by foreign Greek (Milesian and Athenian) entrepreneurs. The Phoenicians enjoyed commercial relations with the neighbouring Aegean islands of Samothrace and Lemnos; according to Homer, the latter received the gift of a decorated 'Sidonian' silver Krater, or mixing bowl.[13] If factual, this Homeric reference would situate such Phoenician trade activity in the eighth century, the presumed period of Phoenician mining operations on Thasos.

THE CENTRAL AEGEAN AND THE GREEK MAINLAND

The distribution of various ceramic, stone, and faience imports from the eastern Mediterranean (Rhodes, Cyprus, and the Syro-Phoenician mainland) allows us to trace the existence of a Phoenician commercial channel to the Greek mainland through the central Aegean. As the archaeological evidence reveals, this route passed in a north-westerly trajectory from Rhodes via Cos and the central Cyclades (Naxos, Delos, Syros[14]) to the island of Aegina in the Saronic Gulf. Delos' centrality to such trade is evident not only from the quantity of its early oriental imports, but from the island's later commercial importance to the Phoenicians in the Hellenistic period. The presence of oriental imports at Thera and neighbouring Melos may point to the existence of an alternate route to the eastern Laconian mainland and the Gulf of Argos through the southern Cyclades. Thera's early association with the Phoenicians is reflected in its Kadmeian foundation legend.

Aegina's role as an entrepot for eastern trade should come as no surprise. Its central location in the Saronic Gulf, with direct access to both Attica and the north-eastern Peloponnese, rendered it an ideal terminus and depot for oriental goods entering Greece. In much the same way that Samos and Rhodes served east Greece, Aegina must have functioned as both a receiving area and a redistribution centre for eastern products aimed at the Greek mainland. The strongly orientalizing character of the island's indigenous ceramic tradition reflects its direct exposure to eastern influence.

As imported finds indicate, Greek coastal centres such as Corinth, Eleusis, and Argos formed major recipients of such Aegean trade, either directly or through the intermediary of an island centre such as Aegina. Herodotus confirms such trade in the opening chapter of his *Histories*. Harking back to a distant era long before the Persian wars, he states that Phoenician vessels loaded with Egyptian and Assyrian wares frequented the coasts of Greece, citing Argos as one of their chief points of destination. To judge from the archaeological record, Corinth, too, served as an active trading partner. Surprisingly, Athens did not. In fact, during the eighth and early seventh centuries, the high point of Phoenician trade in the Aegean, the city has yielded remarkably few eastern imports and none of the Egyptianizing faience trinkets so abundantly represented at other Greek coastal sites. Part of the answer may be rooted in market economics: prior to the late seventh century BC, Athens was a relatively small settlement with limited foreign contact.

Herodotus' comment about the role of the Phoenicians as carriers of others' goods touches upon the larger question of their function as intermediaries in the general commercial trade within the Mediterranean. While actively involved in such trade, they were clearly not responsible for all of the oriental imports that made their way to the west. Many Egyptian goods may have arrived directly, as, for example, on Crete. Others may have come via Greek intermediaries, as on Samos. Historical sources document the active involvement of Samos in Mediterranean commerce by the late seventh century BC.[15]

The example of Samos raises the question of earlier Greek trade initiative with the east. Here, particular attention may be drawn to Euboea, a large island straddling the central Greek mainland. Based upon the wide Mediterranean circulation of its distinctive ceramic wares, it has been postulated that Euboean traders had, by the eighth century BC, launched a commercial enterprise with the northern Levantine coast, utilizing the Syrian port of Al Mina as their base. Yet, the absence of any historical verification for such trade, combined with the strong presence of Cypriot and mainland Phoenician pottery in early levels of Al Mina, argues against the existence of a Greek colony or settlement there. Until compelling evidence to the contrary is produced, the arrival of Euboean pottery in coastal north Syria and Phoenicia (Tyre in particular) must be attributed primarily to Levantine initiative.[16]

CENTRAL MEDITERRANEAN TRADE: THE TYRRHENIAN BASIN

Upon departing from Crete for the central Mediterranean, the Phoenician sea merchant had two options open to him – to set an open course due west to the south-eastern tip of Sicily, or to skirt the Peloponnesian coast and chart a shorter path toward the toe of Italy and the Straits of Messina. Early literary evidence for the second commercial route may, in fact, be found in the Homeric account of Odysseus' passage from the southern coast of Crete to Ithaca aboard a Phoenician trading vessel trammelling the southern and western shores of the Peloponnesus. The hero's passage is clearly described in terms that suggest that the route covered was a well-worn and a familiar one to his Phoenician carriers. It is of no little significance that here and in an account in Book 15 the island of Ithaca is specifically mentioned as a destination for a Phoenician merchant ship.[17] Positioned in the eastern Ionian Sea due west of the mouth of the Corinthian Gulf, Ithaca was strategically situated as a transit station for maritime trade west to Italy, a use to which it was put not only by the Phoenicians but also by the Greeks. (In fact, the Ionian route from Ithaca due west to the harbour of Croton on the eastern Lucanian coast represents the shortest direct open-sea passage from Greece to Italy.)

Sicily

As for the early history of Phoenician contact with Sicily, the Greek historian Thucydides provides a brief but informative account.[18] He states that the Phoenicians had originally established themselves all around the island on promontories and adjacent offshore islets, which were used as posts for trade with the native Sicels. With the arrival of Greek colonists, however, the Phoenicians abandoned most of these settlements, focusing their attentions on Motya, Soluntum, and Panormus in the north-west. The historical veracity of Thucydides' account is confirmed by excavations at Motya, which have revealed early evidence of occupation around 720 BC, shortly after the foundation of the earliest Greek colonies: Naxos (734 BC) and Syracuse (733 BC). Relocation efforts on the part of the Phoenicians thus appear to have been a response to Greek colonial initiative.

As Thucydides implies, the Phoenician withdrawal to the north-western corner of Sicily was a calculated move aimed at consolidating control of its most strategic commercial interests on the island. As the historian himself states, the region was the closest access point to Carthage and the North African mainland. (From Motya to the coast of Cape Bon is a distance of less than 160 kilometres (100 miles).) North-western Sicily also represented the closest point of departure for mineral-rich, southern Sardinia, and for trade north with Campania and Etruria, offering an alternative to passage through the Greek-controlled Straits of Messina. On this route, the Lipari islands off the northern Sicilian coast may have served as a convenient transit stop; incidental finds there of Egyptianizing faience point to the island's participation in eastern trade.

That the Phoenicians had earlier settled along the eastern coast of Sicily is clear from Thucydides' account. The locations of these 'pre-colonial' Phoenician trading establishments can be surmised. One likely candidate is the islet of Vindicari in the harbour of Phoinikous at Sicily's south-eastern tip; it lies directly above Cape Pachynos, the first point of contact for any commercial vessel plying due west across the southern Ionian Sea. Another candidate is the offshore island of Ortygia ('Dove island') located opposite mainland Syracuse; its deep bay, in fact, provides the best anchorage on Sicily's east coast. Recent research has demonstrated that the islet was originally joined at its northern tip with the mainland, creating a promontory with a double harbour in the tradition of the great Phoenician ports. A third possibility for a Phoenician trading post is the site of Naxos along Sicily's north-eastern coast; a natural headland, it represents the first Sicilian landfall for ships rounding the toe of Italy from the north. All three locations conform perfectly with Thucydides' statement about Phoenician trading tactics, i.e. the targeted use of promontories and offshore islets as commercial bases.

As for the beginning of Phoenician commercial contact with Sicily, proposed dates range from the eleventh century or earlier to the late eighth century BC. The evidence once introduced in support of early Phoenician cultural impact upon the island has now been challenged. The first burials at Motya, datable to the final decades of the eighth century, offer the earliest secure archaeological evidence. Thucydides' account itself reveals that the Phoenicians enjoyed a close relationship with the native Elymians at the time of the Greeks' arrival, which suggests that such ties were well nurtured and longstanding. Unlike the Greeks, whose colonial aims brought them into open conflict with the native Sicels of eastern Sicily, the Phoenicians aimed at establishing and maintaining a non-intrusive, peaceful relationship with the indigenous population. Commercial access rather than territorial acquisition formed their primary interest.

Archaeological evidence for the early Phoenician colonial establishments on Sicily remains scant. During its first century, occupation at Motya was confined to a small, unwalled settlement in the islet's north-eastern corner. Situated astride a natural harbour overlooking the mainland, it was clearly sited for trade with the native inhabitants of the Sicilian coast. Ancient Palermo (its Phoenician name remains unknown; the Greeks called it Panormus ('all port')) was situated alongside a natural inlet within a large bay known today as the Conca d'Oro. The ancient walled city, which now lies buried beneath Palermo's historic inner district, stood on a small hill (Paleapoli) originally flanked by two small waterways, the Kemonia and Papireto. Its western portion was marked by an acropolis (now occupied by the Palace of the Normans), beyond which stood an extensive extra-mural cemetery in use from the late seventh to the third centuries BC.

As for Soluntum, recent investigations show that the archaic Phoenician city, yet uninvestigated, stood on the promontory of Solanto and the adjacent plateau of San Cristoforo to Palermo's east. Destroyed, like Motya, in the early fourth century BC, probably during one of the campaigns of the Greek tyrant Dionysius I, the city was then rebuilt, for defensive purposes, on the neighbouring hill of Monte Catalfano, site of the present-day Punic city. Chamber tombs of the sixth- to fifth-centuries from the neighbouring Phoenicio-Punic necropolis of Santa Flavia bear witness to Soluntum's early history.

SARDINIA

As previously stated, Phoenician interest in north-western Sicily was linked directly to its proximity to North Africa and Sardinia, both active regions of early Phoenician colonial activity. Owing to its mineral wealth, Sardinia, in particular, served as a magnet for Phoenician trade. Rich in copper, iron, and silver-bearing lead ores, the island had attracted Mycenaean traders by the fourteenth to thirteenth centuries BC. Following in their commercial footsteps, Cypriot entrepreneurs established contact as early as the late twelfth or eleventh centuries. Early metal-working on Sardinia provides the clearest evidence of such contact. The appearance of bronze tripod-stands of Cypriot variety and the introduction of the lost-wax casting technique both point clearly to influence around this time from the Cypro-Levantine sphere. The early appearance of iron technology suggests that the exploitation of this metal may have served as a catalyst (along with copper) for early Levantine contact.

As the evidence suggests, Phoenician involvement in this 'pre-colonial' phase (eleventh to ninth centuries BC) may have engendered a significant degree of interaction with the native nuraghic population. Phoenician bronze statuettes have been found in the north-western sector of the island, pointing to the probable existence of western trade contacts with Spain. Such an Iberian connection finds an echo in Sardinia's foundation legend as recorded in the classical sources. The development of an active nuraghic industry in cast bronzes and the emergence of native urban settlements at this time may both be tied to Phoenician presence on the island.

The earliest direct archaeological evidence for Phoenician colonization of Sardinia is provided by a monumental inscribed stele found more than 200 years ago at the southern coastal site of Nora. Dated epigraphically to the end of the ninth or early eighth century BC, its text, the interpretation of which remains controversial, appears to commemorate the erection of a sanctuary to the Phoenician god Pumay. The word *Srdn*, if read correctly, would represent the earliest reference to the island's modern name.

The stele's discovery at Nora is not fortuitous. The site's peninsular location along the western shore of the Bay of Cagliari rendered it an ideal landing stage for Phoenician trade both from the eastern Mediterranean and from North Africa. More importantly, it represented a convenient coastal access point to the neighbouring Iglesiente plateau with its abundant deposits of iron- and silver-bearing ores. The Phoenicians were not the earliest of Mediterranean traders to capitalize on this location; recent archaeological finds from the nuraghe of Antigori at neighbouring Saroch confirm that the Mycenaeans had earlier based themselves at the same location. Phoenician commercial activity within the Gulf of Cagliari as a whole appears to have been well established by

71 *Inscribed stele from Nora, Sardinia, late ninth–early eighth century* BC.

the seventh century BC. Focal to control of the region was the port of Cagliari (Punic *Krly*) on the Tuvixeddu promontory. With an extensive lagoon harbour positioned at the southern terminus of the fertile Campidano plain, it was well situated for inland trade. The Phoenician commercial establishment of Cuccureddus near Cape Carbonara at the gulf's eastern extremity may have played a similar role as a landing stage and regional trade centre.

If its late ninth-century dating, now conventionally accepted, is correct, the Nora stele (to which a fragmentary inscription of slightly earlier date from Nora may now be added) is evidence of Phoenician occupation on Sardinia at a period roughly corresponding with the foundation of Carthage and Phoenician Kition. Evidence of cultural ties with Cyprus may be found, above all, in the material culture of Sulcis, which may have been founded, at least in part, by Phoenicians from that island. In this regard, it is worth noting that the god Pumay attested in the Nora stele is uniquely associated with Cyprus.

As archaeology has revealed, by the seventh century the entire south-western coast of Sardinia – from the Bay of Cagliari in the east to the Gulf of Oristano in the west – was literally dotted with Phoenician emporia, largely founded on abandoned early nuraghic settlements located on promontories and offshore islands.[18A] Aside from Nora, the earliest traces of Phoenician occupation, dating back to the mid-eighth century, may be found at modern-day Sulcis (Punic *Slky*). Strategically centred on the eastern shore of the islet of Sant'Antioco in the Gulf of Palmas, Sulcis served as the primary loading port for the mineral wealth of the Iglesiente region. The city, connected to the mainland by a partially artificial isthmus (attributable to Phoenician engineering), housed two protected harbours, located north and south, in the Sant'Antioco basin and the Palmas Gulf. Sulcis' early commercial growth is attested by the eighth-century date of its *tophet* precinct and by the recent discovery of an early Phoenician necropolis in the region of Portoscuso on the adjacent mainland.

Another early major Phoenician coastal foundation was the port of Tharros on the isthmus of Cape San Marco in the Gulf of Oristano. Situated, like Nora, on a narrow promontory with multiple harbours, the city controlled access, through the Campidano plain and Tirso river valley, to an agriculturally rich hinterland. The original settlement, built upon the remains of several abandoned nuraghic villages, appears to have been a modest trading post with an acropolis and a sanctuary situated at the tip of the San Marco headland. By the sixth century BC, however, it had evolved into a major urban centre with an elaborate defence system. As archaeology has revealed, Tharros functioned not only as an international port but as a regional production and distribution centre for a variety of products, including stone funerary sculpture, terracottas, and metal, stone, and faience jewellery. (See fig. 62 and plate VII.)

The seventh and succeeding sixth centuries, indeed, marked a period of territorial consolidation within Phoenician Sardinia, as existing settlements developed and new foundations were established at river arteries on the coast (Bithya, Bosa, Villaputzu) as well as inland (Othoca, Pani Loriga, Monte Sirai) for defensive and commercial purposes. Of the strategic defensive centres, particular attention may be drawn to Monte Sirai, a fortified hilltop settlement established by Sulcis to control and monitor access to the Iglesiente region and Campidano plain. (See fig. 21.) As for external commerce, the mid-seventh century marked a shift in foreign trade initiative within the Tyrrhenian basin – from Pithekoussai and the Campanian coast of Italy to the Etruscan coastal centres (Caere, Populonia) of the north. Trade with the western Mediterranean, North Africa, and the Aegean continued as usual.

CENTRAL ITALY

Phoenician interest in central Italy, as in Sardinia, was motivated primarily by the metals trade; the wealth of the Etruscan cities also rendered them profitable commercial markets for Phoenician goods. The earliest and clearest evidence of Phoenician presence in Italy may be found on the island of Pithekoussai (modern Ischia) off the coast of southern Campania. An early Euboean foundation, the island housed an active community of Phoenician traders by the late eighth century BC, as finds of Phoenician pottery (some with graffiti) attest. In all likelihood, the islet, situated strategically en route to coastal Etruria, served as a 'free port' at which native Greeks and Near Easterners mingled freely.

The primary objective of Phoenician trade in Italy was, however, the northern Etrurian heartland with its ore-rich deposits of copper, lead, iron, and silver. Geological surveys have, in fact, shown that the present-day region of north-western Tuscany, comprising the island of Elba and the opposing mainland between the Ombrone and Cecina rivers, is extremely rich in silver-bearing ores.[19] This mountainous district, the Colline Metallifere, is one of the richest mineralogically in all of Europe; from an early date, it attracted Phoenician prospectors, commerciants, and artisans, who left in their wake a variety of imported goods, including luxury vessels in repoussé silver. (See fig. 56.) The latter, locally produced by resident Phoenician craftsmen, may well have been offered as diplomatic gifts to local leaders in order to secure commercial mineral rights. Phoenician influence is also evident in the dramatic appearance, in the late eighth century BC, of a strongly orientalizing artistic tradition in Etruria.[20]

Imported pottery finds suggest that the flourishing northern Etruscan coastal cities of Populonia and Vetulonia may have formed the primary bases of operation for the Phoenicians. Phoenician knowledge of Etrurian mineral resources may have come through contact with the native inhabitants of Sardinia or through the Cypriots, both of whom were involved in the Tyrrhenian metals trade.[21]

MALTA

In contrast to Sicily and Sardinia, the Maltese archipelago, consisting of the principal islands of Malta (Punic *'nn*) and Gozo (Punic *Gwl*), occupied a very different functional niche for the Phoenicians. Unlike its larger neighbours to the north, Malta possessed little in the way of natural resources. Agricultural potential, confined to two small alluvial plains in the north and south, was extremely limited, while mineral wealth was lacking.

The island's obvious attraction for the Phoenicians lay in its geographic situation midway between two primary Phoenician commercial routes – to the north, along the southern coast of Sicily and, to the south, along the North African littoral. In this respect, Malta differed from the typical Phoenician island port of call, such as Cythera or Motya, whose offshore location rendered it a useful relay point and commercial base for trade with the adjoining mainland. As Diodorus records, the island, with its many natural harbours, served as a place of 'safe retreat' for the Phoenicians in their westward commerce.[22] Located due west of Crete and south of Sicily on the open-sea route to the Tunisian coast, Malta probably served early on as a refuelling point and servicing station for Phoenician merchant ships sailing west through the Mediterranean. This role may have increased in the seventh century BC with the Phoenician loss of eastern Sicily to Greek colonization.

As burial finds and inscriptions have documented, Phoenician presence on the Maltese archipelago was fairly widespread by the late eighth century BC. While Phoenician necropoli have been found throughout both of the main islands, modern construction has severely limited archaeological exploration of habitation levels. As in Gozo, with its interior highland settlement (at Victoria) and southern coastal port (in the bay of Mgarr), Phoenician occupation on the main island of Malta was centred in two zones – to the north, on a central highland plateau, and in the south-east, around the large bay of Marsaxlokk and its neighbouring inlets. From the size and extent of its surrounding necropoli, the northern hill town located inland at Rabat-Mdina apparently formed the main urban nucleus. With its natural harbours, the region around Marsaxlokk functioned as the centre of commercial trade, a fact evident both from the density of surrounding indigenous settlements and from the presence of two major Phoenician sanctuaries to Melqart and Astarte. The latter temple, implanted on the site of an earlier Chalcolithic complex at Tas Silg, has yielded a wealth of evidence for the Phoenician cult, including several hundred ceramic plates bearing dedications to Tanit and Astarte.

As a result of its relatively isolated, open-sea location, the Phoenician cultural stratum on Malta stands apart, in its idiosyncratic nature, from that of other western Phoenician settlements. As the archaeological record underscores, Phoenician settlers on Malta interacted closely with the indigenous population. Such direct and continuous coexistence, evident in the intermingling of Phoenician and native wares, produced a level of cultural assimilation unusual for the Phoenicians, who normally assumed the role of a commercial 'outsider'. The indigenous nature of the settlement at inland Mdina bears this out. The Phoenician cultural facies on Malta, in fact, remains uniquely archaizing and generally resistant to outside influence from the Levant, Carthage, and the west Phoenician realm. In general, Phoenician Malta's cultural orbit appears to have been oriented on a north-south axis extending from eastern Sicily to the opposing North African mainland. This sphere of interaction suggests that the island, like Pantelleria to its west, played an increasingly focal role as an intermediary in Phoenician (and later Punic) trade with the African mainland.

NORTH AFRICA

The story of the Phoenicians in North Africa, or ancient 'Libya', is centred on the northern Tunisian headland around the Bay of Tunis. Here, at the southern apex of the Tyrrhenian triangle, the two earliest and most important Phoenician foundations, Carthage and Utica, were established along a temperate and protected coastal stretch of North Africa situated on the transit route to the central Mediterranean and the far west. According to ancient historical accounts, Utica, at the mouth of the fertile Bagradas (Medjerdeh) river valley, was founded first – some 287 years before Carthage.[23] The classical sources are in agreement about the city's early foundation, which followed shortly after the establishment of Cadiz in 1104/3 BC. According to Pliny the Elder,[24] Utica's ancient temple to Apollo (Melqart) was founded in 1101 BC, 1,178 years before that author's account. Scepticism, however, has persisted over the validity of such an early date for Phoenician presence in North Africa, which has yet to be substantiated by the archaeological record. At Utica itself, no trace of the Phoenician settlement has yet been found, while the city necropolis has yielded tombs datable no earlier than the seventh century BC.[25]

Modern topographical analysis has revealed that Utica, today located some 12 kilometres (7.5 miles) inland, was originally situated on a coastal promontory with an adjoining islet – a typical Phoenician settlement configuration. The city was, in fact, well situated as an emporium and refuelling station on the commercial route both from the Straits of Gibraltar and from the southern Sardinian coast, which lies directly north. Its location, on a coastal promontory overlooking Tunisia's principal river valley, would lend credence to ancient claims made regarding the city's primacy over neighbouring Carthage. If accurate, the early foundation dates proposed for Utica, Cadiz, and Lixus may reflect an early phase of 'pre-colonial' commercial exploration in the central and western Mediterranean. Archaeological documentation of such early Phoenician trade has so far proved elusive. In reality, the earliest Phoenician port establishments may have consisted of little more than seasonal anchorage sites equipped with temporary facilities that would have left little archaeological trace.

By contrast, Carthage (Punic *Qart-hadasht,* 'New City') appears to have assumed its urban character early on in its development. A Tyrian foundation, like Utica, the city was blessed with an excellent natural harbour and a large, accessible hinterland. Recent excavations on the Byrsa hill have yielded architectural vestiges dating to the mid-eighth century – slightly more than 50 years shy of the city's traditional foundation date of 813 BC.

As for Phoenician commercial presence further east along the North African coast, the archaeological record is scant. Practical navigational considerations may have figured largely into the equation. The strong west–east current that runs along the North African littoral from the Straits of Gibraltar to Port Said made a westerly coastal advance toward Carthage from Egypt extremely problematic. So, too, did the buffeting winds, hazardous shoals, and poor visibility encountered along the barren 480-kilometre (300-mile) coastal stretch of central Libya known as the Syrtis. In the face of such difficulties, Phoenician sailors from the eastern mainland heading for Carthage and points beyond would have opted for a more direct westerly route via the open seas.

Such circumstances help to explain why, despite ancient historical claims, the eastern Tunisian and Libyan coasts have yielded little evidence for permanent Phoenician occupation. Indeed, with the exception of Hadrumetum and Leptis Magna, both reputed Phoenician foundations, the great cities of the Sahelian littoral, the Gulf of Gabes, and Tripolitania are marked by settlement strata originating in the Punic period. Leptis Magna (Punic *Lpqy*) alone has yielded evidence of permanent construction associated with its seventh-century origins. Yet even here doubt persists as to the nature of the incipient settlement; according to a recent interpretation, the early stone construction found on virgin soil near Cape Hermaion served as a warehouse for a seasonal way station or entrepot; permanent settlement did not begin until the late sixth century under Carthaginian initiative.[26] The balance of evidence suggests that Phoenician contact along the North African coast east of Carthage amounted, at best, to a series of temporary staging posts for ships returning from the western Mediterranean.

The record of early Phoenician settlement along the North African coast west of the Tunisian headland is equally scant. In fact, the entire coast of western Tunisia and eastern Algeria – from Bizerte to Oran – has produced little evidence for occupation prior to the fifth century BC. Culturally and chronologically, the many emporia dotting the Algerian coastline from Hippo Regius (Annaba) westward to Gunugu (Gouraya) reflect the growing regional influence of Carthage. The sites themselves and their Punic toponyms, which are often prefixed by *'y* (Punic for 'island', as in Iol or Icosium (modern-day Algiers)) or *Rus* (meaning 'cape', as in Rusicade or Rusucurru) underscore their functional significance as emporia for Punic coastal trade.

It is only in the extreme west of Algeria, along the Oranian coast, that evidence of earlier (seventh to sixth century) Phoenician occupation may be found – at Les Andalouses west of Oran and at Rachgoun, a coastal islet situated near the mouth of the Siga (Tafna) river. There, an inland necropolis and coastal settlement have yielded evidence for Phoenician occupation extending back to the seventh century BC. The early pottery, both wheel- and hand-made, is distinct from that of archaic Carthage and finds its closest parallels in Phoenician material from the Spanish Andalusian coast, which lies 165 kilometres (100 miles) opposite; it appears that close reciprocal ties bound these two western regions of the Mediterranean.[27]

SPAIN

Archaeological investigation in recent decades has revealed a great deal about Phoenician settlement in the Iberian peninsula, the westernmost stage of Phoenician Mediterranean expansion. Memory of early Phoenician involvement in southern Spain has been preserved in the accounts of classical authors, who relate Tyre's efforts at founding the emporion of Cadiz (Phoenician Gadir) beyond the Straits of Gibraltar. As their accounts make abundantly clear, Phoenician colonial activity in the region was driven by one overriding motive: the acquisition of ores and precious metals. The Spanish peninsula, in fact, forms one of the richest sources of raw minerals – gold, copper, iron, tin, and silver – in the entire Mediterranean. It was the pursuit of such lucrative trade (in tin and silver, in particular) that propelled the Tyrians into an ambitious long-distance commercial venture into the Atlantic regions of coastal Spain.

The chronology of early Phoenician contact with the Iberian peninsula remains the subject of scholarly controversy, much of which centres upon the relationship of biblical Tarshish to historical Tartessos. Was the fabled, metal-rich land described in the Old Testament – the object of King Solomon's long-distance trade expeditions – equivalent to the silver-bearing region of western Andalusia, historical territory of King Arganthonius?[28] While the current archaeological record of Phoenician presence in Spain extends back no further than the eighth century BC, initial trade exploration may have begun long before, as isolated finds now suggest. Such early commercial activity may have been motivated by a Phoenician interest in the Atlantic tin trade, which was already operative, under native Iberian control, in the ninth century BC.[29] The subsequent Tyrian settlement of Cadiz – in close proximity to the mineral-rich Huelva district and Guadalquivir valley – suggests that the Phoenicians were well aware of the region's mineral resources. While unverified archaeologically, the traditional foundation date assigned to Cadiz (1104/3) may reflect such early trade contact.

Ancient Cadiz (from Punic *Gdr*, 'wall' or 'fortified citadel') was founded on a series of offshore islands in the sheltered Bay of Cadiz beyond the Straits of Gibraltar. As recent geologic and archaeological investigation has shown, the early Phoenician settlement was centred on the small northern islet of Erytheia, the present heart of nineteenth-century Cadiz. In antiquity, this islet was separated from the larger, southern island of Kotinoussa by a deep, narrow channel, the Bahia-Caleta, which served as Cadiz' original harbour. Over the years, alluvial activity from the mainland Guadalete estuary has blocked this channel and filled the adjoining bay, converting the Cadiz archipelago into a peninsula.[30]

Like its mother-city Tyre, the early Phoenician settlement at Cadiz, which lies unexcavated, appears to have been an extremely compact one, covering no more than 10 hectares (25 acres). The colony's three primary sanctuaries to Astarte, Baal Hammon, and Melqart were situated in discrete locations on the city's two main islands – the temple of Astarte on the western cape of Erytheia itself; the sanctuaries of Baal Hammon and Melqart, at the north-western and south-western extremities of Kotinoussa. The latter sanctuary, renowned in antiquity for its oracle, may be localized on the present-day islet of Sancti Petri, where a group of ancient bronze statuettes depicting male deities was discovered in 1984. The city necropolis of Cadiz was situated apart from the settlement on the opposite bank of the Bahia-Caleta channel – in the area of Puertas de Tierra, where numerous burials, the earliest dating to the fifth century BC, have been uncovered.

Cadiz' foundation on Erytheia, directly opposite the mouth of the River Guadalete, was a calculated move: the latter communicated directly with the neighbouring valley of the Guadalquivir, access point to the mineral wealth of Lower Andalusia. Early on, Cadiz established an enclave on the northern shore of the Guadalete estuary at the indigenous

Tartessian settlement of Castillo de Doña Blanca, which served as the island city's continental port and transit station for mainland trade. Excavations conducted there over the past two decades have revealed extensive traces of Phoenician presence.[31]

Tyrian involvement in the Tartessian silver trade, long alluded to in the classical sources, has been elucidated in recent years by archaeological research. Activity focused in two regions: the western area of the province of Seville and the mountainous region of Huelva beyond. In the former, the trade in metals followed a route ending directly at Cadiz via the mouth of the Guadalquivir. The rich silver mines at Aznalcollar along the southern spurs of the Sierra Moreno appear to have been the main source. As archaeological research has demonstrated, the silver-bearing lead ores from these mines were processed and subsequently smelted at the native Tartessian sites of Tejada la Vieja and San Bartolomé de Almonte, respectively. Phoenician activity at Tejada is evinced by the urban character of the native walled settlement, which housed stone-built warehouses and facilities for the grinding and washing of the ores.[32]

The richest deposits of gold- and silver-bearing pyrite ores were, however, to be found in the mountains of Huelva, in the inland region of Rio Tinto. (See fig. 72.) The site of the most extensive mining operations in antiquity, Rio Tinto's silver ore lodes are now completely exhausted. (The last deposit of some 30,000 tons was mined in 1887.) Modern survey of the surviving traces of silver slag, however, reveals the monumental scale of mining activity conducted there in the Iron Age. Estimated at roughly six million tons, the ancient slag is distributed over an area one-and-a-half kilometres by half a kilometre (one mile by a third of a mile). The presence of two indigenous neighbouring hill settlements (Quebranthuesos and Cerro Salomon) confirms that the process of mining and extraction fell in native hands. Phoenician involvement in such mining operations is now well documented by excavations conducted in 1966–7 at Cerro Salomon, where a small settlement, marked by imported Phoenician pottery, revealed obvious traces of metalworking, including mining tools, bellows, and crucibles. Lead droplets found within the houses reveal that at least some of the silver was extracted in situ by cupellation, using locally mined lead. The metal was then transported, in the form of ingots or crude ore, down the Rio Tinto to the native coastal port of Huelva, where the final processing occurred; excavations in the centre of the modern town have revealed the emplacement of actual smelting furnaces dating to the eighth to seventh centuries BC.[33] Phoenician commercial presence at Huelva is likewise attested by the strongly orientalizing character of the burials at La Joya, necropolis of the Huelvan aristocracy.

Beyond Huelva, evidence of Phoenician occupation along the Atlantic coast has proved elusive. Recent excavations, however, have revealed the presence of a substantial settlement of seventh-century date at Alcácer do Sal near the mouth of the River Sado. The presence of this site, located some 400 kilometres (250 miles) north of the Guadalquivir basin, lends credence to the supposition that the Phoenicians had established a series of coastal emporia up to and beyond the Algarve coast of Portugal.[34]

It is along the Andalusian coast east of Gibraltar, however, that the Phoenicians appear

72 *View of the Rio Tinto mining area, Spain.*

to have concentrated their settlement efforts, beginning in the eighth century BC. Archaeological investigation over the past three decades has documented the existence of a series of compact, closely spaced settlements with adjacent necropoli along the coasts of Granada, Malaga, and Almeria, all strategically situated on low coastal headlands within sheltered bays or inlets. Their positions – on riverine estuaries such as the Guadalhorce, Guadalmedina, Velez, and Algarrobo – ensured access to the agriculturally rich interior. The Andalusian coast from the Guadalhorce to the Rio Grande at Adra represents some of the most fertile agricultural land in all of the Iberian peninsula. It was with an eye towards local exploitation of such natural resources that the majority of such settlements, including Cerro del Villar, Toscanos, Moro de Mezquitilla, and Chorreras, must have been founded. The potential for development was apparently great, as much of the coast lay undeveloped and sparsely inhabited at the time of the Phoenicians' arrival; certain establishments, like Moro de Mezquitilla, appear to have been founded on unoccupied soil.

Coastal commerce played a role too, although the economic relationship of the Andalusian settlements both to the Phoenician east and to metropolitan Cadiz remains unclear. With the exception of Malaga (Malaka), Sexi (Almuñécar), and Abdera (Adra), the sites of the eastern Andalusian coast lay unrecorded in the ancient sources. Settlement patterns and faunal evidence at Toscanos point not only to the pursuit of agriculture but to extensive animal husbandry (sheep, goat, and, especially, cattle). The high percentage of cattle bones at this and other Andalusian sites suggests that livestock were raised for both traction and domestic consumption. The timber industry may have contributed significantly to the local economy too; the inland mountains are rich in oak and fir.

Unlike their Levantine coastal equivalents, the settlements of the eastern Andalusian coastal plain, on the whole, are small and unpretentious in their layout, evincing an 'urban' concentration only in their very cores. The majority of settlements, including Morro de Mezquitilla, Chorreras, and Adra, totalled only a few acres (2-5 hectares), with correspondingly small populations.[35] The settlement of Toscanos, at its height, is estimated at no more than fifteen hundred individuals. What the archaeological record reveals, thus, is a series of centrally administered commercial enclaves rather than fully fledged towns.

Toscanos well illustrates this point. Situated on a peninsula within a small coastal bay (now silted up), the early settlement (*c*.750–650 BC) was serviced by a large three-aisled public facility, which functioned as a central warehouse. It was only during the second half of the seventh century that occupation expanded to the surrounding hills of Penon and Alarcon, which were ultimately encompassed by fortification walls and towers; the initial settlement was protected by a simple v-shaped defensive ditch. In addition to farming and cattle-breeding, Toscanos' economic activities, as archaeology has confirmed, consisted of purple-dye manufacture and metallurgy; both copper and iron were worked locally. As in the neighbouring settlement of Morro de Mezquitilla, industrial installations devoted to the processing and smelting of iron have been uncovered on the slopes of the Penon hill. Such activity was apparently intended primarily for domestic consumption rather than export; unlike the Guadalquivir-Huelva region, there is little evidence that the rich ore deposits (iron, copper, lead) of eastern Andalusia's mountainous interior were mined extensively in antiquity.

As with southern Spain in general, Phoenician settlement at Toscanos came to an end before the mid-sixth century BC. The reasons for the site's abandonment remain unclear. Regional demographic and economic factors must have played a contributory role, as did rising commercial competition from emerging powers (Greek and Carthaginian) within the Mediterranean. As some scholars have suggested, the cessation of Phoenician commercial activity in Andalusia (and of mining pursuits in the Huelva region) were the product of a more widespread political and economic crisis in the Phoenician east, culminating in the fall of Tyre to the Babylonians in 573 BC.[36]

Over its 200-year span, the Phoenician occupation of southern Spain left a strong cultural imprint on native Iberian society, which entered a strongly 'orientalizing' phase in the late eighth and seventh centuries BC. Such influence, particularly widespread in the region of Huelva and the lower Guadalquivir, was felt in the realm of architecture (the use of ashlar stone and mudbrick construction), technology (the introduction of iron and the potter's wheel), funerary practice (the adoption of Phoenician tomb types and burial customs), and writing. As seems increasingly clear, the introduction of an alphabetic system in native south-west Iberian script was the direct result of Phoenician influence.[37]

As one might expect, Phoenician cultural impact is particularly apparent in the cemeteries of the Tartessian aristocracy (at Huelva and Setefilla), who benefited directly from the Phoenician silver trade. Many of the luxury objects in gold and silver that accompanied these burials are strongly influenced, both in technique and decoration, by oriental models; others were direct imports, manufactured in regional Phoenician workshops such as Cadiz. The latter were probably issued as diplomatic gifts to secure transit rights into the mineral-rich Andalusian interior.

THE BALEARICS AND IBIZA

Phoenician commercial interests dictated the selection of another settlement site in the western Mediterranean: the island of Ibiza in the Balearic archipelago. Situated off the Levantine coast of Spain, Ibiza (Punic *'ybsm*, 'isle of the Balsam-tree') formed a natural port of call for Phoenician craft plying the Mediterranean to and from the Straits of Gibraltar. Excavation in recent years has confirmed that the island was settled by Phoenician colonists from the Atlantic straits. By the mid-seventh century, an early foothold was established on the peninsula of Sa Caleta for trade east with Sardinia and west with the Iberian coast. In addition to shipping, mining interests appear to have promoted the settlement, a modest entrepot of limestone-and-mudbrick residences and warehouses located along Ibiza's south-western coast. Local exploitation of silver is indicated by the quantities of argentiferous lead found throughout the site, which, as analysis has shown, was extracted from the mines of Santa Argentera in the east. The remains of a blast furnace attest equally to the local smelting of iron, a characteristic Phoenician pursuit.

After a brief occupation of some 50 years, the settlement of Sa Caleta was abandoned, its population transferred to the hill of Puig de Vila overlooking the larger bay of Ibiza a short distance to the east. At the base of this hill within sheltered waters stood the ancient port facility, its emplacement marked by abundant finds of Phoenician pottery dating to the last quarter of the seventh century BC. Salvage excavations undertaken on the lower slopes of the adjacent hill of Puig des Molins (later site of Ibiza's vast Punic necropolis) in the early 1980s have uncovered the remains of the settlement's archaic burial precinct, which was marked by several dozen cremation pithoi burials deposited in excavated pits or natural cavities in the rocky slope.[38]

Ibiza's strategic placement for early Phoenician trade has been elucidated by scattered finds of Phoenician pottery along the north-eastern coast of Spain – in Alicante province (Peña Negra de Crevillente, Los Saladares) and Castellon (Vinarragell) and, further north, in the delta of the River Ebro in southern Catalonia. Such finds, dating from the late seventh and early sixth centuries BC, suggest that Ibiza had served as a conduit for western Phoenician trade with the northern Spanish interior and with southern France, valued outlets for tin arriving overland from the north Atlantic regions of Cornwall and Brittany. This lucrative inland trade, which supplemented the Atlantic coastal shipping route from Galicia and the Atlantic north, probably served the Phoenicians until the mid-sixth century, when the Greek Phocaeans assumed control of such inland routes from their colonial bases at Massalia (Marseilles) and Emporion (Ampurias).

Phoenician Atlantic trade: Morocco

As history records, the city of Lixus (Punic *Lks*) was central to early Phoenician trade in Atlantic Morocco. The classical literary tradition underscores the importance of this key emporium, whose foundation (in 1180 BC) was believed to antedate that of Cadiz.[39] Lixus' location – 4 kilometres (2.5 miles) inland on the north bank of the River Loukkos – has been known since the early nineteenth century. Yet excavations on the upper plateau of the Tchemmich hill, the presumed site of the early city, have failed to produce architectural evidence of early Phoenician occupation. As recent analysis has shown, the earliest of Lixus' monumental temples (Apsis 'H') does not predate the first century BC, the period of the Numidian King Juba II. In all likelihood, the port and its harbour were originally situated below, on the sheltered eastern foot of Tchemmich Hill. The date of this settlement may be surmised from scattered finds of Phoenician red-slip ware of late seventh century date found on the plateau above.[40] Like Cadiz, Lixus monitored riverine access into a mineral-rich hinterland; along the spurs of the Atlas mountains lay rich deposits of gold, copper, iron, and lead.

Beyond Lixus, along a coast largely devoid of natural harbours, archaeological traces of Phoenician coastal trade are sparse. The first clear evidence of occupation may be found at Sala, an emporium situated inland from the Bou Regreg estuary near the heart of modern Rabat. Here, excavations have uncovered the remains of a large ashlar stone building associated with Phoenician red-slip pottery datable to the seventh to sixth centuries BC.

More than 400 kilometres (250 miles) beyond Sala lies the southernmost of Phoenician establishments documented along the Moroccan coast. Here, on the island of Mogador in the bay of Essauoira, excavations have uncovered a seasonal coastal encampment, roughly 50 metres (55 yards) in diameter, marked by hearths and small huts. Mogador's commercial nature is apparent from its ceramic finds, which include a large quantity of red-slip ware sherds (some twenty bearing Phoenician inscriptions) together with Greek (Attic and Ionian) amphorae and Cypriot pottery. A settlement in operation from at least 650 to 500 BC, Mogador, like Sala to the north, functioned as a secondary centre for trade with the indigenous peoples of the Moroccan interior. As its Phoenician inscriptions and pottery types reveal, it was founded by colonists from the Phoenician mainland or from Cadiz, itself a Tyrian foundation. The ceramic repertoire from Mogador is particularly close to that found in Phoenician settlements from Andalusia.[41]

PHOENICIAN EXPLORATION BEYOND

How much further along the coast beyond Mogador the Phoenicians undertook to explore remains an open question. While clearly exaggerated, Strabo's claim[42] that the Tyrians founded three hundred colonies along the west African coast may contain a reminiscence of such exploration, which set the stage for the later expedition of the Carthaginian Hanno. That the Phoenicians themselves had navigated up Africa's western coast is implied in Herodotus' account[43] of their successful circumnavigation of the continent at the behest of the Egyptian pharaoh Necho (610–595 BC).

The same questions pertain to Phoenician exploration within the Atlantic. That Phoenician fishermen from Cadiz sailed well beyond the Straits in search of tuna is a matter of historical record.[44] It is likely that the Phoenicians navigated as far as Madeira and the Canary Islands off the Moroccan coast. (The volcano Teide on Tenerife can today be seen by any coastal navigator.) It is to Madeira that Pseudo-Aristotle and Diodorus apparently refer when they mention the chance discovery of a heavily wooded island in the midst of the Atlantic.[45] A Phoenician or Carthaginian landing in the more distant Azores is more problematic, but may not be entirely ruled out; recent surveys on the island of Corvo, however, have failed to turn up any evidence of their presence.[46]

Punic commercial expansion abroad

In its commercial expansion, Carthage built upon settlement patterns earlier established by the Phoenicians. In contrast to the latter, however, Punic occupation was characterized by a much greater spread and density of settlement. Such was particularly the case on island domains, such as Sardinia, Ibiza, and Malta, where occupation expanded well beyond the coast. On Sardinia, Carthaginian political and economic control had virtually encompassed the island by the fourth century BC, thanks to an extensive network of forts and roads. Unlike the Phoenicians, transit trade and the procurement of metals no longer formed the exclusive focus; the large-scale exploitation of agricultural resources, cereal production in particular, now assumed primary importance.

By the fifth century BC, commercial and colonial interaction within the Punic world was controlled not only by Carthage itself but by a number of other semi-autonomous communities. Ibiza, for example, participated in a widespread commercial network that included southern France, Spain, Sicily, and Sardinia. The prosperous island community of Malta initiated its own colonial activity, establishing settlements on neighbouring Pantelleria and along the North African coast. In the far west, Punic Cadiz controlled an extensive commercial empire centred in the Atlantic regions north and south of Gibraltar. With its large merchant fleet, the city exported fish and other commodities to Corinth and other areas of the Aegean.[47]

CARTHAGINIAN EXPLORATION OVERSEAS

History records two engaging feats of Carthaginian commercial exploration in the Atlantic. The first, preserved in an early medieval manuscript, recounts a remarkable voyage undertaken along the western coast of Africa by a Carthaginian navigator named Hanno in the second half of the fifth century BC. Debate has raged over the identification of ancient place-names mentioned in the account, which was originally set up in the temple of Saturn (Baal Hammon) at Carthage. The more adventurous would take him as far as Sierra Leone or even the Cameroons or Gabon in the Gulf of Guinea. According to a more conservative view, the explorer terminated his voyage at Cape Juby along Morocco's southern boundary.[48]

Roughly contemporary with Hanno's expedition was another voyage, led by Himilco, up the tin route along the Atlantic coast of western Europe. According to the *Ora Maritima* of Avienus, which preserves an account of this event, Himilco's four-month expedition brought him to the coast of northern Britanny and perhaps beyond – across the channel to southern Britain and the coast of Cornwall (Scilly Isles). As with Hanno's voyage, scholars debate the extent of Himilco's expedition.[49] No archaeological proof of Carthaginian commerce with northern Europe has yet been found.

EPILOGUE

Persian rule over Phoenicia ended with the siege and sack of Tyre in 332 BC. The following year saw Darius III's final defeat by Alexander and the Macedonians; the Persian empire was no more. Alexander the Great's rule was short-lived. During the final years of the fourth and ensuing third century, the region was contested by the two Greek dynastic houses that had emerged in the Near East following Alexander's death – the Seleucids and Ptolemies. During this time, most of Phoenicia, with the exception of northerly Arwad, fell under Ptolemaic rule; in 198 BC, the area succumbed to Seleucid control, under which it remained until the final decades of the second century. Following a brief period of autonomy, the region fell to Rome in 64 BC; it would remain under Roman control for more than 600 years until the Arab conquest in the seventh century AD.

Under the Ptolemies and the Seleucids, the process of Hellenization, already well under way since the late fifth century BC, accelerated, and numerous Phoenician cities and sanctuaries underwent marked expansion and redevelopment in the Greek style. The Hellenistic and later Roman periods were prosperous times for the Phoenician ports, which continued to trade actively throughout the Mediterranean. With the increasing adoption of western ways, however, the Phoenicians lost much of their ethnic character, including language. From an urban standpoint, their cities became indistinguishable architecturally from other Greek (and later Roman) metropolises.

The history of Carthage and the Punic west in the third and second centuries was also bound up with the political affairs of the Greek and Roman world. In 279 BC, Carthage and Rome entered into their fourth and final alliance: a mutual defence pact launched against Pyrrhus of Epirus, a Hellenistic king who was then campaigning, at the behest of Greek city of Tarentum, on Italian soil against the Romans. Within a few years of Pyrrhus' departure, however, relations between the two central Mediterranean powers broke down, leading to a series of protracted and costly wars that would ultimately spell the demise of the Carthaginian state.

Responsibility for the eruption of hostilities, whether Carthaginian or Roman, remains the subject of debate; clearly, neither side foresaw the magnitude of events that its outbreak would unleash. The three Punic Wars that followed would embroil the two superpowers intermittently for a period of more than 100 years. The first (264–241 BC) ended in a devastating defeat for Carthage, which was forced to give up Sicily, renounce hostilities towards Rome and its allies, and pay enormous war reparations. The second (217–201 BC), immortalized for posterity by the exploits of Hannibal, dealt the death blow to Carthage's imperial aims; soundly defeated, the Punic state had to relinquish its recently acquired territory in southern Spain, destroy its fleet, and again pay a heavy indemnity – in instalments that would be parcelled out over 50 years. Hannibal, whose daring campaign across the Pyrenees and Alps into Italy achieved stunning success in the early stages of the war, was ultimately defeated on African soil. Subsequently forced into exile, the Carthaginian general took his own life rather than fall into Roman hands.

The early years of the second century BC witnessed a remarkable revival for Carthage. Capitalizing on the enormous agricultural surpluses of its rich hinterland, the city prospered economically. Such signs of economic resurgence and of military 'stirring' raised Rome's suspicions. Urged on by Cato the Elder ('Carthago est delenda'), the Roman Senate resolved to destroy Carthage once and for all. Backed by troops installed at Utica, in 149 BC Rome issued its final ultimatum, which left the city and its inhabitants no alternative but war: in return for their freedom, the Carthaginians had to abandon their city and resettle away from the coast. The brief Third Punic War (149–146 BC) ended in the final assault upon and destruction of Carthage, which was razed by the Romans in the spring of 146 BC. From its ashes arose a new Roman city – Colonia Concordia Iulia Karthago, conceived by Julius Caesar and realized by Augustus. As a political entity, Punic Carthage was no more. Yet, in spite of its destruction, its cultural heritage – its language, beliefs, and customs – would endure for centuries in Africa and its overseas territories; a powerful city and its legacy were not so easily erased.

Appendix: Survey of Cities in the Phoenician Homeland

Tell Dor

See discussion in text.

Atlit

The site of Atlit is situated on the coast of northern Israel 15 kilometres (9.5 miles) south of Haifa. Bounded to the north by the River Oren and to the east by a sandstone ridge running parallel to the coast, it occupies an area of nearly 80 hectares (200 acres) extending to the east and south of a broad headland, which is naturally fortified with cliffs on its north, west, and south sides. The Phoenician Iron Age settlement consisted of a defensible acropolis and an extended lower town, with harbour facility, fortified on its landward side. Two cemeteries have been located outside the main residential area – along the northern shore to the east, and on the sandstone ridge beyond the south-eastern end of the settlement mound. Archaeological soundings have demonstrated that the Phoenician city, which was founded in the seventh century BC, was situated along the shore at the base of the acropolis – near the northern bay, which served as the city's primary port facility. An earlier settlement, dating to the late ninth century, was located further east along the shore in proximity to the River Oren's outlet, which served as the settlement's initial anchorage site.

As underwater finds attest, construction on Atlit's built northern harbour was apparently begun in the late seventh century BC.[1] Protected to the west by a pair of offshore islets, it was connected to the settlement by an ashlar-paved ramp that led from the shore to a twin-towered city gate. In general plan, the port consisted of two ashlar-built moles set at right angles to one another, defining an enclosed rectangular harbour with an entrance 200 metres (220 yards) wide. Each of the jetties was set perpendicular to an ashlar-built quay; the outer mole was anchored to the northern islet, while the inner mole ran parallel to the northern shore from the region of the city gate. Both served not only as breakwaters but as points of anchorage for the loading and unloading of merchandise. The outer, freestanding mole, which extended from the aforementioned islet, may have served as an emporium for foreign ships.

Tell Abu Hawam

Tell Abu Hawam (ancient Aksaph) is situated within the bay of Akko in the delta region of the River Kishon. The ancient settlement, which originally bordered the beach (it is now located roughly 1.5 kilometres (1 mile) inland), covered at least 4 hectares (10 acres).

In antiquity, the town was blessed with three harbour facilities: a natural bay to the north, a lagoon (between Mount Carmel and the tell) to the south-west, and the Kishon estuary to the east. Tell Abu Hawam was served by two neighbouring cemeteries: a rock-cut necropolis of the Persian period situated on the slopes of Mount Carmel, and a maritime cemetery of the Late Bronze Age located along the ancient coastline.

Following its destruction at the end of the Late Bronze Age, Tell Abu Hawam was reoccupied *c.* 1100 BC. The Early Iron Age settlement, which revealed Phoenician bichrome pottery, was marked by a new building orientation and the appearance of the three-room house type. Following its destruction, the city was resettled in the early tenth century BC. This Iron II settlement was characterized by a dense urban arrangement of modestly sized rectangular rooms. During this period, the River Kishon estuary replaced the lagoon as the city's primary harbour facility. Following another destruction in the second half of the eighth century BC, Tell Abu Hawam lay abandoned for two centuries until the Persian period, when the city re-emerged as a strategic stronghold and regional maritime commercial centre. The city saw major urban redevelopment in the fourth century BC. The acropolis was levelled and crowned with a casemate wall and stone glacis, while the lower settlement, newly fortified, was rebuilt according to an axial grid plan.

Akko

The 20-hectare (50-acre) settlement of Akko is situated about 700 metres (765 yards) from the Mediterranean Sea on the northern bank of the River Na'aman. A flourishing fortified city from the Middle Bronze II period onward, Akko was reduced to a much smaller settlement in the Early Iron Age. Beginning in the ninth to eighth centuries BC, the city was refortified and a series of residential quarters and large public buildings were established in the northern and eastern sectors of the tell. Urban growth accelerated greatly in the Persian period, when the city prospered as an administrative centre under the Achaemenids, and expanded along the coast. At this time, a series of well-constructed public buildings was erected on the acropolis; a bowl fragment with Phoenician inscription found in one of them attests to the presence of a temple to Asherath. Residential areas uncovered on the settlement mound show clear signs of city planning. Construction during the Persian and ensuing Hellenistic periods was characterized by the Phoenician pier-and-rubble technique.

In the late second and early first millenium BC, the estuary of the River Na'aman served as the city's harbour. As geomorphological studies have shown, Akko was situated on a peninsula flanked by a bay to its west and a lagoon to its east. During the Persian period, as urban settlement expanded westward, anchorage was transferred to the eastern bay of the present-day Akko peninsula. A large harbour equipped with a pair of breakwaters was built. Initial construction on the southern mole, which extended some 330 metres (360 yards), may be assigned to the late sixth or early fifth century BC. To its east stood an artificial pier of probable Hellenistic date on an ashlar ledge. Like the freestanding mole at Atlit, it may have served as a kind of free port for foreign trading vessels.

Achziv

The site of ancient Achziv (its ancient toponym is preserved in the name of the modern village ez-Zib) is located on the coast of northern Israel between Akko and Tyre. The tell, a double mound, is situated on a sandstone ridge overlooking the Mediterranean. Suitable anchorage is provided by the Kesib river estuary to the north and a deep riverbed and a natural bay to the south. Beyond the southern bay is a well-protected and sizable harbour, Minat ez-Zib. An artificial ditch, cut at the eastern base of the mound between the River Kesib and the southern riverbed, effectively turned the settlement into an island.

A substantial, fortified settlement in the Middle and Late Bronze Age, Achziv saw limited, temporary resettlement at the beginning of the Iron Age. During the Iron II–III period, the city, now refortified, witnessed rapid growth, expanding eastwards beyond its rampart. In the eighth century BC, Achziv attained its maximum extent – about 8 hectares (20 acres). Excavations in the northern part of the mound adjacent to the city's eastern defences have uncovered a number of public buildings of Late Iron Age date, which apparently functioned as royal storerooms. After a decline in the Persian period, the city witnessed a renewal in the Hellenistic period.

Excavations reveal that the Iron Age settlement possessed four distinct cemeteries. The earliest burials, a series of well-dressed stone cist tombs dating back to the eleventh century BC, were uncovered on the eastern slope of the settlement mound. Their handsome construction, rich tomb inventories and privileged location within the settlement mark them as burials of the city élite. The other three necropoli were located outside the settlement to the east, north, and south of the tell. The first, cut into the sandstone ridge east of the settlement mound, contained a series of chamber tombs dating from the late eleventh to the sixth century BC. The second, situated south of the settlement at the southern end of the bay of Achziv, contained rock-cut inhumation tombs and cremation burials dating to the Iron II period. The third, located north of the mound on the northern bank of the Kesib river estuary, consisted of: first, an open-air sanctuary with central stele/altar containing jar cremation burials of the Late Iron Age; and, second, an adjoining precinct with inhumation burials of Persian period date.

Tell Keisan: an inland Phoenician agricultural settlement

Tell Keisan is situated 8 kilometres (5 miles) east of the Mediterranean littoral in the central northern basin of the Akko coastal plain.[2] A prominent, oval-shaped mound of roughly 6 hectares (15 acres), it affords a commanding view of the agriculturally rich surrounding plain. As excavations have revealed, Tell Keisan was an important regional agricultural centre and probably served as Akko's major granary; the surrounding Galilee region was well known in antiquity for the production and export of agricultural produce, especially olive oil. During the Iron Age, Tell Keisan may have been a Tyrian enclave; at any rate, the settlement fell within the cultural orbit of that city. Occupied continuously from the Neolithic period onward, Tell Keisan attained its greatest prosperity and physical extent in the Early and Middle Bronze Ages, when it was fortified with a massive glacis and stone defensive wall. Following a destruction level datable to the early twelfth century BC, the site was soon reoccupied. The occupation levels of the succeeding Early Iron Age are exceptionally thick and stratigraphically undisturbed. Stratum 9, datable to the second half of the eleventh century BC, revealed an urban complex of substantial multi-roomed buildings laid out on a rectangular grid; its town plan appears to have been based on groups of rectangular dwelling units of standardized dimensions (6 by 10 metres (20 by 35 feet)). Following a destruction at the end of the eleventh century BC, the town was rebuilt and inhabited continuously into the eighth century, when it was again destroyed and abandoned. Tell Keisan witnessed a renaissance in the seventh century BC under Assyrian cultural influence; excavations revealed limited, but conclusive, evidence of a new town plan based upon a rectangular grid no longer oriented to the topological features of the plateau. Following yet another destruction toward the end of the seventh century BC, the town was reoccupied and inhabited throughout the Persian and Hellenistic periods; the site was abandoned in the second century BC.

Iron Age Tell Keisan presents an illustrative picture of an unwalled 'proto-urban' agricultural community. Settlement was concentrated on the periphery of the mound, where the earliest and most solidly constructed residences were located; with their principal walls aligned perpendicular to the slope, they presented a formidable defensive façade. Throughout the Iron II period, the residences were organized, according to a clearly conceived plan, in discrete blocks along the slope of the tell. As its excavators have noted, the Iron Age city was not densely built. Its houses were laid out with considerable gaps between; their fills, which included organic material and animal dung, suggest usage as enclosures for livestock.

The settlement at Tell Keisan shows remarkable continuity in plan and construction, with succeeding houses built atop earlier structures, often re- utilizing existing foundations. The town's excavated residential quarters terminate abruptly to the south in a large open precinct of approximately 500 square metres (600 square yards). This sector, which revealed no sign of permanent construction, apparently served as an area of communal domestic, agricultural, and industrial activity (including textile production). The tell's eastern summit, its administrative centre, was also the probable site of a local sanctuary or shrine. Primary access to the settlement was attained from the north and south-west, where zones of depression mark the location of access ramps.

Tyre: a case study in the urban topography of a Phoenician metropolis

The modern city of Tyre is situated on a peninsula off the coast of southern Lebanon, midway between the ports of Akko and Sidon.[3] (See fig. 11.) Tyre's physical setting today differs greatly from that of the ancient city. The headland on which it stands is the result of successive sediments deposited on a mole built in 332 BC by Alexander the Great. In antiquity, Tyre was an island emporium, situated originally on two adjacent offshore reefs. Its ancient name, *Sor* ('rock' in Phoenician), clearly alludes to its geologic origins.

A deep sounding undertaken in 1974 by Patricia Bikai revealed that Tyre was originally occupied in the Early Bronze Age, or early third millennium BC, corroborating an ancient Tyrian tradition that the city was founded around 2750 BC (Hdt. 2.44). Following this initial settlement, which may have lasted 500 years or more, the city was apparently abandoned. A long hiatus in occupation (covering the Middle Bronze Age, 2000–1600 BC) is attested by a thick stratum of pure sand (totalling one metre (one yard) or more) that overlay the last Early Bronze Age level. As the Bikai excavation revealed, Tyre's 'rediscovery' at the start of the Late Bronze Age, or sixteenth century BC, was initially a casual one, marked by an extended period of sporadic visits to the site. Judging from the archaeological record, permanent habitation on the island does not seem to have taken root until the end of the fifteenth century BC, with comprehensive urban development following in the mid-fourteenth century.

Through modern topographical exploration we may gain some idea of the size and urban appearance of the early city. Traces of bedrock on the Tyre's western edge and in the adjacent sea bed reveal that the principal island upon which Tyre was founded was a long narrow reef some 500 metres (550 yards) in extent. The location of the second smaller islet which originally lay adjacent to it remains the subject of conjecture; in all likelihood, it was situated immediately north or east of the main island. The heart of Late Bronze Age and Iron Age Tyre was almost certainly situated on the slope of the ancient city's acropolis, which may be localized on the high ground west of the Crusader cathedral.

The urban character and topography of ancient Tyre was greatly altered in the tenth century BC by the urban expansion efforts of King Hiram I (969–936 BC), who levelled up the eastern part of the settlement with artificial embankments, and connected the main city with the adjoining islet by a causeway (Jos., *C.Ap.*, 1.113). The archaeological record and the ancient sources are in unanimity about the urban character of Iron Age Tyre: the city was densely populated, perhaps far more so than any of its Phoenician mainland counterparts with the possible exception of Arwad. As ancient eyewitness accounts reveal, multi-storeyed buildings dotted its urban landscape (Strabo 16.2.23). By the late fourth century BC, its population may have reached forty thousand, if one accepts Arrian's testimony concerning the number of soldiers slain and inhabitants sold into slavery at the time of Alexander's siege. In all likelihood, the city's ranks were swelled at that time by an influx of refugees and soldiers from the mainland. A survey of the site's early Iron Age stratigraphy suggests that the island city, during its Iron Age heyday, was considerably smaller than the present one – perhaps totalling no more than 16 hectares (40 acres). Some tentative conclusions may be drawn about the general location of the city's major architectural landmarks. The temples of Melqart and Astarte were situated on the ancient acropolis located in the city's south-western sector. According to Herodotus (2.44), Tyre possessed a second temple to Herakles, renowned for its twin columns of emerald and gold. The temple to which Herodotus refers may be equated with the island sanctuary of Baal Shamem, which Hiram ultimately joined to the city by a causeway.

Prominent among the city's landmarks was the royal palace compound with its kingly residence, archives, and treasuries. According to Arrian (2.23.6), it was also located in the south-western sector of the city, no doubt on the slopes of the acropolis, commanding a view of the sea. The city's 'high grounds' no doubt formed the primary residential quarters of the city. Tyre's commercial/industrial district, by contrast, may be localized in the north-east: in proximity to the main harbour and market square: the *Eurychoros*, or 'Broad Place'. Hiram's efforts at broadening this market square may be seen as an integral part of the Tyrian king's overall expansion project, which was concentrated in the eastern sector of the city. It is here that Tyre's large-scale industrial plants – the fisheries, metal foundries, and purple-dye installations – were localized, away from the residential quarters of the élite. As excavation confirms, various forms of cottage industry (pottery production, textile weaving and dyeing, faience jewellery manufacture) took place throughout the city.

In view of Tyre's extended urban history, it is difficult to imagine that there was much opportunity for centralized planning, except in the newly developed areas around the city periphery. What evidence we have suggests a more entrepreneurial approach marked by the improvised use and re-use of available materials. The mid-ninth to the end of the eighth century BC was an especially active period; the Bikai sounding yielded nine distinct building levels from this time that bear witness to continuous efforts at remodelling, levelling, and terracing. From this time, the pier-and-rubble technique was used widely; large-scale buildings were marked by handsomely dressed walls of marginally drafted ashlar masonry. As one would expect, internal access within such a closed urban environment was extremely tight, with routes of communication consisting of long narrow alleys or passageways. The resulting picture is that of a densely built-up urban amalgam. As the Assyrian reliefs reveal, Tyre was surrounded by a multi-storeyed circuit wall with arched gateways and regularly spaced towers; the city appears to have been more strongly defended on its vulnerable eastern side facing the mainland; by the fourth century BC, according to Arrian (2.21.4), this wall had reached a height of 45 metres (150 feet).

Any serious discussion of urban Tyre must consider its relationship to the opposing mainland, upon which it was greatly dependent for natural resources (especially water and fuel). Its mainland territory was contained within a narrow coastal stretch extending from the River Litani in the north to the promontory of Ras en-Naqura (the so-called 'Scales of Tyre') to the south. The focus of Tyre's continental realm was the town of Ushu, which served as the island city's main dependency down to the sixth century BC. Known as Palaetyrus ('ancient Tyre') in the classical sources, Ushu served not only as the primary conduit for raw materials from the surrounding region but as the base for the city's southwards expansion into the Akko plain and the northern Galilee.

As the Amarna correspondence reveals, Ushu was Tyre's primary source of drinking water until the Early Iron Age, when lime-plastered, water-proofed cisterns made possible the catchment and long-term storage of rain water on the island itself. Prior to this time, water was transported by boat to the island city.[4] According to Pseudo-Skylax, the town of Ushu was cut by a watercourse, which may correspond with the Ras el-'Aïn, whose waters later fed Tyre by means of an aqueduct in Roman times. Ushu's location remains an open question. It has been traditionally identified with Tell Rachidiyeh, a small

73 *View of the excavations at the mainland cremation cemetery at Tyre, Lebanon, 1997.*

unexcavated mound located 4 kilometres (2.5 miles) south of Tyre near the source of the Ras el-'Aïn. The much larger settlement mound of Tell el-Mashouk located on the mainland directly east of Tyre has also been proposed. The various cemeteries uncovered on the mainland provide an indication of the extent of Tyrian inland settlement. These include a rock-cut necropolis adjacent to Tell Rachidiyeh, and cemeteries at Joya, in the foothills east of Tyre, and at Qasmieh, on the far side of the River Litani. As recent excavations have revealed, Tyre's primary extramural cemetery, an extensive cremation necropolis in use from the tenth to the seventh century BC, was located along the shoreline on the opposite mainland – adjacent to the later Roman and Byzantine burial precinct. (See fig. 73.) The city's royal burial grounds have not been found; they may well have been located on the city acropolis, as at Byblos.

Tyre's two harbours, to the north and south, were noted by classical authors, including Pliny (*N.H.*, 5.76), who observes that they were connected by a canal which traversed the city.[5] Its northern port (known in antiquity as the 'Sidonian') was a natural bay, sheltered from prevailing winds by the island itself and by a strip of offshore reefs that protected its entrance; it functioned as a closed harbour within the city walls. Tyre's southern port, the 'Egyptian', was a built harbour protected by two great offshore breakwaters.

The chronology and physical configuration of Tyre's two harbours has been the subject of much debate. The northern ('Sidonian') port, the earlier of the two, functioned as the sole harbour facility in Hiram's own day. The southern ('Egyptian') port was constructed at a later date; its development is traditionally ascribed to King Ithobaal I (887–856 BC). With the exception of its two offshore breakwaters, the 'Egyptian' harbour, as presently configured, is the work of the Roman period. Stratigraphically, the southern sector of present-day Tyre rests on successive layers of landfill dating primarily from the Hellenistic and Roman eras, suggesting that the city's Iron Age harbour facility, sculpted from the island's inner reefs, was located much further inland.[6]

Sarepta: a portrait of a Phoenician industrial town

The coastal town of ancient Sarepta (modern Sarafand) is situated between Tyre and Sidon along Phoenicia's southern coast.[7] The settlement, which occupies a low mound, is on the promontory of Ras el-Qantara, overlooking a broad bay with sheltered anchorage. Explored by the University of Pennsylvania from 1969 to 1974, Sarepta represents the first in-depth excavation of an Iron Age mainland Phoenician settlement. Soundings made in two areas on the tell (X and Y) have revealed a continuous sequence of habitation extending from the beginning of the Late Bronze Age – the date of the city's foundation – to the Hellenistic period. Sounding Y was made on the highest part of the mound. This primarily residential area, which revealed an uninterrupted sequence of eleven occupation strata, yielded complexes of courtyard houses equipped with potters' kilns and bread ovens. One of them, Stratum D (1025–800 BC), was marked by a new city plan and repertory of ceramic styles (red-slip finish) and shapes (torpedo-shaped amphorae).

Sounding X revealed an extensive industrial quarter near the harbour at the northern periphery of the settlement. Much of this district was devoted to pottery production; findings included the remains of twenty-two stone-built firing kilns and slip basins and tanks for washing and storing clay. Other industries included purple-dye production jewellery manufacture, and olive oil processing. Sounding X produced an eighth-century stone ashlar shrine to the goddess Tanit-Ashtarte with benches, an offering table, and a central cultic pillar. The ancient settlement was flanked to the north and south by two small harbours; excavation of the south-western port at Ras esh-Shiq uncovered a stone-built quay erected in the first century AD. No evidence has yet been found for the usage of either harbour facility prior to the Roman period.

Sidon: a Phoenician port and its suburban environs

The port city of Sidon (Punic *Ṣdn*), located 35 kilometres (22 miles) north of Tyre, is situated on a small promontory bordered by a line of reefs hugging the coastline. (See fig. 12.) The settlement, which is marked by an oval mound of roughly 58 hectares (145 acres), is circumscribed by two small rivers, the El Kamlé to the north and the El Barghout to the south. The city lies adjacent to two natural harbours: a

74 *An aerial view of Sidon.*

southern circular cove and an enclosed northern port. As at Tyre, the density of modern settlement at Sidon has inhibited archaeological exploration. Excavation, however, has been re-undertaken recently within the old city under the auspices of the Lebanese Directorate General of Antiquities. Centred in the area immediately north and east of the St Louis Castle (on the former location of the American Presbyterian Mission College and the 'Sandikli' site), this work, begun in 1998, has uncovered stratigraphic evidence for the city's Early Bronze Age occupation. In addition, a series of corings was done to determine the ancient extent of the city's mainland harbour.[8]

From the existing evidence, it is possible to construct a general topographical outline of the city and its suburbs. Sidon's oval tell is divided longitudinally by a marked depression into two distinct sections: a low, flat area to the east and an elevated coastal region to the west. The latter comprised the city's upper district, which housed the residences of the élite and its administrative quarters. In all likelihood, a palatial residence or fortress stood at the summit of the hill now marked by the Crusader chateau of St Louis.

To the south of the acropolis, along the shore of the southern circular cove, stands an accumulation 40 metres (130 feet) high of discarded *murex* shells marking the ancient emplacement of a large purple-dye installation. The entire southern cove, which was ill-suited for use as a harbour facility, may have served as an offloading or beaching area for small fishing vessels involved in the procurement of the *murex*. As Poidebard's investigations have shown, Sidon's chief port facility was situated immediately north of the city.[9] This natural harbour, which was sheltered from the prevailing winds by a rocky offshore island and a north-easterly chain of islets and reefs, constituted the city's 'closed port' – first mentioned by Pseudo-Skylax in the mid-fourth century BC. Along the northern perimeter of the city, extending east towards the mouth of the El Kamlé river, stood the city's quays and warehouses.

Recent archaeological and topographical research has led to a better understanding of 'greater' Sidon and its suburban environs. Broadly defined, the city's heartland consisted of a narrow, well-watered agricultural plain 16 kilometres (10 miles) in length extending north from the Ras Sarafand, the headland north of Sarepta, to Ras-al-Jajunieh. In addition to its coastal possessions, Sidon also controlled territory inland; its hinterland extended through the eastern foothills of the Lebanon range and, beyond, into the populous and agriculturally fertile Beqa valley; it was through the latter that Sidon enjoyed crucial trade access to Syria and Transjordan.

An inscribed clay prism of the Assyrian king Sennacherib (704–681 BC) provides a listing of seven satellite towns (including Sarepta) under Sidon's control.[10] Sennacherib's inscription speaks of Sidon's walled fortress cities, which were equipped with provisions for the state garrisons. Two locations represent likely emplacements for such defensive outposts. The first is the hill of Mer Elias, located in the south-eastern flank of the city's suburbs. The elevated coastal mound of Brak et-Tell, located 10 kilometres (6 miles) south of Sidon, may equally mark the site of a fortress guarding Sidon's southern frontier.

Archaeological research over the last century has provided substantial data on the distribution of Sidon's suburban cemeteries. Special attention may be drawn to the necropolis of Dakerman, a vast coastal cemetery precinct located immediately south of the city. Excavations there by the Lebanese Department of Antiquities have yielded several hundred tombs of various types ranging from the fourteenth century BC to the early Roman period. Sidon's royal necropoli of the Persian and Hellenistic periods (Mogheret Ablun and Aya) have been located along a line of hills extending east and southeast of the city. Excavation has documented the existence of other cemeteries that may have served the city and its environs, including a pair of Iron II necropoli located south-east of Sidon at Tambourit and Ain el-Helwé. A large number of Bronze Age burial sites have been located further inland along the northern and eastern foothills.

The most important of Sidon's suburban sanctuaries was the precinct of Eshmun, located to the north of the city on the southern slopes of the Nahr el-Awali valley. Erected over a series of split-level terraces, this temple complex, founded in the sixth century BC, was enlarged during the Achaemenid era. Of Sidon's remaining suburban shrines and sanctuaries, attention may be drawn to a series of sacred grottoes (favoured religious sites by the Phoenicians) located south-east of the city.[11]

Beirut: a newly excavated Phoenician harbour town

The ancient port of Beirut (Punic *B'rt*; Greek *Berytos*), located along the central Lebanese coast, is situated on a rocky promontory with a sheltered harbour. Known previously only from scattered ancient textual references, the ancient city has now been revealed through archaeological research undertaken in connection with the redevelopment of war-devastated downtown Beirut. These excavations, begun in 1993 under the auspices of the Lebanese Department of Antiquities, have unearthed numerous sectors of the pre-Roman city, including the settlement mound and an adjacent residential precinct dating to the Persian period.

The original settlement occupied an elliptical tell roughly 2 hectares (5 acres) in extent, measuring 240 by 120 metres (260 by 130 yards). Its core, site of the ancient acropolis, was completely demolished during construction of the medieval Crusader castle, whose foundations reached bedrock. Recent excavations around this structure have uncovered evidence for a sequence of occupation dating back beyond the Middle Bronze Age, when the site was first fortified and equipped with a monumental gate. The city defences continued in operation until the end of the Late Bronze II period. Beirut's active external trade relations during this time are indicated by the variety of imported pottery finds (Cypriot and Mycenaean) uncovered in a rock-cut chamber of LB IIIA date. Some time before the tenth century BC, the settlement was equipped with a massive new fortification wall and glacis that continued in usage in the succeeding Iron II period. (See fig. 25.) This defensive system was subsequently destroyed, and then abandoned (and apparently reused as a dump site) in the second half of the eighth century. This latter stratum is marked by the first appearance of Phoenician red-slip ware. Some time around the mid-seventh century, the settlement was equipped with a casemate wall; an adjoining warehouse building housed quantities of Phoenician storage jars and local red-slip as well as imported Cypriot and Attic amphorae. A sixth and final fortification wall marked the Persian-period occupation of the site, during which time settlement spread well beyond the confines of the tell. To the west, in the area of the modern Souk, excavations have uncovered the remains of a residential district with well-preserved dwellings of pier-and-rubble construction laid out in an orthogonal plan. (See fig. 27.) In the area immediately adjacent to the north-west, a large quantity of *murex* shells and a basin complex were uncovered, offering possible evidence of local purple-dye production. The close proximity of both areas to the ancient harbour site reveals their commercial focus. As excavations have revealed, Beirut underwent extensive urban development beginning in the third century BC under the Seleucids.[12]

Byblos: an urban reconstruction of a Phoenician coastal emporium

The seaport of Byblos (ancient Gubal) is located at the foot of the Lebanese mountains 37 kilometres (23 miles) north of Beirut.[13] Situated on a promontory with a central spring and two small adjacent harbours, the site was blessed with access to a local copper source and abundant tracts of cedar in the adjacent slopes of the Lebanon range.

Byblos' principal settlement was situated on an elevated circular tract of land approximately 3 hectares (7 acres) in size. A planned city with a massive stone rampart and two gates, Early Bronze Age Byblos was an important coastal emporium. As recent studies have shown, its urban development was centred on a rock-cut well or spring situated in a central depression on the promontory. Beginning in the third millennium BC, the northern sector of the mound was converted into a sacred precinct by the erection of two monumental sanctuaries: a temple to Baalat Gubal and an L-shaped temple dedicated to an unidentified male deity. The latter structure was subsequently dismantled and its foundations re-employed in the construction of a sanctuary (known as the 'Obelisk Temple') dedicated to the god Resef. The Baalat Gubal and Obelisk sanctuaries were maintained with modifications down to the Hellenistic period.

Between the First and Second World Wars, French excavations in the southern sector of the promontory uncovered the remains of a residential district dating to the Middle Bronze Age, which was composed of roughly one hundred two- to four-room house units densely arranged in four blocks. The restricted housing capacity of this quarter (recently estimated at two thousand individuals maximum) has raised questions about its usage. Was this area the residential heart of the Middle Bronze Age city, as originally assumed, or did it serve a more specialized function – as a housing district for the city's temple personnel? If the latter interpretation is true, then the bulk of the city's population must have resided elsewhere by the early second millennium BC.

A possible clue as to the location of the city's residential centre may be found in the remains of a staircase descending from the north-western corner of the city acropolis in the direction of the northern port. In this location, on the culminating point of the upper hill (site of the royal palace), the northern rampart wall turns a curious right angle; this angled return probably marks the emplacement of a portal providing access from the acropolis to a lower neighbourhood in the vicinity of the port. Byblos' urban centre, from the Middle Bronze Age onwards, must be located in the surrounding plains to the north and east of its fortified promontory.

The urban extent of Phoenician Iron Age Byblos remains a complete unknown. None of the city's Iron Age necropoli has yet been found. Scattered clues point to urban development in the plains east of the acropolis. Here, beginning in the ninth century BC, the city's eastern defensive fortifications were successively strengthened in the area of the promontory's southern gate, the main point of access to the surrounding coastal plain. Building activity probably reached a peak in the Persian period, when the city prospered economically as a regional administrative and defensive centre under the Achaemenids. It was at this time that a monumental platform and stone pillared building (marking a Persian governor's reception hall) was erected in the north-east sector of the city walls.

As for the city's harbour facilities, the twin bays located north of the acropolis are both extremely small (the northern harbour – site of the medieval and modern port – measures only 130 by 80 metres (140 by 90 yards)) and is unsuitable for large ships. As has been recently proposed, the city's primary needs may have been served by the larger bay and riverineestuary that stood south of the acropolis.[14] The location of such a southerly port facility may help to explain the city's rapid urban expansion along the eastern coastal plain. If this reconstruction is correct, Byblos' topography would conform with that of a typical Phoenician port, situated on a headland flanked to the north and south by separate harbours. Further archaeological and geomorphological exploration is necessary to verify this hypothesis.

Tripolis: an urban confederation of the Late Iron Age

Tripolis ('triple town' in Greek) is situated 97 kilometres (60 miles) north of Beirut at the western extremity of a peninsula enclosed by the Abu 'Ali and el-Baḥṣaṣ Rivers.[15] According to classical sources (Diod. 16.41; Skylax 104), the city was a confederation of three neighbouring fortified towns founded in the Persian period by Arwad, Tyre and Sidon; during this period, Tripolis served as the headquarters of a pan-Phoenician council. The port of Tripolis may be securely identified with the harbour town of modern Al-Mina, whose fortifications had been noted in medieval sources. Excavations within the Crusader castle located on the hill south-east of its city walls have revealed evidence of occupation in the Late Bronze Age and Persian period. The identification of the other two towns in the confederation is less certain; they are probably to be located on the hills of Abu Samra and Al-Qubba, which occupy defensible positions on either side of the Abu 'Ali river 4 kilometres (2.5 miles) to the south-east of Al-Mina. Like Al-Mina, the first of these two sites revealed traces of discontinuous occupation from the Late Bronze Age and Persian era, suggesting that the ancient city enjoyed two distinct and widely disparate periods of urban activity, as the ancient texts suggest.[16]

Tell Ardé

Tell Ardé (ancient Ardata), an oval settlement mound of approximately 14 hectares (35 acres), is situated 10 kilometres (6 miles) south-east of Tripolis on the eastern fringe of the Akkar plain.[17] Ancient Egyptian texts attest to Ardata's importance in the mid-second millennium (fifteenth to fourteenth centuries BC). The city's complete absence from historical texts of the ensuing first millennium, however, suggests that it played a diminished role in the Iron Age. Limited excavations on the mound have revealed a continuous sequence of occupation from the Neolithic to the present.

Ullasa

Ancient Ullasa may be identified with the Phoenician coastal site of Ard Artusi to the north of Tripolis. Situated at the mouth of the Nar el-Barid, Ullasa served as a strategic harbour in the Late Bronze Age; in the fifteenth century BC, the Egyptian pharaoh Tuthmosis III appropriated it for use as an Egyptian naval and commercial port. Following its mention in the thirteenth-century Amarna correspondence, the site drops from the historical record until the Seleucid period (first century BC), when it reappears under the name Orthosia.

Tell Arqa

Tell Arqa (ancient Arqata) is situated at the mouth of the Akkar plain to the south of the Nahr el-Kebir.[18] The settlement, which is located 12 kilometres (7.5 miles) inland from the Mediterranean, occupies an imposing mound of roughly 12 hectares (30 acres). As the historical and archaeological record has revealed, Tell Arqa was a prosperous town in the first half of the second millennium BC. Following its destruction in the mid-fifteenth century BC (which may be attributed to one of the Syrian campaigns of Tuthmosis III), the site was partially abandoned for an extended period of time. Excavation, in fact, has uncovered only feeble traces of occupation down to the ninth century BC.

Tell Arqa was reoccupied intensively in the Iron II period (late ninth to early seventh centuries BC), when settlement apparently extended northward into the surrounding plain. At this time, the periphery of the tell was occupied by a necropolis with incineration burials.

Sheikh Zenad

Sheikh Zenad is situated to the north-west of Tell Arqa 4 kilometres (2.5 miles) south of the Nahr el-Kebir estuary. The site, yet unexcavated, occupies a low but extensive mound located on the left bank of the Nahr el-Khoreibi. At its base are the remains of a harbour installation datable, on ceramic grounds, to the Iron Age.

Tell Kazel

Tell Kazel is situated in the northern Akkar plain on the right bank of the Nahr el-Abrash 3.5 kilometres (2 miles) from the Syrian coast. An imposing oval tell of 11 hectares (27 acres), it is the largest of the settlements in the Eleutheros river valley. Scholars believe that the site may be identified with ancient Simyra, the fortified Late Bronze Age capital of Amurru that figures prominently in the Amarna correspondence and later Assyrian texts.

Excavations at Tell Kazel since 1985 have uncovered valuable new information about the settlement's occupational history from its origins in the Middle Bronze Age. Extensive architectural remains, including a palace complex and a temple datable to the end of the Late Bronze Age, attest to Tell Kazel's importance in the Amarna period. The latter, situated on the western platform of the tell, yielded an impressive amount of imported pottery from Cyprus and the Mediterranean world as well as an array of seals, amulets and glazed wares that underscore Tell Kazel's strong cultural connections with Ugarit. Architectural evidence for Early Iron Age habitation at the site remains scant. The Iron II settlement, which flourished in the ninth century BC, came to an abrupt end some time in the eighth century; evidence of burnt destruction (followed by architectural disruption) has been associated with an as-yet-unidentified Assyrian incursion. The Iron Age history of Tell Kazel is most fully represented by the Persian-period occupation, architecturally attested by two sizeable stone-built structures uncovered in the acropolis sector (Area I): a tripartite 'warehouse' of pier-and-rubble construction and a defensive installation composed of monumental ashlar blocks. Continued occupation in the Hellenistic period is evidenced by the discovery of a large cemetery on the north-east terrace of the site.[19]

Arwad: a northern Phoenician emporium and its dependencies

Ancient Arwad (Punic *'rwd* ('refuge'); Greek Arados) occupies a roughly oval-shaped island of *c.* 40 hectares (100 acres) situated 2.5 kilometres (1.5 miles) off the Syrian coast opposite mainland Antaradus (modern Tortose). The urban history of this Phoenician island emporium, which remains completely unexcavated, is virtually unknown. Although Arwad was occupied continuously from at least the third millennium BC, its

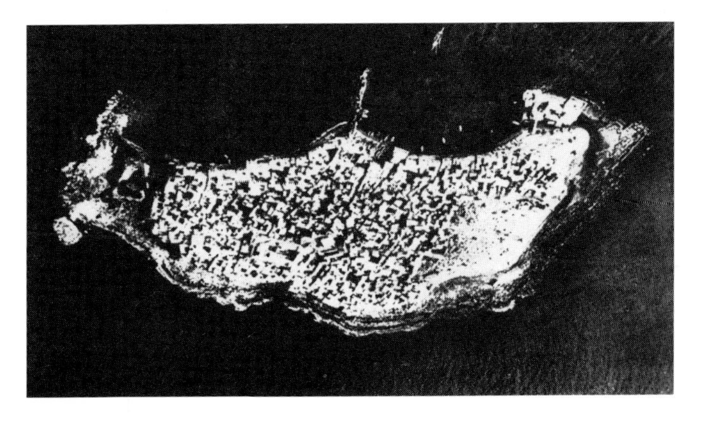

75 *A aerial view of Arwad.*

earliest surviving architectural vestiges (i.e. the monumental city ramparts) date only from the Roman period. Ideally situated for trade, Arwad possessed a twin harbour facing east towards the mainland; its northern and southern bays were separated by a natural jetty some 60 metres (65 yards) in length, which was augmented in antiquity by ashlar stone construction. As the massive Roman fortifications suggest, the Phoenician Iron Age city must have been protected by a fortified defensive wall that ringed the island. As the classical sources reveal, Arwad was densely populated; its city centre, like that of Tyre, was marked by multi-storeyed houses (Strabo 16.2.13). The high ground now occupied by the medieval fortifications undoubtedly marks the ancient city's acropolis and the site of its main sanctuaries. In this regard, reference may be drawn to a Graeco-Phoenician inscription with dedication to Herakles-Melqart and a basalt block with Greek inscription mentioning Zeus Cronos (Baal-Shamem?). As at Tyre, the city's main necropoli were probably located on the mainland opposite – in the region of Tortose, in whose vicinity a Persian-period cemetery of royal character has recently been found. As chance finds from the modern city suggest, a small cremation cemetery may also have been located in the island's southern periphery.

Like Tyre, Arwad was heavily dependent upon the mainland for its raw materials and agricultural staples. In antiquity, it appears that the city's independent water supply was ensured, at least in part, by the emplacement of extramural cisterns cut into the island's rocky counterscarp. In addition to Tortose, Arwad's mainland dependencies included coastal Marathus (Amrit), Arwad's chief continental port. Both Tortose and Amrit, which formed part of the larger mainland confederation controlled by Arwad in Hellenistic times, undoubtedly served as points of transhipment for trade moving through the strategic Akkar plain.[20]

Amrit

The site of Amrit (ancient Marathus) is located 5 kilometres (3 miles) south of Tortose along the southern Syrian coast, 700 metres (765 yards) inland from the Mediterranean. The ancient town, which extends over an area measuring 6 square kilometres (2.3 square miles), is bounded to the north and south by two rivers, the Nahr Amrit and the Nahr al-Qubleh. In antiquity, Amrit served as the continental port for the island city of Arwad; recent excavations have revealed the emplacement of its ancient harbour facility. The actual settlement of Amrit occupies a rectangular tell measuring 110 by 140 metres (120 by 150 yards). Excavations on the mound's northern periphery have revealed a large building dating to the late Persian period, Amrit's floruit. Situated west of the settlement mound is the famous sanctuary known locally as the Ma'abed – a porticoed temple complex consisting of a monumental built chapel set in a rock-cut basin. Phoenician dedications found within a votive trench in the sanctuary reveal the existence of a local cult to the god Eshmun, which flourished during the Persian and early Hellenistic periods (sixth to third centuries BC). To the settlement's south lies an extensive cemetery of the late Persian period (fourth century BC) with rock-cut tombs, three of them surmounted by distinctive pyramidal and cube-shaped funerary towers. Settlement at Amrit continued until the Hellenistic period.[21]

Chronological Chart

Chalcolithic	4500(?)–3100 BC
Early Bronze Age	3100–2000 BC
Middle Bronze Age	2000–1550 BC
Late Bronze Age I	1550–1400 BC
Late Bronze Age II	1400–1200/1150 BC
Iron Age I	1200/1150–1000 BC
Iron Age II	1000–586 BC
Iron Age III (Neo-Babylonian)	586–538 BC
Persian period	538–332 BC
Hellenistic period	332–64/63 BC

Bibliographical Abbreviations

Books

Acquaro, *Arte*
Acquaro, E., *Arte e cultura punica in Sardegna* (Sassari 1984)

Acquaro, *Biblo*
Acquaro, E. et al., *Biblo: una città e la sua cultura* (Rome 1994)

Aubet, *Phoenicians*
Aubet, M.E., *The Phoenicians and the West: Politics, Colonies and Trade* (Cambridge 1993)

Baurain and Bonnet, *Phéniciens*
Baurain, Cl. and C. Bonnet, *Les Phéniciens: marins de trois continents* (Paris 1992)

Betlyon, *Coinage*
Betlyon, J.W., *The Coinage and Mints of Phoenicia, the Pre-alexandrine Period*, Harvard Semitic Monographs 26 (Chicago 1982)

Bikai, *Cyprus*
Bikai, P.M., *The Phoenician Pottery of Cyprus* (Nicosia 1987)

Bikai, *Tyre*
Bikai, P.M., *The Pottery of Tyre* (Warminster 1978)

Biran, *Dan*
Biran, A., *Biblical Dan* (Jerusalem 1994)

Bonnet, *Astarté*
Bonnet, C., *Astarté: dossier documentaire et perspectives historiques* (Rome 1996)

Briend and Humbert, *Tell Keisan*
Briend, J. and J.-B. Humbert, *Tell Keisan, 1971–1976: un cité phénicienne en Galilée* (Freibourg and Paris 1980)

Briquel-Chatonnet and Gubel, *Phéniciens*
Briquel-Chatonnet, F. and E. Gubel, *Les Phéniciens: aux origines du Liban* (Paris 1998)

Casson, *Ships*
Casson, L., *Ships and Seamanship in the Ancient World*, 3rd ed. (Princeton 1995)

Culican, *Merchant Venturers*
Culican, W., *The First Merchant Venturers: The Ancient Levant in History and Commerce* (New York 1971).

Culican, *Opera*
Culican, W., *Opera Selecta: From Tyre to Tartessos* (Göteborg 1986)

Dunand, *Byblos*
Dunand, M., *Byblos: Its History, Ruins, and Legends*, 2nd ed. (Beirut 1968)

Elayi, *Économie*
Elayi, J., *Économie des cités phéniciennes sous l'empire perse* (Naples 1990)

Elayi, *Recherches*
Elayi, J., *Recherches sur les cités phéniciennes a l'époque perse* (Naples 1987)

Elayi, *Sidon*
Elayi, J., *Sidon, cité autunome de l'Empire perse* (Paris 1989)

Elayi and Elayi, *Trésors*
Elayi, J. and A.G. Elayi, *Tresors des monnaies phéniciennes et circulation monetaire: ve–ive siecles avant J.-C.* (Paris 1993)

Fantar, *Carthage*
Fantar, M., *Carthage: approche d'une civilisation*, 2 vols (Tunis 1993)

Ferjaoui, *Recherches*
Ferjaoui, A., *Recherches sur les relations entre l'Orient phénicien et Carthage* (Freibourg, Göttingen, Carthage 1993)

Garbini, *I Fenici*
Garbini, G., *I Fenici: storia e religione* (Naples 1980)

Gras, *Univers*
Gras, M., P. Rouillard and J. Teixidor, eds, *L'univers phénicien* (Paris 1989)

Gubel, *Phéniciens*
Gubel, E., *Les Phéniciens et le monde méditerraneen* (Brussels 1986)

Hachmann, *Frühe Phöniker*
Hachmann, R., ed., *Frühe Phöniker im Libanon: 20 Jahre deutsche Ausgrabungen in Kamid el-Loz* (Mainz am Rhein 1983)

Harden, *Phoenicians*
Harden, D.B., *The Phoenicians* (Harmondsworth 1971)

Harrison, *Spain*
Harrison, R., *Spain at the Dawn of History: Iberians, Phoenicians and Greeks* (London 1988)

Huss, *Geschichte*
Huss, W., *Geschichte der Karthager* (Munich 1985)

Huss, *Karthago*
Huss, W., ed., *Karthago* (Darmstadt 1992)

Jidejian, N., *L'archeologie au Liban* (Beirut 1998).

Joukowsky, *Heritage*
Joukowsky, M.S., ed., *The Heritage of Tyre: Essays on the History, Archaeology, and Preservation of Tyre* (Dubuque, Iowa 1992)

Karageorghis, *View*
Karageorghis, V., *View from the Bronze Age: Mycenaean and Phoenician Discoveries at Kition* (New York 1976)

Katzenstein, *Tyre*
Katzenstein, H.J., *The History of Tyre: From the Beginning of the Second Millennium* B.C.E *until the Fall of the Neo-Babylonian Empire in 539* B.C.E. (Beer Sheva 1997)

Kopcke and Tokumaru, *Greece*
Kopcke, G. and I. Tokumaru, eds, *Greece between East and West: 10th–8th centuries* B.C. (Mainz am Rhein

1982)
Krings, *Civilisation*
Krings, V., ed., *La civilisation phénicienne et punique: manuel de recherche* (Leiden, New York, Cologne 1995)
Lancel, *Byrsa II*
Lancel, S., *Byrsa II: rapports preliminaires sur les fouilles 1977–1978* (Rome 1982)
Lancel, *Carthage*
Lancel, S., *Carthage: A History* (Oxford and Cambridge, M.A. 1995)
Lipinski, *Dictionnaire*
Lipinski, E., ed., *Dictionnaire de la civilisation phénicienne et punique* (Brussels, Paris 1992)
Markoe, *Bowls*
Markoe, G., *Phoenician Bronze and Silver Bowls from Cyprus and the Mediterranean* (Berkeley 1985)
Martín Ruiz, J.A., *Catálogo documental de Los Fenicios en Andalucía* (Junta de Andalucía 1995).
Masson and Sznycer, *Recherches*
Masson, O. and M. Sznycer, *Recherches sur les phéniciens à Chypre* (Geneva 1972)
Montet, *Byblos*
Montet, P., *Byblos et l'Egypte* (Paris 1929)
Moscati, *Phoenicians*
Moscati, S., ed., *The Phoenicians* (New York 1988)
Moscati, *World*
Moscati, S., *The World of the Phoenicians* (London 1968)
Moscati, *I Fenici*
Moscati, S., ed., *I Fenici: ieri, oggi, domani. Richerche, scoperti, progetti* (Rome 1994)
Niemeyer, *Phönizier*
Niemeyer, H.G., ed., *Phönizier im Westen* (Mainz am Rhein 1982)
Niemeyer and Gehrig, *Phönizier*
Niemeyer H.G. and U. Gehrig, *Die Phönizier im Zeitalter Homers* (Mainz am Rhein 1990)
Parrot, *Phéniciens*
Parrot, A., Chéhab M.H. and S. Moscati, *Les Phéniciens: l'expansion phénicienne, Carthage* (Paris 1975)
Picard and Picard, *Carthage*
Picard, G.C. and C. Picard, *Carthage* (London 1987)
Poidebard, *Tyr*
Poidebard, A., *Un gran port disparu, Tyr* (Paris 1939)
Poidebard and Lauffray, *Sidon*
Poidebard, A. and J. Lauffray, *Sidon: aménagements antique du port de Säida* (Beirut 1951)
Pritchard, *Sarepta*
Pritchard, J., *Recovering Sarepta, a Phoenician City* (Princeton 1978)
Raban, *Harbour Archaeology*
Raban, A., ed., *Harbour Archaeology: Proceedings of the First International Workshop on Ancient Mediterranean Harbours* (Oxford 1985)
Redford, *Egypt*
Redford, D.B., *Egypt, Canaan, and Israel in Ancient Times* (Princeton 1992)
Reyes, *Cyprus*
Reyes, A.T., *Archaic Cyprus* (Oxford 1994)
Stern, *Dor*
Stern, E., *Dor, Ruler of the Seas* (Jerusalem 1994)
Stern, *Encyclopedia*
Stern, E., *The New Encyclopedia of Archaeological Excavations in the Holy Land*, 4 vols (New York 1993)
Wagner, *Einfluss*
Wagner, P., *Der Ägyptische Einfluss auf die Phönizische Architektur* (Bonn 1980)
Ward and Joukowsky, *Crisis Years*
Ward, W.A. and M.S. Joukowsky, eds, *The Crisis Years: The 12th Century B.C. From Beyond the Danube to the Tigris* (Dubuque 1992)
Warmington, *Carthage*
Warmington, B.H., *Carthage* (Baltimore 1964)
Wright, *Building*
Wright, G.R.H., *Ancient Building in South Syria and Palestine*, 2 vols (London 1985)

Periodicals

AAAS Annales Archéologiques Arabes Syriennes
AJA American Journal of Archaeology
AM Athenische Mitteilungen: Mitteilungen des Deutschen Archäologischen Instituts. Athenische Abteilung
BAAL Bulletin d'Archéologie et d'Architecture Libanaises
BAR Biblical Achaeological Review
BASOR Bulletin, American Schools of Oriental Research
BCH Bulletin de Correspondance Helléniqiue
BMB Bulletin du Musée de Beyrouth
CA Classical Antiquity
CEDAC Centre d'Études et de Documentation Archéologique de la Conservation de Carthage
CRAI Comptes rendus de l'Académie des Inscriptions et Belles-Lettres
HbÄ Hamburger Beiträge zur Archäologie
IEJ Israel Exploration Journal
JAOS Journal of the American Oriental Society
JCS Journal of Cuneiform Studies
JEA Journal of Egyptian Archaeology
JNES Journal of Near Eastern Studies
MM Madrider Mitteilungen
MUSJ Mélanges de l'Université Saint-Joseph
OLP Orientalia Lovaniensia. Periodica
OpAth Opuscula Atheniensia
OxJA Oxford Journal of Archaeology
PBA Proceedings of the British Academy
PEQ Palestine Exploration Quarterly
PIASH Proceedings of the Israel Academy of Sciences and Humanities
RM Römische Mitteilungen: Mitteilungen des Deutschen Archäologischen Instituts. Römische Abteilung
RSF Rivista di Studi Fenici
UF Ugarit-Forschungen: International Jahrbuch für die Altertumskunde Syrien Palästinas

WO Die Welt des Orients

VOLUMES, SERIES

ACFP 1 *Atti del I Congresso Internazionale di Studi Fenici e Punici* (Rome 1983)

ACFP 2 *Atti del II Congresso Internazionale di Studi Fenici e Punici* (Rome 1991)

ACFP 3 *Atti del III Congresso Internazionale di Studi Fenici e Punici* (Tunis 1995)

ACFP 4 *Atti del IV Congresso Internazionale di Studi Fenici e Punici* (Cadiz, forthcoming)

ARAB Luckenbill, D.D., *Ancient Records of Assyria and Babylonia*, 2 vols (Chicago 1926)

ANET (3) Pritchard, J.B., ed., *Ancient Near Eastern Texts Relating to the Old Testament*, 3rd ed. (Princeton 1969)

CAH *Cambridge Ancient History* (Cambridge 1971–82)

CIG *Corpus Inscriptionum Graecarum*

CIS *Corpus Inscriptionum Semiticarum*

EA Moran, W.L., ed., *The Amarna Letters* (Baltimore 1992)

FGH Jacoby, F., *Die Fragmente der griechischen Historiker* (Berlin, Leyden 1923–58)

KAI Donner, H. and W. Röllig, *Kanaanäische und aramäische Inschriften*, 3 vols (Wiesbaden 1966–9)

OxEANE Meyers, M., ed., *Oxford Encyclopedia of Archaeology in the Near East*, 5 vols (Oxford 1997)

Sarepta I Anderson, W.P., *The Late Bronze and Iron Age Strata of II, Y* (Beirut 1988)

Sarepta II Khalifeh, I.A., *The Late Bronze and Iron Age Strata of Area II, X* (Beirut 1988)

StPhoen 1–2 Gubel, E., E. Lipinski and B. Servez-Soyez, eds, I: *Redt Tyrus/Sauvons Tyre*; II: *Histoire phénicienne/Fenicische geschiedenis* (Leuven 1983)

StPhoen 3 Gubel, E. and E. Lipinski, eds, *Phoenicia and its Neighbors* (Leuven 1985)

StPhoen 4 Bonnet, C., E. Lipinski and P. Marchetti, eds, *Religio Phoenicia* (Namur 1986)

StPhoen 5 Lipinski, E., ed., *Phoenicia and the Eastern Mediterranean in the First Millennium B.C.* (Leuven 1987)

StPhoen 6 Lipinski, E., ed., *Carthago* (Leuven 1988)

StPhoen 7 Gubel, E., *Phoenician Furniture* (Leuven 1987)

StPhoen 8 Bonnet, C., *Melqart: cultes et mythes de l'Heracles tyrien en Mediterranée* (Leuven 1988)

StPhoen 9 Hackens, T. and G. Moucharte, eds, *Numismatique et histoire économique phéniciennes et puniques* (Louvain-la-Neuve 1992)

StPhoen 11 Lipinski, E., ed., *Phoenicia and the Bible* (Leuven 1991)

CLASSICAL SOURCES

Arist., *Pol.* Aristotle, *Politics*

Ath. Athenaeus, *Deipnosophistae*

Curt. Quintus Curtius Rufus, *History of Alexander*

Diod. Diodorus Siculus

Hdt. Herodotus

Hom., *Il.* Homer, *Iliad*

Hom., *Od.* Homer, *Odyssey*

Jos., *A.J.* Josephus, *Antiquities of the Jews*

Jos., *C.Ap.* Josephus, *Contra Apionum*

Pliny, *N.H.* Pliny the Elder, *Naturalis Historia*

Pol. Polybius

Ps.-Arstt., *Mir. ausc.* Pseudo-Aristotle, *De mirabus auscultiorum*

Sil. Silius Italicus, *Punica*

Tac., *An.* Tacitus, *Annals*

Thuc. Thucydides

Xen., *Anab.* Xenophon, *Anabasis*

Xen., *Hell.* Xenophon, *Hellenica*

OLD TESTAMENT

Chr. Chronicles

Deut. Deuteronomy

Ez. Ezekial

Gn. Genesis

Hos. Hosea

Jer. Jeremiah

Jgs Judges

Jos. Joshua

Kgs Kings

Sm. Samuel

NOTES

INTRODUCTION

1 M.G.A. Guzzo in Moscati, *Phoenicians*, 570–72.

CHAPTER ONE

1 Cf. the presence of more than a hundred paste scarabs of Hyksos variety from Byblos; J.-F. Salles, *La nécropole K de Byblos* (Paris 1980) 63 and pl. XXIII.
2 The Egyptian–Byblite timber trade in cedar, already attested in the Egyptian Predynastic period, is documented historically by the Fourth Dynasty.
3 W.F. Albright and W.L. Moran, JCS 4 (1950) 163–68.
4 For the recent discovery of Early Bronze Age settlement at Sidon, see under Sidon in Appendix.
5 R. Gundlach, Lexikon der *Ägyptologie* 3 (1980) 881–82.
6 M. McKay in Berytus 31 (1983) 144–45.
7 *AJA* 90 (1986) 269–96; 92 (1988) 1–37; 93 (1989) 1–29. See, most recently, G.F. Bass in J.E. Coleman and C.A. Walz, eds, *Greeks and Barbarians* (Bethesda, Maryland 1997) 85–92.
8 E. De Vaumas, *Le Liban* (Paris 1954) 287. The greater forested zone occurs at medium altitudes of 1500–2000 metres (5000–6500 feet).
9 J.H. Breasted, *Ancient Records of Egypt* 3 (Chicago 1906) 113, no. 274 (Great Abydos Inscription); G.T. Martin, *The Hidden Tombs of Memphis* (London 1991) 133 (Tomb of Pabes).
10 See Bass (note 7, above) 77–83.
11 As the texts reveal, an Ugaritian commercial firm, the house of Ewr-kl, was established at Beirut to supervise bronze-working production; see Ugaritic Text 2101; 2056:1–4.
12 Bikai, *Tyre*, pl. XLIV, no. 16 and Appendix A.
13 For Sidon and the other Phoenician cities in the Late Bronze Age cuneiform texts, see B. Arnaud, *Studi Micenei ed Egeo-Anatolici* 30 (1992) 179–94. Arnaud points to the Assyrian character of the language and script employed by Sidon in its correspondence with Ugarit.
14 Bikai, *Tyre*, 8; idem in Ward and Joukowsky, *Crisis Years*, 133.
15 *Sarepta* II, 113, 124, 138–39; *Sarepta* I, 380, 386, 388, 424; Pritchard, *Sarepta*, 85.
16 *Berytus* 38 (1990) 76–78; *Syria* 71 (1994) 345.
17 Justin, 18.3.5. B. Mazar, *PIASH* 1:7 (1967) 5, n. 11.
18 A.H. Gardiner, *Ancient Egyptian Onomastica* I (Oxford 1968) 150, no. 257 (Egyptian *kpn(y)*).
19 H. Goedicke, *The Report of Wenamun* (Baltimore and London 1975); *ANET* (3), 25–29.
20 Bikai in Ward and Joukowsky, *Crisis Years*, 133, n. 12.
21 V. Karageorghis and M. Demas, *Excavations at Kition* 5 (Nicosia 1985) 277–80.
22 V. Cook, *OpAth*, 17:3 (1988) 17, 20, 24. For Canaanite jars at Enkomi, see J.-C. Courtois, *Acts of the International Archaeological Symposium 'Cyprus between the Orient and the Occident'* (Nicosia 1986) 88.
23 A. Mazar, *Qedem* 20 (1985) 123–26.
24 *Ibid.*, 75–76, 84–85.
25 For Tell Keisan, see Briend and Humbert, *Tell Keisan*, 197–206; for Tell Dan, see Biran, *Dan*, 138–42.
26 E. Stern, *BASOR* 279 (1990) 28–31.
27 Biran, *Dan*, 135–44.
28 Jgs., 1:31.
29 2 Sm., 24:6–7.
30 E. Stern, *BASOR* 279 (1990) 27–32.
31 Jos., 11:8, 13:4, 19:28; Jgs. 18:7, 18:28.
32 Gn., 10:15.
33 *EA*, 146–55.
34 *EA*, 149.
35 Bikai, *Cyprus*, 58–62.
36 Bikai, *Tyre*, 54, table 13A, and 74; *Sarepta* I, 407, and 517, table 18.
37 See now J.N. Coldstream in S. Gitin, A. Mazar and E. Stern, *Mediterranean Peoples in Transition: Thirteenth to Early Tenth Centuries bce* (Jerusalem 1998) 353–60 for the supposition of high-level diplomatic contacts between élites at Tyre and Lekfandi in the tenth century BC.
38 H.G. Niemeyer, *Biblical Archaeology Today* (Jerusalem 1993) 341–42.
39 1 Kgs, 9:26–28; 10:22ff; 2 Chr., 8:18.
40 H.G. Niemeyer, *Biblical Archaeology Today* (Jerusalem 1993) 340; against, see Aubet, *Phoenicians*, 176–79.
41 I Kgs, 7:13–48.
42 1 Kgs, 5:1.
43 1 Kgs, 5:11.
44 1 Kgs, 9:11–14.
45 A. Lemaire, *StPhoen* 11, 152.
46 2 Chr., 2:14; Katzenstein, *Tyre*, 66–67.
47 F. Volkmar and A. Kempinksi, *Ergebnisse der Ausgrabungen auf der Hirbet el-Msas (Tel Masos), 1972–75* (Wiesbaden 1983) 20–21, 39–43, plans 3, 6, 14. I. Finkelstein, *JNES* 47:4 (1988) 241ff.
48 See A. Raban in Raban, *Harbour Archaeology*, 27.
49 See G. Kestemont, *StPhoen* 3, 135–49.
50 1 Kgs, 16.31.
51 Jos., A.J., 8, 318; cf. 1 Kgs, 18:19.
52 Katzenstein, *Tyre*, 137.
53 Katzenstein, *Tyre*, 130–35.
54 Jos., A.J. 8, 324.
55 *ANET* (3) suppl. 560b.
56 Ez., 27:18.
57 For Phoenician political and military involvement in Cilicia at this time, see the newly discovered stele from Inçirli dated to Shalmaneser V (726–722 BC); see Chapter 5, n. 70.
58 J. Elayi, *Semetica* 35 (1985) 25.
59 Redford, *Egypt*, 354–55.
60 ANET (3) 533–34; most recently, N. Na'aman,

RSF, 22 (1994) 3–8.

61 Redford, *Egypt*, 441–42.

62 Jos., *C.Ap.*, 1,156; *A.J.*, 10,228.

63 Katzenstein, *Tyre*, 324–32. For the Babylonian tablet, see R.P. Dougherty, *Archives from Erech, Time of Nebuchadnezzar and Nabonidus* (New Haven 1923) 61, no. 151.

64 Katzenstein, *Tyre*, 320–21.

65 Alternatively, such restitution may have occurred at the beginning of Cyrus' reign.

66 D.W. Thomas, ed., *Documents from Old Testament Times* (New York 1961) 93 (Cyrus Cylinder).

67 M.A. Dandamaev, *A Political History of the Achaemenid Empire* (Leiden 1989) 60–65.

68 S. Weinberg, *PIASH* 4:5 (1969) 92–94.

69 Hdt.., 4.42.

70 Reyes, *Cyprus*, 70–84.

71 Hdt., 2.112.

72 Hdt., 2.158 (Suez canal); 7.23 (Mount Athos canal). For the Old Persian text of the Suez stelae inscriptions, see R.G. Kent, *Old Persian*, 2nd ed. (New Haven 1953) 147.

73 Diod., 16.41.4.

74 *CIG* 1:126, no. 87.

75 See Elayi and Elayi, *Trésors*, esp. pp. 355–58.

76 Hdt., 7.44; 7.96; 7.98; 8.67.

77 C. Baurain and A. Destrooper-Georgiades in Krings, *Civilisation*, 618–23 and map on p. 598.

78 See I. Michaelidou-Nicolau in *StPhoen*, 5, 333–38; and M. Yon in *StPhoen*, 9, 243–59.

79 Huss, *Geschichte*, 58–65.

80 Hdt., 1.166–67.

81 Huss, *Geschichte*, 58–62.

82 *FGH*, 2C, Ephoros of Kyme F 186; Diod., 11.1.4–5; 11.20.1; see also Huss, *Geschichte*, 98–99.

83 Fantar, *Carthage* 2, 22.

84 S. Lancel, *StPhoen* 9, 272; J.-P. Morel, *ACFP*, 1, 731–40.

85 S.R. Wolff, *Maritime Trade from Punic Carthage* (Ph.D. diss., Chicago 1986) 115–16.

86 F. Rakob, *RM*, 94 (1987) 341–43 and pl. 146.

87 Thuc., 6.34.2.

88 Isocrates, *Panegyric*, 161.

89 M. Yon and M. Sznycer, *CRAI* (1991) 791–823.

90 Xen., *Agesilaus*, 2.30.

91 Betlyon, *Coinage*, 13–14; fig. 1 and pl. 3.

92 Diod., 16.41.2.

93 Betlyon, *Coinage*, 16–18.

94 Diod., 16.44.5–6.

95 Grayson, *Assyrian and Babylonian Chronicles* (Locust Valley 1985) 114.

96 Betlyon, *Coinage*, 18 and n. 70; see also Elayi and Elayi, *Trésors*.

97 Arrian, *Anabasis*, 2.24.5; Diod., 17.46.4; Curt., 4.4.15–17.

98 J. Elayi, *Transeuphratène*, 2 (1990) 59–70; 5 (1992) 143–51.

99 L. Stager, *BAR*, 17:3 (1991) 28–32.

100 J. Elayi, *JNES*, 41 (1982) 83–110; idem, *Recherches*, 11–20.

101 J. Sapin, *Transeuphratène* 4 (1991) 51–62; 5 (1992) 95–110.

102 E. Gubel, *Transeuphratène* 2 (1990) 37–46; also J. Sapin, *Transeuphratène* 2 (1990) 89, 93.

103 P. Lund, *Transeuphratène* 2 (1990) 13–32; J. Sapin, *Transeuphratène* 1 (1989) 21–47.

104 Stern, *Dor*, 157–79.

105 R.A. Stucky, *Tribune d'Echmoun* (Bâle 1984). Idem, *[Beirut] National Museum News* 7 (1998) 4ff; also J. Ferron, *Sarcophagus de Phénicie. Sarcophages à scènes en relief* (Paris 1993) 352ff.

106 For the Etruscan agreements, see Picard and Picard, Carthage, 134–36. For the Rome–Carthage treaty, see Huss, *Geschichte*, 149–55.

107 Diod., 20.8.2–4.

Chapter Two

1 A. Raban in Raban, *Harbour Archaeology*, 30–38.

2 Appian, *Libyca*, 96. For the British excavations, see H. Hurst and S.P. Roskams, *Excavations at Carthage: The British Mission* 1:1 (Sheffield 1984).

3 Z. Gal, *Levant*, 24 (1992) 173–86.

4 H.G. Niemeyer and R.F. Docter, *RM*, 100 (1993) 204–14.

5 For the Late Bronze Age Levantine type, see Courtois, *UF* II (1979) 104–34.

6 Byrsa: S. Lancel, G. Robine, and J.-P. Thuillier in J.G. Pedley, ed., *New Light on Ancient Carthage* (Ann Arbor 1980) 13ff; Kerkouane: M. Fantar, *Kerkouane* I–III (Tunis 1984–86); Monte Sirai: P. Bartoloni, S.F. Bondi and L.A. Marras, *Monte Sirai* (Rome 1992) 43–45.

7 Appian, *Libyca*, 128.

8 A structure of similar type has been found at Toscanos; see H. Schubart in Krings, *Civilisation*, 752–53.

9 Bikai, *Tyre*, 7; *Sarepta* I, 380.

10 *EA*, 89.

11 Pritchard, *Sarepta*, 81–83.

12 L. Badre, *BAAL*, 2 (1997).

13 F. Rakob, *RM*, 96 (1989) 165.

14 F. Rakob, *RM*, 91 (1984) 2, 4.

15 Athlit, Megadim, Shiqmona, and Tell Abu Hawam.

16 Area II, Y: *Sarepta* I, 419 (Stratum B); Area II, X: *Sarepta* II, 140 and pl. 11 (Phase VIIIB).

17 C. Aupert, *BAAL*, 1 (1996) 63, 83.

18 See Wright, *Building* 1, 162.

19 F. Rakob, *RM*, 94 (1987) 334ff.

20 Casson, *Ships*, 53–60, 94–96. I would like to thank Dr Casson for his kind input in this section.

21 L. Badre, *BAAL*, 2 (1997) 48–50, 60–64 and fig. 31a, 76–80 and fig. 40a, 88–90.

22 Stern, *Dor*, 109–15; idem, *IEJ*, 38 (1988) 6ff. On salient and recess trace walls, see Wright, *Building* 1, 84; 2, figs 86, 87.

23 J.-P. Rey-Coquais, *Arados et sa Pérée* (Paris 1974).

24 Ez., 27:11.

25 Dunand, *BMB*, 20 (1967) 30 and figs 2, 3.
26 Dunand, *BMB*, 19 (1966) 98, fig. 1.
27 J. Elayi, *RSF*, 8 (1980) 165–80; idem, *Transeuphratène* 11 (1996) 77–90.
28 Xen., *Anab.* 2.21.
29 Diod., 16.44.5–6.
30 P. and P. Bikai, *Berytus* 35 (1987) 75.
31 Thuc., 1.13.6; Hdt., 1.166–67.
32 Hdt., 7.165 (Ligurians, Iberians, Elisykans).
33 Warmington, *Carthage*, 47.
34 C.R. Whittaker, *Klio*, 60 (1978) 338 and n. 39; and G. Brizzi in Krings, *Civilisation*, 308.
35 R. Duval, *CRAI* (1950) 53–59
36 *EA*, 138 (Byblos); *EA*, 157 (Simyra).
37 *KAI*, no. 31; Masson and Sznycer, *Recherches*, 13ff.
38 Aubet, *Phoenicians*, 125–32.
39 See Fantar, *Carthage* 1, 240; for an earlier date, see S.F. Bondi in Moscati, *Phoenicians*, 128.
40 Cf. Justin, 18.3 for the slave population at Tyre.
41 Fantar, *Carthage*, 1, 185–88.
42 *CIS*, 1, 4808, 5988; Fantar, *Carthage* 1, 204–05.
43 *CIS*, 1, 5948; Fantar, *Carthage* 1, 205.
44 See Fantar, *Carthage* 1, 200–06 for an overview of women in Carthaginian society.

CHAPTER THREE

1 1 Kgs, 5:1–18; the Old Testament text also mentions the assistance of the Byblians, whose services were probably subcontracted by Hiram as part of the agreement: 1 Kgs 5:18. A similar agreement underlay the terms of service of the Tyrian bronzecaster Hiram (1 Kgs 7:13–47).
2 See Elayi, *Économie*, 31–38.
3 Ez., 27:17.
4 Hos., 14:6–7; Pliny, *N.H.*, 14.9.74.
5 Ath., 1.29b; Ps.-Arstt., *Mir. ausc.*, 135; Hdt., 3.6. Here we may note the Phoenician amphorae of Neo-Babylonian and Persian date recently found in Wadi Tumeilat, the site of the ancient canal connecting the Nile and the Red Sea; see A. Lemaire in Lipinski, *StPhoen* 5 (1987) 59.
6 R.F. Docter, *HbÄ* 15–17 (1988–90) 143–88.
7 Ez., 27. See H.J. van Dijk, *Ezekial's Prophecy on Tyre: A New Approach* (Rome 1968).
8 D. Arnaud, *Studi Micenei ed Egeo-Anatolici* 30 (1992) 179–94.
9 For a discussion of the term as it relates to the Wenamun account, see H.J. Katzenstein in *ACFP*, 1:2, 599–602.
10 1 Kgs, 10:22; 2 Chr., 9:21. Cf. the later *hubur* between Kings Jehoshaphat and Ahaziah (2 Chr., 20:35–36)
11 See Aubet, 11.
12 The above information has been excerpted from Casson, *Ships*, 65–69.
13 For a late sixth–early fifth century shipwreck discovered at Ma'agan Micha'el, off the Northern Israeli coast near Haifa, see E. Lindner, *BAR*, 18:6 (1992) 24–35. For two late eighth-century wrecks found in the Bay of Mazarron, off the Southeastern coast of Spain, see I. Negueruela in *ACFP*, 4 (Cadiz forthcoming). Attention may also be drawn to two recent deep-sea finds of Phoenician merchant vessels located with the aid of deepwater side-scan sonar technology and documented by a remotely operated vehicle system (ROV). The first, situated in the Western Mediterranean off the Straits of Gibraltar, contained more than 200 amphorae of Punic variety dating to the mid-fifth century BC. For initial reports, see W.J. Broad, *The New York Times* (12 October 1998); and *Odyssey Update* at www.shipwreck.net. The second comprised two vessels, measuring 15 and 18 metres (48 and 58 feet), respectively, with cargoes of several hundred amphorae dating to the second half of the eighth century BC, discovered 48 kilometres (30 miles) off the coast of Southern Israel near Ashkelon; for initial reports, see D.L. Chandler, *International herald Tribune* (25 June 1999) 1, 6; and at www.ngnews.com.
14 Curt., 4.2.10; Diod., 20.14.
15 For an excellent summary, particularly as it relates to the Persian period, see Elayi, *Économie*, 61–68.
16 S. Frankenstein in M.T. Larsen, ed., *Power and Propaganda: A Symposium on Ancient Empires* (Copenhagen 1979) 272–73.
17 See G. Markoe, *CA*, 8:1 (1989) 103–04.
18 It should be pointed out, however, that the frontal owl does occur in Egypt as the hieroglyphic symbol *m*.
19 Betlyon, *Coinage*, 53–57.
20 Elayi and Elayi, *Trésors* 342, 360.
21 J.M. Turfa, *AJA*, 81 (1977) 368–74.
22 Arstt., *Pol.*, 3.5.10–11 (1280a); see also Hdt., 1.166–67.
23 Polyb., 3.22; 3.24.
24 Diod., 5.35; Pliny, *N.H.*, 33.31.97; Strabo, 3.2.10.
25 Thuc., 6.34.2.
26 G.F. Jenkins and R.B. Lewis, *Carthaginian Gold and Electrum Coins* (London 1963) 25–26; Hdt., 4.196.
27 For the copper mines, see Strabo, 17.3.11; for iron-working at Carthage, see Lancel, *Byrsa*, 2, 217–60, 366.
28 Warmington, Carthage, 82–83; J.D. Muhly in *Early Metallurgy in Cyprus 4000–500 B.C.*, 257; C. Domergue, *Les mines de la péninsule ibérique dans l'antiquité romaine* (Rome 1989) 141–54. For the voyage of Himilco, see Pliny, *N.H.*, 2.169; Festus Avienus, *Ora Maritima*.
29 Plautus, Poenelus.
30 According to Hermippos (fourth to third century BC), Carthage exported its carpets and pillows. For the excavations at Le Kram, see M.K. Annabi, *CEDAC*, 4 (1981) 26–27.
31 Y. Maniatis et al., *Journal of Field Archaeology* 11:2 (1984) 205–22..
32 Amos, 1:9; Joel, 3:6; Ez., 27:13; M. Dietrich, O.

Loretz, and S. Sanmartin, *Die Keilalphabetische Textes aus Ugarit. 1. Transcription* (Kevelaer, Neukirchen, Vlyun 1976) 3, 4.

33 Strabo, 3.2.10.

34 Hdt., 1.1; 2.54–56; cf. also Hom., *Od.*, 14.287ff.

35 Timaeus (apud Ps-Arstt., *Mirab. ausc.* 188): *FGH*, frag. 164, 18–20). Sardinia may have been another source; see S. Gsell, *Histoire ancienne de l'Afrique du nord* 4 (Paris 1920) 135.

36 See P.A. Garnsey and C.R. Whittaker, *Imperialism in the Ancient World* (Cambridge 1978) 65–66; 88–90; according to some scholars, the process of territorial expansion began already in the fifth century BC; see Fantar, *Carthage*, 266.

37 Diod., 20.79.5 (wheat export in 306 BC); Diod., 20.8.4 (Carthaginian estates).

38 The date of the first Sicilian Phoenician coinage is debated, with scholarly opinion divided between an initial date of 480 and 430 BC.

39 See E. Acquaro in Moscati, *Phoenicians*, 204.

40 P. Visona, *American Journal of Numismatics* 10 (1998) 1–27. I am grateful to Dr Visona for the content of this section.

CHAPTER FOUR

1 In its early stage, the following vowels may be postulated: short *i*, *a*, *u*; and long *i*, *e*, *o*, and *u*.

2 P.K. McCarter, Jr, *The Antiquity of the Greek Alphabet and the Early Phoenician Scripts* (Missoula 1975) 34ff, 50ff.

3 For the script, see J.B. Peckham, *The Development of the Late Phoenician Scripts* (Cambridge, M.A. 1968).

4 For the early alphabetic scripts, see McCarter, *op. cit.*; idem, *Ancient Inscriptions: Voices from the Biblical World* (Washington, D.C. 1996) 67–75; and F.M. Cross in Cross, ed., *Symposia Celebrating the 75th Anniversary of the Founding of the American Schools of Oriental Research* (Cambridge, M.A. 1979) 97–111.

5 See B. Sass, *The Genesis of the Alphabet and its Development in the Second Millennium B.C.* (Wiesbaden 1988) 2; 74, n. 48; and 86ff, n. 58.

6 M. Sznycer in J. Leclant, ed., *Le déchiffrement des écritures et des langues* (Paris 1975) 75–84; G.E. Mendenhall, *The Syllabic Inscriptions from Byblos* (Beirut 1975).

7 Hdt., 5.58; Diod., 5.74; Pliny, 5.67; Tac., *An.*, 11.14.

8 For the suggestion of an eleventh-century origin, see E. Lipinski in Gubel, *Phéniciens*, 65. For an early second-millennium dating, see M. Bernal, *BASOR*, 267 (1987) 1–19.

9 Hdt., 5.5.8–61.

10 B.B. Powell, *Homer and the Origin of the Greek Alphabet* (Cambridge 1991) 12–18; C.J. Ruijgh in *Bibliotheca Orientalis*, 54:5/6 (1997) 533–603; and R.D. Woodard, *Greek Writing from Knossos to Homer* (New York 1997).

11 For a study of the Punic language, see S. Segert, *A Grammar of Phoenician and Punic* (Munich 1976), and J. Friedrich, M.G. Amadasi Guzzo and W. Röllig, *Phönizisch-punische Grammatik* (Rome 1995). For the script, see J.B.S. Peckham, *The Development of the Late Phoenician Scripts* (Cambridge, M.A. 1968).

12 See M. Sznycer in Huss, *Karthago*, 321–40.

CHAPTER FIVE

1 Hdt., 2.43–44.

2 Jos., *C.Ap.*, 1:113, 118; *A.J.*, 8:146; also Eupolemus: *FGH*, 3C, 723, frag. 2.

3 See E. Lipinski in Gubel, *Phéniciens*, 74.

4 Aubet, *Phoenicians*, 125–32.

5 *EA*, 108, 147, 149.

6 E. Lipinski in Gubel, *Phéniciens*, 72.

7 Bonnet, *Astarté*, 64–56; R.C. Steiner in *JNES*, 51 (1992) 191–200.

8 W. Röllig in Lipinski, Dictionnaire 48 ('Astarte'). The Ugaritic keret epic locates a shrine of Asherah at Tyre in the Late Bronze Age; see S. Parker, ed., *Ugaritic Narrative Poetry* (Atlanta 1997) 19.

9 R.J. Clifford, *BASOR*, 279 (1990) 60.

10 For the uninterrupted use of *ḥmn* in Ugaritic and Phoenician personal names, see P. Xella, *Baal Hammon* (Rome 1991) 36.

11 M. Yon, *StPhoen*, 4, 132, 137.

12 E. Lipinski in Gubel, *Phéniciens*, 72. See also S. Ribichini in Moscati, *Phoenicians*, 105.

13 A. Lemaire, *StPhoen*, 4, 98.

14 P. Xella in Moscati, *I Fenici*, 146–48; Xella, *WO* 19 (1988) 45–64.

15 H.W. Attridge and R.A. Oden, *The Syrian Goddess (De Dea Syria)* (Missoula 1976).

16 Adonis, whose worship is attested in late classical texts, is now believed to have been a Greek creation, loosely based upon the Semitic concept of a dying god. See S. Ribichini, *Adonis: Aspetti 'orientali' di un mito greco* (Rome 1981).

17 See *ANET* (3) 533–34.

18 *ARAB*, 2, 229 (par. 587). For Mount Saphon, see P.N. Hunt, *StPhoen* 11, 103–15.

19 H.W. Attridge and R.A. Oden, *Philo of Byblos: The Phoenician History* (Washington, D.C. 1981); A.I. Baumgarten, *The Phoenician History of Philo of Byblos* (Leiden 1981).

20 Text of Azitawadda of Adana: *KAI*, 26.III.18–19.

21 Jos., 19: 27.

22 N. Avigad and J.C. Greenfield, *IEJ*, 32:2–3 (1982) 118–28.

23 *CIS*, I, 86.

24 Hdt., 1.199.

25 Sil. Ital., 3.21–28. C. Bonnet, *StPhoen*, 8, 358–61.

26 Karageorghis, *View*, 106.

27 Karageorghis, *View*, 105–06. Cf. the offering of a lamb (*'mr*) in a storage jar at Sarepta (Pritchard, *Sarepta*, 98ff and fig. 97).

28 Markoe, *Bowls*, 56–59.

29 Such a public context is suggested by the two elaborately decorated masks found embedded in the debris of the principal street at Sarepta; see

Pritchard, *Sarepta*, 92 and figs 87, 88.

30 Markoe, *Bowls*, no. E9.

31 Culican, *Opera*, 549–69.

32 Deut., 16:21; Jgs, 6:25–30; 2 Kgs, 17:10; 18:4.

33 J.W. Shaw, *AJA*, 93 (1989) 165–83.

34 Gozzo (height 1.41 metres): E. de Manneville in *Mélanges syriennes offerts à Monsieur Renée Dussaud* 2 (Paris 1939) 895–902. Mogador (height 1.50 metres): Parrot, *Phéniciens*, 161. Motya: Lipinski, *Dictionnaire*, 303, fig. 236.

35 Tac., *An.*, 2, 2.

36 S. Iwry, *JAOS*, 81 (1961) 27–37.

37 Cf. Amen's divine revelation in the report of Wenamun; H. Goedicke, *The Report of Wenamun* (Baltimore and London 1975) 53–54.

38 1 Kgs, 18:20–40.

39 Cf. the *favissa* at Kharayeb north of Tyre, which yielded 1100 terracotta figurines spanning the late fourth to the first centuries BC; see M. Chéhab, *BMB*, 10–11 (1951–52).

40 See Gubel, *Phéniciens*, no. 32 for the textual reference to a private shrine to Astarte outside Tyre.

41 A. Lemaire, *StPhoen*, 4, 87–98.

42 The earliest identifiable representation of Melqart may be found on the Aramaic stele of Barhadad (*c.*800 BC) found near Aleppo (ill. Lipinski, *Dictionnaire*, 286, fig. 223).

43 For the *dea Tyria gravida* type, see Culican, *Opera*, 265–80.

44 Bonnet, *Astarte*, 35.

45 For the Ma'abed at Amrit and the sanctuary at Ain el-Hayat, see Wagner, *Einfluss*, 2–10, pls 15, 33.

46 M. Dunand, *BMB*, 26 (1973) 7–25. Wagner, *Einfluss*, 10–15. See, most recently, R.A. Stucky, *[Beruit] National Museum News* 7 (1998) 3–13 (with bibliography).

47 A. Caubet, *StPhoen*, 4, 153–68.

48 M. Dunand and R. Duru, *Oumm el Amed* (Paris 1962). Wagner, *Einfluss*, 27–35, pl. 16.

49 Wagner, *Einfluss*, 16–26.

50 E. Gubel in *StPhoen*, 4, 263–76.

51 1 Kgs, 7:13–47.

52 1 Kgs, 5:16–32; 9:10–11.

53 C. Bonnet, *StPhoen*, 4, 209–22.

54 Ill. Harden, *Phoenicians*, pl. 41.

55 *CIS*, I, 3914.

56 *CIS*, I, 3776.

57 Sicca Veneria: Valerius Maximus, 2.6.15.

58 *CIS*, I, 6000 bis.

59 *CIS*, I, 1068.

60 For an overview, see Lipinski, *Dictionnaire*, 382–83.

61 Cleitarchus, Scholia to Plato's Republic, 337A: *FGH*, 2B, 745, frag. 9.

62 Plutarch, *De Superstitione*, 171C–D; Pliny, *N.H.*, 36.4.39; Sil. *Ital.*, 4.765–822; Diod., 20.14.

63 The list of *tophet* precincts so far discovered includes: Carthage and Hadrumetum (Tunisia); Cirta (Algeria); Motya (Sicily); Sulcis, Bithya, Nora, Monte Sirai, and Tharros (Sardinia).

64 According to L.E. Stager, as Patricia Smith, physical and forensic anthropologist at Hebrew University, Jerusalem, cautions, one must be extremely careful in approximating age based upon the weight of the charred skeletal remains, particularly if comparison is being made to life tables derived from modern population studies. Infants at term in traditional societies can appear much younger than those in modern ones.

65 For a summary of the most recent excavations, see L.E. Stager in Niemeyer, *Phönizier*, 155–63 (Huss, Karthago, 353–69).

66 See Lancel, *Carthage*, 227–56.

67 Jer., 7:31–2; 2 Kgs, 17:17; 23:10.

68 A. Simonetti, *RSF*, 11 (1983) 91–111; S. Moscati, *Il sacrificio dei fanciulli: realtà o invenzione?* (Rome 1987); S. Ribichini, *Il tofet e il sacrificio dei fanciulli* (Sassari 1987).

69 Curt., 4.3.23.

70 The text of this stele, which bears a primary inscription in Phoenician and secondary texts in Akkadian and Luwian, will be published in a forthcoming volume of *JAOS*. My sincere appreciation to Dr Stephen Kaufman for making a preliminary translation available to me.

71 L.E. Stager and S.R. Wolff, *BAR*, 10 (1984) 30–51.

72 Tertullian, *Apologia*, 9.2–3.

73 R. Nisbet, *RSF*, 8 (1980) 115; F. Fedel and G. Foster, *RSF*, 16 (1988) 29–42.

74 F. Rakob, *RM*, 98 (1991) 33–80.

75 H.G. Niemeyer and R.F. Docter, *RM*, 100 (1993) 211–13, 241–43, and pl. 55,4.

76 Isis situla: P.K. McCarter, *BASOR*, 290–91 (1993) 115–20; Har Mispe Yamim situla: S. Wolff, *AJA*, 97 (1993) 148, fig. 13.

77 *KAI*, no. 13.

78 P.A. Bienkowski, *Levant*, 14 (1982) 8–88. For an excellent overview of Phoenician funerary practices (including child sacrifice), see M. Gras, P. Rouillard and J. Teixidor, *Berytus*, 39 (1991) 127–76.

79 For an overview of Phoenician cemeteries documented on the eastern mainland, see H. Sadae in *Cuadernos di Arqueologia Mediterranea* 1 (1995) 15–30.

80 See P. Bartoloni in *Riti funerari e di olocausto nella Sardegna fenicia e punica* (Cagliari 1989) 69.

81 For the recent excavations at Tyre, see A. Badawi, *[Beirut] National Museum News* 6 (1997) 37, and M.E. Aubet, ed., Excavations in the Necropolis of Tyre-Al Bass (Cambridge, forthcoming). I would like to thank Dr Aubet for making her as yet unpublished findings available to me.

82 The excavated stelae correspond with monuments from the same area illicitly excavated in 1990; for the latter and associated finds, see H. Seeden, *Berytus* 39 (1991) 39–126.

CHAPTER SIX

1 For ivorywork from Kamid el-Loz, see R. Echt in Hachmann, *Frühe Phöniker*, 79–91.

2 For the Annals of Tiglath-Pileser I, see *ARAB*, 1, 98 (paras 302 and 306) and 103 (para. 328).

3 2 Chr. 2: 13–14.

4 For an overview of dating, see G. Markoe, *BASOR* 279 (1990) 18–22.

5 The misuse or more properly 'reuse' of foreign motifs has been traditionally identified as a hallmark of Phoenician art. See the remarks of H. Frankfort, *The Art and Architecture of the Ancient Orient* (Suffolk 1954) 188.

6 M. Mallowan, *Nimrud and Its Remains* 2 (London 1966) 474–75; D. Ciafaloni, *Eburnea Syrophoenicia*, Studia Punica 9 (Rome 1992) 19–30.

7 For a thorough examination of Phoenician furniture, see E. Gubel, *StPhoen* 7.

8 Hom., *Il.*, 12.740–49.

9 The term, however, should not be taken literally as a geographic designation; see Markoe, *Bowls*, 3.

10 Stylistically, a number of the bowls have been assigned to a north Syrian centre of production. In reality, there is very little hard evidence to support such an assumption; see, most recently, P.R.S. Moorey (p. 29) and J.D. Muhly (p. 337) in J. Curtis, ed., *Bronzeworking Centres of Western Asia. c. 1000–539 B.C.* (London 1988). Analysis of the alloy composition of the Nimrud bronze bowls has revealed that their chemical groupings cut across stylistic lines; see *ibid.*, figs 172, 173.

11 M.R. Popham et al., *Archaeological Reports for 1988–89*, 118 and fig. 5; idem, *OxJA*, 14:1 (1995) 103–07 and fig. 2.

12 Markoe, *Bowls*, 7–8.

13 Markoe, *Bowls*, E1-14; idem., *HbA*, 19/20 (1992/3) 11–31.

14 B. Grau-Zimmerman, *MM*, 19 (1978) 161–218.

15 G. Markoe, *Levant*, 22 (1990) 111–22.

16 C. Doumet-Serhal et al., *Stones and Creeds: 100 Artefacts from Lebanon's Antiquity* (Beirut 1997) 68, no. 27.

17 E. Kukahn, *Anthropoide Sarkophage in Beyrouth* (Berlin 1955); M.-L. Buhl, *The Late Egyptian Anthropoid Sarcophagi* (Copenhagen 1959); J. Elayi, *Iranica Antiqua* 23 (1988) 275–322.

18 V. Karageorghis, *Proceedings of symposium on ancient marble, Paros* (forthcoming).

19 Institut du Monde Arabe, *Liban, l'autre rive*, exh. cat. (Paris 1998) 108, 147–49; Culican, *Opera*, 363–84; 541–47.

20 Horvat Rosh Zayit: Z. Gal, *JNES*, 53:1 (1994) 27–31; see also Culican, *Opera*, 385–90; W.A. Ward, *JEA*, 53 (1967) 69–71, pl. XII,1.

21 Pliny, *N.H.*, 36.193; Strabo, 16.2.25.

22 See D.F. Grose, *Early Ancient Glass* (Toledo 1989) 54–56. For the Amarna texts, see D. Barag, *Catalogue of Western Asiatic Glass in the British Museum* 1 (London 1985) 38; for the Ulu Burun cargo, see G.F. Bass, *AJA*, 90 (1986) 281–82.

23 For the juglets, see D. Barag in A. Oppenheim et al., *Glass and Glassmaking in Ancient Mesopotamia* (Corning 1968) 179–80; for the transitional alabastra, see Grose, *op. cit.*, 77–79.

24 Grose, *op. cit.*, 110.

25 For a review and bibliography, see Markoe, *Bowls*, 97–98.

26 T.E. Haevernick, *MM*, 17 (1977) 152–231; M. Seefried, *Les pendentifs en verre sur noyau des pays de la Méditerranée antique* (Rome 1982). For the discovery of glass and faience eye-beads in excavated Chou Dynasty tomb contexts, see G. Markoe, *ACFP*, 4 (Cadiz forthcoming).

27 A. Rathje, *Levant*, 8 (1976) 96–106; also V. Webb, *Archaic Greek Faience* (Warminster 1978) 36–60.

28 A. Caubet and M. Yon in V. Tatton-Brown, ed., *Cyprus and the East Mediterranean in the Iron Age* (London 1989) 28–43.

29 Culican, *Opera*, 265–80.

30 Culican, *Opera*, 481–93.

31 A.M. Bisi in Moscati, *Phoenicians*, 328–53.

32 G. Markoe, *BASOR*, 279 (1990) 14–16.

33 For Phoenician pottery in general, see Bikai, *Tyre*; idem, *Cyprus*; idem, *BASOR*, 229 (1978) 47–56.

34 W.P. Anderson, *BASOR*, 279 (1990) 35–54.

35 Oral communication, P. Bikai, 10 February 1998.

36 Pritchard, *Sarepta*, 111–26.

37 V. Hankey, *PEQ*, 100 (1968) 27–32.

38 For bibliography, see Lipinksi, *Dictionnaire*, 361.

39 Pliny, *N.H.*, 9.60–65.

40 H. Walter and K. Vierniesel, *AM* 74 (1959) 41.

41 R. Stucky, *Dedalo* 19 (1974) 1–170; see, most recently, D.S. Reese and C. Sease in *JNES* 52:2 (1983) 109–28.

42 For the Etruscan tradition, see W.L. Brown, *The Etruscan Lion* (Oxford 1960); Markoe, *Bowls*, 127–41. For the Cretan, see E. Kunze, *Kretische Bronzereliefs* (Stuttgart 1931); H. Matthäus in V. Karageorghis and N. Stambolides, eds, *Eastern Mediterranean: Cyprus-Dodecanese-Crete 16th–6th cent. B.C.* (Athens 1998).

43 M.E. Aubet Semmler in Niemeyer, *Phönizier*, 309–35.

44 G. Markoe, *BASOR* 301 (1996) 47–67.

45 A.M. Bisi, *StPhoen*, 6, 29–41.

46 G. Markoe, *BASOR* 301 (1996) 65, n. 30.

47 M.E. Aubet, *Marfiles fenicios del Bajo Guadalquivir*, 1–2 (Valladolid 1979–80); idem, *Pyrenae*, 17–18 (1981–2) 231–79.

48 For the stelae, see bibliography in Lipinski, *Dictionnaire*, 427; and S. Brown, *Late Carthaginian Child Sacrifice and Sacrificial Monuments in their Mediterranean Context* (Sheffield 1991).

49 S.M. Cecchini in Krings, *Civilisation*, 530–33; A. Rathje in J. Swaddling, ed., *Italian Iron Age Artefacts in the British Museum* (London 1986) 397–404.

50 E. Acquaro, *I rasoi punici* (Rome 1971).

CHAPTER SEVEN

1 For a report of the excavations and analysis of bone remains, see D. Christou, A.P. Agelarakis, A. Kantaand N. Stampolidis in V. Karageorghis and N. Stampolidis, eds, *Eastern Mediterranean: Cyprus-Dodecanese-Crete 16th–6th cent. B.C.* (Athens 1998) 207–29.
2 For an overview of Phoenician presence on Cyprus, see C. Baurain and A. Destrooper-Georgiades in Krings, *Civilisation*, 597–631; also Reyes, *Cyprus*, 18–21.
3 Ez. 27:15.
4 Markoe, *Bowls*, 95–99, 125–27.
5 S. Ribichini, *ACFP*, 3, 341–47.
6 For the finds at Eleutherna, see N. Stampolidis, Kanta, A. and A. Karetsou in V. Karageorghis and N. Stampolidis, eds, *Eastern Mediterranean, Cyprus–Dodecanese–Crete, 16th–6th cent. B.C.* (Athens 1998) 175–84 and 159–73. For Knossos, see J.N. Coldstream and H.W. Catling, *Knossos The North Cemetery: Early Greek Tombs* 1–4 (London 1996).
7 Hom., *Od.*, 13.272–77. For the Mediterranean distribution of Phoenician luxury goods, see G. Markoe, *BASOR* 301 (1996) 58, fig. 18.
8 For the Idaean Cave, Kommos, and the Cretan iron trade, see H. Matthäus, J. Shaw and G. Markoe, respectively in V. Karageorghis and N. Stampolidis, eds, *Eastern Mediterranean: Cyprus-Dodecanese-Crete 16th–6th cent. B.C.* (Athens 1998).
9 Xen., *Hell.*, 4.8.7.
10 Hdt., 1.105.
11 For Cythera, see J.N. Coldstream and G.L. Huxley, eds, Kythera (London 1972) 36–7; for Gytheion, see N. Scoufopoulos-Stavrolakes in Raban, *Harbour Archaeology*, 49–62. According to Aristotle, Cythera was known in antiquity as Porphyroussa, or 'Purple Island'.
12 Hdt., 6.47. F. Salviat and J. Servais, *BCH* 88 (1964) 280–84.
13 Hom., *Il.*, 23.741–45. For the Phoenicians and Thasos, see Hdt., 2.44; 6.46–47; see also Lipinski, *Dictionnaire*, 144.
14 For Syros, cf. Hom., *Od.*, 15.403ff and J. Muhly, *Berytus* 19 (1970) 41ff and nn. 169–72. Direct Levantine influence on Naxos may be seen in the Cycladic vases of the Naxian 'Heraldic Group'.
15 J. Boardman, *The Greeks Overseas* (London 1980) 113–14.
16 J.N. Coldstream (n. 37, chapter 1); for Euboean pottery imports at Tyre, see J.N. Coldstream and P. Bikai, *RDAC* (1988), part 2, 35–44.
17 Hom., *Od.*, 13.272–86; 15.473–82.
18 Thuc., 6.2.6.
18A For Phoenician settlement on Sardinia, see, most recently, F. Barreca, *La civilta fenicio-punica in Sardinia*, 2nd ed.(Sassari 1988); and P. Bernardini, R. D'Oriano and P.G. Spanu, *Phoinikes Bshrn. I Fenici in Sardegna* (Oristano 1997).
19 See Kopcke and Tokumaru, *Greece*, pl. 71, fig. 8.
20 See Chapter 6, n. 42.
21 G. Markoe, *HbÄ* 19/20 (1992/3) 11–31; idem in Kopcke and Tokumaru, *Greece*, 61–84; also D. Ridgway in *op. cit.*, 90–91.
22 Diod., 5.12.
23 Ps.-Arstt., *Mir. ausc.* 134.
24 Pliny, *N.H.*, 16.216.
25 H. Ben Younes in Krings, *Civilisation*, 800; P. Cintas, *Karthago* 2 (1951) 40ff; A. Lezine, *Utique* (Tunis 1970).
26 M. Longerstay in Krings, *Civilisation*, 831–32.
27 M. Bouchenaki in *Richerche Puniche nel Mediterraneo Centrale* (Rome 1970) 47–61; S. Lancel in Krings, *Civilisation*, 786–93. For Rachgoun, see G. Vieullemot, *Reconnaissances aux échelles puniques d'Orante* (Autumn 1965) 55–130.
28 For two sides of the issue, see J. Alvar and J.M. Blazquez, eds, *Los enigmas de Tarteso* (Madrid 1993); and M. Elat, *OLP* 13 (1982) 55–69 or M. Koch, *Tarschisch und Hispanien* (Berlin 1984).
29 Harrison, *Spain*, 34–35.
30 Aubet, *Phoenicians*, 223–30
31 D. Ruiz Mata and C.J. Pérez, *El Poblado Fenicio del Castillo de Doña Blanca* (Cadiz 1995); Mata, *MM* 27 (1986) 87–115.
32 J. Fernandez Jurada, *Tejada la Vieja: un ciudad protohistorica* (Huelva 1987).
33 On the Spanish silver trade in general, see Aubet, *Phoenicians*, 236–47. On the Rio Tinto mines, see Harrison, *Spain*, 149–54.
34 A.A. Tavares, ed., *Os fenicios no territorio Portugues* (Lisbon 1993). J. Soares and C. Tavares da Silva, *Castelo de Alcácer do Sal: descobertas no sul de Portugal* (Setubal 1980).
35 A notable exception is the island settlement of Cerro del Villar in the river estuary of the Guadalhorce; for recent excavations of this industrial-commercial complex, which totals some 10 hectares (25 acres), see M.E. Aubet, *Festschrift fur Wolfgang Röllig* (Neukirchen-Vluyn 1997) 11–22; and idem, Cerro del Villar I (Barcelona 1999).
36 For recent overviews of Phoenician settlement in southern Spain, see Aubet, *Phoenicians*, 218–76; and H. Schubart in Krings, *Civilisation*, 743–61; M.E. Aubet, *PBA* 86 (1996) 47–65; and Martín Ruiz, *Feniciar.*
37 For a general review of the Tartessian orientalizing period, see Harrison, *Spain*, 51–68. For the impact of the Phoenician alphabet on Iberian script, see J. de Hoz in Cl. Baurain, C. Bonnet and V. Krings, eds, *Phoinikeia grammata, lire et écrire en méditerranée* (Liège 1991) 669–82.
38 C. Gomez Bellard in Krings, *Civilisation*, 762–72 with recent bibliography; idem, *MM* 34 (1993) 83–107.
39 Pliny, *N.H.*, 19.63.
40 For a recent analysis of Lixus, see P. Rouillard in Krings, *Civilisation*, 781–83; H.G. Niemeyer, *HbÄ*, 15–17 (1988–90) 189–207.
41 For Phoenician settlement in Morocco, see P. Rouillard in Krings, *Civilisation*, 776–83. For Mogador, see A. Jodin, *Mogador, comptoir phénicien du Maroc atlantique* (Tangier 1966).

42 Strabo, 17.3.3.
43 Hdt., 4.4.2.
44 Strabo, 2.3.4.
45 Ps.-Arstt., *Mirab. ausc.* 84; Diod., 5.19–20.
46 P. and P. Bikai, *Archaeology* (Jan./Feb. 1990) 23.
47 M.E. Aubet, *PBA* 86 (1996) 51–55.
48 For analysis of the text and English translation, see Harden, *Phoenicians*, 171–77; also G.C. Picard in Huss, *Karthago*, 182–92; and Huss, *Geschichte*, 75–83.
49 Avienus, *Ora Maritima*, 114–29, 380–89, 404–15. Huss, *Geschichte*, 84–85.

APPENDIX

For up-to-date information on excavated sites mentioned in the text, see Lipinski, *Dictionnaire*, Stern, *Encyclopedia*, and *OxEANE*.

1 For the ancient harbour site, see A. Raban in Raban, *Harbour Archaeology*, 30–38.
2 Briend and Humbert, *Tell Keisan*.
3 Bikai, *Tyre*; Katzenstein, Tyre; Joukowsky, *Heritage*.
4 Papyrus Anastasi: *ANET* (3), 477.
5 In general, see Poidebard, *Tyr*.
6 For this plausible suggestion, see P. and P. Bikai in *Berytus* 35 (1987) 75.
7 Pritchard, *Sarepta*.
8 For early excavations, see *Syria*, 1 (1920) 198–229; 287–317; 4 (1923) 261ff; 5 (1923) 9–23; 123–34; *BMB* 19 (1966) 103–105; 20 (1967) 27–44; 22 (1969) 101–07. For preliminary reports of 1st season recent excavations, see C. Doumet-Serhal in the [Beirut] *National Museum News* 11 (1999) and *BAAL* 4 (1999) forthcoming.
9 Poidebard and Lauffray, *Sidon*. According to Poidebard, the southern bay was not adequately protected from dominant south-westerly winds to have served effectively as a harbour facility in antiquity.
10 *ANET* (3), 287–88.
11 See F.C. Eiselen, *Sidon. A Study in Oriental History* (New York 1907) 5–6.
12 For the preliminary reports of the recent excavations, see *BAAL* 1 (1996) and 2 (1997). I would like to thank Dr Leila Badre for her generosity in making available her discoveries on the Beirut excavations prior to publication; these findings are published in *BAAL*, 2, 6–94. See also J. Elayi and H. Sayegh, *Un quartier du port phénicien de Beyrouth au Fer III/Perse. Les objets. Transeuphratène* Suppl. 6 192 (Paris 1998).
13 Montet, *Byblos*; M. Dunand, *Fouilles de Byblos*, 5 vols (Paris 1937–58); idem, *Byblos: Its History, Ruins, and Legends*, 2nd ed. (Beirut 1968).
14 See J.-C. Margueron in Acquaro, *Biblo*, 24, n. 27, and fig. 8. For investigation of the southern bay and newly discovered submerged reef, see H. Frost, *[Beruit] National Museum News* 8 (1998) 29 and *BAAL*.
15 J. Elayi, *Transeuphratène* 2 (1990) 59–71.
16 H. Salamé-Sarkis, *MUSJ* 50 (1975–76) 549–65.
17 H. Salamé-Sarkis, *MUSJ* 47 (1972) 123–45.
18 J.-P. Thalmann, *Berytus* 39 (1991) 21–38.
19 For archaeological research at Tell Kazel, see *AAAS* 14 (1964) 3–14; L. Badre et al., *Berytus* 38 (1990) 9–124; idem, *Syria* 71 (1994) 259–346 and *ACFP* 3, 118–27.
20 J.-P. Rey-Coquais, *Arados et sa Pérée* (Paris 1974).
21 For the Ma'abed, see Wagner, *Einfluss*, 2–8, pls 15:1, 33; for the funerary towers, see E. Will, *Syria* 25 (1949) 282–85; Wright, *Building*, 328–29.

GLOSSARY

acropolis upper fortified part of an ancient city
alabastron perfume or ointment jar with a flattened lip and narrow mouth and an elongated body rounded at the bottom
amphora large two-handled earthenware vessel with a narrow cylindrical neck and tapering bottom used for storing wine, oil, or grain
ankh ancient Egyptian hieroglyphic sign for 'life'
aryballos small globular perfume jar
ashlar hewn or squared stone used in wall construction
betyl monolithic standing stone in the form of a cone or tapering pillar marking the presence of a deity
cippus small low pillar used as a votive or grave marker
cothon artificially constructed dry dock used for the building or repairing of ships
faience glazed composition consisting of a sand quartz core with a glassy surface glaze
glacis artificial slope built against a fortification wall for defence against attack
ingot mass of metal or glass cast into a convenient shape for storage or transportation
naiskos shrine in the form of a small columned temple
necropolis the cemetery of an ancient city
oinochoe one-handled wine pitcher or jug, with trefoil-shaped, pinched mouth
ostracon fragment of pottery or limestone bearing a written inscription
phiale shallow bowl with central boss used for drinking or pouring libations
pithos large earthenware storage jar with a wide, round mouth
sarcophagus coffin made of stone, often ornamented in relief
scarab conventionalized representation of a scarab beetle in stone or faience, usually bearing an inscription on the underside
scaraboid engraved scarab-shaped gem with a flat oval base and a rounded back
situla bronze pail or bucket-shaped vessel
stele freestanding upright stone slab used as a votive dedication or a gravestone
suffete one of the two annually appointed chief magistrates at Carthage and other Punic cities in North Africa and the Mediterranean
votive offering object offered or erected in fulfilment of a vow or in gratitude for a prayer answered

ACKNOWLEDGEMENTS

In the preparation of this book I am indebted to a great number of colleagues, who assisted in the acquisition of illustrations, provided scholarly input, or made available to me the results of recent research. I gratefully acknowledge the following individuals: Joan Aruz, Camille Asmar, Maria Eugenia Aubet, Leila Badre, Amelie Beyhum, Pierre and Patricia Bikai, Betsy M. Bryan, Barbara Burrell, Lionel Casson, John Curtis, Joseph A. Greene, David F. Grose, Eric Gubel, Thor Heyerdahl, Vassos Karageorghis, Stephen Kaufman, Serge Lancel, P. Kyle McCarter, Andrew Meadows, P.R.S. Moorey, Paul Mosca, Oscar White Muscarella, Hans George Niemeyer, Lawrence Stager, Andrew F. Stewart, Paolo Visona and David Weisberg.

I would also like to thank Linda M. Pieper, Curatorial Secretary at the Cincinnati Art Museum, for her invaluable assistance in the preparation of the manuscript. Above all, my sincere gratitude goes to former Museum Director Barbara K. Gibbs for her encouragement and her support in granting me sabbatical leave to complete the writing of this work.

ILLUSTRATION ACKNOWLEDGEMENTS

Objects in the British Museum (BM) (Department of Western Asiatic Antiquities) are identified as WAA followed by their accession number.

Colour Plates

I Musée du Louvre, Paris, Département des Antiquités Orientales, AO 9093 © RMN 00499563 – Hervé Lewandwski.

II Photo Pierre Bikai.

III Museo Arquelológico Nacional, Madrid. RCS Libri and Grandi Opere, Milan.

IV Musée du Louvre, Paris, Département des Antiquités Orientales, AO 3988 © Christian Larrieu.

V Photo Philippe Maillard.

VI BM WAA 127412.

VII BM 133316, 133317; BM 133529, 133530; BM WA A133392 (56-12-23, 790); BM 133940 56-12-23, 1399; BM 133395 56-12-23, 792; BM 133486, 56-12-23, 893.

VIII Rome, Museo Archeologico di Villa Giulia. RCS Libri and Grandi Opere, Milan.

IX Musée du Louvre, Paris, Département des Antiquités Orientales, AO 3783 © RMN 00499504.

X Photo M.E. Aubet.

XI District Museum, Limassol. RCS Libri and Grandi Opere, Milan.

XII District Museum, Limassol. RCS Libri and Grandi Opere, Milan.

Black and White Figures

Frontispiece

Musée du Louvre, Paris, Département des Antiquités Orientales, AO 4806 © RMN 00600194 – Chuzeville.

1 BM 29811.

2 Pushkin Museum, Moscow.

3 Musée du Louvre, Paris, Département des Antiquités Orientales, AO 9502.

4 BM WAA124562.

5 BM WAA 124656.

6 BM. Line drawing by Sir Austen Henry Layard.

7 Staatliche Museen zu Berlin Preussischer Kulturbesitz, Vorderasiatisches Museum, VA 2708, VAN 8873.

8 Photo Marguerite Yon, KB 1996. Mission française de Kition-Bamboula.

9 Photo Claudia Kunze, September 1998, courtesy of H.G. Niemeyer.

10 Archaelogical Museum, Instanbul.

11 Musée du Louvre, Paris, Département des Antiquités Orientales, AO, MND 800 © Christian Larrieu.

12 Tyre at http://almashriq.hiof.no.general/930.

13 Drawing A. Raban, ed., *Harbour Archaeology: Proceedings of the First International Workshop on Ancient Mediterranean Harbours* (Oxford 1985), p. 33, fig. 14.

14 Z. Gal, Levant 24 (1992), p. 109.

15 Drawings courtesy of H.G. Niemeyer.

16 Photo Dieter Jahn, 1993, courtesy of H.G. Niemeyer.

17 Photo S. Lancel.

18 Piero Bartoloni, Sandro Filippo Bondí and Luisa Anna Marras, *Monte Sirai* (Rome 1992).

19 From S. Moscati, *The Phoenicians* (New York 1988), p. 189.

20 M.E. Aubet.

21 Line drawing from E. Gubel, E., *Les Phéniciens et le monde méditerraneen* (Brussels 1986), fig. 32.

22 Julian Whittelessey. Photo from *Carthage: A Mosiac of Ancient Tunisia* (New York and London: W.W. Norton and Company 1987), 95, fig. 43.

23 Musées Royaux d'Art et d'Histoire, Brussels, IN VA 1323.

24 BM WAA 124772.

25 Photograph courtesy of the author.

26 BM 123053.

27 Baal, Volume 1, 1996, p. 242, fig. 2.

28 Musée du Louvre, Paris, Département des Antiquités Orientales, AO 19890 © RMN 00310220 – H. Lewandowski.

29 BM: PCG2A43; BMC Tyre 1; 1948.361; BMC Sidon 6; BMC Arad. 11; BMC Arad. 7; BMC Byblos 38; Hirmer Verlag Munich 140684R.

30 BM: A 1946.1.1.1600; B 1946.1.1.1616; C 1987.6.49.197; D 1987.6.49.303.

31 Staatliche Museen zu Berlin Preussischer Kulturbesitz, Vorderasiatisches Museum, S 6579, VAN 12697.
32 S. Moscati, ed., *The Phoenicians* (New York 1988), pp. 94–95. Prof Sergio Nolan.
33 Musée du Louvre, Paris, Départment des Antiquités Orientales, AM 1196 (head), AO 4411 (base).
34 Musée du Louvre, Paris, Départment des Antiquités Orientales, AO 22368.
35 Ny Carlsberg Glyptothek, Copenhagen, No. 837.
36 Cyprus, Nicosia, Kit. 1969 AR11/I435.
37 BM WAA 125096.
38 University of Pennsylvania Museum, Philadelphia. Neg. 306 SAB 16.
39 BM WAA 140864.
40 Musée du Louvre, Paris, Départment des Antiquités Orientales, AO 25952.
41 Seville, Museo Arqueólogico. From E. Lipinski, ed., *Dictionnaire de la civilisation phénicienne et punique* (Brussels, Paris 1992).
42 Direction Générale des Antiquités (Department of Antiquities), National Museum, Beirut, D 6048.
43 Musée du Louvre, Paris, Départment des Antiquités Orientales, AO 27197.
44 Photo Philippe Maillard.
45 BM WAA 125252.
46 Photo Jim Whitred, courtesy of the ASOR Punic Project. Semetic Museum, Harvard University.
47 Bardo Museum, Tunis. Ministere de la Culture Institut Nacional du Patrimoine.
48 Photo Dieter Jahn, KA 93-75-6 1 Neg. 9, courtesy of H.G. Niemeyer.
49 Ministero per i beni Culturali e Ambientali, Sardinia. Photo from Piero Bartoloni, Sandro Filippo Bondí and Luisa Anna Marras, *Monte Sirai*, p. 127, fig. 41.
50 From E. Lipinski, ed., *Dictionnaire de la civilisation phénicienne et punique* (Brussels, Paris 1992), p. 461, figs 355, 356 and 357. Courtesy of H. Benichou-Safar.
51 Musée du Louvre, Paris, Départment des Antiquités Orientales, AO 15557, N 3263.
52 Photo Philippe Maillard.
53 BM WAA 118157.
54 Photographic Services, The Metropolitan Museum of Art, New York, NY 10028, Neg. No. 74.51.4554.
55 Photograph courtesy of the author.
56 BM WAA 115505.
57 The Metropolitan Museum of Art, New York, NY 10028, Neg. No. 159474.
58 Musée du Louvre, Paris, Départment des Antiquités Orientales, AO 22247, RMN 00629938.
59 Musée du Louvre, Paris, Départment des Antiquités Orientales, 64 BL 839, AO 4836.
60 Museo Arquelógico Nacional, Madrid, No. E1. RCS Libri and Grandi Opere, Milan.
61 (a) Musée du Louvre, Paris, Départment des Antiquités Orientales, AO 4803 © Christian Larrieu; (b) BM 125097 64-11-28-1.
62 BM E 48496, PS 249253; BM 134278; BM 134288; BM 68.5-20.22, 136023, PS 173622/136023; BM WAA 117719, PS 285185; BM E 48056, PS 040200; Direction Générale des Antiquités (Department of Antiquities), National Museum, Beirut; BM GR 65.7-12.126, 136021; BM 103305.
63 No. 520, Musée Nationale Tarquiniese.
64 Ibiza, Museo Arqueológico, MAI 1672. RCS Libri and Grandi Opere, Milan.
65 From Patricia Bikai, *Cyprus*, nos 3, 17, 66, 117, 136, 175, 261, 271–2, 355, 373, 402, 468, 497, 565, 588, 591.
66 University of Pennsylvania Museum, Philadelphia, neg. 54-142743.
67 Drawing by Sue Bird; BM GR 1852.1-12.3.
68 Musée du Louvre, Paris, Départment des Antiquités Orientales, 69 EN 2801, AO 3242.
69 Cyprus Museum, Nicosia.
70 Archaeological Museum of Haraklion, Crete, No. 4346.
71 From E. Lipinski, ed., *Dictionnaire de la civilisation phénicienne et punique* (Brussels, Paris 1992).
72 Photo H.G. Niemeyer.
73 Direction Générale des Antiquités (Department of Antiquities), National Museum, Beirut.
74 Sidon at http://almashriq.hiof.no.general/930.
75 Arwad at http://almashriq.hiof.no.general/930.

INDEX